Renaissance Culture and the Everyday

NEW CULTURAL STUDIES

Series Editors
Joan DeJean
Carroll Smith-Rosenberg
Peter Stallybrass
Gary A. Tomlinson

A complete list of books in the series
is available from the publisher.

Renaissance Culture and the Everyday

Edited by Patricia Fumerton and Simon Hunt

PENN

University of Pennsylvania Press

Philadelphia

10 9 8 7 6 5 4 3 2 1

Published by
University of Pennsylvania Press
Philadelphia, Pennsylvania 19104–4011

Library of Congress Cataloging-in-Publication Data
Renaissance culture and the everyday / edited by Patricia Fumerton and Simon Hunt.
    p.   cm. — (New cultural studies)
    Includes bibliographical references and index.
    ISBN 0-8122-3454-5 (cloth : alk. paper). —
    ISBN 0-8122-1663-6 (pbk. : alk. paper)
    1. England — Social life and customs — 16th century. 2. England — Social life and customs —
17th century. 3. Europe — Social life and customs. 4. Renaissance — England. 5. Renaissance.
I. Fumerton, Patricia. II. Hunt, Simon, 1967–   . III. Series.
DA320.R49   1998
942 — dc21   98-35173
                                                                              CIP

Contents

I

Introduction:
A New New Historicism

Patricia Fumerton

WHEN PREPARING A PIG FOR CONSUMPTION in the Renaissance, it was common practice to stick a knife in its side and watch it hurl itself around in agony until it finally collapsed through sheer exhaustion and loss of blood. Alternatively, an Elizabethan manual suggests, with almost tender consideration, you could "gently bait him with muzzled dogs." Or yet again — and decidedly less tenderly — if you were feeling especially energetic, you could beat the animal to death with a whip made from knotted ropes. Fish followed suit, as Philipa Pullar notes in her litany of culinary torments: "salmon and carp were hacked into collops while living," she observes, and "eels were skinned alive, coiled round skewers and fixed through the eye."[1] The common idea behind these diverse preparatory torments, as with the baiting of bulls and boars before eating them, was to render the flesh more tender and tempting. Whereas moderns whack their meat when it is dead and anonymous (cut into steaks and laid out on a kitchen cutting board), the Renaissance pounded its meat when it was alive and identifiable as a feeling creature.[2]

The torture of animals in the service of gustatory gratification was so much a part of everyday life in the early modern period that it found its way into household cookbooks, which proliferated in England in the late sixteenth and seventeenth centuries. Consider, for instance, the popular recipe on how to make a "restorative" broth: "Take a great fatt Capon that is well fleshed," Phioravante instructs, in John Hester's 1582 rendering of the recipe, "and pull it while it is aliue, and take forthe onely the guttes and the belly, and when he is dead, stamp it in a Morter grossly. . . ."[3] Or try Henry Buttes's pain-inducing recipe for eel, which begins thus: "Choake it with white Wine, stop the mouth with a Nut-meg, and the other holes with Cloues. . . ."[4] Pig was similarly dressed, or more accurately "dressed up" (pig was considered lower-class meat) as in its forced translation into higher fare in Vincent La Chapelle's recipe "To make a Pig taste like a wild Boar": "Take a living Pig, and let him swallow the following Drink, *viz.* boil in a Stew-pan a little Water and Vinegar with some Rosemary, Thyme, sweet Basil, Organy, Mirlirot, Bay-leaves, Sage, and Marjoram. This being boiled and then cold, make the Pig swallow it, and whip him to Death. . . ."[5]

Such torturous cookery instructions reached fullest cultivation in the following recipe twice told by John Wecker, in his *Secrets of Nature* (published in Latin, 1582; translated into English by R. Read in 1660):

> "To rost a Goose alive"
> A Goose, or Duck, or some lively Creature, (but the Goose is best) must be pulled all clean off her Feathers, only the head and neck must be spared. Then make a fire round about her, not too close to her, that the smoke do not choke her, and that the fire may not burn her too soon: not too far off, that she may not escape free; within the circle of the fire let there be set small cups and pots full of water, wherein Salt and Honey are mingled, and let there be set also Chargers full of sodden Apples, cut into small pieces in the dish. The Goose must be all Larded and basted over, to make her the more fit to be eaten, and may rost the better, put then fire about her, do not make too much haste, when as you see her begin to Rost; for by walking about, and flying here and there being cooped in by the fire that stops her way out, the unwearied Goose is kept in by drinking of the water, which cools her heart and all her body, and the Apples make her dung, cleanse and empty her. When she grows scalding hot, her inward parts rost also, then wet with a Sponge her head and heart continually; and when you see her giddy with running, and begin to stumble, her heart wants moisture: she is Rosted, take her up, and set her upon the Table to your Guests, and as you cut her up she will cry continually, that she will be almost all eaten before she be dead.

In his second telling of this recipe, Wecker adds the appreciation, "it is very pleasant to behold."[6] The mighty pleasure felt in watching the cooked goose suffer, which is personalized by calling the goose "she" and captured in loving detail (recalling the "gentle" baiting of the pig), finds final satisfaction in hearing her cry out in pain as she is sliced open. So elaborate is the torture here that it seems to the modern eye almost parodic. Our sense of excess may be explained by the writer's efforts to make a common practice more "refined" and thus exciting for his readers (who were mostly of the aspiring middle class). But the effect is only different in degree. In all such cases of animal torment, the torture is the tasty seasoning that flavors the otherwise plain meat. It adds spice to the culinary experience, a mouth-salivating flavoring which — unlike the costly East Indies spices — was economically available to all classes. Indeed, despite La Chapelle's violent efforts to turn the lowly pig into high meat (boar) befitting, as the title-page to his cookbook claims, "the Tables of Princes, Ambassadors, Noblemen, and Magistrates," he also has more common aims in mind: "As also," the title-page continues, "The least

Expensive Methods of providing for private Families." Making or supervising such affordable cookery would be the woman of the house, who is often specifically addressed in cookbook title-pages, prefaces, and recipes of the period.[7] Whereas moderns might add A-1 to their steak, the Renaissance populace — and preeminently its housewives — found assorted tasty ways to torture the steer.

These examples of animal torture, especially the goose recipe, might have served well as appetizer to the kind of new historicism served up in the 1980s. Following its inauguration with Stephen Greenblatt's *Renaissance Self-Fashioning*, new historicism quickly became notable for the opening anecdote that was riveting because bizarre: the horrifying first-person account of how a Baptist minister made his fifteen-month-old son love him by starving the boy; or of the strange contents — embalmed child, unicorn's tail, and the like — of a wonder cabinet; or of a titillating wet dream (Simon Forman's about Queen Elizabeth), or — perhaps the biggest box-office hit of these catchy anecdotes — the improbable story of a stand-in husband, as told in Greenblatt's retelling of Natalie Zemon Davis's account-turned-film of the return of Martin Guerre.[8] Many of these narratives, for all their exotic flavor to our modern taste, share the cookery stories' concern with the middling and low sort, the popular, and the domestic. But the new historicism of the '80s generally employed such common subjects to very uncommon ends: as prolegomena to discussions of royalty, courts, the state, and (male) power. In a word, it was "political" historicism. The work of Greenblatt, Louis Montrose, Steven Mullaney, and Leonard Tennenhouse is exemplary.[9] Even new historicism's more "grounded" British counterpart, cultural materialism, worked primarily in this lofty political mode. Studies in the 1980s by such cultural materialists as Peter Stallybrass, Francis Barker, Jonathan Dollimore, and Catherine Belsey might have given more prominence to the common — pigs, the masses, the bourgeoisie, women — but they did so in the service of arguments about hierarchical power structures (arguing from the bottom up as opposed to new historicism's top-down perspective) that continued to privilege official authority, state ideology, and politics.[10] My more modest reading of anecdotes about daily culinary violence (abbreviated for the purpose of illustration) is a bird of a different feather. It characterizes a new breed of '90s new historicism.

This newly emergent new historicism focuses primarily on the common, but the common in both a class and cultural sense: the low (common people), the ordinary (common speech, common wares, common sense), the familiar (commonly known), the customary or typical or taken-for-granted (common law, commonplace, communal), etc. A new new historicism sites particular clusters of such myriad commonality within the context of the manifold details of cultural practice and representation—what we might call, evoking Michel de Certeau and Henri Lefebvre, the *"everyday."*[11] To the extent that this new historicism of the everyday looks beyond (and below) the politics of the court or the state apparatus and its cultural instruments, it is not so much "political" as "social" historicism (though clearly there is some overlap between these terms and movements). Significantly, the newer methodology of the everyday has as yet no leader, but it can be detected in such published works as Joy Wiltenburg's *Disorderly Women and Female Power in the Street Literature of Early Modern England and Germany* (Virginia, 1992), Frances E. Dolan's *Dangerous Familiars: Representations of Domestic Crime in England, 1550–1700* (Cornell, 1994), Lena Cowen Orlin's *Private Matters and Public Culture in Post-Reformation England* (Cornell, 1994), and Ann Jensen Adams's *Public Faces, Private Identities: Portraiture and the Production of Identity in Seventeenth Century Holland* (Cambridge, 1998), as well as in a host of works-in-progress, including my own project on the spatial mobility of the lower orders in early modern England and Richard Helgerson's cross-Channel investigation into domesticity and nationhood.[12]

What we see in such works of the 1990s is that the shift from the old political historicism to a new social historicism of the everyday is not an absolute break but in many ways a continuum, a filling out, and also a dispersal of the earlier methodology (which is why I have called the new movement "a" new historicism rather than another "the").[13] Introductory anecdotes working in this new mode not only extend what was often but a preliminary focus on low subjects; they also de-privilege while also proliferating the (in)famous riveting detail. Characteristically, early works of new historicism used the single striking story—rendered through what Clifford Geertz calls "thick description"[14]—as an avenue to the culture at large. That is, the anecdote served synecdochally for the whole, though, of course, that "whole" was usually hierarchically defined in a way that privileged the upper echelon. One could *read* a culture's class structure or power relations from a telling particular artifact or event. This approach has come under considerable attack, and while I have defended the anecdote as aptly representative of history as fracture,[15] the idea that a whole culture can be represented by just one of its parts is, indeed, very problematic. What is noticeable among the second generation of new historicists is their implicit recognition of the problematics of this approach through their layering of individual accounts with multifarious supporting details. Consider, for instance, the extraordinary amount of data presented by Lena Orlin in her efforts fully to "place" the domestic murder of Arden of Faversham in *Private Matters and Public Culture* (pp. 15–78). Detail upon fascinating detail is added to her argument in a kind of successive (versus singular) anecdotalism.

Attention to the details of everyday life, in all their plurality, complements a further interest by second-generation new historicists in *materiality*. The *sense* of the everyday is very much caught up in sensuality or physicality. In this sense, we can see a forerunner to the present volume in a recent collection of essays, *Subject and Object in Renaissance Culture*, ed. Margreta de Grazia, Maureen Quilligan, and Peter Stallybrass (Cambridge, 1996), which calls for a more material grounding of cultural studies. (That Peter Stallybrass is one of the editors of this volume demonstrates the substantial continuity and even fluidity between "political" and "social" historicisms.) The concept of the everyday, as we are defining it, foregrounds such materiality as well. However, it is simultaneously more general and more specific than the subject-object dialectic would allow. Everyday life, that is, expands to include not only familiar things but also collective meanings, values, representations, and practices; in this respect, second generation new historicism, like the first, is indebted to cultural anthropologists such as Geertz as well as to cultural historians / sociologists such as Michel Foucault, Pierre Bourdieu, and Norbert Elias. At the same time, the everyday tends to place upfront particular kinds of subjects: the common person, the marginalized, women. In this regard, the methodology is indebted to feminists[16] and in regard to the first of these subjects, the "man-on-the-street" — to de Certeau and postmodern theorists such as Jean Baudrillard, as well as, more generally, to a Marxist sense of powerment / disempowerment as crucial, rock-bottom fissure.

This new array of foci thus does not deny the reality of power or politics. But it does not promote a male-centered or "top down" gaze (or its mirror-image reverse). That is, power is no longer seen by critics of everyday life, as it is by Greenblatt, to be artfully and predominantly wielded by aristocrats or institutions; rather, we find the dominant social order to be used and fractured in complex ways by the lower social groups that inhabit it (in the role of imitators, consumers, audiences, adolescents, intimates, pets, etc.). This is what de Certeau means by *practice* of everyday life. In his or her daily practices, the common person tactically and almost invisibly transforms from within the social structures she or he inhabits. Though de Certeau fixes his gaze on the masses as *opposed* to their strategically organized governors, the ruling aristocracy itself, as producer *and consumer*, is not excluded but involved in such unsettling practices, especially in its eager participation in the expanding consumer economy of the seventeenth century. For this reason, de Certeau's comment about the modern condition — that "marginality is becoming universal" (referring to the mass of users, that is, non-producers, of cultural products) — has relevance for the early modern period as well (de Certeau, p. xvii). As a marginalized consumer group, the aristocracy becomes particularly everyday in its use of the trivial, common, or low — a practice redefined in terms not of a suppression or absorption of that other but of a more nebulous involvement or negotiation with it.

Finally, as marked by my introductory anecdotes, a new new historicist methodology continues to be fascinated with strange and marginal details. But the strange is rethought in terms of the everyday. Questions that necessarily arise as a consequence are: "What stamps particular early modern practices or representations as common as opposed to strange?" and "Can the common itself be strange (and vice versa)?" Certainly the everyday in the Renaissance can be the uncommonly strange to modern taste. It is in fact often very hard to recognize the common or usual practice of a period so far removed from our own that almost everything seems foreign. Yet, as evidenced in my opening examples of culinary gusto, it is also true that the everyday practice of another period (as also of our own) can be charged with strangeness even to its practitioners. One of the values of the everyday is that it provides comfort and reassurance that life is proceeding apace, with no threat of unsettling change. But another, paradoxical value is that it provides a regular outlet for something different and above the regular. In the common act of torturing animals the Renaissance man or woman experienced something uncommon — the rush of adrenaline that added spice to everyday life. In sum, it is often precisely in the trivial details of everyday life that Renaissance men and women invested their lives with extra-ordinary meaning.

This volume marks and advances the emergence of a new new historicism that tackles the above concerns. Organized around the categories of materiality, women, and transgression — and constantly crossing these categories — the collection of essays we here offer promotes a thoughtful entry into the complex matrix of issues involved in the practice and representation of everyday life. Foregrounded are the common person, the marginal, women, the domestic, and everyday speech as well as familiar things: mirrors, horses, books, foodstuffs, paintings, architecture, laundry baskets, embroidery, conduct manuals, money, graffiti. Included, though necessarily given "minor" representation, is the aristocracy in its own everyday practices — investing in dressage, holding to the homely accents of high English, and retreating as women into nunneries and other architectural spaces. In this expansive and variegated and sometimes even contradictory vision of everyday life — for we are nothing if not inconsistent in our day-to-day living — the strange, as the final section illustrates, becomes not an alien other but a defining mark, however disfiguring, of everyday life. Some of the strangeness in familiarity and familiarity in strangeness of the everyday is emphasized in this collection by our inclusion of papers not only by new new historicists working on England, but also by like-minded scholars of Italian history, Dutch art history, and

French and Italian literature. Everyday life can be uncannily similar as we move from one country to another, or one discipline to another, but it can also suddenly seem very, very different. However differently we react, the complexion of this volume makes clear that the everyday is not the sole prerogative of the English (though they might like to think so), nor is it always predictably common.

Part I, "Materials of the Everyday," lays the groundwork for the theme of materiality or physicality that runs throughout the essays of the volume. Debora Shuger's opening paper focuses on the new availability in the early modern period of glass mirrors, which had become a relatively common household item in England by the 1600s. Her concern, like that of so many of the other scholars represented here, is with the much vexed question of identity formation at this time. Since the mirror provides a dominant metaphor for modern subjectivity with its habitual reflexivity and specular gaze, it would seem plausible that representations (both visual and textual) of this everyday artifact would register the emergence of the modern subject. Not so, says Shuger. Before the late seventeenth century, she argues, mirrors virtually never figure introspective self-consciousness; rather the peculiar metaphorics of Renaissance mirrors point to an unfamiliar and unmodern conceptualization of selfhood. Here the everyday early modern artifact produces a strange reading from the modern perspective, forcing us to rethink the history of the subject and subjectivity.

But, once again, it is in the nature of the everyday to be inconsistent. We are different persons depending on the different daily practices in which we engage. Furthermore, our individual contradictions are compounded by such destabilizing social factors as class, gender, and race. Thus Karen L. Raber offers another reading of identity in early modern England when she looks at the English aristocracy and its preoccupation with horses, particularly with the art of dressage. Of course, horses were very much a part of the everyday life of all classes in the early modern period: horses plowed fields, carted goods, transported people, and bore warriors. Because of the importance of horses to all these areas of life, the relationship between man and horse was also the site of important ideological work. Raber's essay examines one locus of such work in the horsemanship treatises of William Cavendish, Duke of Newcastle. She notes that, "Composed during the civil war, Cavendish's books on horsemanship assert the superior skill, intellect, and humanity of the aristocratic horseman." Such higher qualities are demonstrated through the horseman's refinement of a display-oriented luxury pursuit and his election of humane training methods. At the same time, Raber adds, Cavendish's methods endow the horses with independent personalities. In this respect, the horses mirror changes in the human world, where bourgeois individualism and expanding democracy work to marginalize the kind of aristocratic identity Cavendish's writing is intended to recover. Cavendish's treatises thus "encapsulate and contribute to one of the most far-reaching transformations of everyday early modern English life."

If Raber pursues the reevaluation of aristocratic political power as resisted but also embodied in its preoccupation with horses, Don E. Wayne extends the civil politics of the high to include the equally problematic economic reality of the market and its embrace of the masses. Wayne concentrates his investigation on Ben Jonson's uneasy effort to legitimate high culture as distinct from the popular on the basis of the poet's intellectual labor. Working from Pierre Bourdieu's notion of "distinction," Wayne analyzes how the cultural distinctions and the class divisions Jonson attempts to define are blurred by the effects of commodification in the early stages of market capitalism. As seen in Jonson's play *The Staple of News*, the playwright's efforts to relegate the commodity form to the popular (newsmongering, gossip, spectacle), while idealizing poetry as a transcendental cultural medium, repeatedly run up against the reality of the commodity form as it begins to permeate all facets of cultural activity. Jonson sought to establish a place for the intellectual that was independent of the ordinary system of rank in Jacobean society. But, with respect to the court, the intellectual's dependency was bound up with patronage; and, by the 1620s, with respect to the commons, dependency had become an effect of the market. The paper ends with a reference to a later playwright, David Mamet, in a comment on Senator Dole's recent attack on the entertainment industry, and concludes that one characteristic of the modern — "early" or "late" — is that the distinction between high culture and popular culture is never as stable as intellectuals and the elites they serve would like to imagine.

My essay, which concludes this section, finds a similar instability and cohabitation of high and popular in the so-called "rule" of major English at the end of the sixteenth century and its representation in the seventeenth century through another genre adopted by Ben Jonson: the masque. In this study, I rethink the Greenblatt/Mullaney model of language history by which English is seen to gain its major status and rule in the course of the late sixteenth century through a Bakhtinian absorption and then purgation of foreign terms. Drawing on the postmodern work of Gilles Deleuze and Félix Guattari, I argue that such a language history is myth. Every major language is always from the start what Deleuze-Guattari call a "becoming-minoritarian" or "becoming-minor of the major language." This is especially the case of English in the early seventeenth century, given its submission to a Scots-speaking king,

James I. To further illustrate this point, I turn to Jonson's masque, *For the Honor of Wales*, which, it has been assumed, celebrated James's and English's majority or "rule." But in fact the masque's distinction between an interior subdiscourse and its enveloping major discourse — between the Welsh language and dialect of the antimasque and the "King's English" of the main masque — is factitious. Throughout the masque we hear a many-voiced, intra-linguistic minoritarianism, a continuous variation within Welsh, Scots, and English that pronounces them all, in the Deleuze-Guattarian spirit of dispersal and modulation, *collaborators* in the "becoming-minoritarian" of language. Jonson thus speaks up to his Scottish-English king, ensconced on his high dais, by speaking low. Furthermore such low speech was textually and historically situated in the materiality of the homely and domestic; therein lay its allure. In this sense, minoritarian discourse has the status of an everyday, household "thing."

In concluding with the home, my paper introduces a major concern of Part II of this volume, "The Everyday Making of Women." That is, it raises the intimate association between the everyday and domestic space, which increasingly in the sixteenth and seventeenth centuries was seen to be the arena of women, and which in differing ways is the focus of the next section. The first paper, however, by Judith C. Brown situates women in other places entirely: convents. Here women are dis-placed from their home-base physically, psychologically, and socially. That sense of displacement may be enhanced for English literary scholars in reading Brown's historical study of the everyday life of nuns in early modern Florence. But Brown's study offers its own version of becoming-minoritarian. The foreignness of internal dialects to "major" English complements the strange remove from England that we experience in entering a Florentine nunnery and statistical (as opposed to cultural) historicism. And just as strange terms were found to be *a part* of English, exposing the minoritarianism of all discourse, so the unfamiliar focus and methodology of Brown's paper, when viewed from the perspective of English cultural studies, actually results in a reenvisioning of female space that is at home with the other papers in this section, where seemingly marginalized women can in practice be empowered.

Brown opens her discussion by questioning the traditionally-held tie between family life and long life. Since the mid-eighteenth century, Brown observes, scholars have tended to agree with Antoine Deparcieux, one of the founders of demography, who concluded that married people live longer than monks and nuns primarily because the latter are deprived of those "*mille petites douceurs*" of family life so essential to longevity. "Yet for much of the European past," Brown counters, "the choice was not between a long life in marriage and a short life of solitude." Religious institutions in fact proffered a life-sustaining experience of collaborative support often missing from other social settings. How this could be so, however, has to date been largely unknown because of a paucity of necessary historical records, especially for women. But Brown has found detailed entrance and death registers for two Florentine convents, San Jacopo di Ripoli and Santa Maria Annunziata delle Murate. Reading these hard facts with the same attentiveness that a new new historicist brings to the manifold details of cultural practice, Brown establishes the longevity of nuns dwelling in these institutions and surmises the kind of everyday experiences there that contributed to their long lives from the mid-fifteenth to the early nineteenth centuries. "When examined in the wider context of family strategies for biological, social, and economic reproduction," Brown finds, "such documents elucidate the larger demographic and social world of a large and important segment of European women."

Shannon Miller's essay transports us back to England in focusing on one aristocratic woman, Lady Mary Wroth. Unlike the Florentine nuns Brown studies, Miller's Englishwoman was marginalized not through her placement in a nunnery but rather through her audacious act of writing. Like Brown's nuns, however, Wroth resorts to architectural spaces beyond the home (though also including it) in her efforts to legitimate and empower herself. These physical spaces, Miller finds, were explicitly marked as male but turned to female ends. That is, denied access to a unified subjectivity ideally granted to men through political theory and systems of learning such as humanism, women like Wroth turned to external, man-made structures (rooms, castles, even poems) in order to find opportunities to articulate the "self." Miller thus discovers through everyday spatial structures the modern notion of subjectivity not found by Shuger in looking at mirrors. At the same time, however, Miller exposes a gender split in the way early modern subjectivity was conceived. Furthermore, the project that Wroth undertook as a female author carried with it an implicit danger: the splintering or fracturing of that female self. The danger is illustrated in the final sequences of the *Urania,* where a figure for Wroth as writer is metaphorically erased by an alternate figure for Wroth in the text, thus showing the constituted female self to be tenuous and perhaps ultimately untenable. Unlike the nuns of Brown's study, Wroth's empowered female subject spatially imagined in her writing is dangerously short-lived.

Richard Helgerson's paper leads the turn, in the next three papers, to a more specifically middle-class and female domestic space in which women variously and sometimes quite powerfully assert themselves. Helgerson focuses on the activities of the women in *The Merry Wives of Windsor* (of all

Shakespeare's plays the one most obviously concerned with the everyday), which Helgerson dubs Shakespeare's "genre painting." But this everyday world is invaded by a would-be sexual marauder from the generically distant realm of the English history play: the carnival king and sometime soldier, Sir John Falstaff. Helgerson examines the devices Windsor's merry wives use to humiliate and defeat the invader—the laundry basket, the witch, and the queen of fairies—arguing that each situates the local and domestic differently: the laundry basket suggesting the autonomy of the female-dominated household; the witch, a regional network of subversive female gossips; and the queen of fairies, a covert filiation of Windsor women with the national monarch. If we take "genre" (as in "genre painting") to stand for the local and domestic and "history" (as in "history play") to stand for the court-based and political, he notes, genre repels history in ways that assert in succession its independence of history, its antagonism to it, and its symbolic dependence on it. But, however accomplished, this victory is not decisive. Though Falstaff is defeated, Fenton, Falstaff's younger and better-looking doppelganger, succeeds—and succeeds precisely where Falstaff has failed. He gains access to Windsor's wealth through the affections of a Windsor woman. *Merry Wives,* Helgerson suggests, is engaged in the ideological negotiation between these two outcomes and between its three rival situatings of the local and domestic. It thus works to shape the everyday world it pretends only to represent.

Suggested in Helgerson's paper is the notion that the everyday space of the home might in fact on occasion be a space of transgression, depending on its "use." This idea is pursued in the following two papers by Lena Cowen Orlin and Frances E. Dolan, which thus look forward to the next section. Orlin focuses her paper on the common domestic activity of needlework. In particular, she sees needlework as a cloaking behavior related to two other "invisibilities" of women in the English Renaissance: the idea of the "feme covert" as a legal status and the idea of the silent woman as a prescriptive model. Studying many of the huge number of sewing scenes in Elizabethan drama, Orlin finds that needlework regularly functions as an overt signal of chastity and circumspection—signaling that the woman is properly "cloaked"—but that needlework can also serve as the cue for an impending attack upon the sewer's chastity or even as her own smokescreen for transgressive activity. Here de Certeau's notion of practice as a sometimes subversive *use* of a sanctioned space, behavior, or product is important. Despite the historical evidence of Mary Stuart's notoriously treasonous embroidered messages (to the Duke of Norfolk, for example), the *product* of needlework was not generally subversive. The *practice,* however, may have been, if evidence from playtexts is considered.

But it is also the case that a domestic practice which might at times appear subversive from the modern perspective is actually a regular feature of women's household duties. Frances E. Dolan finds this to be true in investigating the role of the household, and especially of women, in what some critics have labeled the early modern "culture of violence." Analyzing efforts by the period to make qualitative distinctions between parties involved as well as between contexts and kinds of violence in the household, Dolan asks, "Under what conditions were women licensed to discipline others?" Like Orlin, Helgerson, and many others in this volume, her concern in answering this question lies less with the historical "fact" than with its representation. That is, Dolan says, she is "less interested in evidence of the extent to which women actually harmed, coerced, or threatened others than in a range of representations, including books on personal conduct, ballads, and plays such as *The Taming of the Shrew,* in which women's verbal and physical domination of others is constructed positively." As represented in the material form of the text, she finds, certain kinds of female violence are not transgressive at all. They are accepted everyday practice.

So what then constitutes blatantly transgressive behavior in early modern everyday life? As the preceding papers illustrate, such a question is often extremely difficult, if not impossible, to answer, not only because of the gap between modern and early modern sensibilities but because, in the early modern period (and even today), transgressive behavior often found expression *within and through* everyday practices and representations. Indeed, sometimes one can become the other. Each of the essays in the concluding section to this volume, "Transgressions of the Everyday," discovers a version of this problematic.

Ann Jensen Adams introduces this section by situating us on foreign soil — Holland and Dutch painting — and focusing on what we would expect to be an obviously transgressive, if everyday, behavior: prostitution. But the pairing in seventeenth-century Holland of prostitution with the market problematizes our conceptualization of such transgression. Just as Wayne finds the English to be preoccupied with the market's blurring of social distinction, so Adams finds the Dutch (England's arch economic rivals) troubled by the market's disturbing of social order, that is, its potential to run out of control, particularly in the realm of prices and monetary value. Seventeenth-century Holland, like England, witnessed the rise of commodity and capital markets whose functioning was both unpredictable and relatively unregulated. What to do when a country's economic life-blood is itself thus transgressive? The answer: imaginatively think through anxieties in a removed, marginal realm such as that of the prostitute and her frequent economic partner, the mercenary soldier. In a detailed examination of a painting by Gerard Terborch, the so-called *Paternal Admonition*, and building upon the work of historians Lotte van de Pol and Rudolf Dekker among others, Adams argues that the prostitute and the mercenary soldier, along with their representations, became one of the sites onto which moral and economic anxieties were unconsciously displaced. At the same time such displacement allowed for a reimagining of transgressive consumerism. The prostitute and the mercenary soldier both functioned in commercial spheres that were not only marginal but also highly regulated or disciplined. Their image covertly implies that, far from racing out of control through man's unlicensed greed, the very circulation of money can actually be self-regulating. Because it transgressed the boundaries of contemporary morality, in sum, prostitution provided a site for the consideration of a much larger question of the morality and the regulation of emerging capital and commodity markets.

If Adams sees prostitution as serving in seventeenth-century Holland as a site for the considered regulation of (formerly) transgressive market activities in general, Stephanie H Jed rather seeks out the transgressiveness in the everyday acts of regulating — that is, recording and organizing — the facts of Florentine history. Beginning with de Certeau's *The Writing of History* and proceeding to adopt an unorthodox feminist style as well as position, Jed "reorganizes" knowledge about Florentine history through a study of various cultural and social environments in which such a history was constructed. By making visible the rhetorics of inventories, catalogues, and the construction of categories in the texts of bureaucrats (of the sixteenth century), feminist political theorists (of the seventeenth and nineteenth centuries), and editors and erudites (of the nineteenth century), her research envisions alternative, non-humanistic, and feminist possibilities for making sense of political acts and projects. Like de Certeau and feminists in many other fields, in other words, Jed is here interested in historicizing and situating experience and, in particular, our experience of books. She understands such experience, Jed asserts, "not as the origin of knowledge but as a series of everyday practices of looking for, listening to, stumbling across, handling, compiling, and transcribing texts — practices which situate us in particular social relations and produce our visions, identities, and interpretations." Once again, then, it is the *practice* of everyday life that opens up possibilities for both regulation and transgression.

Richard Corum also situates that notion of practice in the work of de Certeau, where it is loaded with transgressive "tactical" signification, and re-reads *Love's Labor's Lost* as an emergent-transgressive play. After surveying the production and critical history of the play, wherein it is either perceived as a failed comedy or reimagined as a successful one in the form of *Love's Labor's Won*, Corum offers an alternative. He argues that, as it stands, *Love's Labor's*

Lost is a successful comedy if it is retroactively resignified as a practice of *tactics* in an imaginary French setting and in everyday Elizabethan life. By conflating these two contexts *Love's Labor's Lost* accomplishes the socio-cultural task it was designed to perform for its audiences: that is, to initiate, shape, and record the emergence of *adolescence* (as opposed to youth) as a deconstructive force in early modern England. To understand this subversive practice, Corum asserts, we must rethink the Lawrence Stone-Alan Macfarlane debate as to the proper way of writing English social history with the aid not only of de Certeauian tactics but also of Lacanian psychoanalytic theory.

Corum thus offers a tactical reading of transgressive behavior *from within* social orders that allows us to escape the new historical dialectic of high versus low, subversive versus contained. Simon Hunt also reenvisions this binding dialectic. He begins by examining one of the ways in which the writers of English history plays in the 1580s and '90s negotiated the representational problem created by the necessity of depicting popular rebellion onstage. Can rebellious peasants be allowed to speak onstage without inviting identification with their concerns? Is it possible, as the Master of the Revels Edmund Tilney demanded of one play, to "leave out the insurrection wholly"? Anthony Munday and his collaborators in *The Book of Sir Thomas More*, Shakespeare in *2 Henry VI*, and the anonymous author of *The Life and Death of Jack Straw* all respond to this dilemma by mapping rebellion onto the temporary license of carnival (inevitably to be subsumed into everyday order) and the ordinary embodiment of carnival on the early modern stage, the clown. Then turning to a discussion of Thomas Heywood's *1 Edward IV*, a play which combines rebellion, clowning, and carnival in a very different way, Hunt demonstrates that this pattern of what some might call "containment" is by no means inevitable. In fact, he demonstrates the inadequacy of the subversion/containment reading of history and its analogues, arguing that they are insufficiently attentive to processes of historical change. Instead, he proposes a "hermeneutics of advocacy" as a way to read everyday phenomena both early modern and modern.

As a final tribute to the problematics of transgression when viewed in terms of everyday practice, Juliet Fleming completes this section with an historical re-imagining of modern notions of graffiti. Her essay argues that our definition of graffiti, as of its bedfellow, pornography, is a product of modern classification. That is, graffiti finds its meaningful place for us as a result of being set within our peculiar understanding of a series of oppositions: between public and private, present and absent, sanctioned and transgressive. Set within this modern grid, graffiti appears as a present and public transgression. But faults arise, Fleming points out, when we overlay this grid onto the graffiti of the past. What strikes us as graffiti in Elizabethan England, she finds, was in fact generally sanctioned practice both within and without the home. Such a finding upsets the categories by which we have learned to read graffiti and may well unsettle our aesthetic appreciation of the age of Shakespeare. Fleming concludes that "the uncanny (unhomelike) effects of Elizabethan domestic wall-writing depend in part on the dizzying collapse of the distinction between 'a symbol and the thing it symbolizes' that graffiti may be taken to enact—a collapse of language into its material forms with which Elizabethans, unlike ourselves, seem to have been thoroughly at home."

From mirrors that reflect an unmodern sense of self to domestic graffiti that is to us unhomelike—so concludes our round of everyday representations and practices in the early modern period. Our circle of essays is hardly complete; it offers more accurately but a slice of early modern daily life. But that is in accord with the volume's modest aims: to advance a new kind of new historicism that holds up familiar subjects of inquiry—about materiality, women, domesticity, transgression—to the ordinary, and sometimes quite extra-ordinary, light of the everyday.

Notes

I would like to thank especially Juliet Fleming, Richard Helgerson, Simon Hunt, Debora Shuger, and Don Wayne for their helpful comments on my argument about the everyday, as well as all my fellow contributors for their aid in the wording of the descriptions of their individual papers.

1. The manual is cited by Peter Stallybrass and Allon White, *The Politics of Poetics of Transgression* (Ithaca and New York: Cornell University Press, 1986), p. 47; Philippa Pullar, *Consuming Passions: Being an Historic Inquiry into Certain English Appetites* (Boston: Little, Brown, 1970), p. 150; see also p. 151.

2. This is not to say that moderns don't treat cruelly their animals marked for consumption. The force-feeding of geese to enlarge their livers (for paté) and the abusive treatment of calves (for veal) are two such instances of which I am aware. But the big difference between us and the early moderns is that we moderns don't relish hearing about such mistreatment, would prefer not knowing about it, even that it did not occur, and situate such practices at several removes from the household purchase, preparation, and cooking of meats.

3. *A Compendium of the rational Secretes of . . . Leonardo Phioravante Bolognese. . . ,* trans. John Hester (London, 1582), pp. 59–60. Though Phioravante offers his broth concoction as a "medical" recipe, versions of it (and other such medicinal formulae) often appeared in Renaissance cookbooks. On "cock broth," see also C. Anne Wilson, *Food & Drink in Britain, from the Stone Age to Recent Times* (London: Constable, 1973), pp. 133–34; and Pullar, p. 151.

4. Henry Buttes, *Dyets Dry Dinner: Consisting of eight seuerall Courses . . .* (London, 1599), p. 184.

5. Vincent La Chapelle, *The Modern Cook . . . ,* 3rd ed. (London, 1744); direc-

tions follow for gutting the sweetly-tortured pig, stuffing it (with "the same sweet Herbs used in the Draught"), selective skinning ("not the Head"), and roasting, after which one must "serve it up with hot Pepper and Vinegar sauce over it." On pig as lower-class meat, see Andrew B. Appleby, "Diet in Sixteenth-Century England," in *Health, Medicine, and Mortality in the Sixteenth Century*, ed. Charles Webster (Cambridge: Cambridge University Press, 1979), p. 99.

6. *Eighteen Books of the Secrets of Art & Nature . . . First designed by John Wecker Dr in Physick, and now much Augumented and Inlarged by Dr. R. Read* (London, 1660), pp. 148, 309. The first recipe appears under the section titled, "The secrets of Geese" (and is attributed to Varro); the second recipe appears under the section titled, "Of the Art of Cookery" (and is attributed to Mizald). Each recipe is slightly different, most notably in the gender of the bird ("she" in the first citing; "he" in the second). The goose recipe is later recited disapprovingly by William Kitchiner, in the preface to his *The Cook's Oracle. . .* , 2nd ed. (London, 1818), B5r–B6v.

7. Stephen Mennell, *All Manners of Food: Eating and Taste in England and France from the Middle Ages to the Present* (Oxford: Basil Blackwell, 1985), p. 84.

8. Stephen Greenblatt, *Renaissance Self-Fashioning: From More to Shakespeare* (Chicago: University of Chicago Press, 1980); Greenblatt, "The Cultivation of Anxiety: King Lear and His Heirs," in his *Learning to Curse: Essays in Early Modern Culture* (New York and London: Routledge, 1990), pp. 80–82; Steven Mullaney, "The Rehearsal of Cultures," in his *The Place of the Stage: License, Play, and Power in Renaissance England* (Chicago: University of Chicago Press, 1988), pp. 60–61; Louis Adrian Montrose, "'Shaping Fantasies': Gender and Power in Elizabethan Culture," *Representations* 1 (1983): 61–94; Greenblatt, "Psychoanalysis and Renaissance Culture," in *Learning to Curse*, pp. 131–45.

9. Greenblatt, *Renaissance Self-Fashioning* and, as a later example of his methodology, his *Learning to Curse* and *Shakespearean Negotiations: The Circulation of Social Energy in Renaissance England* (Berkeley: University of California Press, 1988); Montrose, "'Shaping Fantasies,'" and his "'Eliza, Queene of shepheardes,' and the Pastoral of Power," in *Renaissance Historicism*, ed. Arthur F. Kinney and Dan S. Collins (Amherst: University of Massachusetts Press, 1987), among a host of other articles; Mullaney, *The Place of the Stage*; Leonard Tennenhouse, *Power on Display: The Politics of Shakespeare's Genres* (New York and London: Methuen, 1986).

10. See, for example, Stallybrass and White, *The Politics and Poetics of Transgression*; Francis Barker, *The Tremulous Private Body: Essays on Subjection* (New York and London: Methuen, 1984); Jonathan Dollimore, *Radical Tragedy: Religion, Ideology, and Power in the Drama of Shakespeare and His Contemporaries* (Chicago: University of Chicago Press, 1984); Dollimore and Alan Sinfield, eds., *Political Shakespeare: New Essays in Cultural Materialism* (Ithaca and London: Cornell University Press, 1985); and Catherine Belsey, *The Subject of Tragedy: Identity and Difference in Renaissance Drama* (New York and London: Methuen, 1985).

11. Michel de Certeau, *The Practice of Everyday Life,* trans. Steven Rendall (Berkeley: University of California Press, 1984); Henri Lefebvre, *Critique of Everyday Life*, trans. John Moore (London and New York: Verso, 1991).

12. Patricia Fumerton, "Spacious Voices/Vagrant Subjects in Early Modern England"; Richard Helgerson, "Adulterous Alliances: Home, State, and History in Early Modern European Drama and Painting." See also the work-in-progress listed in this

volume in the Notes on Contributors, especially those of Dolan, Orlin, and Raber. Another newly published work of social history that embraces the common and marginal is Paul Griffiths, *Youth and Authority: Formative Experiences in England, 1560–1640* (Oxford: Clarendon Press, 1996). Of course, as I will argue in this introduction, the ordinary or trivial need not exclude the aristocracy, who also had an everyday life.

13. Heather Dubrow, in "The Newer Historicism," also finds both continuity and some methodological shift in moving from the new historicism of the 1980s to that of the '90s, though she describes the change somewhat differently and more locally than I do here (in her review of four second-generation new historicist books); *Clio* 25, 4 (1996): 421–38. Of course, we should heed Dubrow's caution against making overgeneralizations about new historicism (pp. 422–23), a warning vigorously advanced by Louis Montrose in his craftily titled essay, "New Historicisms"; in *Redrawing the Boundaries,* ed. Stephen Greenblatt and Giles Gunn (New York: MLA, 1992), pp. 392–418. Rather than fixing first-generation new historicism into a "homogeneous body of doctrines and techniques," Montrose argues, we should recognize "the heterogeneous and changing dimensions of the work." While we may acknowledge the uniqueness of individual new historicist approaches, such as Montrose's own, however, we can still detect a strain of shared concerns and methodology. Montrose's emphasis in this article on ideology and on "a ceaseless contest among dominant and subordinate positions," for instance, is typical of what I have characterized as the "political" (though not necessarily activist) character of first-generation new historicism; pp. 392, 405. For an argument that remains "political" but moves toward a more social historicism of the everyday, see John Fiske, "Cultural Studies and the Culture of Everyday Life," in *Cultural Studies,* ed. Lawrence Grossberg, Cary Nelson, and Paula A. Treichler (New York and London: Routledge, 1992), pp. 154–73.

14. See Clifford Geertz, "Thick Description: Toward an Interpretive Theory of Culture," in *The Interpretation of Culture* (New York: Basic Books, 1973), pp. 3–32.

15. Patricia Fumerton, *Cultural Aesthetics: Renaissance Literature and the Practice of Social Ornament* (Chicago: University of Chicago Press, 1991), pp. 11–18.

16. In "Gender and the Invention of Everyday Life," the feminist critic Rita Felsky discusses the varied and often contradictory meanings of the everyday but sees it as especially associated with women (paper presented at the 1997 Modern Language Association Convention, Toronto); see also Fiske, p. 168. Dubrow notes as well the interest by second-generation new historicists in the "domestic" (including in her examples two contributors to the present volume, Frances Dolan and Lena Orlin); p. 429.

PART I

MATERIALS OF THE EVERYDAY

2

The "I" of the Beholder

Renaissance Mirrors and the Reflexive Mind

Debora Shuger

THIS ESSAY BEGAN AS AN ATTEMPT to document an hypothesis that turned out to be false. While preparing a course on early modern autobiography, I ran across an intriguing essay by Georges Gusdorf which hypothesized that the invention of the clear glass mirror in the sixteenth century gave rise to modern, reflexive self-consciousness, which, in turn, led to the sudden proliferation of autobiographical genres.[1] I thought it might be worthwhile to trace the role this novel everyday artifact played in the emergence of early modern selfhood; at the time it seemed a plausible and suitably materialist alternative to current narratives of the modern self as a capitalist epiphenomenon.

The part about mirrors ended up being quite straightforward. Mirrors date from antiquity, but prior to the sixteenth century they were made either of brass or of a greenish dark glass, both producing only a shadowy, imperfect reflection: as in Saint Paul's "through a glass darkly." The Venetian discovery in 1507 of a method for making clear or "crystal" glass mirrors was, in the words of Herbert Grabes, the "technological marvel of the age."[2] Venetian glass spread throughout Europe; by the early seventeenth century, cheap crystal mirrors, now of English manufacture, had become widely available. For the first time, people could see what they looked like (and whether they had spinach on their teeth), although Renaissance mirrors were generally convex and hence, unlike the modern flat mirror, miniaturized objects. In fact, most Renaissance mirrors resemble miniatures: small, oval or circular, worn as an ornament—usually on a ribbon attached to one's waist—often lavishly encased.[3] They seem, moreover, to have made a deeper impression on the Renaissance imagination than did the miniature. Grabes, with most Germanic diligence, has ferreted out 398 English books with mirror-titles between 1500 and 1700; mirror-imagery traverses Renaissance drama, sonnets, satire, theology, emblem books, biographies, almanacs, encyclopedias, and what have you. This pervasive fascination with mirroring would seem to suggest that the mirror both registered and elicited a new awareness of individual identity — what do I look like — and a new reflexive self-consciousness: the specular gaze or Cartesian subjectivity where the perceiving "I" separates from and beholds — as in a mirror — an objectified "me."[4]

The problem with this suggestion is that, up to the late seventeenth century, references to mirrors, whether literal or metaphorical, are very odd. They are odd in several ways.

First, the object viewed in the mirror is almost never the self. The viewer sees a great many things in Renaissance mirrors but not, as a rule, his or her own face. Encyclopedias and how-to books thus frequently have mirror-titles, not because readers somehow see themselves in the text but because, like convex mirrors, such epitomes provide a small-scale version of a large subject. Hence one finds numerous titles on the order of *Speculum Britanniae. The first parte an historicall, & chorographicall description of Middlesex* (1593), *Speculum nauticum. A looking glasse for sea-men* (1624), *Europae speculum. Or, a view or survey of the state of religion in the westerne parts of the world* (1629), *Speculum mercativum, or the young merchants glass, wherein are exact rules of all weights, coins, measures, exchanges, and other matters necessary used in commerce* (1674), or *The sick womans priuate looking glass. Wherein methodically are handled all uterine affects, or diseases arising from the wombe* (1636). These mirrors obviously have nothing to do with self-consciousness.

The majority of Renaissance mirrors — or rather, mirror metaphors — do reflect a face, but not the face of the person in front of the mirror. Typically, the person looking in the mirror sees an exemplary image, either positive or negative. Thus in Jan David's woodcut entitled *Speculum exemplare* (from his 1610 volume, *Duodecim specula*) the couple kneeling in front of the mirror see Christ and the Blessed Virgin reflected in the glass (Figure 1); another woodcut, this one from Stephen Batman's *The trauayled Pylgrime* (1569), shows a knight gazing into a convex "glasse of reformation," which (presumably) reproduces not his own face but an ideal image on which he should model his new life (Figure 2). George Wither's *A Collection of Embleames* (1635) includes a picture of what appears to be a woman looking at herself in a mirror, but the appended verses erase any trace of reflexivity; the "faithfull glasse" she holds before her face turns out to signify "the good Examples of those pious men, / Who liv'd in elder times" or "a wise Companion, and, a loving Friend" (Figure 3).

The notion that viewers should attempt to mold their own features so as

Figure 1. Jan David, *Speculum exemplare*, from *Duodecim specula* (1610). By permission of the Huntington Library, San Marino, California.

The Author being caried by his horse Will to the palace of disordered liuers, seeing then the abuse of all vertues, and the maintenance of filthy luxuria, remembreth his promise made to Age, looketh in the glasse of reformation, straight taketh his iorney, forsaking vtterly those abuses.

The Author seeing Abusion of all ordered vertues, so deckt like a foole, suspecteth that all the rest inhabiters, are no fit companions, concerning his promise to Age, leaueth all and departeth with Memorie.

G.i.

Figure 2. Stephen Batman, the "glasse of reformation," from *The trauayled Pylgrime* (1569). By permission of the Huntington Library, San Marino, California.

In all thine Actions, have a care,
That no unseemlinesse appeare.

249

91

DECEAT·VT·NE·QVID

ILLVSTR. XLI.

Book. 4

THe *Virgine*, or the *Wife*, that much desires,
To please her *Lovers*, or her *Husband's* Eyes,
In all her costl'est *Robes*, her selfe attires;
And, seekes the coml'est *Dresse*, shee can devise.
Then, to her trustie *Looking-glasse*, shee goes,
(Where, often, shee her person turnes and winds)
To view, how seemely her attiring showes;
Or, whether ought amisse therein she finds.
Which praisefull *Diligence*, is figur'd thus
In this our *Emblem*; that, it may be made
A documentall signe, remembring us,
What care of all our *Actions*, must bee had.
For, hee that in G*o*d's presence would appeare
An acceptable *Soule*; or, gracious grow
With men, that of approv'd conditions are,
Must by some faithfull *Glasse*, be trimmed so.
The good Examples of those pious men,
Who liv'd in elder times, may much availe:
Yea, and by others evills, now and then,
Men see how grossely, they themselves, doe faile.
  A wise Companion, and, a loving Friend,
Stands nearer, than those ancient glasses doe;
And, serveth well to such an usefull end:
For, hee may bee thy *Glasse*, and *Fountaine* too.
His good *Example*, shewes thee what is fit;
His *Admonition*, checks what is awry;
Hee, by his *Good-advise*, reformeth it;
And, by his *Love*, thou mend'st it pleasedly.
  But, if thou doe desire the perfect'st *Glasse*,
Ioyne to the *Morall-Law*, the *Law of Grace*.

L l   Wee

Figure 3. George Wither, from *A Collection of Embleames*
(1635). By permission of the Huntington Library, San Marino, California.

to resemble what they behold in their mirrors—with its curious implication
that the face seen in the mirror is not their own—recurs in countless early
modern texts. Thus Shakespeare terms Henry V a "mirror of all Christian
kings" (2.Chorus.6); likewise in *1 Henry VI,* Talbot describes Salisbury as the
"mirror of all martial men" (1.4.75). Mirrors reflect biblical exemplars, as in
The myrrour or glasse of Christes passion (1534) and *A mirrour of mercie: or,
the prodigals conversion* (1614). Encomia on historical persons are likewise
mirrors—for example, Philip Stubbes's eulogy on his wife entitled *A christal
glasse for Christian women* (1591) or George Whetstone's *A mirror of treue
honnour and Christian nobilitie: exposing the life, death and deuine vertues of the
most noble and godly Lorde Frauncis Earle of Bedford* (1585). In Whetstone's *A
mirour for magistrates of cyties. Representing the ordinaunces, policies, and diligence,
of the noble Emperour, Alexander (surnamed) Severus* (1584) and Edmund Rich's
The myrrour of the Chyrche (1521), the glass portrays models for institutional
reform. These are not quite platonic mirrors—the Earl of Bedford is not a
platonic Idea—but they are, as it were, platonically angled, tilted upwards in
order to reflect paradigms rather than the perceiving eye.

A third standard type of Renaissance mirror does explicitly reflect what
Davies's *Nosce teipsum* calls "my inward selfe," but that self turns out to be
generic rather than individual.[5] Davies's poem, in fact, exemplifies this quite
nicely, since it seems to use the mirror precisely as a metaphor for reflexive self-
consciousness:

That *Powre* which gave my eyes, the world to view;
   To view my selfe enfus'd an *inward light*;
   Whereby my *Soule*, as by a Mirror true,
   Of her owne forme may take a perfect sight. . . .

As now me thinks, I do distinguish plaine,
Each subtill line of her immortall face.
                (ll. 193–96, 263–64)

But the "face" Davies then proceeds to sketch has an unexpectedly garden-
variety look; the description begins: *"The soule a substance*, and a *spirit* is,/
Which *God* him selfe doth in the Bodie make" (ll. 265–66). This self-portrait is
pretty clearly not the fruit of rigorous introspection. Davies's mirror reflects
theological commonplaces rather than anything we would be likely to call a
person's "inward selfe."

The generic face reflected by early modern mirrors can be less metaphorically flattering. Thus in a passage that, like the corresponding one
in Davies, initially seems to describe reflexive self-consciousness, Anthonie

Fletcher (1595) observes that "our eies, which do behold heauen and earth, and other innumerable creatures of God, do not see themselues, but looking in a glasse, by that meane, they perfectly see themselues." The next sentence, however, pursues the mirror-metaphor in an unanticipated direction: "So . . . if we will set before our eies, the glasse of the remembrance of death, and the true knowledge of our selues, . . . we cannot choose but very plainly see our selues and what we be."[6] David's *Speculum propriae vilitatis* illustrates this sort of "true knowledge of our selues": the foregrounded figure in the woodcut does not even look in the mirror placed behind him; instead, the mirror's entire surface is filled by a grinning skull, which, as the motto makes clear, reflects the authentic selfhood of each person who beholds it: "Approach and see what you are, what you will be, what you will have been. For this mirror, the title shall be 'know thyself' " (Figure 4). The "self" to be known here is distinctly not modern. Similarly, in Laux Furtnagel's *Portrait of Hans Burgk-mair and His Wife* (1529), the mirror does not reflect the middle-aged couple who stand alongside it, but once again the unindividuated skulls they shall become and, in some real sense, already are (Figure 5). Furtenagel's painting may depict an actual type of mirror; at least in the fifteenth century, some mirrors (called *miroirs de mort*) had skulls drawn on their linings, so that viewers would in fact see a sort of holographic deathshead rather than their own image.[7]

Instead of skull or soul, other generic mirrors reflect the mutability of earthly glory. In the final scene of Skelton's *Magnificence*, Sad Circumspection thus explains: "A mirror encircled is this interlude, / This life inconstant for to behold and see: / Suddenly advanced, and suddenly subdued, / Suddenly riches, and suddenly poverty."[8] The subtitle of the massively influential *Mirror for Magistrates* makes the same point; the text is a glass "Wherein may be seen by example of other, with howe grevous plages vices are punished: and howe frayle and vnstable worldly prosperitie is founde, euen of those, whom Fortune seemeth most highly to fauour."[9] The mirror reflects what is likely to happen to a given class of persons — namely, magistrates; the image is "realistic" only in the Thomist sense.

A second oddity characteristic of Renaissance mirrors is implicit in the first: as they do not reflect the face of the person who looks into them, so they ignore the viewer's subject-position — his or her "subjectivity." That is, if one tries to follow Hamlet's advice and "hold, as 'twere, the mirror up to nature" — using the typical Renaissance small hand-mirror — one of two things happens. Either you cannot see the reflected images at all, or, in attempting to glimpse the mirror's surface, you end up staring at your own face.[10] A similar difficulty crops up in *Nosce teipsum*, which describes the eyes as "Mirrors [that] take into

Figure 4. Jan David, *Speculum propriae vilitatis,* from *Duodecim specula* (1610). By permission of the Huntington Library, San Marino, California.

Figure 5. Lukas Furtenagel, *Portrait of Hans Burgkmair and His Wife*, 1529. Kunsthistorisches Museum, Vienna. Courtesy Erich Lessing / Art Resource NY.

their litle space, / The formes of *Moone*, and *Sunne*, and every *Starre*" (ll. 973–74). But who is looking into this mirror and from what vantage point? Davies, presumably, does not hold that vision requires the soul to stand in front of its own eyes; rather he just seems indifferent to questions of spatial / subject positioning.

Even when the text specifies the viewer's subject-position, its relation to the mirrored image remains peculiar. A sermon by St. John Chrysostom describes what seems an ordinary enough procedure: "when thou art sitting at a hairdresser's, and having thine hair cut, thou takest the mirror, and dost examine with care the arrangement of thy locks." But the analogy he then goes on to draw between this sort of mirror and one "spiritual, and far more excellent" confounds this straightforward relation between gaze and glass. The spiritual mirror, Chrysostom explains, "is the memory of good men, and the history of their blessed lives. . . . If you be willing once only to look upon the portraitures of those holy men, thou wilt both see the foulness of thine own mind, and having seen this, wilt need nothing else to be set free from that deformity."[11] In both cases, the mirror-image enables self-correction, but the physical mirror reflects the face before it while the spiritual one does not. In the spiritual mirror, the position of the gazing subject becomes irrelevant because, as the term "portraiture" suggests, the mirror is really a painting.

The mirrors depicted in Renaissance texts are, in fact, often paintings. The concepts frequently seem interchangeable; Caxton's *Mirrour of the world*, for example, translates the French *Image du monde*.[12] Caxton presumably considers image and mirror equivalent since both give a miniaturized version of the actual object; the convexity of Renaissance mirrors — not their reflexivity — grounds the metaphor. Renaissance practice, moreover, tends to elide mirrors and paintings: in the *miroirs de mort*, as we have seen, the skull is drawn on the glass's lining. Mirror and painting also overlap, although in a different manner, in Renaissance artistic practice, where mirrors were used to achieve a perspectively correct representation of external objects; the mirror showed how one might transpose three-dimensional objects on to a small-scale, flat surface. Gerard Dou, a student of Rembrandt, thus invented a mirror-stand by fixing a convex glass into a screen, which "formed a species of partition between the object to be represented and the artist." Dou then put a wire mesh grid over the mirror and traced its outline on to the canvas to indicate corresponding spatial coordinates, so that "the artist had only to copy . . . [the object] seen in a reduced scale in the glass."[13] Painting here copies — reflects, as it were — the mirror-image, but the mirror in turn does not reflect the "I" of the beholder.

In some contexts, mirrors seem closer to windows than to pictures: one looks through rather than at them (as, for example, Davies's eye-mirrors and St. Paul's "through a glass darkly" [per speculum]) — an association strengthened by the etymological link between "mirror" (*speculum*) and "window" (*specularia*). Hence in Jan David's *Speculum creaturarum*, the mirror reflects the visible world — the moon, sun, and stars imaged on its surface — but simultaneously functions as a window, allowing the kneeling spectators to see through it to the invisible things of God, depicted in the circle behind and above the circular mirror (Figure 6). Again, the self-reflexive function of the mirror seems to be its least essential or interesting aspect.

The exceptions tend to confirm the rule: when mirrors are used to view one's own face, they almost invariably signify vanity or related vices; so Stephen Batman's 1569 woodcut of a woman adjusting her headdress with the aid of a mirror, oblivious to the devil lurking at her back, is titled simply *Of Pride* (Figure 7). One would be hard-pressed to find any early modern English instance of mirroring used as a paradigm for reflexive self-consciousness. With the exception of Shakespeare's Richard II, no one looks in a mirror to find out what he looks like, to view himself — and Richard finds the result so unsatisfactory that he throws the mirror down and breaks it.[14]

But presumably early modern persons did not, in fact, generally hold mirrors up to nature or find saints staring back at them from their glass, but used them to see their own reflections. Representations (whether textual or pictorial) seem not to register everyday life — although some qualification may be in order here, since Renaissance persons seem to have tried to see a fair number of odd things in their mirrors. Fifteenth-century pilgrims, for example, held up mirrors to the relics displayed in Aachen's Liebfrauen Cathedral, boasting on their return (we are told) "that they had brought back physical evidence . . . because their mirrors had captured the reflection of the sacred scene."[15] A century later, magic mirrors capable of reflecting the future — a procedure known as "scrying" — still sparked at least half-serious interest among the educated elite; Queen Elizabeth thus requested John Dee to demonstrate the magical properties of his famous black mirror, which he performed, Dee reports, to "her Majestie's great contentment and delight."[16]

Yet if some mirrors were used for magical or similarly esoteric purposes, most were not; the practices of necromancers and pilgrims do not explain the pervasive absence of reflexivity in Renaissance mirror-images. The verbal and pictorial representations of mirrors, which seem so oddly irrelevant to what we can assume to have been the usages of everyday life, however, correspond exactly to the standard Renaissance model of cognition. Prior to the late seventeenth century, the mirror does not, as I had originally hypothesized, generate a new epistemic or psychological construct but is understood in terms of the

Figure 6. Jan David, *Speculum creaturarum*, from *Duodecim specula* (1610). By permission of the Huntington Library, San Marino, California.

Figure 7. Stephen Batman, "Of Pride," from *A christall glasse of Christian Reformation* (1569).

traditional, largely Aristotelian, account of mental operations. The oddness of Renaissance mirror-imagery points to the oddness of the pre-modern theory of mind.

Juan Luis Vives's 1538 *De anima et vita* is instructive here, partly because its epistemology is more or less standard Aristotelianism, but also because it makes frequent recourse to mirror-analogies. Reading Vives, one is struck by his total omission of any faculty or mental operation that might be designated self-consciousness. The only faculty by which the mind reflects on its own operations is *iudicium*, but judgment is the impersonal and objective process of scanning one's own thoughts for their logical validity, not self-consciousness.[17] The absence of the latter follows from Aristotelian theory, in which knowledge derives from sense-perception; hence, cognition is invariably conceived on the model of vision, and the eye does not see itself. Thought, Vives observes, "is, as it were, an image of things imprinted on the mind as in a mirror" — a mirror held up to nature, for, he continues, "our minds know that which comes from the outside."[18] In this mortal body, the mind is like "a person shut in a small room, which has no other aperture through which he can see outdoors except a glass window (*vitrea*); he thus can see only what the window permits."[19] The mind has mirrors, but they function like windows, allowing the inner "I" to perceive external objects, not to reflect the self to itself. Vives thus notes that writing about the soul is difficult and "unnatural," for "we do not have another mind above our mind, which could view and analyze the lower one. . . . God gives us these faculties so that we might use, not inspect, them."[20] We are simply not creatures designed to see ourselves.

This claim, of course, needs qualification. Both the Middle Ages and the Renaissance in fact stress certain types of self-scrutiny, but these are ethical rather than epistemic procedures, acts of conscience not self-consciousness. The examination of conscience, in fact, works very much like Chrysostom's spiritual mirror and the exemplary mirrors depicted in figures 1 and 2: one beholds in the synderesis — what Melanchthon calls the inward "mirror of God" — the exemplary images of good and evil.[21] This interior mirror reveals what one *should* look like, enabling the penitent to correct his or her present self so that it will, so to speak, reflect this interior reflection of the transcendent and transpersonal moral law.[22] Similarly, when Hamlet tells his mother that he will set before her "a glass / Where you may see the inmost part of you" (3.4.19– 20), what he apparently presents her with is not a mirror but the exemplary miniatures of her dead husband and his brother: "Look here, upon this picture, and on this, / The counterfeit presentment of two brothers" (3.4.54–55). Gertrude's response suggests that she too elides the miniature portraits with the inward mirror of conscience: "O Hamlet, speak no more! / Thou turn'st mine eyes into my very soul" (3.4.89–90). The idealized image of the man she should have loved, like Chrysostom's "memory of good men," shows her "the foulness of thine own mind." As before, the mirror of conscience reflects an ideal image, whose perfection discloses, by contrast, one's own deformities.

In this respect, mystical theology resembles moral. Works like Augustine's *Confessions* and Bonaventure's *Iter mentis ad Deum* do require what David Aers terms an "introspective search for self-knowledge."[23] But although medievalists have recently cited such works as evidence for backdating the emergence of the modern self by a millennium, mystical — and more generally, devout — introspection seeks to discover not one's self but God. Augustine explains, "Into myself I went, and with the eyes of my soul (such as it was) I discovered . . . the unchangeable light of the Lord."[24] So in Langland, Piers reports, "Clerkes kenne me that crist is in alle places / Ac I saw hym nevere soothly but as myself in a Mirour."[25] The self (or more properly, soul) that the contemplative seeks to know is not an individual subjectivity but the *imago Dei*.[26]

Although exceptions exist (the most obvious one in this case being Montaigne), the preponderance of evidence suggests that the Renaissance self lacks reflexivity, self-consciousness, and individuation, and hence differs fundamentally from what we usually think of as the modern self. To grasp the radical difference between these constructs it seems instructive to contrast the Renaissance models of selfhood discussed above with Leibniz's account.

Leibniz's early "Paris Notes" (1676) capture something of the excitement and wonder accompanying the modern discovery of the self:

> It seems that when I think of myself thinking and already know, between the thoughts themselves, what I think of my thoughts, and a little later marvel at this triplication of reflection, then I turn upon myself wondering and do not know how to admire this admiration. . . . Anyone who desires an experience of these matters should begin to think of himself and his thinking sometime in the middle of the night, perhaps when he cannot sleep, and think of the perception of perceptions and marvel at this condition of his, so that he comes gradually to turn more and more within himself or to rise above himself, as if by a succession of spurts of his mind. He will wonder that he has never before experienced this state of mind.[27]

Echoes of this nocturnal *Turmerlebnis* suffuse Leibniz's later works. In these, reflexivity (what he calls "apperception") becomes the distinctive property of human selfhood, for the "intelligent soul" is defined by "knowing that it is and having the ability to say that word 'I' so full of meaning," by its capacity for "*Reflexive Acts*, which enable us to think of what is called *I* and to consider that this or that lies within ourselves."[28]

For Leibniz, this "intelligent soul" is, as all things are, a monad; what this means, as he explains in the *Monadology*, is that the soul has (*pace* Vives) no windows — nothing enters it from without; rather, it itself is "the true immediate cause of all its actions and inward passions."[29] The soul (or self) thus is radically and strictly autonomous: "Nothing can happen to us but thoughts and perceptions, and all our future thoughts and perceptions are only consequences . . . of our previous thoughts and perceptions." Our experiences — the modifications and modulations of psychic life — are not caused by external objects or events but are exfoliations of our own nature, the unfolding of "an *internal principle*."[30]

But if the self has no windows, it is itself a "living mirror" of the entire universe, which it reflects from its particular "point of view," "as the same city is variously represented according to the various situations of him who is regarding it" or "as one and the same town viewed from different sides looks altogether different and is, as it were *perspectively* multiplied."[31] To say that the self mirrors the universe *from its point of view* is to define selfhood in terms of subject-position — of *subjectivity*; each self reflects the universe from a particu-

lar angle. And because no two selves occupy the same point of view, each subjectivity — each specular gaze — is radically individual.

Leibnizian monads are modern selves: reflexive, autonomous, individu-
ated, subjective. But Leibniz belongs to the generation of Locke and Newton,
not Shakespeare. While aspects of Leibniz's model derive from Descartes, one
cannot backdate this selfhood to the Renaissance, which seems to operate with
a fundamentally different — and in many respects antithetic — paradigm.

I want to end with two accounts of children seeing themselves in a mirror.
The first is by a twentieth-century psychologist, Fritz Wittels, who reports,

> When I was still a small boy, I woke one day with the overwhelming realization that I
> was an "I," that I looked externally, to be sure like other children but nonetheless was
> fundamentally different and tremendously more important. I stood before the mirror,
> observed myself attentively. . . . I do not know if I kissed my reflection, but I have seen
> other children kissing theirs; they come to terms with their ego by loving it.[32]

This is all I have ever read of Wittels; the passage reminds me more of Mister
Rogers than of Lacan, but its interest lies precisely in its banality.[33] For Wittels,
kissing one's reflection bespeaks a healthy "self-esteem," and one acquires this
sense of being special — a unique, valuable "ego" — in front of a mirror.

Three hundred years earlier, Vives briefly noted a similar phenomenon.
"Likeness," he observed, "is the cause of love, as if toward another self. Thus
children embrace and kiss mirrors in which they view their image because they
think another child like themselves to be inside."[34] In Vives, however, the children kissing themselves in the mirror are not coming to terms with their ego,
for they do not recognize the reflected face as their own. That Vives (unlike
Wittels) assumes this to be the "natural" response to one's mirror-image suggests that pre-modern people may have found the division of the self into
beholder and beheld — the habitual stance of modern self-consciousness — a
rather unfamiliar experience. Moreover, if Wittels's anecdote delineates an
auto-erotic primal scene, Vives's children, like Narcissus and Milton's Eve, do
not fall in love with themselves but with their image — an image that they
perceive as another. In a much-quoted passage from De amicitia, Cicero thus
remarks, "when a man thinks of a true friend, he is looking at himself in the
mirror."[35] For Vives likewise the object of love is always one's own image — but
not, however, one's own self. Hence his account of childish mirror-play concludes rather differently than Wittels's: "How great, think you, was the flame
of love that Adam felt at first beholding Eve, in whom he saw his very self
under a wholly different form?" So in Paradise Lost, when God draws the
newly-created Eve from the pool, where she has been gazing longingly at her

own reflection, and brings her to Adam, the divine voice enjoins her to love him "whose image thou art" and their children who will be "like thyself."[36] One's "likeness," the image of one's self, in the Renaissance, is not identical to one's self but *like* it — a significantly similar other. The early modern mirror functions according to an ontology of similitude rather than identity/difference; it reflects those whom one will or can or does resemble; conversely, before the late seventeenth century, its objectification of the viewing subject, allowing one to watch oneself, elicits virtually no theoretical interest.

Yet because mirrors provide an obvious metaphor for such self-objectification, the infrequency with which those depicted in Renaissance texts reflect the person looking at them suggests, as I have now argued at some length, the unimportance of reflexive self-consciousness during this period. It would also seem to suggest a second key difference between pre-modern versions of selfhood and later ones: the earlier versions do not construe selfhood in psychosexual terms.[37] There is nothing remotely Freudian about *Nosce teipsum*; for Davies, to know oneself has no more to do with the analysis of fantasies and traumas than it does with Cartesian introspection. What Renaissance mirror imagery implies is that these characteristically modern types of self-knowledge are related, since both (in contrast to the textual and pictorial mirrors of the Renaissance) require that the viewing subject also be the object viewed — and viewed largely in isolation; the mirror faces the one holding it up, so that it reflects *only* the form and pressure of this individual subjectivity. The modern self stands alone in front of the glass.

In the Renaissance, the self's internal mirror angles outward, toward the windows, permitting only an oblique glimpse of the surrounding mental furniture, whether cognitive or psychological. What Renaissance persons *do* see in the mirror are instead saints, skulls, friends, offspring, spouses, magistrates, Christ. The mirror reflects these figures because they are images of oneself; one encounters one's own likeness only in the mirror of the other. Renaissance texts and emblems consistently describe mirroring in these terms, which suggests that early modern selfhood was not experienced reflexively but, as it were, relationally.

The mirror-imagery, of course, merely implies this, but there are passages in Renaissance texts that make the relational character of the self quite explicit. William Perkins, the foremost Calvinist theologian under Elizabeth, gives a particularly striking formulation. "Every person," he thus argues, "is a double person"; spiritually and inwardly "I am a person of mine own self, under Christ." In secular life, however, one is "a person in respect of another": a "husband, father, mother, daughter, wife, lord, subject."[38] For Perkins, secular identity is by definition relational, existing solely "in respect of" other people.

While "in respect of" does not entail resemblance, the submerged visual meta-phor (*respicere* means "to look back upon") suggests mirroring; to be "in respect of another" implies that one's identity "reflects" that relationship. Thus in *Paradise Lost* Eve images her husband as both his "likeness" and "fit help" (8.450); she is Adam's "other self" because she is his counterpart—which is pretty much what Perkins means by "in respect of."[39]

In Perkins, moreover, inwardness is likewise relational. His "person of mine own self" remains "under Christ." The Renaissance mirrors of con-science, of the soul, even the mirrors of death with their grinning skulls, present inwardness along similar lines; they reflect a selfhood that, while not constituted by social bonds, is beheld—and beholds itself—in relation to God. Thus in David's *Speculum propriae vilitatis* the scenes above the death's-head portray, on the left, God reminding Adam and Moses of their own mortality, and on the right, penitents kneeling for the ritual imposition of ashes (Figure 4). The mirror of death positions the viewer *sub specie aeter-nitatis*, not in existential solitude. In *Nosce teipsum*, the soul, viewing itself "as by a Mirror true" (l. 195), likewise discovers that it is *not* a "dividual being,"[40] but "*kin to God, and Gods bright ray*,/A Citizen of heaven to earth confin'd" (ll. 711–12).

Only in Montaigne does one find selfhood imagined as a recessed space (*arrière-boutique*) where one goes to be alone: to get away from other people and, perhaps, to get out from under Christ.[41] Before the mid-seventeenth century, most people seem rather to have encountered their image reflected in another—for us, a deeply unfamiliar sort of mirroring. We do not, as a rule, describe friends and family as our reflections. We generally make a clear dis-tinction between self and other, whether God, ideal cultural types, or those to whom we are bound by affection, kinship, class, or collegiality. It is, I think, hard for us to conceive how a self could be relationally constituted—how others could mirror oneself, how self-knowledge could not entail reflexivity. Early modern persons seem to have known themselves in strange ways—a strangeness palpable in the extraordinary scene from Act 3 of Shakespeare's *Troilus and Cressida* where Ulysses holds up a "glass" for Achilles (3.3.47). The scene both enacts the process by which the self beholds its image in the mirror of the other and, more important for our purposes, attempts to describe how this process works. The two warriors having exchanged a brief greeting, Ulys-ses proceeds to inform his sulking compatriot that a man "feels not what he owes [i.e., owns], but by reflection." Not, however, by viewing his own reflec-tion, since the sentence continues: "As when his virtues shining upon oth-ers/Heat them, and they retort that heat again/To the first giver" (3.3.99–102). In reply, Achilles simply restates Ulysses's account, but in optical rather than thermal terms. The eye does not, he thus observes,

behold itself,
Not going from itself; but eye to eye oppos'd
Salutes each other with each other's form.
For speculation turns not to itself
Till it hath travl'd and is married there
Where it may see itself.

(3.3.106–11)

In this context, "speculation" apparently means "sight," but the etymological link to *speculum* implicitly configures seeing as a kind of mirroring. For Achilles, as for Ulysses, "speculation" is not reflexive, "turns not to itself." Instead, the structure of self-knowledge is, in the fullest sense, relational. Unlike its glass counterpart, the mirror of the other does not reflect on compulsion; to see oneself, another person must return the salute, must choose to respond, and, by responding, give back one's image.[42] Mirroring thus, as Achilles's wording indicates, resembles marrying.[43] And this, he quite startlingly concludes, "is not strange at all" (3.3.111).

Notes

1. Georges Gusdorf, "Conditions et limites de l'autobiographie," *Formen der Selbstdarstellung: analekten zu einer Geschichte des literarischen Selbstportraits*, ed. Guenter Reichenkron and Erich Haase (Berlin: Duncker and Humbolt, 1956), pp. 108–9.

2. Herbert Grabes, *The Mutable Glass: Mirror-Imagery in Titles and Texts of the Middle Ages and English Renaissance*, trans. Gordon Collier (Cambridge: Cambridge University Press, 1982), p. 4.

3. Ibid., pp. 4–5, 43.

4. For a succinct and lucid description of modern reflexive self-consciousness, see W. H. Auden's essay "Hic et Ille," which, significantly enough, begins "Every man carries with him through life a mirror, as unique and impossible to get rid of as his shadow" (*The Dyer's Hand and Other Essays* [New York: Vintage, 1989], pp. 93–96).

5. Sir John Davies, *Nosce teipsum*, in *The Poems of Sir John Davies*, ed. Robert Krueger (Oxford: Clarendon Press, 1973), l. 190. Subsequent line references to Davies's poem will be given parenthetically in the text.

6. Grabes, *Mutable Glass*, p. 89.

7. Ibid., p. 119.

8. John Skelton, *Magnificence*, in *The Complete Poems of John Skelton, Laureate*, ed. Philip Henderson, 2nd ed. (London: J. M. Dent, 1948), p. 243.

9. *Mirror for Magistrates*, ed. Lily B. Campbell (Cambridge: Cambridge University Press, 1938), p. 62.

10. The passage makes a good deal more sense if it is the audience who view their own "nature" in the dramatic *speculum*, but that is not quite what Hamlet says. Rather, the mirror "show[s] virtue her own feature, scorn her own image, and the very age and body of the time his form and pressure" (3.2.23–25). The mirror is beheld neither by the one holding it up nor by the "whole theater" (3.2.29), but by personified abstractions, leaving the precise scenario still rather hard to visualize.

11. Saint John Chrysostom, *The Homilies of St. John Chrysostom . . . on the Gospel of St. Matthew*, 3 vols., ed. and trans. Sir George Prevost, Library of Fathers of the Holy Catholic Church (Oxford, 1843–51), 1: 57–58.

12. Grabes, *Mutable Glass*, p. 43.

13. Benjamin Goldberg, *The Mirror and Man* (Charlottesville: University Press of Virginia, 1985), pp. 152–55.

14. Other passages likewise suggest that early modern persons might not always have been impressed by how accurately the new glass mirrors reproduced their own features; rather, like Richard II, they seem at times to have had the opposite response: what strikes them is the inadequacy of the reflected image. In *The Passions of the Minde in Generall* (ca. 1598), Thomas Wright argues that we find it easier to inspect "the corners of other mens soules" than our own, just as "no man knoweth exactly his owne face, because he neuer see it, but by reflexion from a glasse, & other mens countenances he conceiueth most perfectly, because he vieweth them directly, & in themselues" (ed. Thomas Sloan [Urbana: University of Illinois Press, 1971], p. 313). Gascoigne's *The Steele Glas* (1576) hinges on the rather odd claim that the old polished metal mirrors (the ones I have seen work about as well as a stainless-steel potlid) "shewde al things, even as they were in deede" (l. 186), while the "christal glas" distorts by showing "the thing much better than it is" (l. 189; in *English Sixteenth-Century Verse: An Anthology*, ed. Richard Sylvester [New York: Norton, 1984], pp. 275–317). I'm not sure how literally to take this claim; sixteenth-century glass mirrors were often quite poor, making objects look dark and blurry but not, one would think, better.

15. Goldberg, *The Mirror and Man*, p. 139.

16. Ibid., pp. 15–16.

17. Juan Luis Vives, *De anima et vita*, in volume 3 of *Opera omnia*, 8 vols., ed. Gregorio Mayans y Siscar (Valencia, 1782; rpt. London: Gregg Press, 1964), p. 362.

18. Ibid., pp. 407, 342.

19. Ibid., p. 364.

20. Ibid., p. 342.

21. Philip Melanchthon, *Liber de anima*, in *A Melanchthon Reader*, trans. Ralph Keen, American University Studies: Theology and Religion (New York: Peter Lang, 1988), p. 255.

22. See, for example, William Bouwsma's splendid *John Calvin: A Sixteenth-Century Portrait* (New York: Oxford University Press, 1988), pp. 179–80.

23. David Aers, "A Whisper in the Ear of Early Modernists; or, Reflections on Literary Critics Writing the 'History of the Subject,'" *Culture and History, 1350–1600: Essays on English Communities, Identities and Writing*, ed. David Aers (Detroit: Wayne State University Press, 1992), p. 183.

24. Augustine, *Confessions*, trans. William Watts, Loeb Classical Library (Cambridge, Mass.: Harvard University Press, 1950), 7.10. Quoted in Aers, "A Whisper," p. 183.

25. *Piers Plowman: The B Version*, ed. George Kane and E. Talbot Donaldson (London: Athlone Press, 15.161–62. Quoted in Aers, "A Whisper," p. 184.

26. See Debora K. Shuger, *Habits of Thought in the English Renaissance: Religion, Politics, and the Dominant Culture*, The New Historicism: Studies in Cultural Poetics 13 (Berkeley: University of California Press, 1990), p. 100.

27. Gottfried Wilhelm Leibniz, *G. W. Leibniz's "Monadology": An Edition for Students*, ed. Nicholas Rescher (Pittsburgh: University of Pittsburgh Press, 1991), p. 77.

28. Ibid., pp. 109–111.

29. Ibid., pp. 58, 69.

30. Ibid., pp. 97, 68.

31. Ibid., pp. 198, 200.

32. Goldberg, *The Mirror and Man,* p. 249.

33. Lacan's account of the mirror stage (*Ecrits,* 12) at times seems quite close to Wittels—especially the former's claim that the "jubilant assumption of his specular image by the little man . . . [or] the mirror stage is interesting in that it manifests the affective dynamism by which the subject originally identifies himself with the visual *Gestalt* of his own body" as "an ideal unity, a salutary *imago*." But Lacan does not claim that the infant initially and, as it were, instinctively recognizes the mirrored image as his own; this self-recognition occurs during the mirror stage. See Anika Lemaire, *Jaques Lacan,* trans. David Macey (London: Routledge & Kegan Paul, 1977), pp. 80, 177.

34. Vives, *De anima,* p. 155.

35. Marcus Tullius Cicero, *Laelius: On Friendship* [*De amicitia*], in *Cicero on the Good Life,* trans. Michael Grant (Middlesex: Penguin Books, 1971), p. 189.

36. John Milton, *Paradise Lost,* ed. Merritt Hughes (New York: Odyssey Press, 1935), 4.472–74.

37. On this, see Stephen Greenblatt, "Psychoanalysis and Renaissance Culture," *Literary Theory/Renaissance Texts,* ed. Patricia Parker and David Quint (Baltimore: Johns Hopkins University Press, 1986), pp. 210–24.

38. William Perkins, *The Work of William Perkins,* ed. Ian Breward, The Courtenay Library of Reformation Classics (Appleford, Eng.: Sutton Courtenay Press, 1970), p. 382. I have discussed this passage and its sources in *Habits,* 94–95. See also Katharine Eisaman Maus, *Inwardness and Theater in the English Renaissance* (Chicago: University of Chicago Press, 1995), p. 11.

39. Even in modern English, the phrase "mirror image" can refer not only to an exact likeness but, since mirrors reverse right and left, also to an inverse or complementary one. Thus on the one-sex model of Galenic physiology, the female and male genitals constitute mirror-images of each other; they are, that is, counterparts.

40. The phrase is from *Paradise Lost* 12.85. By "dividual" Milton, of course, means something close to what we would call "individual."

41. Michel de Montaigne, "Of Solitude," *The Complete Essays of Montaigne,* trans. Donald Frame, 174–82 (Stanford, Calif.: Stanford University Press, 1957), p. 177; quoted in Greenblatt, *Renaissance Self-Fashioning from More to Shakespeare* (Chicago: University of Chicago Press, 1980), p. 46. Montaigne, to be sure, does not say this latter part. Yet most private spaces in the Renaissance are devotional; Montaigne's *arrière-boutique* conspicuously is not.

42. This is less complicated than it sounds; e.g., one knows he or she is funny by the fact that people laugh at one's jokes. Their response *reflects* one's sense of humor.

43. This is very close to the claim, which goes back to antiquity, that the beloved functions as a mirror in which the lover beholds himself (or, conversely, that the lover functions as a mirror in which the beloved beholds herself). See, for example, Plato, *Phaedrus,* 255d; Spenser, *Amoretti* 45.

3

"Reasonable Creatures"

William Cavendish and the Art of Dressage

Karen L. Raber

HORSES IN EARLY MODERN ENGLAND plowed fields, transported humans and goods across the countryside, and carried men into war. Perhaps because horses are so ubiquitous a part of the early modern world, yet so foreign to our own context, the social and political ramifications of their use in early modern culture have rarely been foregrounded in recent criticism. Anthony Dent, one exception to this rule, laments that contemporary scholars blithely accept their own ignorance of what has become a "special interest" in the twentieth century.[1] I agree with Dent—we lose tremendously if we do not attempt to recover something of that early fundamental material dependence on the horse. I would emphasize, however, that the intellectual, emotional, and financial relationship between man and horse was also the site of important ideological work. The amount of money, time, and effort expended on a horse was, for instance, a significant indicator of class difference: the cost of daily feed for one horse exceeded the daily income of the average laborer. The quality of a horse spoke volumes about the distinction and taste of its owner, and its maintenance for carriage-pulling, racing, or pleasure riding made it a sign of surplus income invested in ostentatious consumption.[2] Above all, the skill a rider demonstrated in horsemanship could instantly and efficiently indicate nuances of his educational background, political sympathies, and temperament to any observer.

This essay examines one locus where the horse's ideological significance is most prominently and complexly explored, namely the seventeenth-century horsemanship treatises of William Cavendish, Duke of Newcastle. Composed during the civil war, Cavendish's books on horsemanship assert the superior skill, intellect, and humanity of the aristocratic horseman, demonstrated through his refinement of a display-oriented style of riding and his adoption of humane training methods to accomplish mastery over his animal. In so doing, however, the treatises also reformulate codes for aristocratic behavior and purpose: the aristocrat becomes in Cavendish's works a leader of men not by virtue of his power with the court but by virtue of his superior taste, sensitivity, and refinement; rather than depleting the country's resources for war, the aristocrat becomes their diligent protector.[3] Such redefinition of the aristocrat's role represents a partial defense against the renewed but less secure class distinctions the Restoration brings to English society. Yet the methods Cavendish's texts describe and advocate inadvertently endow his horses with will, agency, and character. In this essay I argue that Cavendish's depiction of his animals is at odds with his conscious purpose in authoring the treatises. Cavendish's horses embody elements of a subtle yet sweeping historical change in the world of human relationships: definitions of individualism eventually appropriated by the middle classes toward the end of the eighteenth century are already germinating in Cavendish's Restoration England. Concepts of individualism, individual rights, and rational participation in self-government have begun, despite the return of monarchy, to transform English political and social life; these concepts, reflected in Cavendish's descriptions of his beloved horses, are precisely those that will ultimately marginalize the kind of aristocratic identity their author himself exemplified before the Civil War. Thus, although Cavendish's treatises appear to be intended to recuperate the privilege and power of Caroline England, their construction of horses who are "reasonable creatures" valorizes a definition of individual consciousness that will ultimately subvert aristocratic claims to special status. This essay looks at how Cavendish's treatises thus both resist and unconsciously encapsulate and contribute to one of the most far-reaching transformations of everyday early modern English life.

In 1667 William Cavendish's treatise *A New Method and Extraordinary Invention to Dress Horses* was published in England, a redaction for the English public of his great work outlining a design for selecting, breeding, and training horses, the *General System of Horsemanship*.[4] Together these texts articulate a training method now considered one of the most advanced of its time. The art of riding detailed in Cavendish's text has become known as "dressage," from the French word for training. But this simple term obscures the rigorous complexity of Cavendish's method. Page after page is filled with intense and detailed technical instruction for horse and rider, accompanied by drawings that show the placement and movement of the horse's hooves in strict patterns. The highest goal of this style of horsemanship is the perfection of the *haute école* or battle maneuvers for horse and rider, which include the *levade*, the *capriole*, and the *courbette* (respectively, balanced rearing with the front legs held tight to the body, the leap with a rearward kick, and the balanced leap on hind legs). These movements, which demand extreme precision and physical exertion, were initially taught because of their usefulness to cavalry for repelling attackers: the *levade* allows the mounted soldier to cut and slash at infantry from a height, while his horse's legs, positioned defensively, protect its belly from blows; the *courbette* repeats this effect, but the horse progresses by leaping forward in balance, driving its rider's target before it; and the *capriole* is suited to a horse wearing spiked shoes, as it allows the horse's hind legs to serve as additional striking weapons, clearing a space for maneuvering in battle. Cavendish's treatises anatomize the lengthy process of conditioning and educating the horse to the pinnacle of performance these movements represent.

Cavendish's commitment to dressage flowered during the lowest period of his life. Exiled to the Continent after his ignominious defeat at Marston Moor, Cavendish had lost everything that gave his life meaning. A staunch defender of the throne, descended from an aristocratic family known for its service to the government and the king, Cavendish found himself during the latter part of the civil war not only financially impoverished, forced to beg forbearance from his creditors in Holland, but banished as well from all the social structures and physical landmarks that had shaped his sense of self. To fill the vacuum of his loss, Cavendish threw himself into his equestrian pursuits, borrowing horses or the money to buy them. At various times, Cavendish owned five Barbs, five Spanish horses, and a host of Dutch animals. Although the Cavendishes suffered extreme financial hardship during their exile and William Cavendish was frequently reduced to begging his creditors' forbearance, he refused to sell any of these, his most valuable assets. He notes proudly in the Preface to his *New Method*, "I was then too great a Beggar, to think to be made Rich by the Sale of a Horse: I have bestow'd many Thousands of Pounds in Horses, and I have given many, but never was a good Hourse-Courser; Selling being none of my Professions." His determination to hold on to his prized possessions is yet easier to understand when Cavendish describes how his training of his animals to extraordinary levels of obedience and accomplishment attracted the admiration of some of Europe's most powerful royalty:

Many French Gentlemen, and Persons of the greatest quality of that Nation, did me the favour to see my Horses; and the Prince of Conde himself, with several Noble-men, and Officers, was pleased to take the pains to goe twice to my Mannage [dressage]. . . .

Among many great Persons . . . the Landgrave of Hesse, did not only do me the honour to Visit me and see my Horse; but, being return'd to his Country, was pleased to shew, by a very kind Letter, That he had not forgotten me. (*NM*, Preface)[5]

The extent to which Cavendish's pastime underwrote his self-esteem is revealed not only in his own writing, but in the many works of his wife,

Margaret Cavendish. Her *Playes*, also written during the couple's exile, defend her husband's judgment of military matters by emphasizing his attention to the importance of choosing good war horses. For instance, a character in her play *Bell in Campo* praises the General of the good Kingdom of Reformation for choosing "such horses as are usefull in War, such as have been made subject to the hand and heel, that have been taught to Trot on the Hanches, to change, to Gallop, to stop"[6] and other sound traits described in her husband's works. In her *Description of the New World, Called the Blazing World*, Margaret Cavendish pleads her husband's case repeatedly, lamenting the reduction of his estates and fortunes. Her disembodied soul traveling the cosmos with the soul of the Empress of the World at one point leads the Empress to her husband's estate at Welbeck, where the Empress comments on the beautiful forests there, giving the duchess the opportunity to deplore the war's devastation of the woods her husband had once cultivated. As part of the Empress's entertainment, Newcastle rides his best horses for her, demonstrating his skill at the "manage."[7]

Cavendish defends his dressage training method from criticism for being mere "Tricks, Dancing and Gamballs, and of no use" (*NM*, p. 11), on the basis that it is crucial to contemporary warfare: "Every thing and Particle of it Useful, and so Useful that a Good Horseman, upon such a Horse, would have so much advantage . . . either in a single Combat, or in the Warres" (*NM*, p. 6). But such a claim is patently false: the use of pikes had made mounted cavalry less effective as a shock force to cut through enemy infantry, and by the 1660s the perfection of firepower meant that the mounted cavalry had lost virtually all its value to the army as a fighting unit.[8] Battles as early as the Middle Ages showed that the cavalry as a heavy-armored attack force was ineffective: at Crécy and Agincourt, the English had watched the French cavalry decimated by English archers; horses and riders were mowed down long before they could reach enemy lines to engage. Even amongst the English, however, the tradition of cavalry as a fighting force died hard, partly because of its class associations. Attempted adaptations to new military developments included extremely heavy armor for horsemen (which made speed impossible, and James I himself was reputed to have commented that all armor did was prevent the rider from doing injury to his enemies), and the use of firearms from horseback (a Swedish tactic only effective once, because of delays in reloading, and at close range against massed infantry). The Civil War saw a brief resurgence for the cavalry, mainly because they learned a new approach, the close-order advance. Cromwell's forces were successful in making good use of cavalry once they honed this tactic — but again, these are not military uses that require anything remotely like the *haute école*. Although Cavendish may have been impressed with Cromwell's cavalry, he had personally experienced the limited effect they had in battle when he and Prince Rupert were defeated at Marston Moor, despite the fact that both Royalist generals were famous for their horsemanship skills and commanded troops who also had strong skills in horsemanship.

Thus precisely those maneuvers of horse and rider which Cavendish's system offers as its aim are obsolete. Cavendish tacitly concedes this fact by observing that the principal benefit of the *haute école* is that "to make a horse go in leaps, firms him on the Hand, which is good for a Souldiers Horse" (*NM*, p. 12). The goal of dressage, then, the *haute école*, is only useful to the soldier for inculcating an extra degree of obedience and skill at ground work. The final proof that Cavendish's techniques are not really battle-oriented is found in the apparel of the dressage rider: he wears no armor at all since anything that would interfere with the rider's balance or delicate communication of leg to horse must be discarded. As Anthony Dent observes "school-riding" in fact had little to do with terrorizing enemies: "the military side of it was really an elaborate pretense."[9]

What dressage does provide, and what is repeatedly emphasized in Cavendish's work, is a mode of display of both horse and rider, one which derives from a tradition associating control of the unruly, wild, irrational beast by human hand with the control, and consequent social and political dominance, of the upper classes over the mass of mankind. By the sixteenth and seventeenth centuries only one of the feudal aristocrat's roles survived — mounted escort for the monarch. What had once been a practical service was refined into a symbolic performance in state processions, with aristocrats parading their skill to remind the masses of their monarch's magnificence and their own consequence.[10] Cavendish's work also reflects the growing interest during the late sixteenth and early seventeenth centuries in the horse as a specific kind of commodity — his advice on selecting and breeding horses emphasizes beauty and "character" as much as utility. Dressage, as Cavendish practices it, constructs a new relationship between horse and rider in which skillful horsemanship, based on a cooperative and sensitive understanding between horse and rider, affirms class distinctions. Only the high-born are capable of such refined communication. Of course this also incidentally creates a new, self-consciously non-utilitarian leisure pursuit for the aristocracy.

Early modern literary depictions of horse and rider generally affirm the place of good horsemanship as an image of good rule, whether over the passions in the individual, or over the state as a collective. When Spenser has his hero Guyon "unhorsed" at the outset of Book II of the *Faerie Queene*, the gesture literalizes Guyon's journey of self-discovery, his transcendence through self-control and the containment of passion. Shakespeare fills his plays with such imagery, used to signal both the personal and the political dimension of the horse-rider relationship: in *1 Henry IV*, Harry Hotspur, pressed by his wife to tell her he loves her, replies "When I am a-horseback, I will swear / I love thee infinitely."[11] Hotspur's bawdy remark is only half jesting, since everything Hotspur says in this scene suggests that indeed he loves his horse better than his wife. Robert Watson, in an article entitled "Horsemanship in Shakespeare's Second Tetralogy," notes that images of horsemanship could be used either to celebrate the ruler's command over his subjects, or to suggest that the confusion of military with political authority is dangerous to the state.[12] Hotspur is the quintessential example of the latter use. His very name indicates his unruly, passionate temperament, but it is his glorification of death in military endeavor that signals his unfitness to rule even before Prince Hal emerges as the king's "true" heir. Richard II is similarly compared to a hotblooded stallion by York in the first play of the tetralogy (I.iv.70), and when he is deposed he laments, "Down, down I come like glist'ring Phaethon / Wanting the manage of unruly jades" (III.iii.178–79). Richard is unable to command his subjects because he refuses to allow that a monarch must be, like Bolingbroke, a Machiavellian politician as well as a divinely ordained ruler — he plummets from the heights of divine rule toward the unyielding ground of a new political era. Bolingbroke's usurpation extends to the commandeering of Richard's favorite mount: "That jade hath eat bread from my royal hand; / This hand that made him proud with clapping him. / Would he not stumble?" Richard asks the groom, "Would he not fall down?" (V.v.85–87). After blaming his Barbary's treason, Richard shifts to *identification with* his misused mount, complaining that he is "spurred, galled . . . by jauncing Bolingbroke."[13]

The absolute monarch's right to reign was metaphorically represented by his "right reining" of his mount in statuary and portraiture from fifteenth-century Italy to seventeenth-century England. But only with the advent of dressage as an art form in its own right did such representation take on the subtleties that I will indicate it achieves in Cavendish's works. The old connection between good horsemanship and good rule could be expressed through images of the rider's control of a dynamic rearing or galloping horse; painters like Rubens and Velasquez, though, who are credited with introducing the *haute école* to royal portraiture, used the more rarified image of the ruler engaged in an aristocratic exercise of military precision riding for its own sake. The artistic and political implications of this new formula are far-reaching. To clarify how they work, we might compare Rubens' depiction of St. George and the Dragon (1606) (Figure 1) with a much earlier (1505) version by Raphael of the same subject (Figure 2). Raphael's horse is lunging over the

Figure 1. Rubens, *Saint George and the Dragon*, c. 1606. Museo del Prado, Madrid.

Figure 2. Raphael, *St. George and the Dragon*, 1506. Andrew W. Mellon Collection, National Gallery of Art, Washington, D.C.

body of the slain dragon. Its position is static and unrealistic — it would be impossible for it to balance at such a point long enough for its rider to kill the dragon. Dent terms this a "classicizing tendency," which imitates the ancient style exemplified in the second-century Roman statue of Marcus Aurelius.[14] Alternatively, we might term Raphael's painting a more "medieval" model: showing the galloping horse in an unbalanced forward gait, it images all that was required of it in the age of lances and broadswords. Rubens, in contrast, even in this early work has suspended his horse and rider in a position — wheeling in a near-*levade* or *courbette* — which might conceivably have been performed by any horse trained in the *haute école*.[15] Although Rubens clearly is thinking of Raphael's earlier painting, his own animal is muscled and full of detail — note its wild mane, the lovingly detailed contours of its muzzle, even the inclusion of details of the shoes it wears. This is not precisely a naturalistic style, but it certainly revels in the minutiae of the horse's physical appearance and demonstrates intimate knowledge of equine anatomy. More restrained, but equally suggestive, is Velasquez's 1634 portrait of Philip IV (Figure 3), in which Philip executes the *levade*. Again, Velasquez accentuates the horse's musculature, flowing mane and tail, and focuses intensely on the combined relaxation and balance of the rider. This horse is slightly wild-eyed and its mouth is open against the bit, suggesting a fiery nature contained by the rider's confident hand.

The height of such emphasis on formally correct dressage in portraiture is found in Jacob Jordaens's painting, *A Cavalier on a Horse Executing a Levade* (Figure 4), which frames the rider with an elaborately decorated arch. This horse too is rendered with loving attention to anatomical detail — yet the arch removes the rider and his animal entirely from the "natural" realm. No longer does the rider master the ungoverned power of the horse; instead, horse and rider are crystallized abstractions, signaling man's triumph over nature through his ability to transform the natural into the artificial. Jordaens's horse has no fiery eye or open mouth, but looks out of the painting at the observer with soft, intelligent eyes. Meanwhile the rider focuses his gaze ahead and downward, as if channeling his own rational capacity through his horse's head and outward through his horse's eyes — as indeed the good dressage rider should do. Nature cooperates and is elevated to near-human understanding. As in Cavendish's treatises, this redefinition of the natural is accomplished through partnership rather than a struggle for dominance.

Van Dyck's famous 1635 portrait of Charles I on horseback (Figure 5) perhaps most comprehensively reproduces the complex relationship between man and horse charted in Cavendish's treatises. This painting has already been treated to an exhaustive critical analysis by Roy Strong. Strong examines the

Figure 3. Velasquez, *Equestrian Portrait of Philip IV*, 1634–35. Museo del Prado, Madrid.

painting's synthesis of imperial power, chivalry on behalf of God and love, Neo-Platonic philosophy, and the king's claim to rule by divine right.[16] We should approach the painting with these elements in mind, but I want to focus more specifically on its equine participant. First, Charles's supremacy as king is communicated through the armor he wears, the seal about his neck, his demeanor, and most obviously the tablet calling him King of Great Britain. Van Dyck portrays Charles with a meditative gaze and flowing locks to suggest both the poetic and the philosophical dimensions of the king's role. If we look at Charles's horse, we notice that its flowing locks imitate its rider's, reproducing a romanticized heroism, powerful, yet mannered and beautiful. Despite the massive size of the king's mount, an expression of its and its rider's substance

Figure 4. Jordaens, *A Cavalier on a Horse Executing a Levade*, 1634–35. Gilbert H. Montague Collection, Museum of Fine Arts, Springfield, Massachusetts.

and power, its head is far smaller than is proportional: Van Dyck adjusts equine anatomy to show that the horse's intelligence defers to its rider's authority.

What I want to highlight in Van Dyck's painting is an interesting tension between the artist's need to show the king *in control* as a horseman on a worthy mount, and the tendency of the mount to *mirror* its rider's identity. While the horse's body is big and imposing and its head deferentially small, its general richness of texture, its flowing mane, even its abstracted gaze, reproduce rather

Figure 5. Van Dyck, *Equestrian Portrait of Charles I*, c. 1638. Photo, National Gallery Picture Library, London.

than submit to its rider's identity. In this respect the portrait balances human dominance over the beast with a parallelism — even equity — between horse and rider. Of another Van Dyck painting, also of Charles on horseback, the painter Northcote would later remark that these equine companions are "not exactly like . . . horse[s]" but "might be admitted into a drawing room without offence."[17] A horse that might share tea and conversation in polite company is hardly the best vehicle for demonstrating the rider's metaphoric triumph over "bestial" nature. The validity of the horse-rider image as a metaphor for the imposition of rule, so prevalent in sixteenth- and early seventeenth-century literary works, is thus troubled by the introduction of the ideals of dressage to equestrian art. These beautiful, cultivated animals, which respond so completely to their riders as to mimic human qualities or even embody human attributes, shift the metaphor's emphasis from externally imposed control to mutuality and cooperation.

Like the Van Dyck portrait, and to some extent like those by Rubens and Jordaens, Cavendish's treatises find themselves balancing two not entirely compatible imperatives. While all these works glorify the physicality of the horse, lovingly investigating every contour, every muscle and movement, they engage in this anatomizing study as a means of establishing the claim of the rider to a certain class status. The art of dressage (and here I mean both the practice on horseback and its representation in paintings) strives above all to conceal the labor of the rider and the host of trainers, grooms, farriers, and others who contribute to the horse's training and upkeep, so that the monarch's or aristocrat's authority can be evidenced in his superior horsemanship and the *sprezzatura* of his artistry. Although Cavendish himself allows that dressage takes great "Labour, Study, and Practice," he intends the reader to understand that mastering the art thus requires vast financial resources and leisure time. Figure 6 demonstrates the connections Cavendish wishes to draw between horsemanship, display, birthright, and class superiority. The picture shows Cavendish on his estate at Welbeck, which was one of those he reclaimed after the civil war and one of his most regal and productive family possessions. Cavendish and his horse execute the *levade* on a broad pathway through his bountiful land holdings. We should recall Margaret Cavendish's complaint that the stands of trees, stags and deer, and plentiful birds took Cavendish years to replenish after the property's Parliamentarian owner plundered the estate's resources. In this engraving, the aristocrat has restored paradise — an artful paradise comprised of those beings that belong to the aristocratic estate's Arcadian past. Cavendish's commanding presence carrying the whip that indicates his status as a horse master is the perfected, ideal image of the many other riders to left and right who hunt on horseback with the help of servants and hounds. In this plate, riding is clearly a fitting pursuit for aristocratic leisure time, part of an aristocratic production of effortless and expansive beauty and bounty.

But Cavendish's treatises also unintentionally complicate this picture. Their depiction of the relationship Cavendish advocates between horse and rider introduces elements that work against the class hierarchy meant to sustain both the position of the absolute monarch and, by extension, the identity

Figure 6. Lucas Vorsteman the Younger after Abraham von Diepenbeck, engraving for Cavendish, *General System of Horsemanship*, Plate 38.

and position of the aristocracy who have traditionally been defined by their service to him. In much the same way that Van Dyck's painting partially subverts its apparent message, Cavendish's belief that his horses are "reasonable creatures," his endowment of them with a form of subjectivity that transcends dull brutishness, puts horse and rider into a cooperative partnership in which the horse must be coerced to participate willingly and gladly rather than forced to submit by the imposition of superior power or even reason. Such a relationship, although it assumes that the rider will still achieve a kind of dominance, is no longer fully, fixedly, or naturally hierarchical.

Cavendish criticizes earlier writers on dressage, most specifically the early sixteenth-century Italian master Federigo Grisone, for their cruel or silly practices:

For a Resty Horse, they Raise a whole Town with Staves to Beat him . . . with Squirts, Fire, Whelps, Hedg-hoggs . . . and the same they do Before a Horse that Runs Away . . . For a Horse that is Afraid, and Starts, they appoint Whirlegiggs of several Colours, which will make him Ten times Worse. (*NM*, 18–19)

These methods, relying on external enforcement, cannot work, Cavendish argues.[18] The rider must "cherish" his animal—a word Cavendish uses frequently—educate it, work with its natural instincts. Cavendish's more "humane" approach in fact *humanizes* the horse much further than mere anthropomorphization might. He insists that "a horse's reason is to be wrought upon" (*GS*, 13). Failures in training horses can be traced to the failures of human, not equine, intellect:

Don't then expect more understanding from a horse than a man, since the horse is dress'd in the same manner that children are taught to read. The horse is taught first to know, and then by frequent repetition to convert that knowledge into habit. (*GS*, 11)

Cavendish disputes Descartes's argument that animals do not think:

If he does not think . . . it would be impossible to teach him what he should do. But by the hope of reward, and fear of punishment; when he has been rewarded or punished, he thinks of it, and retains it in his memory (for memory is thought) and forms a judgment by what is past or what is to come (which again is thought;) insomuch that he obeys his rider not only for fear of correction, but also in hopes of being cherish'd. (*GS*, 12)

Indeed, regarding passions Cavendish claims "a horse knows as much of ours, as we do of his; because we know perfectly the passions of one another; a love, hatred, thirst of revenge, envy, etc." (*GS*, 13).

The new, humane, and rational methods Cavendish employs require studious application, to encourage which Cavendish includes detailed drawings to show how the horse's feet should be placed to execute a movement correctly. He gives precise advice on when to correct, how, and how to avoid overcorrection: "[W]hen any Prince of Nobleman comes to see his Manege [the horse master's training] he is sure to find him *Whip in Hand*, which, as he fancies, is the most becoming aire he can assume, whereas it is the most ridiculous; wherefore never use it when it can be avoided" (*GS*, 19). The best analogies Cavendish finds for training animals compare them to school children or soldiers. Horses must even have their days of rest in Cavendish's method: "Have not all Schollers Play-dayes? and certain Hours of Rest in their daies of Study? All Tradesmen, Holy-dayes to Rejoyce themselves in? States-Men, Divertisements from Business?" (*NM*, p. 39). From a plate in the *General System* (Figure 7) we find what Cavendish expects his scholars to be doing while on holiday: while many prance or relax, some of these horses, like schoolboys conning their lessons, are practicing their *haute école* on their time off, perhaps the better to encourage their masters to cherish them well.

Keith Thomas, in *Man and the Natural World*, observes that "humane" training methods for animals coincide with more humane treatment of young

Figure 7. Cavendish, *General System of Horsemanship*, Plate 12.

boys at school.[19] Like women, children were often considered in need of "taming"—indeed, as Thomas notes, the language of bridling, haltering, and breaking linked the status and education of animals with that of women and children. But emphasis on the correction of undesirable behavior among women and children through external devices and punishments was gradually rejected in favor of methods that inculcated the desire for correct behavior based on a more subtle system of reward, dependence, and sentiment. Instead of being beaten like beasts with no rational capacity, school children could be coerced by the promise of practical or spiritual enrichment if they demonstrated self-control, just as wives could be persuaded to accept marital subordination if it meant God's and their husbands' love.

We should find it significant, then, that Michel Foucault begins a chapter of *Discipline and Punish* principally on discipline in schools and prisons with an account of the *dressage* or training of soldiers:

The classical age discovered the body as object and target of power. It is easy enough to find signs of the attention then paid to the body—to the body that is manipulated, shaped, trained, which obeys, responds, becomes skilful and increases its forces. The great book of Man-the-Machine was written simultaneously on two registers: the anatomic-metaphysical register, of which Descartes wrote the first pages and which the physicians and philosophers continued, and the technico-political register, which was constituted by a whole set of regulations and by empirical and calculated methods relating to the army, the school and the hospital, for controlling or correcting the operations of the body.[20]

Foucault argues that the modern era replaces the mechanistic view of the body with an even higher art of dressage: the cultivation of the "docile body," which "may be subjected, used, transformed and improved." Unlike its mechanistic precursor, this "disciplined" body was the product of a "policy of coercions" aimed at making it at once more thoroughly subjected, yet at the same time more useful.[21] The shift from classical to modern methods relies in large part on the construction of human interiority, of a type of human consciousness capable of more thoroughly policing itself from within as well as accepting external correction.

   Foucault's analysis of "gentle punishment," the exploitation of individual subjects achieved through discipline and punishment, and his affirmation of the state's interest in a more coercive exercise of power resonate with early modern changes in the treatment of animals and children and with Cavendish's insistence that his training methods are judicious, flexible, and rational. This is precisely my main point: Cavendish's construction of his horses in his treatises participates in discourses that run counter to his own politics and social beliefs. Cavendish was a committed Hobbesian. His close association with Hobbes is mentioned in Thomas Slaughter's introduction to his translation of Cavendish's letter of advice to Charles II (1659). Further, however, Slaughter points out that Cavendish's political theory, such as it is, fully embraces the view that England's great unwashed masses need a strong monarch to restrain their brutish natures: "The heart of his philosophy stands opposed to all theories . . . that emphasized the reason and quality of men above the ruthless competitiveness of human nature and the necessity for established hierarchy to maintain that order."[22] Yet in his depictions of his equine companions Cavendish seems to resort to notions of identity and the construction of an equine subjectivity that do not at all resemble the political agenda he applied to his human peers.

   As I have indicated, Cavendish's *General System* insistently opposes the Cartesian notion that animals are merely machines; yet his scientific method, which probes and manipulates every muscle of horse and rider, surely works on the body at the most mechanical level. Cavendish seems appalled only that the Cartesian view cannot allow for the manipulation of emotion or reason, the interior space of the animal's mind and heart. Insisting that this interior space is the target of his training scheme, Cavendish resurrects the horse, body *and* soul, as a suitable subject for disciplined training. His animals are intelligent, self-motivated creatures whose loving response is best provoked through respectful suggestion—only with extremely recalcitrant individuals should physical correction be necessary. These horses are capable of having their wills "colonized", so to speak, only if their rider appreciates and preserves their individual identities. This is what makes them worthy of the kind of art Cavendish creates with their cooperation. It is, perhaps, a smaller step than we might have believed from Foucault's new methods for disciplining soldiers and schoolchildren to Cavendish's horses.

In the introduction to his first treatise, Cavendish goes so far as to draw a parallel between human and equine contributions to the state:

When a commonwealth is to be form'd, that men may live together in society, those who make feathers to put into their masters hats, are as useful in the republick . . . as those who sell beef and mutton; for the tendency of the whole is to live by aiding one another, without wronging or offending any body. As for a managed [trained] horse, which they call dancer and prauncer; if those gentlemen were to fight a duel, or go to wars, they would find their error; for these horses perform a journey as well as they do the high airs. (*GS*, 14)

Cavendish again accentuates the cooperative nature of the horse-rider partnership, extending it analogically to the state. This passage sounds like an anxious self-defense (his horses are, after all, being compared to those who "make feathers to put in their masters' hats," which accurately represents the true purpose and outcome of his method). In the very next breath, Cavendish again insists that his method is for "giving Kings, Princes, and persons of quality . . . an exercise that is very noble, and that which makes them appear most graceful when they shew themselves to their subjects, or at the head of an army . . . so that the pleasure in this case is as useful as anything else" (*GS*, 14). The battle between utility and pleasing display is resolved in Cavendish's text with relief once he asserts the utility *of* display, the practical political dimension of this essentially frivolous pastime.

Let us return for a moment to Van Dyck's painting of royal Charles I on horseback, to situate what it and Cavendish share more clearly in an historical context. Van Dyck's Charles I is, in 1635, still as much of an absolute monarch as England has known since Elizabeth. The portrait is painted during the years of his "personal rule" when the hierarchical national culture which legitimizes his reign is still intact, if only barely. The suggestion of parallels between horse and rider I have pointed out, along with its implications both political and ideological, is there but is overlaid with the artful blend of *personae* which validate Charles's rule. Cavendish, however, writes his dressage treatises after the devastating events of 1642, having faithfully followed the king he once tutored into exile. Even after this devastating dislocation, Cavendish worked hard to maintain what he had once had: during Charles's first doomed campaign to regain the throne, Cavendish provided liaison with the Scottish support, eventually earning Charles's resentment when the collaboration fell apart. Cavendish's wife, Margaret, attests in her biography of her husband to his dedication to the ideals of an absolute monarchy. Not only was he willing to bankrupt himself for his king, he literally saw no identity for himself outside a relationship to the ruler. Margaret Cavendish recounts that when she tried to lighten the misery of exile by telling her husband that at least he was subject to no state or prince, he replied "as he was subject to no prince, so he was a prince of no subjects."[23] Cavendish could imagine no other identity, underwritten by no other system, than the aristocratic identity he had held before the war as servant to his king, a member of a class hierarchy which guaranteed his superior status by birth and power.

After the Restoration, however, the success and even the necessity of the class values Cavendish upholds to a new English political and social environment was in doubt. He wrote his *New Method* in 1666, dedicating it to England's newly restored king. Certainly he hoped that English civil and political life would literally be "restored" without change to their prior state. But years of civil war, experiments with government, and the influence of Puritan values during the Interregnum could not so easily be erased. Aristocratic power in post-civil war England could no longer be manifested exclusively through a strict hierarchy or a system of political rewards tied to the supposed absolute power of the monarch—that institution had proven more shaky than any could have expected. And the court of Charles II was infamous for its encouragement of license, libertinism, corruption, and ostentatious consumption, which put the newly returned aristocracy in a bad odor, something Cavendish tacitly acknowledged in his preference for a quiet retreat to his country estates. Ultimately, a strong legacy of Puritan morality, a denatured form of which was embraced by a growing and more powerful middle class, extended this opprobrium to the aristocracy as a whole, until by the eighteenth century the idea of the corrupt, licentious, parasitical aristocrat was available as a commonplace. While the aristocracy and middle classes fought a kind of ongoing battle for possession of the moral high ground, prudence, sexual morality, and rational behavior eventually seemed to become the property of the industrious and devout middle class. Although it would take nearly a century and a half before such clear class divisions would be fully realized,[24] the seeds had been planted in the years of unrest, war and negotiation over the place of the new king. As I have pointed out, Cavendish began to make his stand in this battle by stressing his role as preserver and protector of a regal legacy, manifested in his determined restoration of his estates and in his promotion of dressage as a gentlemanly pursuit. The lord of the manor who "cherishes" his land, the gentleman who engages in leisure pastimes and spends his money on the cultivation of beautiful things and beautiful actions — these were important images that helped to accommodate change, while preserving at least the ideological importance of the aristocracy, even if they often sacrificed the aristocrat's former military relevance. Cavendish's horsemanship treatises help to illustrate the other side of the story of the Restoration court: license is, in his case, translated into freedom to indulge aesthetic values, while inherited wealth liberates him from the constraints of economy and allows him to salvage an idealized, Arcadian past. His superiority of birth and education gives him special insight into the nobility of his equine companions.

Yet the potential we might see in Cavendish's horsemanship treatises to redefine and reconstruct aristocratic power must be balanced by the implications of their endowment of his subjects with reason, sense, and emotion. Cavendish's emphasis on riding as a partnership, and on the rational, characterful nature of the horse, invests the horse with a nascent subjectivity, an individualized and self-motivated identity which mirrors cultural and political transformations of human subjectivity across class lines in seventeenth-century England, and one which, as I have suggested, ultimately subverts his ostensible purpose. By the century following Cavendish's return to England and the publication of his treatises, political control of England by Parliament rather than the king and his aristocratic supporters would be defended on the basis of every man's rational ability to govern himself. John Locke, writing after the war and soon after Cavendish published his treatises, describes the nascent formulae of possessive individualism: every man is possessor of his self, his body, and his labor, and every man is capable of entering into rational contracts for governance. While Locke may not have imagined himself part of a complex of ideas about human nature and human identity that would lead to democracy, his work is just one manifestation of a long-term and broadly expressed set of transformations that permit later philosophers to arrive at that destination. Unless we wish to believe that Locke's notions of identity and self-possession spring fully-formed, Athena-like, from a single intellect, we must accept that his writings mainly codify, clarify, and develop what is already an available cultural trend. Like other critics before me, I situate many of Locke's theories and comparable contemporary explorations of identity, individuality, and self-government on a continuum.[25] We can find elements and demonstrations, some more obvious than others, of these ideas scattered among cultural media long before they are given a name. Yet these early glimpses can and

Figure 8. Engraving for Cavendish, *General System of Horsemanship*, Plate 4.

should be understood as part of the same gradual shift that will lead centuries later to general suffrage for humans.[26] Cavendish's treatises are such a glimpse. The identity, the interiority, the integrity of his horses—all these are being defended as properties of humanity, which Cavendish's horses (as schoolboys, good children, partners in creating art) are always mirroring.

So even as Cavendish's texts seek to bolster the authority of the ruling class, the changing nature of human subjectivity which underpins a new concept of human political and social nature is reflected, even promoted, through his description of the loving, respectful, mutually accommodating treatment he accords his horses. Like the horse and rider that are, as Van Dyck represents them, as much images of each other as antagonists in the battle for domination, Cavendish's horses possess an integrity and rationality that might be said to represent the fitful, yet profound, political transformation which eventually reshaped England's government as a representative republic. The treatises suggest that these two possibilities—the conservative and the subversive—are held in uneasy balance.

To further indicate the nature of this precarious balance, I want to conclude with one last image, another plate from Cavendish's *General System of Horsemanship* (Figure 8). Here, Cavendish, re-enacting the mythical flight Shakespeare's Richard II once blamed for his fall from power, holds the reins of his winged steeds, lifted in his chariot high above the ground in a sort of cosmic *haute école*. Around him, the horses of his stable rise in perfect *levade* to honor their master. Like many of the other images I have offered in this essay, this one must be read for its ambiguity: the transcendence Cavendish attains can be read either as a statement about the significance of his method for reasserting aristocratic class values, or it can be read as a sign that those class values, as Cavendish imagines them, are already being transformed, dislocated, detached from their former place in the "real" world of political power.

Notes

1. "The learned glossator will cheerfully . . . gloss 'riggish' as wanton without thinking it worthwhile to explain that it qualifies, literally, the behaviour of a rig — he has moved so much further away from the horse-borne world than his counterpart of Shakespeare's day as not even to know what a rig is." Anthony Dent, *Horses in Shakespeare's England* (London, J. A. Allen, 1987), p. ix.

2. For information on the costs of maintaining a stable and the various uses horses were put to by the aristocracy and the peasantry, see Joan Thirsk, *Horses in Early Modern England: For Service, for Pleasure, for Power* (Reading: University of Reading Press, 1978).

3. The image of the aristocrat as preserver of his country's wealth is clearly opposed to the characterization of other class groups as blind predators of English resources. We find these oppositions demarcated in poetry like Marvell's "Upon Appleton House," which defends aristocratic measures for land improvement, and in husbandry treatises like Sir John Evelyn's *Sylva, or a Discourse of Forest-Trees* (London: Martyn and Allestry, 1664). A founding member of the Royal Academy, Evelyn writes "But what shall I say of our late prodigious Spoilers whose furious devastation of so many goodly woods and forests have left an infamy of their names and memories not quickly to be forgotten! I mean our unhappy Usurpers, and injurious Sequestrators" (Preface to the Reader), heavy-handedly asserting the moral superiority of the royalists now returned to power over their temporary supplanters, the classless rabble of the Commonwealth.

4. William Cavendish, Duke of Newcastle, *A New Method and Extraordinary Invention to Dress Horses* (London: Thomas Milbourn, 1667). Further references use *NM* to indicate this version of the treatise. *A General System of Horsemanship* (abbreviated as *GS* in further references to this version) was first published in French in 1657/8 at Antwerp (the title in French was also *La méthode nouvelle*, but this text and the English version with the same title are actually entirely different works). The text of the *General System* used in this paper is the facsimile of the London edition, published by J. Brindley of 1743. This later translation from the French includes the plates intended for, but not reproduced with, the original.

5. Cavendish's passion also probably inspired another visitor to his household in Holland: Thomas Hobbes wrote a pamphlet on *Considerations touching the facility or Difficulty of the Motions of a Horse on straight lines and Circular*, most likely pursuant to the many discussions he and Cavendish had about the nature of the horse. For this and other discussion of Cavendish's horsemanship pursuits see Geoffrey Trease, *Portrait of a Cavalier: William Cavendish, First Duke of Newcastle* (London: Macmillan, 1979), pp. 74 ff. Cavendish elaborates on the debate between Descartes's view of horses as irrational machines and Hobbes's of the animals as capable of non-linguistic reasoning in the *General System*, p. 12.

6. *Playes Written by the thrice Noble, illustrious and Excellent Princess, the Lady Marchioness of Newcastle* (London, 1662).

7. *Description of a New World Called the Blazing World, and Other Writings*, ed. Kate Lilley, NYU Press Women's Classics (Washington Square, N.Y.: New York University Press, 1992), p. 124.

8. The maneuvers Cavendish describes presume close fighting in which the horse is as much a weapon as the rider, but this kind of close fighting traditionally ensued only after a heavy cavalry charge, a massed assault on enemy infantry ridden at a trot or slow canter which broke up ground soldiers' lines. Pikes and palisades first made the cavalry shock force less effective — rather than breaking through enemy lines, horses and riders ended up impaled on the pikes or held at bay while archers and arquebusiers picked them off. For a brief time, once these setbacks were understood and accepted, cavalry could be used after artillery softened an infantry line (rarely were forces so coordinated, however) or to charge in smaller groups during reloading (of course, arrows were still efficient repellents). Firepower, once the speed and distance of shot increased, made cavalry hopelessly outmoded. "Heavy horse" were gradually replaced by "light horse" which were useful for scouting or performing flanking maneuvers on the battlefield. For a simple history of the horse in battle which covers these and many more details of military development, see John Ellis, *Cavalry: The History of Mounted Warfare* (New York: Putnam's, 1978), pp. 6–107.

9. Dent, *Horses in Shakespeare*, p. 92.

10. As Dent puts it, "In order that all manner of subjects might be duly impressed with the monarch's majesty, the nobleman . . . must make a brave show on horseback" (*Horses in Shakespeare*, p. 96). Dent includes a wonderful plate of the henchmen (professional riders) at Elizabeth's accession executing movements of the "haute ecole" (p. 65) to impress the crowds.

11. *The First Part of King Henry the Fourth*, II. ii. 97–98, *William Shakespeare: The Complete Works*, ed. Alfred Harbage (New York: Viking Press, 1984). All references to Shakespeare's plays are to this edition.

12. *ELR* 13, 3 (Autumn 1983).

13. References to horsemanship in *Richard II* are legion: the usurper is called "mounting Bolingbroke," he rides before the people on a "hot and fiery steed" which he keeps to a "slow and stately pace" (V. ii. 7–10). Mowbray is curbed by Richard from "giving reigns and spurs" to his "free speech" (I. i. 54–55). Elsewhere horses and horsemanship appear with tremendous frequency in early modern literature. In Philip Sidney's *Defense of Poetry*, for example, an Italian horsemaster's preference for his beasts stands for the potential logical absurdity of the whole process of the defense; throughout the *Faerie Queene*, as in its precursor the *Orlando Furioso*, numerous characters

prove their worth, or lack thereof, through their relationship to their mounts. I mention Spenser and Shakespeare here only because in them we find the closest corollary to the intended messages of the European painters.

14. *Horses in Shakespeare*, pp. 85–86. Dent notes that the fact that sixteenth-century artists painted from live models didn't impinge upon artists' commitment to this classical ideal.

15. Rubens was fond of depicting horses lunging in this pose, a cross between true motion and a battle maneuver. A thorough and informed analysis of the rearing horse in seventeenth-century art can be found in Walter Liedtke's *The Royal Horse and Rider: Painting, Sculpture, and Horsemanship 1500–1800* (New York: Abaris Books, 1989). Liedtke discounts many modern interpretations of the "dynamism" of the rearing horse (14–16), arguing quite rightly that artists like Rubens and Van Dyck and sculptors like Tacca relied on contemporary practices of horsemanship rather than general concepts like dynamism in depicting horses and riders.

16. Roy Strong, *Van Dyck: Charles I on Horseback* (New York: Viking Press, 1972).

17. Quoted in Strong, *Van Dyck*, p. 38.

18. Cavendish is not the first to advocate humane methods; in fact, he misrepresents Grisone to some extent. John Astley provided a rough paraphrase of both Grisone and Xenophon in 1584, *The Art of Riding* (Amsterdam: Theatrum Orbis Terrarium and New York: Da Capo Press, 1968) which also condemned beating horses. Likewise, Gervase Markham's many works on horsemanship and farriery in the early seventeenth century tend to agree that horses need to be praised as much as punished. His *Cheape and Good Husbandry for the Well-Ordering of all Beasts and Fowles . . . Shewing further the whole Art of Riding great Horses* (1698) discusses the "three main points of a Horsemans knowledge, which are helpes, corrections and cherishings (15)." Cherishings are the positive reinforcements of the other aids, including "the voice, which being delivered smoothly and lovingly . . . gives the horse both a cheerfulnesse of spirit, & a knowledge that he hath done well" (17). The most famous continental horseman of Cavendish's era, Antoine Pluvinel, master of the king's horse in France, was a noted defender of humane training. However, Cavendish's texts are the most widely disseminated and the most extensive of his day, and his use of a term like "cherish" goes far beyond the context and meaning it has in these other writers' works — more than a mere use of voice or touch, it is a mental attitude of friendship or even love. Keith Thomas in *Man and the Natural World: a History of the Modern Sensibility* (New York: Pantheon, 1983) points out that although Renaissance Englishmen valued their horses, that did not mean they treated them especially well (see pp. 100–101) — hence the famous saying "England is a hell for horses." Humane training techniques took many years to filter down to everyday relations with horses used for less specialized pursuits.

19. Thomas, *Man and the Natural World*, p. 45: "The training of youth was frequently compared to the breaking of horses; and it was no accident that the emergence in the seventeenth and eighteenth centuries of more humane methods of horse-breaking would coincide with a reaction against the use of corporal punishment in education."

20. Michel Foucault, *Discipline and Punish: The Birth of the Prison* (New York: Vintage, 1979), p. 136.

21. Ibid., pp. 136, 137. It is worth noting also that Foucault is historicizing the development of an individual "interiority," which can be acted upon by the "rational"

methods of discipline and punishment, in much the same way that Cavendish needs to establish the interiority of his horses to argue that his methods are preferable.

22. Thomas P. Slaughter, *Ideology and Politics on the Eve of Restoration: Newcastle's Advice to Charles II* (Philadelphia: American Philosophical Society, 1984), p. xviii. Slaughter's lengthy introduction compares actual passages from Cavendish's letter to Hobbes's writing; whether or not we agree with Slaughter about actual passages, Cavendish makes clear in nearly all his writings that he prefers the most authoritarian style of leadership.

23. Margaret Cavendish, Duchess of Newcastle, *Life of William Cavendish* (London, Routledge, 189?), p. 137.

24. I am drawing class divisions with an admittedly broad brush; the subtleties of "aristocratic" class structure in England are more carefully represented in works like R. Malcolm Smuts's *Court Culture and the Origins of a Royalist Tradition in Early Stuart England* (Philadelphia: University of Pennsylvania Press, 1987), Christopher Hill's *Change and Continuity in Seventeenth-Century England* (Cambridge, Mass.: Harvard University Press, 1975), and of course, Lawrence Stone's *Crisis of the Aristocracy 1558–1641* (Oxford: Clarendon Press, 1965).

25. Two notable examples: Don E. Wayne's *Penshurst: The Semiotics of Place and the Poetics of History* (Madison: University of Wisconsin Press, 1984) argues that Locke's theory of "possessive individualism" actually dominates representations of property and "home" in the early seventeenth century. More recently Annabel Patterson, at the 1997 Arizona Center for Medieval and Renaissance Studies Conference, has argued in a talk on "Virtual Reality: The Portrait and Identity from Locke to Chaucer" (note the implied reversal of history in the title) that ideas of individuality which we normally associate with Locke and others of his generation are found here and there in English art and culture long before Locke was born. Like Wayne, she referred more than once specifically to Locke, and connected these moments in portraiture with larger changes in political democracy and what most critics call "bourgeois individualism," the valorization of individual identity that marks eighteenth- through twentieth-century middle class culture.

26. In fact, by the twentieth century animal protectionists extend "rights" to animals generally as part of a strategy to enforce legal defense against their abuse. Such rights theory, now found most prominently argued in the U.S. in the publications of People for the Ethical Treatment of Animals (PETA), and codified in Tom Regan's *The Case for Animal Rights* (Berkeley: University of California Press, 1983), awards animals rights like control over one's body (a prominent Lockean concept), and tends to connect its goals to those of the women's suffrage movement or the civil rights movement of the 1960s. For an example of that connection, see Marjorie Speigel, *The Dreaded Comparison: Human and Animal Slavery* (New York: Mirror Books, 1989).

4

"Pox on Your Distinction!"

Humanist Reformation and Deformations of the Everyday in *The Staple of News*

Don E. Wayne

It should not be thought that the relationship of distinction (which may or may not imply the conscious intention of distinguishing oneself from common people) is only an incidental component in the aesthetic disposition. The pure gaze implies a break with the ordinary attitude towards the world which, as such, is a social break. One can agree with Ortega y Gasset when he attributes to modern art — which merely takes to its extreme conclusions an intention implicit in art since the Renaissance — a systematic refusal of all that is 'human,' by which he means the passions, emotions and feelings which *ordinary* people put into their *ordinary* existence, and consequently all the themes and objects capable of evoking them.

— Pierre Bourdieu, *Distinction*[1]

I HEARD A JOKE RECENTLY: outside a theater, a homeless man approaches a well-dressed member of the audience for a handout. The theater patron says, archly: "'Neither a borrower, nor a lender be' — William Shakespeare!" To which the homeless man replies: "'Fuck you' — David Mamet!" Now I can tell this joke in the context of a scholarly essay and have some reasonable expectation that a reputable academic press will print it; that is, of course, if the rest of my essay meets certain standards. Fifteen years ago this would not have been a reasonable expectation. But the situation in academic discourse is now comparable to that of the New York theater in the late 1970s when David Mamet assumed the license to eschew euphemisms and to use the actual expletives of the city's streets on the Broadway stage. Popular culture, the passions, the body, consumption, and the circulation of commodities are at the foreground of discourse in the humanities. Does this mean that the relationship of distinction as described by Bourdieu no longer obtains, or that the status it accords has been devalued? Not necessarily. It does mean that academic elites — like playwrights and screen-writers — have had to adjust to new demographies and new markets in ways that produce hybrid discourses.

Until recently, when intellectuals thought of culture, they thought of *distinction*. Bourdieu's magisterial study of that self-legitimating category made a habit of thought an object of inquiry and in so doing brought a formerly neglected, if not excluded, area of study into the focal plane of critical social theory. In his 1984 preface to the English-language edition, Bourdieu writes that his book "transgresses one of the fundamental taboos of the intellectual world, in relating intellectual products and producers to their social conditions of existence."[2] Little more than a decade has passed, and it already seems somewhat quaint to hear such relations described as "fundamental taboos." We are now so aware of the commodity nature of cultural production at all levels that many intellectuals find it embarrassing to persist in representing their mission in the high-minded language of Enlightenment humanism. (Of course, there are other options to embarrassment: some relish the scandal of demystifying Enlightenment ideologies; others cling to those ideologies while mourning the demise of their authority.)

Indeed, in the present historical context it has become a mark of distinction among intellectuals to acknowledge in practice the connection between culture and commodity exchange: research on the history of relations between literature and market ideology has proliferated in the past decade, and academics routinely identify their status with their market value in negotiating salaries and perks in the corporate university. And it has become a mark of distinction among vanguard intellectuals to acknowledge in theory the connection between cultural distinction and social hierarchy: witness recent curricular debates over the relative value of traditional and emergent literatures; the developing critique of distinctions between "high" and "low" culture; and the growing fault line in the humanities provoked by the institutional shift in some quarters from literary to cultural studies.

Yet the incorporation by intellectuals of the "popular" or the "mass" or the "ordinary" or the "body" into their ways of thinking about culture is not in itself necessarily a very radical break with tradition, especially if such incorporation remains at a high level of abstraction regulated by institutional protocols for the production of knowledge. While, in the humanities, the traditional taboo against relating intellectual products and their producers to the market system of commodity exchange may no longer be in effect, it remains to be seen whether we are any better able than previous generations of scholars to understand the social conditions that enable (or require) the present forms in which knowledge about culture is produced. What Bourdieu terms the "social break" legitimated by the aesthetic disposition of the pure gaze may be reinforced by an intellectual appropriation of the "popular," of the "mass," of the "ordinary," of the "everyday." In other words, social hierarchies marked by divisions of race, class, and gender are not necessarily overridden by the apparent deconstruction of cultural distinctions.

I want to look here at an early modern instance of a similar phenomenon, a time when new flows of capital (in agriculture and in expanding world trade) combined with new communication technologies (the public stage, print) to produce a hybrid culture, combining elite and popular forms. The particular case in question, Ben Jonson's *The Staple of News*, performed by the King's Men in 1626, exploits the representation of everyday practices while expressing anxiety about their encroachment into the area of elite culture, a terrain that Jonson, more than any author of his time, actively sought to delineate.[3] In describing this play as a "hybrid," I refer primarily to its mixing of genres and cultural practices that articulate divisions of class, gender, and competing versions of national identity, because these are the primary operators of social distinction in *The Staple of News*. But I want also to bear in mind Paul Gilroy's use of the term in arguing against national and "racial" exceptionalism, and to follow his suggestion that "cultural historians could take the Atlantic as one single, complex unit of analysis in their discussions of the modern world and use it to produce an explicitly transnational and intercultural perspective."[4] In this particular play, race or ethnicity figure only in passing satiric references to "news" concerning international politics, foreign trade, Jesuit missions to Asia, and the conversion of "cannibals" in America. Yet I want to keep these categories in the background of my discussion; first, because race and ethnicity were significant factors in the cultural distinctions and social divisions dramatized in both the public playhouses and the court entertainments of early seventeenth-century England,[5] and probably in more ephemeral everyday gossip and "news" of which we have little material record; second, because in my conclusion I shall return to the issue of hybridity in Gilroy's wider sense as it pertains to the cultural politics of intellectual elites in the present.

Like the two Jonsonian comedies that preceded it, *Bartholomew Fair* (1614) and *The Devil Is an Ass* (1616), *The Staple of News* is located in the environs of London, registers the intensification of consumption in the period,[6] and satirizes commodification as a disease of the urban populace. The obsession to consume transforms the consumers into mere commodities themselves. This play is also like its immediate predecessors in its extreme self-consciousness: the satire is troubled by the author's recognition of his complicity in the system he criticizes. At the same time, *The Staple of News* is different from the earlier plays in that its action and allegory concern not only consumption, but production and the division of labor. Jonson's satire on commodity consumption modulates here into a homily on putting wealth to work: "The use of things is all, and not the store" (V. vi. 26).[7] Culture is idealized as the product of intellectual labor, and distinguished from the popular, the everyday, and, by implication, ordinary manual labor. Yet the very idealization of high culture as a new basis of distinction registers the materiality of social relations in Jonson's time. The poet/scholar becomes a figure for an administrative elite; intellectual labor is marked with respect not only to those below, but to those above in the order of social rank.

The fact that ten years had elapsed since the last of Jonson's stage comedies is, perhaps, indicative of his ambivalence or embarrassment about writing in a dramatic medium that might undermine the intellectual distinction and moral authority he had worked to achieve in his early career. From 1616 to 1626 Jonson concentrated on developing the masque as a genre of court entertainment. At court, Jonson might be constantly reminded of his lesser status in terms of rank, but he could also maintain a distance from "ordinary" commoners by having his taste and judgment authorized by the king. Some of that authority was no doubt lost following the death of James I in 1625, and the ensuing alterations in taste at the court of Charles I and Queen Henrietta Maria.

Whatever may have driven Jonson back to the theater, the play he wrote for his return constitutes a more developed stage in the satire of commodification. Where Jonson's earlier comedies recognize contract as the principal regulatory device in an emerging capitalist society, they still tend to satirize avarice in the manner of the medieval morality play. In *The Staple of News*, however, avarice is not the central concern. Rather, in a manner that is strikingly consistent with arguments for free trade that began to appear in the 1620s, Jonson's new play emphasizes the proper circulation and reproduction of money regulated by contract.[8] A central metaphor for such reproduction under lawful regulation is marriage, and the action of the play involves a number of rival suitors for the hand of the great lady Pecunia Do-All, Infanta of the Mines ("She is/The talk o'the time, th'adventure o'the age!" [1. vi. 63–64]). She appears with a retinue of attendants whose names are drawn from legal discourse, and particularly from the law pertaining to real property and contracts: her ladies-in-waiting are named Mortgage, Statute, Band (i.e., Bond), Wax; her secretary and gentleman usher is named Broker. Her guardian is the usurer and miser, Richer Pennyboy (also called Pennyboy Senior), whose nephew, the prodigal Pennyboy Junior, is her chief suitor. The father of Pennyboy Junior is thought by both his brother and son to have died. He lives, however, disguised as a beggar known as Pennyboy Canter, and functions as the play's moral commentator (his true given and allegorical name is Frank).

In addition to drawing an equivalence between the proper exchange of *women* and of *money*, Jonson brings in a third term, *information*. In fact, the play's title would suggest that its primary object of satire is commodified information. Portions of the action are set in a "staple [i.e., an emporium or market] of news," a topical reference to early English ventures in periodical "news" publication.[9] The business of the news office is an early representation of what we call today the media. In Jonson's exaggerated depiction, the officers and "emissaries" (reporters) of the staple of news are purveyors of nonsense to their gullible customers. The satire on newsmongering is linked to another misuse of information, gossip, which is feminized and personified in the characters of "four gentlewomen ladylike attired," Gossip Mirth, Gossip Tattle, Gossip Expectation, and Gossip Censure.[10] Their dialogue frames the main action. They interrupt the Prologue, demanding to be seated on the stage — "We are persons of quality, I assure you, and women of fashion, and come to see and to be seen" (Induction, 8–9) — and function as an ignorant chorus arraigning the play and the playwright in the "Intermeans" between acts. In theory, Jonson distinguishes his own work as a poet — a "maker" as he called himself, displaying his knowledge of Greek roots and deliberately implying the association with divine creation — from the promiscuous circulation of information associated with gossip and newsmongering. But in the actual practice of making plays Jonson discovers, repeatedly, that the distinction between high and low cultural effects is a problematic one.[11]

When Cymbal, the master of the news office, seeks the hand of the Lady Pecunia, he offers to give her guardian half of his share of the staple's annual profits of £6,000 if Pennyboy Senior will only permit his ward to sojourn at the staple. Pennyboy Senior questions the legitimacy of Cymbal's business — "Is it a certain business or a casual?" — then launches into a diatribe against the misuse of money and the decay of honest trade:

Is it a certain business or a casual?
For I am loath to seek out doubtful courses,
Run any hazardous paths. I love straight ways,
A just and upright man! Now all trade totters.
The trade of money is fall'n two i'the hundred.
That was a certain trade while th'age was thrifty
And men good husbands, look'd unto their stocks,
Had their minds bounded. Now the public riot
Prostitutes all, scatters away in coaches,
In footmen's coats, and waitingwomen's gowns. . . .
. . . .
What stews, ponds, parks, coops, garners, magazines,
What velvets, tissues, scarfs, embroideries,
And laces they might lack? They covet things

Superfluous still, when it were much more honor
They could want necessary. . . .
. . . .
                        All that excess
Appear'd as little yours as the spectators'.
It scarce fills up the expectation
Of a few hours that entertains men's lives. (III. iv. 30–39, 48–52, 65–68)

Pennyboy Senior is a satirized character. But his tirade concludes in terms that are hardly different from those used by Jonson to distinguish between the "spectators" who come to the theater merely to see and be seen, and those idealized Courtiers addressed as "scholars, that can judge and fair report/The sense they hear above the vulgar sort/Of nutcrackers, that only come for sight" (Prologue for the Court, 6–8). In addressing the audience of the public playhouse, Jonson distinguishes between the actors who "must provide for those/ Who are our guests here in the way of shows," and himself, "the maker," who would "have you wise/Much rather by your ears than by your eyes . . ." This privileging of language over spectacle, of the aural over the visual, is a frequent trope in prologues and epilogues to Jonson's plays. Like his character the usurer Richer Pennyboy, Jonson the poet wants to distinguish between "a certain business or a casual" — not with respect to money and trade, but with respect to information and truth.

    So, whatever else it may concern, *The Staple of News* is about distinction — distinction among different kinds of women, different kinds of trade, different kinds of knowledge. The last of these is perhaps the most essential from the standpoint of the play, and it involves the sort of differentiation of *taste* that Bourdieu has criticized retrospectively as the aesthetic domination peculiar to bourgeois ideology since the Renaissance. It is by marking a difference in intellectual terms that Jonson provides an early formulation of the notion of *taste* as the guarantor of social distinction. Given this playwright's self-conscious preoccupation throughout his work with a defense of the role of the humanist intellectual, it is not surprising that the fundamental distinction around which the play's economic and social themes revolve should be that between elite and everyday cultures. The play is an odd amalgam of the characteristic features of city comedy with the allegorical method that Jonson had developed in his court masques. As such, *The Staple of News* is an experiment in genre, appropriating the device of the *antimasque* (a sequence involving grotesque characters or comic representations of the common people, usually played by professionals, and serving as a foil for the masque proper in which courtiers played the parts) for more extended use in a play written for the mixed audience of the playhouse.

The mixing of high and low genres is especially evident in the middle acts of the play. Act III takes place in the staple and includes a scene in which Cymbal engages in an absurd parody of courtly love while trying to win the lady Pecunia away from the prodigal heir Pennyboy Junior. Act IV is situated in a tavern room called, ironically, Apollo, the name of the celebrated tavern room where Jonson himself purportedly held forth as the "father" of a group of younger writers who called themselves the Tribe of Ben.[12]

When Pennyboy Junior hosts a dinner in the Apollo in Pecunia's honor, the poetaster Madrigal reads the text of a sarabande he has composed in praise of the lady:

As bright as is the Sun her sire,
Or Earth, her mother, in her best attire,
Or Mint, the midwife, with her fire,
Comes forth her grace!
. . . .
She makes good cheer, she keeps full boards,
She holds a fair of knights and lords,
A market of all offices
And shops of honor more or less. (IV. ii. 95–98, 113–16)

Madrigal's composition is then sung by a boy to the accompaniment of fiddlers. The effect is of an embourgeoisement of the masque form, a comment, perhaps, on the embourgeoisement of nobility in the recently ended reign of James I. This scene parodies Jonson's own vocation in the courts of James and Charles Stuart, but the audience is also guided in a critical understanding of the scene by Pennyboy Canter's comments given in several asides.

Canter describes the society we have witnessed to this point in words that, again, evoke the antimasque:

Pennyboy Canter [aside]:
  Look, look, how all their eyes
  Dance i' their heads (observe) scatter'd with lust
  At sight o' their brave idol! How they are tickl'd
  With a light air, the bawdy sarabande!
  They are a kind of dancing engines all,
  And set by nature, thus to run alone
  To every sound! All things within, without them,
  Move, but their brain, and that stands still! Mere monsters,
  Here in a chamber, of most subtle feet! (IV. ii. 134–42)

Though the language is moralistic and obsessively anti-erotic, it manages to convey a striking early image of what later social theorists—Marx, Weber, Lukacs, the Frankfurt School—would describe as the reification of subjectivity that occurs when commodity exchange comes to dominate social relationships and when the circulation of social energy is expressed as the circulation of money.[13] The phrase "circulation of social energy" is, of course, Stephen Greenblatt's.[14] While I share Greenblatt's sense that early modern theater in England is the product of a collective "social energy," I think the economic metaphors in which he frames his account—foregrounding such terms as production, consumption, exchange, negotiation, acquisition, circulation—could stand further explication. The moment of Shakespearean drama may be one of "felt community"[15] expressing or recognizing its energy in the secular ritual space of theater, but it is also a moment when the social effects of human agency—including aesthetic effects—are beginning to be inextricable from the circulation of capital (a point implied though not explicit in Greenblatt's analysis). If Shakespearean drama represents the most affirmative moment in the early modern literary representation of social energy, I would suggest that Jonsonian drama represents an early registering of the deformation of social energy that occurs when the material aspect of power in human relations becomes hidden in the "materials" of commodity exchange.

When the singing of Madrigal's sarabande is concluded, Pennyboy Junior, Fitton (Cymbal's emissary to the Court), Almanac (a quack doctor), and Shunfield (a military sea-captain) join in applauding the poetaster but fall immediately into a dispute over distinctions:

Fitton:
       Oh, he's a dainty poet
  When he sets to't.
Pennyboy Junior:
       And a dainty scholar!
Almanac:
  No, no great scholar, he writes like a gentleman.
Shunfield:
  Pox o' your scholar!
Pennyboy Canter [aside]:
   Pox o' your distinction!
  As if a scholar were no gentleman.
  With these, to write like a gentleman will in time
  Become all one as to write like an ass.
  These gentlemen? These rascals! I am sick
  Of indignation at 'em. (IV. ii. 150–58)

Canter's "pox o' your distinction!" deconstructs the boundary maintained by Almanac and Shunfield between "scholar" (associated with labor) and "gentleman" (associated with leisure), but sets up another binary distinction in its place. The older, aristocratic ethos of *otium* is rendered absurd in Shunfield's mouth (the very name Shun-field is an immediate index of the captain's failure to fulfill the military obligation on which his distinction is based). But Canter's lines go beyond the mere ridicule of a character unworthy of his ideology. Canter raises the question of what constitutes the true mark of quality in an elite, and answers with a version of the work ethic. It is a version involving the distinction between intellectual and manual labor, the foundation of a humanist elitism linked to managerial power in the state and in business. This is quite unlike the anti-elitist version of the work ethic in the earlier, more romantic authors of city comedy, Dekker and Heywood.

Thomas Dekker's *The Shoemakers' Holiday* (1599)[16] is an early staging of class conflict around the distinction between *otium* and the work ethic. Dekker celebrates the shoemakers, those of "the gentle craft," in a highly idealized manner. But there is also a palpable realism to the way in which his play portrays the energy and industry of the burgeoning crafts and trades in early modern England, particularly in the scenes depicting Simon Eyre's workshop. Though the prefatory Epistle insists that "nothing is purposed but mirth," an undercurrent of class conflict runs through the play right from the opening dialogue between two men of status but of different rank and ideology, one a member of the Court, the Earl of Lincoln, the other, a powerful merchant-citizen and Lord Mayor of London, Sir Roger Otley. Lincoln and Otley disclose their mutual distrust in asides to the audience, but they share an anxiety about the attraction of Lincoln's cousin Rowland Lacy for Otley's daughter Rose. While they collaborate in obstructing a marriage that would join their families, there is no mistaking the element of hostility that governs their dialogue.

In the denouement of *The Shomakers' Holiday* this class antagonism is mitigated by the mediating authority of the king, who approves the marriage of Lacy and Rose and who, unlike the Earl of Lincoln, extends his courtesy to those beneath him, mingling with his subjects, commending and rewarding their industry. The ideological shift is comparable to that of Shakespeare's *Henry V*, with the monarch now portrayed as a heroic national leader. But Dekker's king, though hardly developed as a character, is far more engaged with his subjects than Shakespeare's.[17] In Dekker's play, the king represents an alliance between the monarch and the upwardly mobile tradespeople of whom Simon Eyre is emblematic.[18] With the king's warrant, aristocratic display and *otium* have been to some degree displaced by the virtues of thrift and industry; the standard of blood has conceded somewhat to the standard of merit. And merit is measured by productivity.

Jonson does not thematize material production in this way. His plays are concerned with the circulation of capital and of commodities. Characters of

middle and lower rank are portrayed with no less vitality than in Dekker, but
with a good deal less virtue. Where Dekker questions the aristocratic basis of
distinction, idealizes the social atomization produced by intensified commerce,[19] celebrates the energy of popular culture, and asserts its importance to
an imagined national destiny, Jonson appropriates that energy in order to
attract his audience's attention long enough to teach them the difference between popular and high culture. In this latter respect, Jonson does thematize
production—only in his plays and poems the standard of merit is intellectual
production.

The work ethic in Jonson's conception involves a distinction between
intellectual and manual labor. In his non-dramatic verse and in prologues
composed for Court performances of his plays, Jonson idealizes his patrons
primarily in terms of their intellectual qualities. At the same time, when he
addresses these patrons, it is always with a qualified deference that acknowledges the function of his own intellectual labor in legitimating their rank and
their roles as public administrators of the state apparatus. As Alan Sinfield
notes, for intellectuals of lesser rank, "Writing, even when it is purposefully in
the service of an ideology, will very often manifest a slant towards the interests
of the writer *as writer*."[20] In a time when rank was still largely determined by
birth, the standard of intellectual labor had the advantage for the writer who
was not an aristocrat of making quality dependent on merit. For the poet
commoner it constituted an implicit claim to entitlement, if not to equality
with his aristocratic patron. At the same time, such a standard depended on
the reassertion of hierarchy in a natural distinction between intellectual and
manual labor, a distinction Jonson would have readily discovered in his classical sources.

One source for the exaltation of intellectual labor and the subordination
of manual labor by early modern humanist writers was the first book of Aristotle's *Politics*, in which it is argued that the distinction between master and
slave is not just a matter of law but of character, therefore, of nature. Aristotle's
case is based on the distinction between soul and body: "Where then there is
such a difference as that between soul and body, or between men and animals
(as in the case of those whose business is to use their body, and who can do
nothing better), the lower sort are by nature slaves, and it is better for them as
for all inferiors that they should be under the rule of a master (i. 5. 1254^{b}15).
Aristotle also distinguishes between instruments of production (the shuttle)
and instruments of action (the slave): ". . . Life is action and not production,
and therefore the slave is the minister of action" (i. 4. 1254^{a}7). But to what
does "action" refer? It does not refer primarily to warfare, though that is the
means of "justly acquiring" slaves. Rather, it refers to intellectual activity:

"Hence those who are in a position which places them above toil have stewards who attend to their households while they occupy themselves with philosophy or with politics" (i. 7. 1255ᵇ35). Similarly, the *Nichomachean Ethics*, where the foundational assumption is that all human activities aim at the *good*, begins with the designation of politics as the master of all arts and the highest of all forms of action (*N. Eth.* i. 2. 1094ᵇ1).[21]

Towards the end of the sixteenth century, when the modern institutional separation between state and civil society was in its formative stage and the English aristocracy began to represent its primary role in political rather than military terms,[22] a space was opened for the legitimation of quality on the basis of intellectual work. Into that space moved writers who were increasingly conscious of themselves *as writers*. When, in his book of epigrams, Jonson addresses one of the most powerful politicians in the realm, Robert Cecil, Earl of Salisbury, with the question: "What need hast thou of me? or of my Muse?" (*Epig.* 43), he has already given a partial answer in the dedication of the book to the Earl of Pembroke to whom he gives "the honor of leading forth so many good, and great names (as my verses mention on the better part) to their remembrance with posterity." Poetry is itself a form of politics in that it gives historical legitimation to the acts of politicians. In another epigram celebrating Salisbury's accession to the post of Lord Treasurer (1608), Jonson refers to his own "labor" in making a poem that rehearses the virtues of its immediate subject and of the king who is commended for choosing his ministers wisely:

These (noblest Cecil) labour'd in my thought,
    Wherein what wonder see thy name hath wrought?
That whil'st I meant but thine to gratulate,
    I'have sung the greater fortune of our state. (*Epig.* 64)[23]

Salisbury was an appropriate target of Jonson's self-conscious epideictic. He recognized the value to the state of the sort of learning Jonson claimed to embody. Writing in 1610, Salisbury remarked, "Most of our lawyers and judges, though learned in their profession, yet, not having other learning, they upon a question demanded, bluntly answer it, and go no further, having no vehiculum to carry it by discourse or insinuation to the understanding of others."[24] In a time when the English landowning elite collaborated with the crown in refashioning the state apparatus, intellectual labor acquired status both for its practical value (in politics) and its value as an instrument of cultural hegemony (in aesthetics).

Based on the duality of mind/body, the distinction between intellectual and manual labor has a corollary in the realm of pleasure according to Jonson's aesthetic: common (material) pleasure is associated with the eyes, cultured (ideal) pleasure with the ears; common pleasure with the appetite, cultured with the intellect. I referred earlier to the distinction between visual and aural, "spectators" and "hearers," a leitmotif in Jonson's prologues and epilogues. The distinction between appetite and intellect was elaborated in the Jonsonian masque as early as 1618 in *Pleasure Reconciled to Virtue*. The masque opens with a riotous procession in behalf of Comus — "Room, room, make room for the bouncing belly, / First father of sauce, and diviser of jelly. . . ." One of the revelers, bearing the bowl of Hercules, warns "Beware of dealing with the belly; the belly will not be talked to, especially when he is full. Then there is no venturing upon Venter; he will blow you all up; he will thunder indeed, la: some in derision call him the father of farts. But I say he was the first inventor of great ordnance, and taught us to discharge them on festival days." Hercules appears and condemns the vulgarity and the abuse of his cup in such drunken orgies. Ultimately, Pleasure is reconciled to a triumphant Virtue through the medium of art in the person of Daedalus.

In a later masque, *Neptune's Triumph* (1624), the distinction between appetite and intellect is staged by Jonson in the form of a witty dialogue between a Master Cook and a Master Poet. The scene is the Banqueting House where the masque is being performed. The Cook asks the Poet's business, to which the Poet replies that he is there to present a masque. The Cook, claiming authority over the space ("This is my room and region too, the Banqueting House!"), asks the poet, "What are you sir?" The Poet replies:

Poet: The most unprofitable of [his majesty's] servants, I, sir, the poet. A kind of a Christmas engine, one that is used at least once a year for a trifling instrument of wit, or so.
Cook: Were you ever a cook?
Poet: A cook? No, surely.
Cook: Then you can be no good poet, for a good poet differs nothing at all from a master-cook. Either's art is the wisdom of the mind. (ll. 13–26)

The cook ultimately addresses his interlocutor as "brother poet," and the poet confirms the bond with the reply, "Brother!" (ll. 83–84).

Jonson's self-irony is amusing but in no way compromises his purpose of reminding his courtly audience of the difference between kinds of "taste." According to Jonson, understanding that difference is a measure of one's entitlement to the distinction of rank. The cook's conflation of these kinds is rendered comical, anticipating a similar comic moment in the full-fledged aesthetic philosophy of the Enlightenment where the distinction between "tastes" is marked by race as much as it is by class. In his *Critique of Judgment* (1790), Kant punctuates his opening distinction between the mere satisfaction

of desire and the "distinterested" judgment of the beautiful with a wry reference to "that Iroquois sachem, who was pleased in Paris by nothing more than
by the cook shops";[25] Coleridge, borrowing Kant's example, interprets its
meaning for his English readership: "When the Iroquois Sachem after having
been led to the most perfect specimen of Architecture in Paris said, that he saw
nothing so beautiful as the cook's shops, we attribute this without hesitation
to savagery of intellect, and infer with certainty that the sense of the beautiful
was either altogether dormant in his mind, or at best very imperfect."[26] But this
"certainty" of inference which Coleridge could take for granted in 1814 was
not yet codified in Jonson's time. In Jonson's aesthetic, the "beautiful" is still
dependent on the moral and the functional, and therefore not yet *disinterested*
in the Kantian sense. But the Kantian distinction between the higher contemplative pleasure of the "beautiful" and the bodily pleasure of mere sensa-
tion is one that we can observe Jonson already straining to articulate within the
hybrid entertainments he produced for the court and the public playhouse.

A portion of the dialogue between the Master Cook and the Master Poet
of *Neptune's Triumph* is reprised by Jonson two years later in *The Staple of News*.
In the scene at the Apollo, after dinner and before the performance of Madrigal's sarabande, the cook, Lickfinger, asks the Lady Pecunia if the fare was
satisfactory. Her affirmative reply sends the cook into a rapture over his calling,
and into a competition with Madrigal. Lickfinger's speech is, with minor alterations, taken verbatim from the Master Cook in *Neptune's Triumph* (ll. 50–
79). But the difference here is that Lickfinger's interlocutor is allowed few
words. In the earlier masque at court, the part of the Master Poet was an ironic
self-portrait. Here, in the playhouse, the comparable role is assigned to Madrigal, who is not permitted to serve as an ironic alter ego for the author. Madrigal remains no more than a poetaster, and no less ridiculous than the cook.

Among its themes, *The Staple of News* is concerned with the distinction
between elite and everyday culture, between the transcendental and the material. Yet while Jonson ridicules the confusion of metaphorical and literal
"taste," the fact is that his later masques and plays depend on the appropriation
of energy from popular cultural forms.[27] Jonson's strategy is to admit that
energy while attempting to control it through dramatic device. In both the
genres of court masque and city comedy, the popular is staged as an object of
derision and disgust. But the energy of the popular is what animates the
drama. It is a surplus energy that threatens to transport audience and reader
beyond the bounds of satiric intent. So Jonson reasserts authorial control by
means of didactic prologues and epilogues and in notes to the reader. An
extreme instance of this tactic occurs in the 1631 printed text of *The Staple of
News*, where a note "To The Readers" appears not in the usual place at the front

of the play text, but immediately following the Gossips' Second Intermean at the end of Act II — in which Gossip Censure complains, "Why this is duller and duller, intolerable, scurvy!"; Gossip Tattle demands a Vice in the manner of the old morality play, with "a wooden dagger to snap at everybody he meets"; to which the more fashion-conscious Gossip Mirth replies: "That was the old way. . . . But now they are attir'd like men and women o' the time, the Vices, male and female!"; and Gossip Expectation expresses impatience at the author's delay in showing the Staple, "They have talk'd on't, but we see't not open yet." Here, before Act III, in which Cymbal's news office is revealed for the first time, Jonson inserts the following:

> To The Readers
> In this following Act, the Office is open'd and show'n to the Prodigal and his Princess Pecunia, wherein the allegory and purpose of the author hath hitherto been wholly mistaken, and so sinister an interpretation been made as if the souls of most of the spectators had liv'd in the eyes and ears of these ridiculous gossips that tattle between the Acts. But he prays you thus to mend it. To consider the news here vented to be none of his news or any reasonable man's, but news made like the time's news (a weekly cheat to draw money) and could not be fitter reprehended than in raising this ridiculous Office of the Staple.

It is as though Jonson's satiric strategy in the theater and at court had backfired, as though the demand for novelty had been intensified in audiences by the Gossips' commentary in prior stage performances of the play. The necessity to regulate his readers' response by interrupting the play — an extraordinary controlling mechanism even for Jonson — bespeaks a fear of being unable to contain the effects of misreadings pronounced in the theater by characters of his own making. Jean E. Howard has argued that the material conditions of production and reception in the public theater "had ideological consequences for the audience that were in some instances at odds with the ideological import of the dramatic fables which that theater disseminated."[28] In performance, the feminine Gossips of *The Staple of News* already functioned as a screen for masculine authorial anxiety about audience consumption of playtexts. Jonson's subsequent effort to regulate reader response is indicative of the degree to which the material conditions of dramatic production impinged on his program for a humanist reformation of patriarchal power.

Robert Weimann distinguishes between the genial "comedy of solidarity," which he associates with Shakespeare, and the bitter humor of Jonson's plays, written in the tradition of Menander, in which "the audience, if indeed it laughs at all, definitely laughs *at* but never *with* the comic figure. . . . The resulting [satiric] laughter is inspired not by a more or less traditional feeling of social unity between audience and actor but by a critical view of the contradictions between norms of society and the unconventional standards of comic characters, be they dupes or intriguers, the cheats or butts of society."[29] But Jonson's note warning the reader to discount his characters' pronouncements in a previous scene suggests that, by 1631, at least some members of the audience were laughing *with* the characters at the author's expense! This was not, however, the laughter of solidarity; nor was it the traditional sort of satiric laughter which Jonson's earlier plays successfully elicited. Rather, the laughter Jonson strains to fend off in his note "To the Readers" is something relatively new, a laughter that arises from the audience's recognition of its power in a relationship of contractual and commodity exchange. Jonson wants his audience to distinguish between Cymbal's commodity and his own art. But the audience sees this hybrid play as a commodity, and enjoys its judgment as a right purchased with the price of admission. The Gossips who deride the author of *The Staple of News* between acts, though objects of satire, reflect the degree to which Caroline audiences and readers of play texts were beginning to take on an active and demanding role as consumers in establishing the canons of taste in the theater.[30]

It is generally accepted that, with the publication of his *Works* in 1616, and with his role in the publication of the *Shakespeare First Folio* in 1623, Ben Jonson had a formative influence on the construction of modern notions of authorship and of literature as high art. At approximately the same time, literature first became a commodity through the media of playhouse and print. In *The Staple of News*, Jonson perceived commodification as a threat to the high moral purpose he had worked to confer on poetry. But by this point in time the process was already well under way. Jonson sought to educate his audiences as to the distinction between high and low culture. But the stability of that distinction at its inception was shaky. It would take more than a hundred years of English literature for the distinction to be so stabilized that Coleridge and his readers could "without hesitation . . . infer with certainty that the sense of the beautiful" was something beyond the capacity of the Iroquois sachem.

In our own time the distinctions on which the "sense of the beautiful" were based for more than two centuries are once more destabilized. And once more this instability is largely an effect of new flows of capital, new demographies, new technologies, and new everyday practices. Senator Dole's recent scourging of Hollywood and the pop-music business is reminiscent of Puritan attacks on the public playhouses in seventeenth-century London, and of other historic moments when the rapid expansion of capital outstripped the ideology that legitimated it. Among those responding to Dole's attack was David Mamet, whose comments were solicited for a *Time* magazine forum on the entertainment industry. As a playwright, Mamet is known for a hybrid dramatic decorum that appropriates the violence and vulgarity of the popular in a stylish way for the "serious" theater, a decorum that is comparable — allowing for the difference in historical context that enables similar formal features to serve different ends — to that of Jonson's satires. Mamet's reaction to Dole is interesting in the present context. He starts with a strikingly Jonsonian satiric reduction of the politician to the mountebank: "Politics seems to me much like the practice of stage magic . . . we know in our hearts, that politicians running for office are, in the main, mountebanks. They promise us an impossible future, or in the case of Senator Dole, a return to an imaginary pristine past." Mamet transforms Dole into a latter-day version of Zeal-of-the-Land-Busy, a character in Jonson's *Bartholomew Fair*; the G.O.P. is rendered the equivalent of Jonson's satirized Puritans. But then Mamet's commentary concludes with a surprising rhetorical — if not logical — twist: "Yes, popular culture, in the main, is garbage. Perhaps it always has been, I don't know. I know we have a legitimate desire for leadership, and Senator Dole's demagoguery corrupts this desire into a search for a victim and a longing for revenge."[31] Now, I may share Mamet's reading of Dole; but how am I to read Mamet? Is the assertion that "popular culture, in the main, is garbage" an admission or an ascription? Does Mamet identify himself with the "popular culture" to which he refers — and on which he relies in his own plays and screenplays? Or is he drawing a distinction in the earlier manner of Ben Jonson? I suspect the latter. Mamet, like Jonson, reduces the zealot to ridicule, but then claims the higher moral ground of an *authentic* arbiter of taste. Mamet can simultaneously appropriate and deploy popular culture in a stylized fashion for the elite theater, while treating it with contempt in its own everyday social space.

The fact that Mamet's relation to the popular may be more ambiguous, more playful (and yet, more cynical?) than Jonson's is a measure of the difference in their respective historical and social contexts. Jonson's "Pox o' your distinction!" is set in opposition to a system of status based on rank. In its place Jonson constructs the humanist system of status based on judgment and taste acquired through intellectual labor. In appropriating the popular, Jonson seeks to regulate it for its own improvement. Mamet, like many intellectuals at the present time, is more ironic, if not more cynical. As a dramatist he aims more to stylize social deformity than to reform it. His appropriation of the popular may be seen as a dramaturgical deconstructive exercise; the old category of "legitimate theater" is deconstructed, and a new theater of hybrid forms set in its place. At the same time, in each moment, Jonsons's and Mamet's, the popular is appropriated by the dominant culture, cant is granted a certain linguistic currency and becomes a portion of the dramatist's symbolic capital. Intellect legitimates itself as distinct from what it regards as ordinary and common, if only by how well it succeeds in managing the ordinary and common. In the process, however, the boundaries between high and low, between what is represented as transcendental value and as commodity value, are blurred.

From the standpoint of political economy there is a historical basis to the resemblance between cultural practices in the pre-industrial stage of capitalism in England when commercial capital — as distinct from landed capital — was highly liquid, and those at the present moment when corporate capitalism expands beyond national boundaries through more flexible forms of accumulation,[32] and when capital can move with greater fluidity in the medium of "cyberspace."[33] At the beginning of the seventeenth century capital existed primarily in the relatively fixed form of land; and, if one accepts the argument of Robert Brenner in two influential essays, capitalism emerged in England principally through the transformation of social relations of production on the land.[34] At the same time, in this early, pre-industrial stage of capitalist development, merchant capital existed in the sphere of circulation but was relatively detached from direct production, a situation acknowledged by Jean-Christophe Agnew in his study of the market and the theater in England: "In many respects, the detached assets of England's mercantile estate bore a closer resemblance to the mobile resources of twentieth-century finance capital than to the relatively fixed investments of nineteenth-century industrial capital."[35] This resemblance of early and later capitalism in contrast to the moment of industrial capitalism is striking, but it requires qualification. The circulation of capital and the commodification of culture in early modern England were tied to a system of national state formation,[36] whereas the postmodern commodification of culture is related to the development of more fluid corporate structures in the current system of transnational capitalism.[37] In the early modern context, a great corporation such as the East India Company acquired its charter and was regulated as an instrument of national policy; in the postmodern context, national policy appears to be more and more an instrument of transnational corporate economic interest.

Historically, the opening up of markets intensifies commodification and alters demographies of consumption; when that occurs, distinctions that support relatively rigid notions of status break down. Indeed, in the seventeenth century, a whole social system based on status was called into question with the rise of contractual institutions. Aesthetic distinctions then came into being as a way of retaining some criteria of status within the market/contract system of social order. Today, the flexibility of capital has its corollary in the fluidity with which intellectual elites can move among culturally marked subject positions without a necessary loss of status. The judgment of taste can now be manifested in an extraordinary range of media, of styles, of fashion that represent a far greater cultural diversity than ever before.[38] It is a condition that intellectual elites have reason to enjoy and to celebrate, a condition in which we all derive a certain benefit from decades of struggle for cultural recognition by racial and ethnic minorities, by women, and by the gay and lesbian community. But to the extent that such pleasure is incorporated into a revitalized *elite* aesthetic, it also entails the social privilege of renewed status. In that event, the undermining of an old binarism of "high" and "low" culture may prove to be less the result of cultural struggle than a reflex of the new, transnational corporate ideology in which token cultural diversity is tolerated within a global system of economic and political inequity. Cultural studies attempts to define culture in materialist terms as a site of struggle, and to trouble distinctions by giving academic legitimacy to the heterogeneous, the material, the everyday. Bringing pop culture into the university classroom and the professional journals is a form of recognition brought about through patterns of wider consumption and circulation across social boundaries But recognition may be little more than appropriation if intellectuals do not take the further step of relating the popular culture they study to the social divisions that generated the distinction between elite and popular, high and low, in the first place.

As the twentieth century draws to a close and as the universalism of Enlightenment aesthetics is subjected to critique, a new aesthetic of difference has emerged, an aesthetic in which world culture is conceived not in terms of uniformity but of hybridity. It is significant and ironic that this post-Enlightenment aesthetic derives much of its strength from what Paul Gilroy describes as "the vernacular arts of the children of slaves." Gilroy acknowledges the convergence of his work on black Atlantic culture with Marxist critical theory while, at the same time, pointing to a significant difference: "Where lived crisis and systemic crisis come together, Marxism allocates priority to the latter while the memory of slavery insists on the priority of the former. . . . in the critical thought of blacks in the West, social self-creation through labour is not the centre-piece of emancipatory hopes. For the descendants of slaves, work signifies only servitude, misery, and subordination. Artistic expression, expanded beyond recognition from the grudging gifts offered by the masters as a token substitute for freedom from bondage, therefore becomes the means towards both individual self-fashioning and communal liberation."[39] This contradiction between artistic expression arising from "lived crisis" (everyday struggle in its most fundamental material sense) and the Marxist critique of "systemic crisis" (the absorption of the everyday into materialist macro-theory under the overarching concept of the mode of production) is a definite and as yet unsolved problem for a critical history of culture. Gilroy's work on the hybrid culture of the modern world is innovative precisely because it resists both systemic, global abstraction and particularist, local essentialism while constructing a counter-narrative of modernity that provides a historical basis for a transnational cultural history and criticism. It is, moreover, a narrative that manages to be neither assimilationist nor exceptionalist, while avoiding the trap of falling into a benign multiculturalism in which all hybrid forms of culture are represented as equivalent.

In at least one respect, the hybrid culture of today's elites is not unlike the hybrid culture of Jonson's Court masques and stage comedies. It is a culture that draws on the energy of the popular, which it identifies with the body (now often a site of pleasure rather than disgust), while, at the same time, asserting its distinction — and justifying its authority — on the basis of superior intellect, which is increasingly judged by managerial standards of efficiency in short-term commodity production. Those of us who are fortunate to have jobs and who perform the functions of an institutional intellectual elite (in high-tech industrial research, the universities, the media, the arts) fall on one side of this division and may constitute a "new aristocracy of labor."[40] On the other side are the industrial workers, now dispersed globally rather than concentrated in the "postindustrial" West, and a huge underclass of the impoverished and disempowered unemployed in the former industrialized sectors and in parts of the world that have been abandoned by capital. While flexible capital has itself ironically and cynically made "diversity" its watchword, intellectuals in the postindustrial sectors have a difficult time recognizing their relationship to a racially and ethnically diversified global labor force or to the unemployed poor. Postmodern intellectuals are well aware that what they produce are commodities. But, impelled by structuralist and poststructuralist notions of the signifier and the consumer society — which notoriously ignore the international division of labor[41] — they often restrict the study of commodity culture to the economic context of *circulation* and *consumption* — in a manner not unlike Jonson's concerns with circulation and consumption at the incipient stage of capitalist development when news, gossip, broadside ballads, and literature competed for an emerging market of urban cultural consumers. While "commodification" may be a buzzword of contemporary cultural criticism today, the taboo remarked on by Bourdieu against "relating intellectual products and producers to their social conditions of existence" nevertheless persists. In the strategic effort to bring the popular, the material, the everyday into the academic theater of the dominant culture there is a danger of limiting the status of *producer* to the professional and of losing touch with those whose labor produces not only a part of our culture but everything else we consume. The difficult task of investigating how intellectual producers are related to the general social conditions of production is to a degree obstructed by the very professionalism and careerism promoted in late twentieth-century corporate institutions for the pursuit of knowledge. It is not "presentist" to suggest that even those intellectuals whose work focuses on cultures of the past need to be concerned about this institutional constraint on what we can know.

While I have relied on Bourdieu in arguing that distinction based on taste played a role in the modern capitalist division of labor, I have also tried to suggest that, even in its early modern forms, artistic expression was a medium of contestation in which authorial self-fashioning in opposition to aristocratic *otium* depended on the appropriation of popular social energy. Given the governing thesis of the present volume, I want to emphasize that in my view the social relations of production are as "material" as the "things" of everyday circulation and consumption. At the end of *The Staple of News*, Pennyboy Canter informs his brother, his son, and the audience on the proper way of relating to Pecunia: "The use of things is all, and not the store." The immediate double referent of "things" — money and wife — is symptomatic of the reification of human agency and of material social relations in the commodity form. Women's productive labor is collapsed into capital, into circulation and exchange. Marriage and domesticity are the model for a more general economy represented as a reproductive mechanism of equivalence rather than inequity. Yet, ironically, the Gossips of the Intermeans are a telltale sign of the playwright's inability to keep his own house in order. In contesting his masters' criteria of distinction, the playwright is unable to disguise the fact that he takes the productive labor and the material culture of everyday London life and turns it into aesthetic capital.

Notes

1. Pierre Bourdieu, *Distinction: A Social Critique of the Judgement of Taste*, trans. Richard Nice (Cambridge, Mass.: Harvard University Press, 1984), pp. 31–32. In the domain of French social theory, Bourdieu's text is of particular relevance to my immediate concerns with the aesthetic. At the same time, like other contributors to the present collection, I am indebted to the work on social space and everyday practices of Henri Lefebvre and Michel de Certeau.

2. Ibid., p. xiii. In the introduction to her translation of Jacques Rancière's *The Ignorant Schoolmaster* (Stanford, Calif.: Stanford University Press, 1991), Kristin Ross points out that Rancière and other French leftists attacked Bourdieu's sociology "as the latest and most influential form of a discourse deriving its authority from the presumed naiveté or ignorance of its objects of study" (Ross, xi). While this judgment may seem harsh, I do think there is evidence to support it in the passage from Bourdieu I have used as an epigraph, with its uninterrogated categories of the "common" and the

"ordinary." Bourdieu's citation of Ortega y Gasset is repeated twice (Bourdieu, *Distinction*, pp. 4, 31–32), each time in a descriptive mode that appears to rely on irony rather than critique as a way of distancing himself from Ortega's elitism. Whatever may have been its intent, the effect of this rhetorical strategy is ambiguous. Ross's discussion of Rancière's reaction to Bourdieu may be a powerful caveat to those who would too easily accept post-May 1968 social theory as anything other than elitist. But one must also read Rancière's critique of Bourdieu in the context of Parisian intellectual and political polemic. When transplanted to a context of U.S. academic discourse, where — ever since the McCarthy era — there has been a less energetic tradition of debate and theory concerning cultural forms of class conflict than in Europe, Bourdieu's analysis is in certain respects still salutary.

   3. My focus here is on the play's development of an ambiguous distinction between the elite and the popular within cultural production. See also Don E. Wayne, "The 'Exchange of Letters': Early Modern Contradictions and Postmodern Conundrums," in *The Consumption of Culture, 1600–1800: Image, Object, Text*, ed. Ann Bermingham and John Brewer (London and New York: Routledge, 1995), pp. 143–65, for analysis of other aspects of *The Staple of News*: its general concern with consumption and commodity exchange, and, in particular, its author's anxiety about the commodification of literature which I discuss in the context of Jonson's ironic role in the production of the Shakespeare First Folio.

   4. Paul Gilroy, *The Black Atlantic: Modernity and Double Consciousness* (Cambridge, Mass.: Harvard University Press, 1993), pp. 2, 15.

   5. See the collection *Women, "Race," and Writing in the Early Modern Period*, ed. Margo Hendricks and Patricia Parker (London and New York: Routledge, 1994).

   6. Joan Thirsk, *Economic Policy and Projects: The Development of a Consumer Society in Early Modern England* (Oxford: Clarendon Press, 1978), pp. 106–7.

   7. Citations from *The Staple of News* employ the modernized and regularized spelling of Devra Rowland Kifer in, Ben Jonson, *The Staple of News*, ed. Kifer (Lincoln: University of Nebraska Press, 1975). I have also consulted the standard edition of Jonson's works, *Ben Jonson*, ed. C. H. Herford, Percy Simpson, and Evelyn Simpson, 11 vols. (Oxford: Clarendon Press, 1925–52), cited hereafter as H & S, *Ben Jonson*. Citations from the masques are from *Ben Jonson: The Complete Masques*, ed. Stephen Orgel (New Haven and London: Yale University Press, 1969).

   8. Pamphlets and tracts in defense of "free trade" appeared in the 1620s as part of a debate over the purported causes and proposed remedies of the depressed English economy, a debate that revolved around the East India trade, for which see B. E. Supple, *Commercial Crisis and Change in England, 1600–1642* (Cambridge: Cambridge University Press, 1959), chap. 9; and Terence Hutchison, *Before Adam Smith: The Emergence of Political Economy, 1662–1776* (Oxford: Basil Blackwell, 1988), pp. 6–7, 21–23, 83. Regardless of their differences, contributors to the debate were in general agreement that the fundamental problem was a shortage of money: "The want of money," wrote Gerard Malynes in *The Maintenance of Free Trade* (1622), "is the first cause of the decay of trade, for without money commodities are out of request" (quoted in Hutchison, p. 21). Thomas Culpeper's *A Tract Against Usury* (1621) called for the freeing of money for trade through government control of interest rates, a position shared by Bacon in his essay "Of Usury" (1625). Thomas Mun's *England's Treasure by Foreign Trade, or The Ballance of Our Forraign Trade is The Rule of Our*

Treasure, in *Early English tracts on Commerce*, ed. J. R. McCulloch (London: Political Economy Club, 1856; rpt. Cambridge: Cambridge University Press, 1970), pp. 115–209, first printed in 1664 but written and possibly circulated in the 1620s, argued against government prohibitions on the export of money and specie. Mun was an officer of the East India Company, the interests of which he defended in attempting to undermine the bullionist and protectionist restraints advocated in more conventional mercantilist doctrine. Instead, Mun set forth the doctrine of the "balance of trade," in which the nation's wealth depended on an excess of exports over imports: "For so much Treasure only will be brought in or carried out of a Commonwealth, as the Forraign Trade doth over or under ballance in value. And this must come to pass by a Necessity beyond all resistance. So that all other courses (which tend not to this end) howsoever they may seem to force mony into a Kingdom for a time, yet are they (in the end) not only fruitless but also hurtful: they are like to violent flouds which bear down their banks, and suddenly remain dry again for want of waters" (Mun, p. 209). The theory depended on the somewhat contradictory principle of depending on consumerism abroad while discouraging it at home: "Wee must ever observe this rule; to sell more to strangers yearly than wee consume of theirs in value" (Mun, p. 125).

9. On the historical background to the play's exaggerated representation of an early modern business in news, see H & S, *Ben Jonson*, 2: 171–75; Joseph Frank, *The Beginnings of the English Newspaper, 1620–1660* (Cambridge, Mass.: Harvard University Press, 1961), pp. 12–13; for a more recent account that includes interesting commentary on Jonson's possible motives for attacking the emergent practice of periodical news publication in London, see C. John Sommerville, *The News Revolution in England: Cultural Dynamics of Daily Information* (New York: Oxford University Press, 1996), esp. ch. 2.

10. On Jonson's equation of talking women with "voracious sexuality" and "avid consumerism," see Karen Newman, "City Talk: Women and Commodification in Jonson's *Epicoene*," *ELH* 56 (1989): 506–7.

11. Jonson's effort to stabilize the English language was just as problematic. Patricia Fumerton, "Subdiscourse: Jonson Speaking Low," *ELR* 25, 1 (1995): 76–96, argues that while Jonson's *Grammar* (published in 1640 but probably written before 1623) sought to "fix" and "rule" a standard for English, it was written with a sense of English as "minor" or "low" with respect to Latin. Similarly, in Jonson's masques, the linguistic "rule" of "high" (main masque) over "low" (antimasque) "could only be maintained . . . by patterning English upon 'high' foreign models and thus rendering it 'minor' first of all in relation to an external standard" (Fumerton, p. 86).

12. H & S, *Ben Jonson*, 1: 85.

13. Among the classic treatments of the phenomenon of reification, in addition to Marx's well-known discussion of the fetishism of the commodity in *Capital* vol. I, chap. 1, sect. 4, see Karl Marx, *Grundrisse*, trans. Martin Nicolaus (New York: Vintage Books, 1973), pp. 163–64; Max Weber, "The Market: Its Impersonality and Ethic (Fragment)," in Weber, *Economy and Society: An Outline of Interpretive Sociology*, ed. Guenther Roth and Claus Wittich, 3 vols. (Berkeley: University of California Press, 1978), 1: 635–40; Georg Lukacs, *History and Class Consciousness* (London: Merlin Press, 1971), pp. 83–110; Max Horkheimer and Theodor W. Adorno, *Dialectic of Enlightenment*, trans. John Cumming (New York: Herder and Herder, 1972), p. 37.

14. Stephen Greenblatt, *Shakespearean Negotiations: The Circulation of Social Energy in Renaissance England* (Oxford: Clarendon Press, 1988).

15. Ibid., p. 5.

16. Citations are from Thomas Dekker, *The Shoemakers' Holiday*, ed. D. J. Palmer (London and Tonbridge: Ernest Benn, 1975).

17. See Richard Helgerson, *Forms of Nationhood: The Elizabethan Writing of England* (Chicago and London: University of Chicago Press, 1992), pp. 231–40, for a critical comparison of the figure of the exemplary monarch in Shakespeare and in the work of playwrights like Dekker in the employ of Philip Henslowe.

18. Laura Caroline Stevenson, *Praise and Paradox: Merchants and Craftsmen in Elizabethan Popular Literature* (Cambridge: Cambridge University Press, 1984), p. 117.

19. David Scott Kastan, "Workshop and/as Playhouse: Comedy and Commerce in *The Shoemakers' Holiday,*" *Studies in Philology* 84 (1987): 324–37.

20. Alan Sinfield, *Faultlines: Cultural Materialism and the Politics of Dissident Reading* (Berkeley: University of California Press, 1992), p. 92.

21. Citations of Aristotle are from *The Basic Works of Aristotle*, ed. Richard McKeon (New York: Random House, 1941).

22. Robert Brenner, "The Agrarian Roots of European Capitalism," in *The Brenner Debate: Agrarian Class Structure and Economic Development in Pre-Industrial Europe*, ed. T. H. Aston and C. H. E. Philpin (Cambridge: Cambridge University Press, 1985), pp. 298–99.

23. Citations from Jonson's *Epigrammes* are from H & S, *Ben Jonson*, 8: 40, 25–26, 47–48.

24. Robert Cecil, Earl of Salisbury, quoted in W. J. Jones, *Politics and the Bench: The Judges and the Origins of the English Civil War* (London: George Allen and Unwin, 1971), p. 34.

25. Immanuel Kant, *Critique of Judgment* (1790), trans. J. H. Bernard (London and New York: Hafner Press, 1951), p. 38.

26. Samuel Taylor Coleridge, *Essays on the Principles of Genial Criticism* (Bristol, 1814), in Coleridge, *Shorter Works and Fragments*, ed. H. J. Jackson and J. R. de J. Jackson, *The Collected Works of Samuel Taylor Coleridge*, gen. ed. Kathleen Coburn. Bollingen Series 75, 13 vols. (Princeton, N.J., Princeton University Press; London: Routledge, 1995), 11.1: 381. The phrases *"we attribute this without hesitation,"* and *"[we] infer with certainty"* mark a grammatical strategy in Coleridge that is similar to passages in Kant analyzed by Bourdieu: "The statements on taste are written in the imperative, or rather in that sort of spurious constative which allows the author to remain silent as to the conditions of realization of what is in fact a performative utterance" (Bourdieu, *Distinction*, pp. 488–89).

27. My use of the term "appropriation" here and elsewhere is indebted to Robert Weimann's analysis of this cultural and social function throughout his work on Renaissance drama and fiction, most recently in Weimann's *Authority and Representation in Early Modern Discourse*, ed. David Hillman (Baltimore and London: Johns Hopkins University Press, 1996); see also Michael D. Bristol, *Carnival and Theater: Plebeian Culture and the Structure of Authority in Renaissance England* (London: Methuen, 1986); Scott Cutler Shershow, *Puppets and "Popular" Culture* (Ithaca and London: Cornell University Press, 1995), contains interesting analysis of the interrelatedness of elite and popular culture that is convergent with my argument here; for a discussion of Jonson's appropriation of the popular with different emphasis from my own, see Tom Hayes, *The Birth of Popular Culture: Ben Jonson, Maid Marian and Robin Hood* (Pittsburgh: Duquesne University Press, 1992).

28. Jean E. Howard, *The Stage and Social Struggle in Early Modern England* (London and New York: Routledge, 1994), p. 7; and, in this context, see esp. chap. 4.

29. Robert Weimann, *Shakespeare and the Popular Tradition in the Theater: Studies in the Social Dimension of Dramatic Form and Function*, ed. Robert Schwartz (Baltimore: Johns Hopkins University Press, 1978), pp. 254, 260.

30. On the growing sophistication of audiences, the purchasing of playbooks, and the general establishment of a "flourishing literary world" around the Caroline theaters, see Martin Butler, *Theater and Crisis 1632–1642* (Cambridge: Cambridge University Press, 1984), ch. 6. Marx W. Wartofsky, "Art, Artworlds, and Ideology," *Journal of Aesthetics and Art Criticism* 38, 3 (1980): 239–47, argues similarly with respect to the visual arts that in the seventeenth century "The artwork begins to become a commodity produced not for a patron, or the church, but for a market. The work is no longer defined by commissions, but in a riskier and wider way, as a product for prospective sale to a new class of buyers, through intermediaries who act either as agents for the artists or for the buyers of art" (p. 245).

31. David Mamet quoted in "Tough Talk on Entertainment," a *Time Forum*, comp. by Andrea Sachs and Susanne Washburn, *Time*, 12 June 1995: 35.

32. David Harvey, *The Condition of Postmodernity: An Inquiry into the Origins of Cultural Change* (Cambridge, Mass., and Oxford: Basil Blackwell, 1990), pp. 147–97.

33. At a recent conference called "Technology's Impact on Society," sponsored by the Progress and Freedom Foundation and broadcast on the C-SPAN network (December 1995), a panelist claimed that the global economy was now one of "friction free capitalism resulting from highly lubricated markets as a result of new information technologies." The metaphor invites at least a paragraph's worth of interpretation concerning the relevant semantic contexts: gender, sexuality, perpetual motion machines, etc. But the fellow conferees appeared to treat the statement as a datum, without irony, without humor. If anything, their approbation was devotional, the satisfaction of a congregation that had just listened to a mild and uplifting sermon. The desire to imagine a benign capitalism, in which the actual friction of competition is dissolved into the virtual community of the Internet, reminds one of the more utopian contractual communities of the Reformation.

34. See *The Brenner Debate*, ed. Aston and Philpin, pp. 49–50, 296–99. Brenner's argument has been debated both by non-Marxists and within Marxist theory. His analysis may be economistic from the standpoint of political or cultural historiography, but in emphasizing class struggle in the process of direct agricultural production as a corrective to a strict commercialization model, Brenner provides a compelling argument for why, by the seventeenth century, capitalism was at a more developed stage in England than on the European continent.

35. Jean-Christophe Agnew, *Worlds Apart: The Market and the Theater in Anglo-American Thought, 1550–1750* (Cambridge: Cambridge University Press, 1986), p. 53.

36. Theodor K. Rabb distinguishes the economic preoccupations of merchant investors from the motives of personal and national glory that inspired investors of higher rank. He argues that the records of the East India Company show little concern for national ideals: "Even the tracts written in its behalf dealt more with economics than glory" (quoted in Helgerson, *Forms of Nationhood*, p. 172). Rabb's analysis of the language of the company's records must be considered while bearing in mind that the East India Company acquired its charter from and operated under the regulatory

power of the crown. For a consideration of Rabb's work in the context of the process of national state formation in Tudor and early Stuart England, see Philip Corrigan and Derek Sayer, *The Great Arch: English State Formation as Cultural Revolution* (Oxford: Basil Blackwell, 1985), pp. 66–67. From another perspective, Robert Brenner, *Merchants and Revolution: Commercial Change, Political Conflict, and London's Overseas Traders, 1550–1653* (Princeton, N.J.: Princeton University Press, 1993), emphasizes the political dependency of the merchant companies on the state, from the moment they were granted monopoly privileges by charter: "Ironically . . . there remained in the very constitution of the company merchants' property . . . a critical, irreducibly political-jurisdictional element of the sort that had long been transcended in the property of the landlord class. This was a crucial determinant of their perspective on politics and led, inexorably, to the closest alliance with the monarchy" (pp. 669–70).

37. For which, see the essays collected in *Global/Local: Cultural Production and the Transnational Imaginary*, ed. Rob Wilson and Wimal Dissanayake (Durham and London: Duke University Press, 1996).

38. Witness the kinds of music and dance that characterized the first Clinton inaugural festivities, which, incidentally, bore some resemblance to the hybrid cultural apparatus of the later Jonsonian masques. The Democratic Party hierarchy may have been less condescending than the members of a Stuart Court, but not necessarily less appropriative of popular cultural forms. After Clinton's reelection, hindsight tells us that the representation of cultural diversity at the inaugural was not much more than an allegorical device for an administration that has governed by fearful compromise on issues of the greatest import to people of color, to the poor regardless of race, and even to women despite the outspokenness on their behalf of Hillary Rodham Clinton.

39. Gilroy, *The Black Atlantic*, pp. 38–40.

40. Harvey, *The Condition of Postmodernity*, p. 192.

41. Gayatri Chakravorty Spivak, "Can the Subaltern Speak?" in *Marxism and the Interpretation of Culture*, ed. Cary Nelson and Lawrence Grossberg (Urbana: University of Illinois Press, 1988), p. 272.

5

Homely Accents

Ben Jonson Speaking Low

Patricia Fumerton

COMPLAINING AGAINST ARDUOUS TRAINING under his tutors in Latin, the boy-king, James VI of Scotland, grumbled: "Thay gar me speik latin ar I could speik Scotis."[1] "Scotis" originally meant "Gaelic," the language of social dominance in Scotland until the Middle Ages. In the course of the Middle Ages, however, Gaelic lost dominance, retired to the Highlands, and came to be known as "Yrisch" or "Ersch." The term "Scotis" had found a new voice. By the late fifteenth century, it meant "Inglis," a language of the Lowlands that I shall risk calling a dialect of English.[2] It is this dialect to which James referred and which he evidently felt was his native or natural tongue. Most of his early works were in Scots; the most famous is his manuscript *Basilikon Doron* (1598). But Scots itself was soon to lose dominance. Although the first edition of the *Basilikon Doron* was published in Scotland (1599), James there rendered his Scots more like Southern English, eliminating much of his Scots spelling, grammar, and vocabulary. And in the second edition of the work, published in London on his accession to the English throne in 1603, he purified the text of Scots even more drastically, translating his language into an elevated or "high" English style.[3]

What we witness here, of course, is the process by which English assumed its majority: Gaelic ceded dominance to Scots, which in turn ceded it to English. But consider as well the paradoxical counter-development by which the same evolution of language involved a *devolution* from the major to the minor. Such devolution appears not only in the lost status or gradual death of a major language, as in the case of Gaelic and Scots. It occupies even the moment of majority rule. The very act of translating a minor into a major language, for instance, could cause the latter to degenerate. James recognized this phenomenon in a 1609 letter to Robert Cecil, in which he responds to Cecil's praise of one of his early works written around 1583–1584 (unidentified and now lost). "The language" of the work, James declared, "is extremely bad, for although it was first written all with my own hand it was first marred in the orthography by Geddes copying it . . . in very rude Scottish spelling, and next was it copied by Sir Peter Young's son, who pressing to English hath marred it quite and made it neither, so it is now good Britaine language or rather Welsh."[4] Pressing Scots into English results in a transmutation of both languages into "minor" modes. If only orthographically speaking, good written Scots can become "rude" Scots, which can become an English most like Welsh. Courtiers under James I of England heard English rendered in such a minor chord all the time. As Sir Francis Bacon observed, James spoke English "in the full dialect of his country" — *Scotland* — and he surrounded himself with Scots speakers, not to mention the hordes of unwelcome brogue-voiced petitioners who followed him south.[5]

My concern in this essay is with the manner in which Renaissance English, even in the course of consolidating its majority, also perpetually engaged in a complex process of becoming "sub" or "low." Such lowly speaking grounded high discourse in the homely or everyday, as we shall see in the final section of this paper. At issue here is our very notion of a major or dominant language, which in the wake of postmodern studies ranging from Mikhail Bakhtin to Gilles Deleuze and Félix Guattari has undergone a sea change. Deleuze and Guattari's analysis seems to me especially germane to the situation of Renaissance English. To borrow the terminology of their *A Thousand Plateaus*, we can say that there really was no such thing as a major language to be resisted in the spirit of Bakhtinian "heteroglossia." Rather, every major language — and especially a language as unstable as English in the Renaissance — was from the start a "becoming-minoritarian" or "becoming-minor of the major language."[6]

We can test Deleuze and Guattari's thesis (and its variation upon Bakhtin) by looking to the "high" Jacobean genre mastered by Ben Jonson: the masque. The Jonsonian masque spoke directly to King James in a celebration of his and England's majority or "rule." But how was such "majoritarianism" *voiced*? Put another way, what does it mean to speak "The King's English" under a Scottish/English king? Before we can begin to answer that question, we need to examine more fully the newly established "high" status of English in our age and trace its "becoming-majoritarian" through a simultaneous "becoming-*minoritarian*."

I

In our context, English was a "becoming-minoritarian" language in two important ways, both arising from an unruly foreign or alien presence: in the first case external, in the second internal (although, as we shall see below, such distinctions are difficult to make: the alien outside is imported within).

First of all, English created its majority status only in a manner that made it feel minor relative to other languages from across the channel deemed even "higher." As Richard Foster Jones notes in *The Triumph of the English Language*, sixteenth-century England sought eloquence most especially by importing neologisms from such foreign tongues as Latin, Greek, and French. The seventeenth century then sought to secure the majority of the language by compiling orthographies, grammars, and dictionaries.[7] But this search for security implicitly acknowledged that English yet lacked "major" status or "*rule*." Although the absorption of alien terms had "purged" the vernacular of its felt deficiency, it had also introduced the specter of a language forever mutating.[8] Confirming this impression, the authors of *A History of the English Language* estimate that Renaissance English spilled over with some 10,000 new words.[9]

By the seventeenth century, moreover, the influx of new and foreign terms sparked the beginnings of an antiquarian interest (by William Camden, Richard Verstegan, John Selden, John Speed, Samuel Daniel, Michael Drayton, Richard Carew, Henry Spelman, and many followers) that furthered the sense of language's instability. Led by Verstegan's *Restitvtion of Decayed Intelligence* (1605) and Camden's *Remaines* (1605, and particularly the revised edition of 1614), such studies privileged the theory that English derived from the pride of Teutonic languages, Saxon. At the same time, they questioned the long-held belief in the Celtic or British origins of the language and downplayed the influence of the Danish and Norman invasions.[10] But such revisionism was not secure, even among its most avid proponents. Camden, for example, was torn between exalting the "purity" of the Saxon language and embracing neologisms imported from foreign tongues.[11] Indeed, comparative research into different languages in the service of a history of English called into question not simply its single origin but the very concept of an emerging "major" language. "In the midst of varying and sometimes contradictory views of the mother tongue," Jones observes, "the conviction of the instability of modern languages remained fixed and unchanged." English seemed especially mutable relative to classical languages. But it also suffered from inherent instability, and this points us toward our second model of "becoming-minoritarian." Thus, noting how English had varied since Saxon times, Camden points out "that you may see by what degrees our tongue is risen, and thereby coniecture how in time it may alter and fall againe." Only after keen recognition of such language variation or "becoming-minoritarian" did the seventeenth century embark upon efforts to stabilize, "fix," and "rule" English.[12]

Ben Jonson participated directly in this self-undermining effort. A friend of Camden and Selden, Jonson shared their philological interests and acquired a collection of foreign grammars. He also produced sometime before 1623 an English grammar, which he then rewrote (probably in the early 1630s) after it perished by fire.[13] This *Grammar* (1640) reveals acute sensitivity to the foreign languages shaping the English vernacular — Jonson makes links especially to Latin, Greek, French, and Italian. At the same time he seeks to fix such influences in a ruled and thus "major" English. The imposition of rule took the form of an opening analysis of the proper pronunciation of vowels, consonants, and diphthongs; frequent asides on the proper spelling of words; and a discussion of the proper parts of speech and syntax. Just how tenuous was Jonson's hold on such stability, however, is evident from the revised edition of 1692. Here the editors amply altered Jonson's "rules" and examples to fit yet a new age's linguistic usages.[14] It was not only subsequent generations who rendered Jonson's rule of English minor, however. At the time of composition Jonson himself thought of English in a minor mode. This is clear from the fact that he imposed on the English language the whole Latin system of gender, conjugations, and declensions. Jonson's work is the grammar of "the little language that could" (or rather would) be Latin.[15]

But there is a second, and to my mind much more interesting, sense in which major English was inevitably "minoritarian" — a sense that *internalizes* the problem of English's relation to higher foreign languages. We can begin to see this in the antiquarians' awareness of the historical changes English had undergone, specifically in Camden's observation that the Saxon language had risen in status (and might fall again). Camden here alludes to the low opinion held of Saxon English in the sixteenth century, when the Germanic tribes who had invaded England were considered brute aliens uttering a barbarous speech. But with the rise in the status of the Germanic (and especially Saxon) race in the seventeenth century, Saxon sounded a new note: now it was considered a civilized and uncontaminated language, and was embraced as England's "natural tongue."[16] What interests me here is both the translation of the foreign "low" into the "high" and its internalization. The base alien, we see, has become a ruling native.

The antiquarians' elevating domestication of the "alien" Saxon points us to an even more audible internalization of foreignness in the seventeenth century. I refer to the insistent retention, and even revival, of such "alien" speech from within Britain as the Irish, Gaelic, and Welsh tongues, as well as the cacophony of native dialects increasingly subjected to study. Alexander Gil, whose *Logonomia Anglica* (1619) was a source for Jonson's *Grammar*, for example, promoted the study of the Northern dialect (because it was nearest to the Saxon). And as early as the 1580s, Camden prepared to write his history of England, *Britannia* (1586), by studying the British language of Welsh as well as the Germanic language of Old English.[17] Unlike classical and continental languages, such native idioms and dialects — even that of Wales, whose mythic history of the Trojans and Arthur the Elizabethans so enthusiastically embraced — were definitively "low" in relation to English. But they played upon "major" English as if in a minor chord so that we hear, in the words of Deleuze and Guattari, "continuous variations" that realize "intralinguistic, endogenous, internal minorities."[18]

    This second concept of "becoming-minoritarian," conceived in the manner of Deleuze and Guattari — that of an internal alienness continuously and creatively inflecting the "major" language — tellingly realigns the Bakhtinian model of discourse embraced by many recent Renaissance scholars. Both Bakhtin and Deleuze-Guattari have a keen sense of the alien voiced within language. What Bakhtin calls "the internal dialogism of the word," whereby "the word is shaped in dialogic interaction with an alien word that is already in the object," Deleuze-Guattari would call being "a foreigner, but in one's own tongue."[19] But, however conversational or, as Michael Holquist insists, "relative" Bakhtin's dialogism may be,[20] the concept depends on hierarchy. The term "stratification," for instance, insistently echoes through Bakhtin's work. To cite but one example from *The Dialogic Imagination*, Bakhtin affirms that "the *internal stratification* of any single national language into social dialects, characteristic group behavior, professional jargons, generic languages . . . — this *internal stratification* present in every language at any given moment of its historical existence is the indispensable prerequisite for the novel as a genre" (my emphasis).[21] "Stratification" or hierarchy, as the above reference to multiple voices suggests, further allies Bakhtin's dialogism to its brother-term "heteroglossia." Bakhtin thus hypothesizes an established "unitary" culture and discourse that "*reigns over*" and in essence determines the heteroglossia of the "low." "A unitary language," he observes, "is not something given [*dan*] but is always in essence posited [*zadan*] — and at every moment of its linguistic life it is opposed to the realities of heteroglossia. But at the same time it makes its real presence felt as a force for overcoming this heteroglossia, imposing specific limits to it, guaranteeing a certain maximum of mutual understanding and crystalizing into a real, although still relative, unity — the unity of the reigning conversational (everyday) and literary language, "correct language."[22] It is against such "correct" or "high" discourse, which always asserts itself, that the alien "low," in Bakhtin's mind, launches an aggressive battle. "High" and "low," "major" and "minor" are opposed as if in a Manichean struggle.[23]

    Instead of such a model of discourse built on hierarchy and conflict,

Deleuze and Guattari propose one based on dispersal and modulation (hence their title, "A Thousand *Plateaus*," and their fondness for analogies to music). Rather than "systemic rupture," they suggest, linguistic change occurs by "a gradual modification of frequency, by a coexistence and continuity of different usages." They offer as example the statement, "I swear":

["I swear"] is a different statement depending on whether it is said by a child to his or her father, by a man in love to his loved one, or by a witness before the court. These are like three sequences . . . there is no reason to say that the variables are merely situational, and that the statement remains constant in principle. Not only are there as many statements as there are effectuations, but all of the statements are present in the effectuation of one among them, so that the line of variation is virtual, in other words, real without being actual, and consequently continuous regardless of the leaps the statement makes.[24]

Rejecting any "scientific model" that would argue for a constant in the expression "I swear" (or any other such expression, for that matter), Deleuze and Guattari go on to criticize the analogous "political model by which language is homogenized, centralized, standardized, becoming a language of power, a major or dominant language." They argue instead that "the more a language has or acquires the characteristics of a major language, the more it is affected by continuous variations that transpose it into a 'minor' language." They point out, for example, that

if a language such as British English or American English is major on a world scale, it is necessarily worked upon by all the minorities of the world, using very diverse procedures of variation. Take the way Gaelic and Irish English set English in variation. Or the way Black English and any number of "ghetto languages" set American English in variation, to the point that New York is virtually a city without a language. (Furthermore, American English could not have *constituted* itself without this linguistic labor of the minorities.) . . . *You will never find a homogeneous system that is not still or already affected by a regulated, continuous, immanent process of variation*.[25]

Thus Deleuze and Guattari reject Bakhtinian distinctions between "high" and "low" or "major" and "minor," and the combativeness such oppositions imply, in favor of an "immanent process" of "continuous variation" or "a becoming-minor of the major language." They insist that "the problem is not the distinction between major and minor language; it is one of a becoming." Along these lines, "there is no becoming-majoritarian; majority is never becoming. All becoming is minoritarian."[26]

When applied to Renaissance English, this concept of "becoming-minoritarian" extends and inverts the language story so finely told by Stephen Greenblatt in "Invisible Bullets" and Steven Mullaney in "The Rehearsal of Cultures." Both narrate what one might call a Bakhtinian allegory of the "becoming-*majoritarian*" of English whereby the vernacular produced, reveled in, and then suppressed alien discourses—foreign and native languages as well as dialects—in order to emerge "pure."[27] Their studies are precisely situated: in sixteenth-century England and in Shakespeare's Henry IV and V plays (making the latter now canonical for language study of the English Renaissance). But, to repeat the insight of Deleuze and Guattari: "The more a language has or acquires the characteristics of a major language, the more it is affected by continuous variations that transpose it into a 'minor' language."[28] This seems especially true of the seventeenth century, with its increased sense of language's instability and variation, especially into native languages and dialects—and, of course, with a *Scots*-speaking king on the English throne.

We might do well, then, to look beyond Greenblatt and Mullaney's stage-play "majoritarianism" of the sixteenth century to a seventeenth-century dramatization that directly addressed James: the Jonsonian masque. To this genre I now turn, particularly to a masque that employed dialect and an internal foreign language to talk to the king. Jonson's *For the Honor of Wales* (1618), we will see, demonstrates the full "becoming-minoritarianism" of "major" Renaissance English.

<h1 style="text-align:center">II</h1>

In the course of James's reign, internal, "low" or "sub"-discourses proliferated in Jonson's masques: witches' talk, popular-speak, lingua franca, alchemical lingo, body language, obscenity, gossip, and—my focus here—"native" foreign languages and dialects. Addressing such subdiscourses to his English/Scottish king, Jonson spoke to James in two voices that echo the two models of "becoming-minoritarian" (and the double linguistic side to James) discussed above. But it is the second version, internalizing the foreign, that we hear especially loud and clear.

We might begin, following our first model of "becoming-minoritarian," with "rule." As in his *Grammar*, Jonson sought to exert rule over "continuous variations" upon "major" English in order to celebrate the reign of his *English*/Scottish king. Increasingly, for example, he attempted to quarantine the low from the high: unruly antimasquers mostly speak the "low" language of prose, whereas those who introduce the masquers (after banishing the antimasque in which the audience revels) speak a "high" language of poetry that in every way (rhythm, rhyme, and tone) suggests rule. To the extent that the "low" and "high" are opposed in a conflict over which the "purified" high finally reigns, Jonson's masques, like Shakespeare's history plays, could be described as Bakhtinian. (I say this, of course, aware that Bakhtin is firmly on the side of the "low" even as he continually recognizes the "reign" of the "high.") In fact, the movement by which the main masque breaks into and dispels the antimasque dramatizes the consolidation of "poetry" described by Bakhtin:

> The poetic word (in the narrow sense) must break through to its object, penetrate the alien word in which the object is entangled; it also encounters heteroglot language and must break through in order to create a unity and a pure intentionality (which is neither given nor ready-made) . . . The records of the passage remain in the slag of the creative process, which is then cleared away (as scaffolding is cleared away once construction is finished), so that the finished work may rise as unitary speech, one coextensive with its object, as if it were speech about an "Edenic" world.

This art of poetry, Bakhtin goes on to say, "gives rise to the conception of a purely poetic, extrahistorical language, a language far removed from the petty rounds of everyday life, a language of the gods."[29] Such is the language Jonson's main masques aspired to as the god-like masquers descended and broke through the antimasques, clearing away all traces of the alien and prosaic "low." What remains in this creative process is a purified, unitary, ruled, and "high" English discourse. What could be a higher compliment not only to the political but also to the linguistic rule of James's English reign?

The problem was that such regal poetic "rule" in the main masque could only be maintained, as in Jonson's *Grammar*, by patterning English upon "high" foreign models and thus rendering it "minor" first of all in relation to an external standard. In *Pleasure Reconciled to Virtue* (the companion piece to *For the Honor of Wales*), for instance, the masque celebrated Prince Charles's new ruling title as "Prince of Wales" in a noticeably foreign manner: the masquers danced *Spanish* dances, their doublets were "cut in the manner of ancient *Roman* corselets,"[30] and the figures who introduced them—indeed, who alone spoke the main masque's high poetic discourse—were not English but Roman and Greek (specifically, Mercury and Daedalus).

More significantly, the problem was interiorized in the second manner of "becoming-minoritarian" when Jonson then rapidly remade *Pleasure Reconciled to Virtue* into *For the Honor of Wales*. Performed on February 17, 1618, only six weeks after the performance of *Pleasure Reconciled*, *For the Honor of Wales* would at first glance appear to substantiate the emergence in the main masque of a stable, ruled, and "high" English discourse. The main masques in both entertainments are entirely the same. Only the antimasques, filled with prose subdiscourses, are changed. Yet despite such superficial ratification of the stable "high" discourse, *For the Honor of Wales* brings home to us the internal minoritarianism that subtly modulates England's major language.

Let me first set the stage by documenting that the language contained in the antimasque of *For the Honor of Wales* was indeed "interior," "low," and engaged in "continuous variation." In *Pleasure Reconciled*, we observe, the antimasque is full of drunken, obscene, and violent discourses spoken by Comus's revelers and savage pygmies. But in *For the Honor of Wales* these subdiscourses become Welsh or, rather, a language mutating undecidably between Welsh and Gaelic. The antimasquers speak actual, untranslated Welsh (sometimes whole sentences) as well as a Welshman's pronunciation of English, which I will refer to as Welsh dialect. But this splitting of the antimasque language into a foreign language and a dialect exactly mirrored the language situation in Scotland, where the Gaelic language and Scots dialect cohabited.[31] Indeed, the antimasque's Welshmen, echoing comparisons made by their countrymen, directly liken Wales to Scotland.[32] Most obviously, in inviting James to visit Wales, they cite as precedent his recent journey into Scotland. "Come it downe once a day and trie," the Welshman Jenkin offers, "I tell yow now, yow s'all be as welcomely there [in Wales], as where yow were in your owne Cyntries [Scotland] last two Symmers, and pershance wee'll made yow as good s'eere [cheer] too."[33] Even more tellingly, the Welshmen make etymological claims that in effect embed Gaelic within Welsh. This was easy enough to do since both were Celtic languages. Thus, when the Welshmen argue that the name "Car" (of the masquer, Robert Carr) "is plaine Welse" and give examples of place names — "*Caerleon, Caermardin, Cardiffe*" (172– 73) — the audience, and certainly James, could easily have added the Scottish placenames: "Cairnie," "Cardross," "Cargill."[34] The antimasque of *For the Honor of Wales*, in other words, speaks to the king in a loose and variable Scots-Welsh patois epitomizing the principle of a continuously variable, "minoritarian" discourse embedded within English.

As if to deny such instability, the antimasque of *For the Honor of Wales* is preoccupied with stabilizing the names of things and people. In the opening, for example, the Welshmen declare their anger at the king for allowing Charles and his masquers in *Pleasure Reconciled* to be placed in a foreign, "outlandis" mountain — Atlas — when "his Highnesse has as goodly Mountaines, and as tawll a Hills of his own" in Wales (59–60). Proposing "onely shanging his [the mountain's] name" (149–50), the Welshmen then launch upon a series of alternative Welsh namings:

EVAN. Why, there is *Talgar*⟨*th*⟩.
JENKIN. Well sayd.
EVAN. *Eliennieth*.
JENKIN. Well sayd, *Evan*.
EVAN. *Cadier Arthur*.
JENKIN. Toudge him, toudge him.

EVAN. *Pen-maen-maur*.
JENKIN. 'Is good boyes, *Evan*.
EVAN. And *Craig-eriri*.
JENKIN. *Aw? vellhy?* [so?] why, law yow now? 'Is not *Pen-/maen-maur*, and *Craig-Eriri* as good sound, as *Adlas* every/whit of him? (65–76)

It is as if the Welshmen seek to pin down the relation between words and things and so to confer stability upon their subdiscourse. In this sense they vocalize a pressing contemporary need. Welsh humanists of the period, whom we might dub minoritarian countervoices to the English antiquarians, were themselves attempting to stabilize and assert, or reassert, the "rule" of the Welsh language. As in England, dictionaries, orthographies, and grammars appeared, such as John Davies's renowned Welsh Grammar (1621), which Jonson requested from his friend James Howell. But, even more than in England, the Welsh humanists' efforts were doomed to failure. Undergoing rapid devolution, Welsh "rule" succumbed to the "minor" mode (testified by the fact that Davies's Grammar was written in Latin).[35] So too, within Jonson's masque, the Welsh antimasquers cannot stabilize their language. On the contrary, their continual Welsh variations upon "Adlas" speak the very slipperiness of their subdiscourse. The Welsh language of the antimasque persistently slips from name to name in a proliferation of exchangeable signs. Thus consider another burst of listing over the name "Abercromy" (Abercrombie):

JENKIN. And *Abercromy*, is aull one as *Abermarlys*.
EVAN. Or *Abertau*.
HOWELL. Or *Aber du gledhaw*.
RHYS. Or *Aberhodney*.
JENKIN. Or *Abergevenny*.
HOWELL. Or *Aberconway*.
EVAN. *Aberconway* is very like *Abercromy*, a liddel hard/s'ifte has pit 'em aull into *Wales*.
(177–84)

To get from the "English" courtier "Abercromy" to his Welsh likeness "Aberconway," we have to pass through five transmutations of Welsh place names, and the list could be further extended with some good Scottish place names as well: "Aberfoyle," "Aberlour," "Abernethy."[36]

What makes these slippery etymologies fascinating is the difficulty of knowing to what extent they are actually sham. Deriving the Scotsman's name *"Acmooty"* (Auchmouty) from Welsh *"Ap mouth-wye of Llanmouthwye"* (176) is a big stretch. But Welsh (and Gaelic, for that matter) was a largely oral language and thus highly unstable — spellings of names changed dramatically. The problem was compounded by Anglicizations of Welsh names beginning in the fifteenth century. Sir Robert Cecil, for instance, was of Welsh descent; but his father Englished the Welsh family name, "Seisyllt."[37] When one of the Welshmen thus refers to the masquer Palmer (an *English* name) and says "his Ancestors was call him *Pen-maure*" (174–75), he may very well have been right.[38]

Other such lists in the antimasque provide gazetteers of Welsh nouns that rename what had been Hercules and the Garden of Hesperides in *Pleasure Reconciled* and that further demonstrate the instability of language. "What need of *Ercules*," Evan insists, "when *Cadwallader*—" "Or *Lluellin*," Jenkin breaks in, "or *Reese ap Griphin*, or *Cradock*, or *Owen Glendower*, with a Welse hooke, and a Goats skinne on his backe, had done very better, and twice as well?" (189–92). What need of "Garden of Hesperides," when Welsh can proffer "*Driffindore*, that is the *Gilden Valley*, or *Gelthleedore*, that is the *Gilden Grove*, and is in *Care Marden*, the *Welse Garden*?" "'Is a thousand place in *Wales*," Jenkin asserts, threatening infinite variation, "as finely places as the *Esperides* every crum of him" (363–66). Though the mountain or Hercules or the Garden remain essentially the same, the Welsh language for these places varies not only from "foreign" terms to "native" Welsh, but even within Welsh. In sum, everywhere we look in the antimasque of *For the Honor of Wales*, we see a "low" language characterized by radical mutability.

The full sense in which *For the Honor of Wales* is about the "becoming-minoritarian" of language, however, only emerges when we then look beyond the Welsh itself to its effect on the supposedly separate English linguistic universe of the masquers. Indeed, what *For the Honor of Wales* finally suggests is that the distinction between an interior subdiscourse and its enveloping major discourse—between the antimasque and the masque—is factitious. In reading the Welsh of the antimasquers, in fact, we have really already been reading the English of the main masque—or more accurately a "continuous variation" played upon that English. Thus, for example, notice what happens to the very concept of English when at one point the Welshmen insist that the "English" masquers soon to emerge from the mountain are "aull Welse" (158). Through a fantastic feat of etymology, they locate every masquer's name—whether Montgomery (of Norman French origin), Erwin (Flemish), Hamilton, Carr, Auchmouty, and Abercrombie (all Scots names), or Palmer (decidedly English) in Wales. Exposed to the mutating, viral presence of its subdiscourses, that is, the "English" language itself undergoes a "continuous variation," changing it into French, into Flemish, into minoritarian Scots, into Welsh. Finally, all foreign variations played upon English are "Welshified" or internalized (as Wales is internal to Britain). What we have been hearing all along, in other words, is a many-voiced, intralinguistic minoritarianism that speaks for "major" English.

Minoritarianism then more fully infects English when the Welshmen offer English anagrams to the king. *"Charles James Stuart"* (James's full name) is rearranged to reveal *"Claimes Arthurs Seate"*; *"Charles Stuart"* (his eldest son's name) becomes *"cals true hearts"* (371–77). Voiced in the "minor" key of Welshmen, that is, the English language fully destabilizes: it turns completely, anagrammatically, around to play endless variations in a minor key. Or, rather, it plays variations now so undecidable between major and minor that in the final analysis it is difficult to decide whether it is Welsh pride or the very state of the English language that encourages the antimasquers' anagrammatic flourish. In Renaissance England anagrams depended for their possibility upon erratic English orthography. "Charles Stuart," for example, could only be translated into "cals true hearts" if one spelled calls "cals" and true "tru" (or, alternatively, heart "hart").[39] Such orthography, indeed, was the very touchstone of all the potential minoritarianisms layered within the major tongue. Because of unstable spelling, we know, "minor" dialect and "major" English became at times indistinguishable. Thus Stephen Orgel, working from the 1640 folio text of *For the Honor of Wales*, often modernizes spellings of words that may very well have been meant by Jonson to indicate the broad-voweled Welsh dialect: "all" spelled "aull," "called" spelled "caulld," "talk" spelled "tauke," and so on.[40] Significantly, the Renaissance printer of Jonson's text himself had problems distinguishing Welsh dialect from erratic English and thus badly botched the printing of the Welsh scenes. C. H. Herford and Percy and Evelyn Simpson, aided by the Welsh expert James Fraser, have tried to restore the Welsh language and dialect to Jonson's "intended" form (7: 495–96). And yet they too may have erred in over-standardizing Jonson's dialect. My own feeling is that Jonson went further than most of his contemporaries in his efforts to represent the Welsh dialect accurately, but that his usage was erratic. Whether intentionally so or not, such inconsistency mimed the instability not only of the largely oral Welsh tongue but of English.

In the end *For the Honor of Wales* leaves us with the sense that the minoritarian language represented by "Welshness" has taken over all the discourse of the masque. It is telling that in the published version of the masque Jonson did not actually go to the trouble of reprinting the main masque from *Pleasure Reconciled to Virtue*. What we see on the page is tacitly a discourse-universe surrendered to the "minor." Even more tellingly, at the point where *For the Honor of Wales* was to have segued from its antimasque to the original main masque there is no abrupt dispelling of the antimasquers. The final word, spoken by Griffith (whose dialect now begins to glide into a higher discourse), embraces as much as it rejects his fellow Welshmen. "Very homely done it is," he affirms, "if not very rudely" (384–85). He then proceeds to praise Wales as "a very garden and seed-plot of honest mindes and men" that have, in all learned disciplines, worked diligently in service of the English crown (392–93). One could argue that this inclusion of the Welsh within "high" England is an act of "becoming-majoritarian." Or to put a more insidious twist on the argument, one could contend that the final sequence of *For the Honor of Wales* proves that when major languages "become minoritarian" they are really just "containing" or "appropriating" the languages of their internal minorities (like a Hollywood movie that exploits black ghetto street talk). But Jonson's antimasque, taken as a whole, would seem to argue the reverse. Throughout the antimasque of *For the Honor of Wales*, we witness a "continuous variation" within Welsh, Scottish, and English declaring them all—in the Deleuze-Guattarian spirit of dispersal and modulation—*collaborators* in the "becoming-minoritarian" of language.

III

Finally—and here the importance of minoritarian discourse for the topic of this volume fully comes home—some further thoughts on what Griffith, as we have just heard, calls the "homely" and "rude." I would like to close by reflecting on what it is that makes subdiscourses, despite all the derision and condescension aimed their way, so alluring that "major" languages cannot help but take on their accents. That James and his contemporaries were attracted to "low" or "minor" language is indisputable, and the attraction goes beyond a detached, philological interest. In fact, I suggest, the strong appeal of subdiscourses—of the captivating "minor" at the heart of any language—may very well be their perceived contact with the "homely" and "rude." The mutability of "minor" Welsh, I have argued, is a variation upon the mutability of "major" English. But it also expresses a constant facet of experience inexpressible in "major" discourse with all its foreign importations: the familiarity with the everyday.

There is a strong sense in which the Welsh language and dialect of *For the Honor of Wales* lives in the here and now of everyday life. We might here recall the grounding of the English courtiers' names in Welsh place names—Jonson's doing, since Welsh personal names in fact rarely derived from place names.[41] Such "grounding" is not in some inaccessible historical past. The antimasquers dismiss the ancient bardic tradition (for which Wales was so famous) of recording the past history and pedigree of the Welsh Brutus, Welsh princes, and Welsh saints:

'Is not come here to tauke of Brut,
  from whence the Welse do's take his root;

Nor tell long pedegree of Prince Camber,
   whose linage would fill aull this Chamber;
Nor sing the deeds of old Saint Davy,
   the ursip of which would fill a Navy. (217–22)

Rejecting such grand "old" chronicles, the antimasquers declare to James, "But harke yow me now, for a liddell tales/s'all make a gread deale to the credit of Wales" (223–24). That is, listen for a short while to my stories, but also listen to my little or small-scale songs; these are what make Wales important. Such trivial but somehow meaningful songs will "ground" the antimasquers' discourse in an immediate historical present. They will "toudge [touch]" James's ears with praise of Wales's thirteen shires (only recently formed under Henry VIII)[42] and make him "as glad, and merrie/as fourteene pot of Perrie [pear cider]" (227–28). In other words, the antimasquers promise to sing tales of the commonplace that have a kind of sensory immediacy, tales that James can both touch and taste. In the light of such at-hand consumability of the everyday, it is significant that the only bard referred to in the songs that follow — "Harper Ellis" (270) — is an ordinary, lower-order bard in the nature of a wandering minstrel.[43]

    My point is not simply that the minoritarian is seen as only existing in a kind of here-and-now at any moment being consumed, wandering, or transmuting; it is the fact that such here-and-nowness has a level of reality to it missing from more "ruled" forms of speech. We might in this context look back for a moment to criticisms of the English vernacular at the time contemporaries began to seek eloquence and rule. What we detect amidst the complaints is just such an appreciation for the quotidian. Frequently cited metaphors for the vernacular, Jones observes, were "homespun cloth, coarse bread, wooden casket." These images were meant to indicate the uncouth and low state of English. But, as Jones goes on to remark, they "do not always suggest entire displeasure with its character."[44] There is something down-to-earth and comforting in things that are homespun, or plain, or made of a natural material like wood. They are "homely" in the sense of rude but they also make one feel "at home." The subdiscoursive Welsh songs of *For the Honor of Wales* are full of just such "homely" goods: lists of Welsh clothing, food, drink, music, and dance by which the antimasquers attempt to lure James to Wales. Consider but this sampling from their larder of "provisions for the bellie." They promise James

. . . Cid [kid], and Goat, and great Goates mother,
   and Runt [Welsh ox], and Cow, and good Cowes Vther;
And once but taste o' the Welse-mutton,
   your Englis-s'eep's not worth a button.

And then for your Fiss, s'all shoose it your diss.
  looke but about, and there is a Trout.
     A Salmon, Cor [salt cod], or Chevin [chub]
     Will feed you six, or seven,
     As taull man as ever swagger,
     With Welse-hooke, or long dagger. (247–56)

Each of these promised foodstuffs spoken in "low" dialect is plain and simple, assembled in a rude accumulation or list that continuously varies without any more rule than a swaggering Welshman. They are as unadorned and unruly as the much criticized English vernacular. But as with the criticisms of English, that is their allure.

   In the end all such "homely" discourse culminates in a dance of ordinary Welshmen, whom the antimasquers oppose to the exotic "monsters" of *Pleasure Reconciled to Virtue*: "Is not better this now then *Pigmies*? This is men, this is no monsters" (312–13). The Welshmen conclude the antimasque dances by taking Welsh women in hand. In between, as if the marriage link between these ordinary folk, occurs another "properly naturall devise" opposed by the antimasquers to yet another monstrosity of *Pleasure Reconciled*: Comus's dancing bottles and tuns (314–16). I refer to the dance of Welsh goats. Although the dancing goats approach the idea of subdiscourses as monstrous aberrations (perhaps triggering memory of the dancing satyrs in *Oberon*), the dance is introduced with the familiar, homely, and natural image of the workaday: "Is the Goatheard and his dog, and his sonne, and his wife make musiques to the Goates as they come from the Hills" (321–23). According to Gwyn Williams, the Welsh themselves began to think of their language in just such customary terms as it increasingly lost its major status within Wales. From the Welsh tongue, Williams affirms, native speakers no longer sought high culture or challenge but "comfort and familiarity and reassurance."[45]

   The same could be said for the "cousins" of the Welsh language and dialect in *For the Honor of Wales*: Gaelic and Scots.[46] Of special concern for us here is Scots. We might remember that the young James resented learning "high" foreign languages over his own native Scots, and that the mature James spoke English with a thick Scots brogue—a complement to his "familiar and homely manner" at the elevated English court.[47] Furthermore, we might note, even though James gradually purged his *Basilikon Doron* of most of its Scots forms, his prose remains, in the words of C. J. Sisson, "everywhere thickly strewn . . . with images and phrases from familiar life and his own experience, often full of a pawky Scottish humour."[48] Especially for James, I would thus propose, the comic Welsh subdiscourse would have spoken a familiar and "homey" language. Such a language was not monstrous or alien, and therefore in need of suppression. It was expressive of thoughts and emotions valued by speakers of "major" English but inexpressible otherwise than as "low" discourse or a "becoming-minor of the major language." In *For the Honor of Wales*, in sum, Jonson speaks up to his *Scottish*-English king, seated on his high dais, by speaking low.

Notes

1. Recorded by James's tutor Peter Young on the manuscript list he compiled of the young king's library. See C. J. Sisson, "King James the First of England as Poet and Political Writer," in *Seventeenth Century Studies Presented to Sir Herbert Grierson* (Oxford: Clarendon Press, 1938), p. 50.

2. Charles W. J. Withers, *Gaelic in Scotland, 1698–1981: The Geographical History of a Language* (Edinburgh: John Donald, 1984), pp. 2–9, 16–24; Glanville Price, *The Languages of Britain* (London: Edward Arnold, 1984), p. 187. There is an ongoing debate as to whether Scots is a separate language or a dialect of English; see Price, pp. 186–87, and J. Derrick McClure, "Scots: Its Range of Uses," in *Languages of Scotland*, ed. A. J. Aitken and Tom McArthur (Edinburgh: W. and R. Chambers, 1979), pp. 26–27. McClure classes "Scots and English together as dialects of *Anglic* (using that word as a cover-term to include the language of the Anglo-Saxon invaders of the fifth century and all the speech-forms derived from it)," p. 27. Whatever the actual status of Scots, the term "Inglis" or "Inglisch" would imply that contemporaries at least thought of Scots as a form of English (Price, p. 187).

3. *The Basilicon Doron of King James VI*, ed. James Craigie (Edinburgh and London: William Blackwood and Sons, 1950), 2: 88–135. The revisions to James's text were not based on the author's autograph manuscript but rather on an intermediary fair copy (pp. 89–92); nevertheless, they certainly were made with James's approval, and possibly under his direction. One way the 1603 edition further elevated, through Anglicization, the *style* of the 1599 edition was by elaborating upon a single word in the earlier edition, adding "and" together with another word that extended the meaning — a practice common in "high" Elizabethan English. For example, "the bookes of Moses interpreted *and applyed* by the Prophets"; "the resurrection *and ascention* of Christ"; "*passions & inordinate* appetites"; "*false and* vnreuerent writing"; "ashamed *and offended* with their *temeritie and* presumption"; "*a light &* a veniall sinne"; "the vice of delicacie *& monstrous gluttony*" (cited in Craigie, p. 109). On the process of Anglicization of James's writings (as well as those of his contemporaries), see also M. A. Bald, "The Pioneers of Anglicised Speech in Scotland," *Scottish Historical Review* 24 (1926): 179–93.

4. Historical Manuscripts Commission, *Calendar of the Manuscripts of the Most Honourable The Marquess of Salisbury Preserved at Hatfield House, Hertfordshire*, 1609–1612 (London: Her Majesty's Stationery Office, 1970), 21: 83. James goes on to describe the work: "It contains a short compend of the history of the church, the grounds and antiquity of our religion, and the special times when the grossest papish errors were introduced, which last ye will see specially collected in the table at the end of the book" (p. 83).

5. Quoted in David Harris Willson, *King James VI and I* (London: Jonathan Cape, 1956), p. 166. On James's appointment of Scots to court offices and on the swell of Scottish (as well as English) place-hunters, see pp. 175–76 and p. 161.

6. Gilles Deleuze and Félix Guattari, *A Thousand Plateaus: Capitalism and Schizophrenia*, trans. Brian Massumi (Minneapolis: University of Minnesota Press, 1987), p. 106.

7. Richard Foster Jones, *The Triumph of the English Language: A Survey of Opinions Concerning the Vernacular from the Introduction of Printing to the Restoration* (London: Geoffrey Cumberlege, Oxford University Press, 1953), pp. 75–83, 272–92. Although efforts to "fix" the language began in the late sixteenth century, they dominated the seventeenth century (Jones, pp. 286–87).

8. Jones, *Triumph of the English Language*, pp. 173, 263–71. See also discussion below.

9. Albert C. Baugh and Thomas Cable, *A History of the English Language*, 3rd ed. (Englewood Cliffs, N.J.: Prentice Hall, 1978), p. 232. I am indebted for this reference to Paula C. Blank and her "Challenging the King's English: Attitudes Toward Standard English Language in Renaissance England" (talk delivered at the 1990 Modern Language Association Convention, Chicago); I am grateful to Professor Blank for sharing her manuscript and sources with me. See also her recent *Broken English: Dialects and the Politics of Language in Renaissance Writings* (London and New York: Routledge, 1996).

10. Jones, *Triumph of the English Language*, pp. 214–36. Taking a more extreme stance, John Hare deplored the Norman invasion and wished to expunge from the English language all traces of Norman French (pp. 228–32).

11. Jones, *Triumph of the English Language*, pp. 243–44. Camden is symptomatic of the torn loyalties of his time (see pp. 237–71).

12. Jones, *Triumph of the English Language*, p. 263; Camden's *Remaines* (cited in Jones, p. 267). As Jones further notes (p. 266), demands to "fix" English culminated in the eighteenth century with Dr. Johnson's dictionary.

13. *Ben Jonson*, ed. C. H. Herford, Percy Simpson, and Evelyn Simpson, 11 vols. (Oxford: Clarendon Press, 1925–52), 1: 105. Cited hereafter as H&S, *Jonson*.

14. *Ben Jonson's English Grammar*, ed. Strickland Gibson (London: Lanston Monotype Corporation, 1928), p. v; and following notes.

15. Many of Jonson's contemporaries also resorted to Latin in an effort to regulate English (Jones, pp. 263–64, 287–88).

16. Jones, *Triumph of the English Language*, pp. 218–27.

17. Jones, *Triumph of the English Language*, p. 247; Stuart Piggott, *Celts, Saxons, and the Early Antiquaries* (n.p., n.d.), p. 13. Equally divided, Peter Heylyn as late as 1656 speaks of "our Ancestors (whether we look upon them as the *Brittish* or *Saxon* race)" (*Observations on the Historie of the Reign of King Charles*, p. 5; quoted in Jones, p. 226 n. 35).

18. Deleuze and Guattari, *A Thousand Plateaus*, pp. 102, 103. For another version of the intralinguistic low — perceived as female — see Juliet Fleming, "Dictionary English and the Female Tongue," in *Privileging Gender in Early Modern England*, ed. Jean R. Brink (Kirksville, Mo.: Sixteenth Century Journal Publishers, 1993), pp. 175–204.

19. Mikhail M. Bakhtin, *The Dialogic Imagination*, ed. Michael Holquist, trans. Caryl Emerson and Michael Holquist (Austin: University of Texas Press, 1981), p. 279; Deleuze and Guattari, *Thousand Plateaus*, p. 98.

20. Michael Holquist, *Dialogism: Bakhtin and His World* (London: Routledge, 1990), p. 20 and throughout.

21. Bakhtin, *The Dialogic Imagination*, pp. 262–63. Even more layered with "stratification" is the following passage:

Literary language . . . is itself *stratified* and heteroglot in its aspect as an expressive system, that is, in the forms that carry its meanings.

This *stratification* is accomplished first of all by the specific organisms called *genres*. . . .

In addition, there is interwoven with this generic *stratification* of language a *professional stratification* of language . . . and these sometimes coincide with, and sometimes depart from, the *stratification* into genres. (pp. 288–89; my emphasis on "stratified" and "stratification")

22. Ibid., p. 270.

23. Ibid., p. xviii.

24. Deleuze and Guattari, *Thousand Plateaus*, p. 94.

25. Ibid., pp. 101, 102–3.

26. Ibid., pp. 103–4, 106.

27. Stephen Greenblatt, "Invisible Bullets," in his *Shakespearean Negotiations: The Circulation of Social Energy in Renaissance England* (Berkeley: University of California Press, 1988), pp. 21–65; Steven Mullaney, "The Rehearsal of Cultures," in his *The Place of the Stage: License, Play, and Power in Renaissance England* (Chicago: University of Chicago Press, 1988), pp. 60–87.

28. Deleuze and Guattari, *Thousand Plateaus*, p. 102.

29. Bakhtin, *The Dialogic Imagination*, p. 331.

30. Orazio Busino's description of the masque, translated in *Inigo Jones: The Theatre of the Stuart Court*, ed. Stephen Orgel and Roy Strong, 2 vols. (Berkeley: University of California Press, 1973), 1: 283.

31. In this sense, Scotland was (and still is) a bilingual country (Tom McArthur, "The Status of English in and Firth of Scotland," in *Languages of Scotland*, ed. Aitken and McArthur, p. 59).

32. In the thirteenth century, for example, the prince of Gwynedd drew comparisons between himself and the king of Scotland, and Llywelyn ap Gruffydd (recognized as the first Welsh Prince of Wales) insisted that his realm "enjoy the same privileges as Scotland and other free peoples" (Gwyn A. Williams, *When Was Wales?: A History of the Welsh* [London: Black Raven, 1985], pp. 80, 85). In the seventeenth century, James looked to the amalgamation of Wales with England as proof of the certain success of a union between Scotland and England. In this belief, he appointed two Welsh members of the House of Commons, Sir Richard Bulkeley and Sir Robert Mansel, to the commission established to discuss the issue with the Scots. Another Welsh M.P., Sir William Maurice, was an enthusiastic supporter of the cause and presented to the House a bill advancing the union, as well as the title for James of King of Great Britain (G. Dyfnallt Owen, *Wales in the Reign of James I* [Suffolk: Boydell, 1988], pp. 45–46). See also Glanmor Williams, *Recovery, Reorientation, and Reformation: Wales, c. 1415–1642* (Oxford: Oxford University Press, 1987), p. 474.

33. H & S, *Jonson*, 7, ll. 23–26. All citations to Jonson's masques, unless otherwise

specified, are to this edition and to line numbers, and will appear in the body of the paper. James had actually traveled to Scotland from late March until September 1617 (not, as Jenkin states, two summers earlier). For a full discussion of the allusions of *Pleasure Reconciled* to James's Scottish journey, see Leah S. Marcus, *The Politics of Mirth: Jonson, Herrick, Milton, Marvell, and the Defense of Old Holiday Pastimes* (Chicago: University of Chicago Press, 1986), pp. 108–127.

34. See the lists of Highland parish names in Withers, *Gaelic in Scotland*, pp. 11, 67.

35. This, even though Howell, addressing Jonson, praised Davies's Grammar for successfully taming "A wild and wealthy language," and framing "Grammatic toils to curb her so that she / Now speaks by rules and sings by prosody" (Glanmor Williams, *Recovery, Reorientation, and Reformation*, pp. 450). As Davies's writing his Welsh Grammar in Latin shows, the Welsh found themselves in a similar predicament to the English. Just as the English aspired to assert the "rule" of their language by importing foreign neologisms, so, as Gwyn Williams notes in *When Was Wales?*, the Welsh argued that their tongue could only regain its dignity and sovereignty by following contemporary European models of rhetoric and learning (p. 130). But such an importation of foreign models could only render Welsh minor according to our first model of "becoming-minoritarian." On efforts to revivify "minor" Welsh in the face of the "majoritarianism" of both European languages and English (increasingly favored by the Welsh gentry), see W. Ogwen Williams, "The Survival of the Welsh Language after the Union of England and Wales: The First Phase, 1536–1642," *Welsh History Review* 2 (1964–65): 80–81, 89–91; Gwyn Williams, *When Was Wales?*, pp. 128–31; A. H. Dodd, "Wales and the Scottish Succession, 1570–1605," *Transactions of the Honourable Society of Cymmrodorion* (1937), pp. 205–6; and R. Brinley Jones, *The Old British Tongue: The Vernacular in Wales, 1540–1640* (Cardiff: Avalon, 1970). What sustained the declining Welsh language, allowing for its survival to the present day, was the Elizabethan Act of 1563, which allowed the Bible and Book of Common Prayer to be translated into Welsh—and sparked a flurry of other religious translations and antiquarian studies as well as dictionaries and grammars (W. Ogwen Williams, "Survival of the Welsh Language," pp. 90–91; also Glanmor Williams, *Religion, Language, and Nationality in Wales* [Cardiff: University of Wales Press, 1979], pp. 133–35). On Jonson's requesting Davies's Grammar (which Howell with difficulty procured for him), see H & S, *Jonson*, 1: 105.

36. Withers, *Gaelic*, p. 11.

37. See Gwyn Williams, *When Was Wales?*, p. 121, and Owen, *Wales*, p. 4. As Owen notes, the Welsh "Seisyllt" (or as his source spells it, "Sitsilt") underwent an intermediary transfiguration to Welsh-sounding "Syssell" (the spelling adopted by Robert Cecil's grandfather) before finally emerging as the Anglicized "Cecil" (p. 4). One further finds that a Welsh name "may have besides several Welsh spellings, several English ones too" (John Rhys and David Brynmor-Jones, *The Welsh People: Chapters on Their Origin, History and Laws, Language, Literature and Characteristics*, 4th ed. [New York: Haskell House, 1906; rpt. 1969], p. x). Bishop Rowland Lee, a hanging judge appointed by Henry VIII, began the process of giving the Welsh surnames; see Gwyn Williams, *When Was Wales?*, pp. 118–19. See also Prys Morgan and David Thomas, *Wales: The Shaping of a Nation* (North Pomfret, Vt.: David & Charles, 1984), pp. 231–36.

38. Ivor James, surveying Welsh registries, lists "Palmer" as a decidedly English

name; but he also includes its Welsh spelling, "Pawmer" (*The Welsh Language in the Sixteenth and Seventeenth Centuries* [n.p., n.d.], p. 30).

39. It is a further testimony to the vagaries of Jacobean spelling that neither anagram comes out right in the 1640 folio text.

40. Compare Stephen Orgel's edition of *For the Honor of Wales*, in *Ben Jonson: The Complete Masques* (New Haven, Conn.: Yale University Press, 1969; rpt. 1975), ll. 7–8, with the Herford and Simpson edition (which here maintains the folio spellings), 7: 11. 4–6.

41. Morgen and Thomas, *Wales*, p. 233.

42. The six shires of Wales, established in 1284, were expanded to thirteen (thus encompassing the entire country) by Henry VIII in 1536; William Rees, *An Historical Atlas of Wales: From Early to Modern Times*, 2nd ed. (London: Faber and Faber, 1972), pp. 52–54.

43. H & S, *Jonson*, 10: 594.

44. Jones, *Triumph of the English Language*, p. 31. As Jones goes on to note, such qualities were actually embraced by Puritans who distrusted the humanists' privileging of eloquence or rhetoric.

45. Gwyn Williams, *When Was Wales?*, p. 130.

46. On Gaelic's retreat into the home, see Ronald Wardhaugh, *Languages in Competition: Dominance, Diversity, and Decline* (Oxford: Basil Blackwell, 1987), pp. 88–89. On the retreat of Scots, see Aitken and McArthur, *Languages of Scotland*.

47. Willson, *King James VI*, p. 166.

48. Sisson, "King James the First," p. 61.

PART II

THE EVERYDAY MAKING OF WOMEN

6

Everyday Life, Longevity, and Nuns in Early Modern Florence

Judith C. Brown

IN A LETTER TO A FRIEND, Sylvia Townsend Warner, the author of a historical novel about early modern nuns, wrote that she was "inclined to call it 'People Growing Old.'" Sensibly, she jettisoned the title, knowing full well that it would not garner readers. But she probably did not realize the extent of its historical accuracy or how contrary to the opinions of scholars were her beliefs about the longevity of nuns and its causes.[1] Since the mid-eighteenth century, scholars have tended to agree with Antoine Deparcieux, one of the founders of demography, that "it is a false prejudice to believe that monks and nuns live longer than people who live in the world."[2] His studies of monastic and secular records led him to affirm that, contrary to common belief, marriage was the best path to achieve a long life. Despite the sheltered environment of religious institutions on one side of the convent wall, and the effect of childbirth-related mortalities on the other, married people, he argued, lived longer. Decades of living under the rigors of monastic life adversely affected the longevity of monks and nuns. But above all, their lives were cut short by being deprived of those "mille petites douceurs" that even modest artisans experienced within the bosom of the family.[3] This paean to marriage is echoed in more recent literature. William Farr wrote in the nineteenth century that "marriage is a healthy estate. The single individual is more likely to be wrecked on his voyage than the lives joined together in matrimony," even if that individual is part of a monastic community.[4] Though shorn of the Victorian cult of domesticity, the work of contemporary demographers on the mortalities of single and widowed people echoes these conclusions.[5]

Yet, for much of the European past, the choice was not between a long life in marriage and a short life of solitude. Convents and monasteries provided a communal life with material and social supports that other settings often lacked and that contribute to a longer life. Whether and how this affected the lives of individuals in religious institutions, however, is still largely unknown because the necessary information about pre-modern populations is rare, and particularly so for women, who were often left out of the historical records.[6]

Fortunately, detailed entrance and death registers have survived for two Florentine convents, San Jacopo di Ripoli and Santa Maria Annunziata delle Murate.[7] These records allow us to show that the nuns at these institutions lived astoundingly long lives that exceeded by far those of secular women of all classes, even when adjusting for childbearing mortalities. Florentine nuns, moreover, like their counterparts in Venice, also lived much longer than monks, who were shielded from some of the same life-threatening experiences. This essay will advance some hypotheses about the practices of everyday life that contributed to the remarkable longevity of Florentine nuns from the mid-fifteenth to the early nineteenth centuries. When examined in the wider context of family strategies for biological, social, and economic reproduction, these practices elucidate the larger demographic and social world of a large and important segment of European women.

In Florence, as in most other cities of Catholic Europe, the proportion of women in convents was linked to the economy of marriage within families and to the norms governing inheritance practices. The rate of female monacation, a practice confined to the upper strata of society, increased in the late fifteenth and sixteenth centuries as primogeniture dislodged the earlier system of partible inheritance among male heirs of those classes.[8] As fewer males inherited property, more of them remained bachelors, raising their proportion among patrician men from about one-fifth in the early fifteenth century to about 60% in the seventeenth. Families with young girls soon grew desperate to find husbands whose status and honor were commensurate with their own. Their plight is reflected both in the well-noted inflation of dowries and in the proportion of women sent to convents as a less costly and socially acceptable alternative to marriage.[9] In 1427, when Florence had about 43,000 people, the city's convents contained close to 935 female religious, including lay sisters (*converse*). This represents about 6.5% of the female population of the city over age 14 and close to 20% of women from the elite.[10] By 1622 the number of female religious had grown to 4,200 out of a total population of 76,000. As a proportion of the adult female population, they had more than doubled since the early fifteenth century; one study shows that nearly half of the females born into patrician families in the sixteenth century became nuns.[11] This proportion may have grown until the eighteenth century, when changing social practices, legal restrictions on primogeniture, and mortmain laws reversed the trend. By 1738, the proportion of nuns was about half of what it had been a century earlier and by the early nineteenth century, when Napoleon suppressed the remaining convents of the city, there were fewer than 1,800 nuns in a city of 83,000 people.[12]

Having placed the monastic life within the context of the economy of marriage, we can see that the institutional life of the convents of S. Jacopo Ripoli and S. Maria delle Murate, as well as the life course of the nuns in them, reflected these trends. By the early Renaissance, the Dominican convent of S. Jacopo Ripoli, the older of the two, had become a decimated shadow of its pre-plague self. The general dearth of population and the improvement in the marriage market in the wake of the plague had left only 28 nuns and 4 *converse* by 1428, where once there had been close to one hundred. The situation did not improve until the last quarter of the fifteenth century, when the Florentine population began to increase once more, making a suitable marriage more difficult. The number of nuns grew to 47 by 1476, to 56 by the 1520s and to 63 by the early seventeenth century — a peak in enrollments until the convent was transformed by ducal edict into a conservatory for the education of girls and young women in 1785.[13]

The second convent, S. Maria Annunziata delle Murate, was founded in the late fourteenth century, when a follower of St. Catherine of Siena persuaded thirteen women of modest social origins to live an austere religious life in common. As they inspired others, pious donations and patrician girls began to pour in. By 1461, as a formally organized Benedictine convent, they numbered 150 nuns from the city's most select patrician families. By the end of the fifteenth century there were 170 nuns, and by 1552 there were 190.[14] As the convent became more aristocratic in the late fifteenth century, it also began to take in *converse*. These relieved the nuns of the burdens of domestic or heavy manual labor so that they could spend their time singing and making luxury items for sale — fine miniature paintings and gold or silver-embroidered silk cloth, for which they were reproved by Savonarola, who thought they were becoming too worldly.[15] By the late sixteenth century, the nuns' superiors encouraged them to create another convent, S. Stefano (1592), to reduce the pressure of excess demand. This measure, aided undoubtedly by several epidemic outbreaks which reduced the population of the city, succeeded in diminishing the convent's population. The census taken after the plague of 1630–1632 lists 128 residents.[16] By 1779, when different cultural norms had begun to influence both family and religious life, only 33 nuns and 11 *converse* remained. In the convent's remaining decades the numbers grew slightly simply because of transfers from other convents slated for closure or conversion into other types of institutions. These efforts, however, ended in 1808 with the Napoleonic suppression of all convents, after which the vast buildings that had once housed a thriving female community were turned first into a prison and then into soldiers' barracks.

Spiritual Marriage

Just as demographers often study the life course of individuals in biological families by starting with marriage, it may be helpful to follow the life course of the women who entered the institutional family of the convent by starting with their spiritual marriage as brides of Christ. Families tended to bring their daughters into the convent in the autumn, possibly because at that time harvest settlements on family estates could be applied toward the dowry.[17] This pattern was more pronounced among nuns than among *converse* and more so at the Murate than at Ripoli. If religious vocation or individual choice had been the primary motives in selecting the monastic life, the pattern of entrances would have been more evenly distributed throughout the year, or would have clustered on certain feast days. This is indeed what occurred in the eighteenth century, when new cultural norms about religious vocation and individual choice, rather than family preference, began to play a stronger role in the decision.[18]

Once a girl entered the convent, she had to pass through several theoretically distinct and well-spaced phases marked by veiling and profession, so that she could reflect on the depth of her commitment. In practice, however, these distinctions were often blurred, both in the record keeping and in the actual passage from one stage to another, probably because those who entered the convent to become nuns almost never left.[19] More than half of the 80 or so girls who entered S. Jacopo Ripoli to become nuns between 1532 and 1699, and for whom entrance and veiling dates are available, were veiled within days of entrance, some as soon as the next day—a pattern that held true also for *converse*.[20] A greater time period, averaging two years, elapsed between veiling and profession, especially before the eighteenth century, although on occasion professions took place before the one-year minimum established by the Council of Trent.

The time elapsed between entrance into a convent and the date of profession was related to the ages when girls entered the convent. In the Renaissance and early modern period, the time was greater because the girls were younger (see Table 1). Among 40 nuns who entered Ripoli in the last half of the fifteenth century and whose entrance age we can determine, 11 were under age 10. The number dropped to 10 out of 69 in the next half century, after which

TABLE I   Age at Entrance and Profession of Nuns S. Jacopo Ripoli and the Murate

| | S. Jacopo Ripoli | | | | S. Maria delle Murate | | | |
| | Entrance | | Profession | | Entrance | | Profession | |
Years	Mean	Median	Mean	Median	Mean	Median	Mean	Median
1443–99	13.4	13 (40)[a]						
1500–49	14.9	14 (67)	17	16 (58)				
1550–99	13.5	13 (65)	15.8	16 (65)				
1600–55[b]	14.7	14 (52)	16	16 (51)	14.8[c]	14 (27)		
1650–99			17.7	17 (41)	16.0	15 (45)		
1700–49					17.4	16 (41)	19	18 (19)
1750–99					20.3	20 (49)	21.2	19 (28)

[a]Numbers in parenthesis are the number of observations.
[b]After 1655 the register does not record entrances although it does record professions.
[c]The years for these observations are 1629–49.

virtually no girls entered before age 12. Since age at profession, even before the Council of Trent, hovered in the early to mid-teens, the early entrances in the first century of our study meant a longer waiting time to profession for some of the entrants.

What is most striking, however, is that both ages of entrance and profession rose. In the first half of the sixteenth century, 9 out of 58 girls professed before reaching age 14, nearly half of them by age 15 or less. These were child-nuns, hardly at the age to make informed vows of their own free will, as the church prescribed. By the first half of the eighteenth century, the mean age at entrance and profession had risen to 17.4 and 19 respectively and then rose still further later in the century.[21] Changing social practice was reinforced by a ducal edict issued in 1775 establishing 18 years as the minimum age for veiling and 21 as the minimum for final vows. The latter were moved up to 30 years in 1785.[22]

The rising age at which young women became nuns in the eighteenth century was undoubtedly related to the improvement in the secular marriage market as well as new ideas about the education and the role of women. By the 1730s, it was less acceptable to place a girl in a convent as a child in order to monacate her the moment she turned 16. Equally important were ducal policies that reflected simultaneously the social values of the enlightenment and the political desires of enlightenment government to extend its prerogatives to previously ecclesiastical jurisdictions. The Austrian dynasty that succeeded the Medici in 1737 enacted a series of edicts that made convent life a less attractive option for the daughters of the aristocracy. The mortmain law of 1751 threat-

ened the standard of living of the nuns, as did the edicts issued by Peter
Leopold two decades later, with the announced purpose of closing the smaller
convents and bringing more discipline and religious poverty to the rest. The
intent of these laws was not to "liberate" women from the convent or to
suppress religion, but rather to assert ducal prerogatives against the claims of
the papacy.[23] Nonetheless, the unintended consequences of these measures for
women on both sides of the convent wall would be great.

Who Entered the Convent?

Most convents in the late Renaissance and early modern period were aristocratic institutions, because a spiritual marriage, like a secular one, required a
dowry, although a much smaller one. Given the link between spiritual and
secular marriages, it is not surprising that convent dowries also experienced
inflation. Whereas in the early fifteenth century it took about 100 florins to
become a nun, a century later it was not unusual to spend several thousand
scudi for a monastic dowry.[24] The chronicle of the Murate kept by Sister
Giustina Niccolini reveals many large contributions in cash and in kind. In
1493 Elena Orsini, a sister-in-law of Alessandro Farnese, brought 2,000 scudi,
which Alessandro later supplemented with gifts valued at over 7,000 scudi. In
1587 Leonora Cibo brought a dowry of 3,000 scudi, in addition to 960 scudi to
purchase cloth so that every nun in the convent could have a new habit.[25] At
Ripoli, the dowries were smaller but still considerable. In the late seventeenth
century, nuns brought dowries of about 750 scudi plus rich gifts of furniture,
gold brocade for the decoration of the church, gold-embroidered silk shirts,
and so on.[26] *Converse*, who came from more modest rural and artisanal origins,
obviously paid much less, ca. 300 scudi each, and do not appear to have
brought gifts in kind.[27]

　　The dowry system and the trends in the marriage market had obvious
repercussions for the nuns who entered the convents. Whereas in the early
fifteenth century, as Richard Trexler observed, nuns tended to come from the
impoverished or medium ranks of the patriciate, this was no longer the case by
the sixteenth century. Indeed, some of these families had difficulties amassing a
dowry sufficiently large to place their daughters in a prestigious convent, let
alone to find a secular husband. To meet the need, one benefactor of the
Murate left a 20,000 scudi endowment to pay the dowry for deserving but
poor girls of the nobility who might be admitted from time to time.[28]

　　The aristocratization of convents in the late Renaissance and early modern period is by now a well-noted phenomenon. S. Jacopo Ripoli and the

Murate were filled with the daughters of the Pazzi, the Strozzi, the Pitti, the Ruccellai, and other prominent families. The convent of the Murate in particular seems to have been the depository for the most elite members of the Florentine aristocracy in the sixteenth and seventeenth centuries.

Frequently the girls came as part of families, despite the prohibition against this practice issued by the archbishop of Florence in 1517.[29] Some entered on the same day as their relatives. At S. Jacopo Ripoli there were at least 28 sets of sisters, 8 of which were brought on the same day. At the Murate there were 29 sets of sisters and 5 sets of half-sisters, of which 9 sets entered the same day.

The extent to which the convents became extensions of families on the outside is evident from the record of the Murate. Out of 194 nuns, 119 had relatives among the nuns of the convent at some point between 1629 and 1800. The Malaspina were the largest single family, with 16 individuals in the convent, among whom were two sets of sisters, three sets of half-sisters, and several cousins and aunts. Indeed, from 1636 until the end of the register, there were always at least two Malaspina women in the convent and from the late seventeenth century through the 1730s there were as many as six. At Ripoli, of 246 individuals, 119 had relatives in the same patrilinear lineage.

Given these familial ties, it would be mistaken to view the life of the nuns in convents as separate from the life of their families outside. Nuns were supposed to be "dead" to the world, an impression reinforced by the term "murate" and the ritual immurement at entrance that gave rise to it.[30] But the aristocratization of convents meant that these institutions were closely intertwined with the lives of families, not only because families were well represented in them but because the style of life in convents began to reflect the life led by the families outside. The presence of patrician women brought visits from prominent individuals and an outpouring of large donations from their relatives that transformed the convents' daily life from one of strict religious poverty to a life of greater ease, not to say luxury. This transformation is evident in the artistic patronage and the very building fabric of convents. Whereas the Murate and similar institutions had originally housed the nuns in common dormitories, during the sixteenth century the families of the nuns began to donate funds for the construction of private cells. These were to be reserved for members of a family who might be admitted to the convent at a later date. Indeed, the existence of these cells virtually ensured that family members would be accepted in the future. Thus, the chronicle of Sister Niccolini records that sometime in 1595–96 "three cells were built above the dormitory, at a cost of 560 scudi, incurred by relatives of the nuns from the Cavalcanti, Gaetani, and Del Riccio families."[31] As Gabriella Zarri has pointed out, the reorganization of convents around cells, a common phenomenon in sixteenth-century Italy, undoubtedly intensified the social hierarchies and the family identities within the convent.[32]

The sense of family and the social networks among families on the outside also made themselves felt in quarrels and divisions among the nuns. The reason stated for the episcopal prohibition against relatives living in the same convent was that "Experience has shown that factions and divisions are often engendered by the multiplicity of familial relationships in the monasteries."[33] This was a well-placed fear. Richard Trexler has noted that, during the 1530 siege of Florence, the convent of the Murate was torn by divisions between the pro and anti-Medici camps, so that the young Catherine de' Medici, who had been sent there to be educated in a sheltered environment, had to be moved for her own safety.[34] These influences of family may not be quite the "petites douceurs" Deparcieux had in mind when he contrasted the supportive environment of family to the "isolated" life of nuns and other single people. Yet, whether for good or ill, the family had a strong presence in the life of Florentine convents and provided much of the social world within which nuns operated.

Advancement in the Convent

One arena where family ties mattered was in the hierarchy of the convent. The position of abbess or prioress was a coveted prize, fought over by families for its prestige and the avenues it opened to further power and wealth. For this reason, the church adopted regulations to limit the abuses of power associated with the office: the Council of Trent decreed that nuns would have a secret vote in the selection of abbesses and that the latter should be at least 40 years old. In 1583 the duration of office was limited to three years without the possibility of immediate renewal. Relatives were also prohibited from succeeding each other in office.[35]

Most of these rules were broken at both S. Jacopo Ripoli and the Murate, as Table 2 reveals. Both convents limited the duration of each term of office. At S. Jacopo Ripoli, even before the Council of Trent, a term of office was two years. At the Murate, it was three. Both convents elected nuns over 40 years old; however it is clear from the list of office holders that certain families were favored over others, that some nuns occupied the office repeatedly, and sometimes consecutively, and that often the incumbent was succeeded by a biological sister or other relative. At S. Jacopo Ripoli, the daughters of Jacopo Bellacci succeeded each other in the early 1500s, the Panciatichi sisters succeeded each other in the 1520s, the daughters of Jacopo Gianfigliazzi occupied the position

TABLE 2   Abbesses of the Murate and Prioresses of Ripoli

No. of appearances of surname	Ripoli	Murate	No. of terms in office	Ripoli	Murate
1	30	12	1	29	10
2	9	2	2	27	9
3	4	1	3	4	1
4	0	1	4	2	3
			5	4	
			6	1	
Sets of			7	0	
sisters	8	2	8	1	

seven times between 1546 and 1572, and the Pitti sisters together were prioresses nine times in the eighteenth century. A similar pattern can be found at the Murate, where the Malaspina, the Berardi, and the Pitti repeatedly held the position of abbess.

Yet the series of abbesses at the Murate also reveals the beginning of the end of this aristocratic world of spiritual hierarchy and privilege. In the early years of the series, the abbesses of the Murate, like their counterparts at Ripoli by the seventeenth century, tended to be in their sixties and seventies (see Figure 1). This was a gerontocracy, where the nuns had to wait a long time between entrance into the convent and attaining the coveted position of abbess. By the 1770s, the wait became shorter — the abbesses were younger and they held the position less frequently than their predecessors. As the size of the convent shrank under the onslaught of ducal measures to regulate monastic life, the pool of potential candidates to lead these institutions became smaller and those who held the post, with a few exceptions, tended to come from less distinguished families than before.

The lower age of the abbesses, their less distinguished social background, and the reduced population of the convent are all responses to the ducal measures enacted in the 1770s and 1780s. These regulated the donations that could be made to a convent, mandated a life in common, outlawed family quarters within the convents, limited the dowries of *converse*, and broke the nexus between dowries and the treatment received by nuns by decreeing that dowries go to nearby hospitals or other charity institutions. Convents where nuns did not want to accept communal life were to be transformed into educational conservatories and shelters for widows and *malmaritate*. The life in common was to be a life of poverty, where a minimum standard was assured,

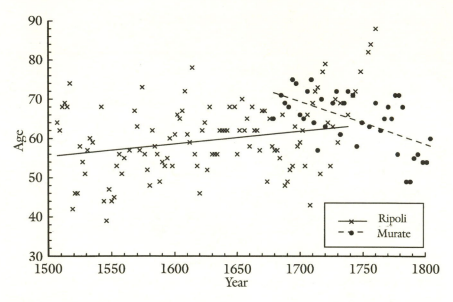

Figure 1. Ages of abbesses of the Murate and prioresses of Ripoli, 1500–1800 (least squares regression analysis).

but where the conspicuous consumption of the aristocracy would have no place. Given these choices, the women in more than half of the institutions, including S. Jacopo Ripoli, voted to join conservatories. The Murate voted to remain a convent, but the remaining number of nuns was so small that transfers were accepted from other suppressed convents, some of whose residents wished to continue the religious life.

Death

The demise of convents still leaves unanswered the questions with which we began: how did living in them affect the longevity of their residents, how did those life-spans compare to those on the outside, and what aspects of everyday life account for the differences? Convents were supposed to be enclosed, a practice that could have protected their residents against the worst ravages of epidemic diseases, although even the most well-enclosed convents had legitimate reasons for social contacts with the outside for provisioning, as well as for medical and religious services. In practice, of course, the lives of the nuns were often less sheltered than the degree prescribed by the monastic ideal or by the Council of Trent. Sister Niccolini's chronicle of the Murate, for example, re-

TABLE 3   Clusters of Years with Higher Than Expected Mortalities
(Excludes Converse)

	Years	Observed deaths	Expected deaths
Ripoli	1530–34	10	5.0
	1535–39	12	5.3
	1540–44	13	4.3
	1585–89	10	5.9
	1600–04	9	5.8
	1620–24	11	7.3
	1645–49	16	6.7
	1680–84	7	3.5
	1695–99	6	2.3
Murate	1710–14	12	6.7
	1775–79	10	5.9
	1805–09	9	5.8

cords that many nuns succumbed to an epidemic of "mal di castrone"[36] that hit
Florence in 1580 and that also afflicted the nuns of S. Jacopo Ripoli. Despite an
earlier visit by Archbishop Altoviti to tighten enclosure in all Florentine convents, enclosure was probably not as effective as he would have liked.

Demographers have compiled extensive information on the years of crisis
mortality in Florence.[37] Some, such as the crisis of 1528–1530, which saw
petechial typhus, bubonic plague, food shortages, and war-related casualties,
affected the deaths of nuns behind the convent walls. The chronicle of Sister
Niccolini reports that at the time of the siege, in addition to Catherine de'
Medici, "a large number of ladies, widows, married women, and girls of all
ages and status took refuge in this monastery."[38] It is not surprising that diseases would spread under those circumstances. Bubonic plague and petechial
typhus, which were frequent in sixteenth- and seventeenth-century Tuscany,
thrived where underwashing and overcrowding were common.

Yet other crises, such as the plague of 1522, left no trace in the death
records of the convents examined. For this reason, it is useful to look for
larger-than-expected mortalities in clusters of years, when they may be more
readily discernible than on an annual basis. For example, in the 1530s 22 nuns
and 3 *converse* died at Ripoli, instead of the expected 10.[39] Other years of high
mortalities were the early 1540s, the 1580s, the early 1620s, and the late 1640s.
At Ripoli the clusters of years when deaths considerably exceeded expectations
occurred more frequently in the early decades analyzed.[40] In keeping with this
downward trend, from 1638 to 1710 the deaths at the Murate did not greatly

exceed expectations in any cluster of years, despite three clusters of higher-than-expected mortalities after 1710 that were too small to be statistically significant.[41]

What seems most notable in both convents is that they were well protected against many of the crisis mortalities that affected Florence. The last big outbreak of bubonic plague in 1630–32, for example, did not touch Ripoli. Of the seven deaths registered during those years only one involved a nun as young as 58, the others were aged 82, 77, 77, 74, 73, 71. Moreover, none of the symptoms described in some of these cases by the recording nun suggest the classic signs of bubonic plague: "she was sick for 6 months," "she was not very healthy, having remained crippled from a fall," "great fever," and so on. Unfortunately, we have no comparable information for 1630–32 on the Murate, because the deaths of nuns who had entered before 1629 would have been recorded in a now-lost register. Perhaps the large number of entrances in the 1630s — 22 in all — replaced vacancies created by the plague. But it is more likely that these entrances were the result of plague-related social dislocations that took place outside the convent rather than inside.

Clues to the reasons for fewer crisis mortalities can be sought in two areas of monastic life, though definitive explanations are not possible. The first is the altered architectural configuration that accompanied the aristocratization of convents. As has already been observed for English monastic institutions, contagious diseases were more likely to spread in dormitory-style sleeping quarters than where individual cells were the norm.[42] It is quite possible that the construction of private cells ensured not only a better life but a longer and healthier one for the daughters of the Florentine aristocracy who were relegated to convents. The second feature of monastic life that deserves attention is effective enclosure. The efforts of religious authorities to restrict contact between nuns and outsiders were supplemented, particularly during epidemics, by more highly organized government measures to enforce quarantines.

Corroborating evidence for this latter explanation comes from the diary of a nun at another Florentine convent, SS. Girolamo e Francesco.[43] Having survived the 1630–1632 epidemic, Sister Gabriella Baldovinetti wrote with pride of the measures undertaken by her convent and others to prevent the spread of disease. The nuns added a glass partition to the parlor bars separating them from outsiders; they dipped in vinegar all money exchanged with outsiders; they smoked other objects coming into the convent, and they observed the strictest quarantine, made possible by subsidies from the grand duke Ferdinand II that helped them minimize contacts with the outside world. Last but not least, they appealed for divine help. Not only did they kneel in prayer for two hours as the ritual procession carrying the Virgin of Impruneta passed by the convent's open door, but upon the request of the Health Board and receipt of an alms-payment of 50 scudi from them, they prayed for 40 days and 40 nights in an uninterrupted vigil kept up by four nuns at a time. The results of these measures, Sister Gabriella concluded, were worth the effort: "[During] the above contagion, when it was at its peak, which was in 1630, there died one hundred people a day and more, and the number reached 150. In our monastery, *as in all the others, there was no infection whatsoever* and we were entirely free of this disease due to God's grace and that of the Blessed Virgin Mary."[44]

Subsequent epidemics also seem to have had little effect on the Murate or other convents. Neither the 1667 typhus and influenza wave, the flu of 1752, or the typhus of 1767 are reflected in higher deaths at the Murate. It is likely that by mid-seventeenth century the enforcement of the government's public health measures to contain epidemics was more effectively applied to institutions than to secular individuals, judging from the fact that epidemics, albeit at a less dramatic level, continued to recur in Florence, as in most premodern cities.

If the nuns did not die from epidemic diseases, what then did they die from? Mostly they died of old age, complicated in the end by strokes and pneumonic diseases. The register of S. Jacopo Ripoli describes symptoms for 152 deaths. Many are, of course, difficult to interpret. A nun who died at age 60 and was "sick for 40 years" could have had any number of ailments. Many deaths are simply attributed to fever (39 cases). There were a few strokes and possible heart disease, perhaps several cases of breast cancer (*chancro nel petto*). But the most common descriptions include consumption, catarrh, chest problems, influenza, and shortness of breath, which together account for at least 40 cases whose symptoms are named.

This is borne out by the seasonality of deaths (Figure 2). Although at Ripoli many deaths took place in late August and September, overall a larger number of deaths occurred in the colder months, which suggests pneumonic illnesses rather than plague-related summer mortalities. If we compare the monthly deaths against those expected if they had occurred evenly each month, we find that at S. Jacopo Ripoli there is less than a 2.5 percent probability of obtaining such results by a chance departure from an even distribution and at the Murate it is less than 1 percent.

In addition to offering protection from some of the diseases common on the outside, the monastic life allowed the nuns to escape from the childbirth-related mortalities that affected secular women. The nuns of S. Jacopo Ripoli and the Murate lived to a ripe old age in all the periods observed. At most times, roughly half of the nuns lived to age 70 and a quarter to their late 70s. Even the *converse* lived to quite advanced ages, despite harsher living condi-

TABLE 4   Seasonality of Deaths Among Nuns (Excludes *Converse*)

	J	F	M	A	M	J	J	A	S	O	N	D	Total
Ripoli (1508–1713)[a]	25	23	17	23	14	12	13	27	29	26	10	19	238
Murate (1629–1809)[b]	22	23	21	13	9	7	2	10	12	8	8	14	149

[a] $\chi^2 = 23.6$, with 11 degrees of freedom, significant at .025 level.
[b] $\chi^2 = 38.2$, with 11 degrees of freedom, significant at .001 level.

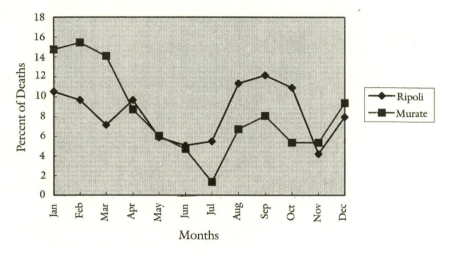

Figure 2. Percentages by month of deaths among nuns at the Murate and Ripoli.

tions and the manual labor they were expected to perform. This longevity, moreover, may not have been unusual for convents in central and northern Italy. In Venice, the nuns of San Daniele, for example, also died at around age 70 and a third of them lived to their late 70s.[45]

If we compare the ages at death of the nuns to those of secular women from similar socioeconomic backgrounds, the advantages of convent life for achieving longevity become readily apparent. Because for this period such information is available only for women of the Milanese patriciate, our comparison perforce has been made with them, but there is no *a priori* reason to think that this would introduce significant distortions, and in any event, we can compare the results against those of other European elites.[46] Not surprisingly, Table 7 shows that, especially during the childbearing years, the mortality rates of nuns were much lower than those of women exposed to the risks of childbearing, which in Milan came to 9.6 deaths per 1,000 births.[47] Less

TABLE 5   Ages at Death of Nuns

| Percentile of deaths at given age | Ripoli | | | | Murate | | |
| | Birth cohort | | | | Birth cohort | | |
	1443–99[a]	1500–49	1550–99	1600–49	1600–49	1650–99	1700–43
25	54.5	53	50	56	56.5	56.8	53.3
50	64	70	67	70	72.1	70.9	69.1
75	75	77	79	76	78.8	75.2	76.5
Mean	64.0	63.0	63.1	64.3	63.1	65.7	64.7
Standard error	1.8	2.4	2.2	2.7	3.2	2.0	2.4
No. observed	(60)	(63)	(73)	(44)	(43)	(48)	(44)

[a]For this birth cohort the figures are based on known ages at death; a slightly different calculation to include 7 nuns who died before 1508 and are therefore unrecorded yields ages from 30 to 48.7, which pulls down ages at death as follows: 25% = 49 years, 50% = 62.5, 75% = 74, mean = 61.8.

TABLE 6   Ages at Death of *Converse*

| Percentile | Ripoli | | Murate | |
| | Birth cohorts | | Birth cohorts | |
	1443–1549	1550–1700	1600–1671	1672–1743
25	46.5	56	51.0	58.4
50	66.5	71	70.1	68.0
75	73.5	78	74.4	75.1
Mean	63.1	66.2	64.4	66.0
Standard error	2.7	2.7	2.6	2.3
No. observed	(36)	(37)	(30)	(30)

obvious, as the accompanying figures show, is that even past the child bearing years the nuns outlived married women on the outside at all ages and in all periods and that these differences are statistically significant. Even in the mid-eighteenth century, when women of the Milanese patriciate could expect to live longer than before, they never reached the longevity of the Murate nuns or those of San Daniele in Venice.[48]

There are probably many reasons for this difference between nuns and secular women. Women who lived outside the convent were exposed to more diseases and other risks than nuns. It is also likely that childbearing had long-term negative repercussions for women even past childbearing age. One way to measure this is to compare the probabilities of survival for women of the

TABLE 7   Ages at Death of Nuns Compared to Married Women of the Milanese Patriciate

| | Birth cohort 1600–1649 | | | Birth cohort 1650–1699 | | Birth cohort 1700–1743 | |
| | Ripoli | Murate | Milan | Murate | Milan | Murate | Milan |
Percentile	nuns	nuns	married	nuns	married	nuns	married
20	52	39.6	38.5	54.5	43.3	50.5	40.2
30	60	61.6	43.3	60.8	54.5	57.4	51.3
40	66	65.5	49.6	68.5	60.3	61.8	60.6
50	70	72.1	55.5	70.9	62.5	69.1	66.2
60	70	73.8	62.7	71.6	66.1	70.6	69.8
70	76	77.5	68.5	73.8	71.7	73.4	73.1
Mean	64.3	63.1	54.5	65.7	59.5	64.7	60.2
Standard error	2.7	3.2	2.6	2.0	2.1	2.4	2.1
No. observed	(44)	(43)	(55)	(48)	(77)	(44)	(77)

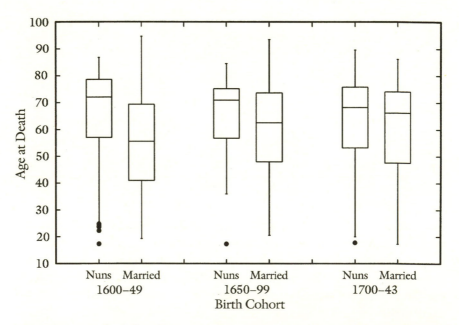

Figure 3. Ages at death for Murate nuns compared to married women of the Milanese patriciate.

TABLE 8   Survival Probabilities for Milanese Mothers with Different Numbers of Children

	Probability of Survival to				Number of observations
	Age 40	Age 50	Age 60	Age 70	
20-year-old mothers with					
1–2 children	87%	76%	61%	31%	36
>2 children	69%	53%	39%	11%	26
25-year-old mothers with					
1–3 children	90%	76%	65%	44%	43
>3 children	89%	76%	58%	30%	66
30-year-old mothers with					
1–5 children	90%	74%	61%	34%	63
>5 children	88%	70%	52%	34%	51

same age who had different numbers of children. Table 8 shows that the women of the Milanese patriciate who at age 20 had only 1 or 2 children had higher probabilities of surviving to all ages than did their sisters who had more children by that age. Indeed, the gap between the two groups widened as they reached their sixties and seventies, which lends support to the argument that repeated childbearing had long-term deleterious effects on the health of these women. The same trend may be observed for women at later ages and with larger numbers of children.

One might claim that the advantage the nuns had was largely due to the unusually large fertility rates of the Milanese women — rates that were among the highest of any European population and that undoubtedly reduced their life expectancy from what it might otherwise have been.[49] Yet, despite this handicap, until the mid-eighteenth century the Milanese women had a higher expectation of life than did the women of the English aristocracy, the women of all the European ruling families, and the women of the Genevan bourgeoisie.[50] This underscores the advantage of convent life for attaining longevity. The nuns of Florence lived longer than did the patrician women of Milan, the bourgeois women of Geneva, the women of the English aristocracy, and those of all the ruling families of Europe. In short, from a demographic point of view, they fared better than the best nourished and the most privileged women in Europe. It hardly needs saying that they also did better than their male counterparts either within or outside religious institutions. Whereas from the fifteenth to the late eighteenth century the Florentine nuns could expect to live into their late sixties and seventies, the fifteenth-century Benedictine monks of Christ Church in Canterbury could, at age twenty, expect to live only to ages 54 to 62; and in the next two centuries the French Benedictine monks of St. Maur could, at age 25, expect at best to live to age 61, which was much longer than the lives of Italian Jesuits who lived more strenuous lives out in the world.[51]

Conclusion

As reformers rejoiced in the closing of convents in the late eighteenth century, few thought of the effect this might have on the life expectancies of women. Indeed, even in our time, scholars who have analyzed the demographic consequences of different forms of religious and secular life have tended to neglect female religious institutions. Implicitly, the life experience of men has become the norm. A recent reexamination of Deparcieux's eighteenth-century study, for example, confirms his findings that the religious life was also the briefer life.[52] The authors speculate that by the time monks reached their mature years, they were more ready than their secular brothers to meet their maker. While this may have been true for monks, it does not appear to be so for Florentine or Venetian nuns, and this raises the issue for other female religious as well. To be sure, convent registers often note the fervor with which the nuns met death in their last moments. But the demographic facts suggest that the nuns of Florence lingered long on this earth and were not in a rush to embrace their bridegroom on the other side. For centuries convents in Catholic Europe were havens from many of the biological risks that faced women in premodern times. Just as important, they were also communities that provided social and psychological supports whose beneficial effects, particularly for women, are just now beginning to be explored by medical research.[53] Rather than being solitary and harsh, the everyday lives of nuns continued to be linked to family, though family relations had to be redefined. Their lives also acquired a sense of purpose that was recognized and respected by city officials and nuns alike. As the Florentine health board acknowledged with its payments for prayers, the pleas of virgins who had made of their lives a gift to God were perceived as especially effective, perhaps even more so than the quarantines and other sanitary measures that became the stock preventatives against disease. This is not to idealize convent life, which had its own glaring limitations. But lest we join the reformers of the Enlightenment and of Victorian times in singing unreflective songs of praise for marriage, we might consider that despite its shortcomings, particularly when it was not freely chosen, convent life contributed to the remarkable longevity of the women who lived it. As European women entered the modern age many of them exchanged the quasi-familial community of the convent and an honored place in the economy of salvation for risky roles as mothers and dubious places as "old maids" (*zitelle*) at the margins of families that had little desire to harbor them in their midst.

Notes

Work on this essay was prepared while the author was a Fellow at the Center for Advanced Study in the Behavioral Sciences. I am grateful for financial support provided by the National Endowment for the Humanities #RA-20037-88 and the Andrew W. Mellon Foundation. Additional support was provided by the Marilyn Yalom Fund at Stanford University's Institute for Research on Women and Gender. Lynn Gale of the Center for Advanced Study in the Behavioral Sciences and Lincoln Moses of Stanford University provided invaluable help with the statistical portions of this article. Additional thanks go to David Brown, Carlo Corsini, Alberto Palloni, Eliot Rowlands, Sharon Strocchia, Larry Wu, and the members of the Life Course Seminar at the Center for Advanced Study in the Behavioral Sciences.

1. Sylvia Townsend Warner, *The Corner That Held Them* (New York: Popular Press, 1948).

2. Antoine Deparcieux, *Essai sur les probabilités de la durée de la vie humaine* (1746; rpt. Paris: Editions d'Histoire Sociale, 1973), p. 85.

3. "Ceux qu'un bon tempérament fait aller jusqu'à un age un peu avancé, pourroient aller bien plus loin s'ils avoient dans les Couvents mille petites douceurs qu'ils n'ont pas, & que les gens du monde trouvent che eux, non seulement les riches, mais aussi ceux qui ne sont que médiocrement aidés, & même les simples artisans qui scavent s'arranger dans leur ménage" (ibid., pp. 84–85).

4. William Farr, "Influence of Marriage on the Mortality of the French People," *Transactions of the National Association for the Promotion of Social Science* (1858): 505, 507.

5. See, among others, W. R. Gove, "Sex, Marital Status, and Mortality, *American Journal of Sociology* 79 (1973): 45–66; J. S. House et al., "The Association of Social Relationship and Activities with Mortality," *American Journal of Epidemiology* 116 (1982): 123–40; L. M. Verbrugge, "Marital Status and Health," *Journal of Marriage and the Family* 41 (1982): 267–85; D. Umberson, "Family Status and Health Behaviors: Social Control as a Dimension of Social Integration," *Journal of Health and Social Behavior* 28 (1987): 301–19; Massimo Livi-Bacci, "Selectivity of Marriage and Mortality: Notes for Future Research," in *Population and Biology: Bridge Between Disciplines*, ed. Nathan Keyfitz (Liège: Ordina, 1985), pp. 99–108; Yuanreng Hu and Noreen Goldman, "Mortality Differentials by Marital Status: An International Comparison," *Demography* 27, 2 (1990): 233–50.

6. For this reason, Richard Trexler concludes that we do not know whether the longevity of women in religious institutions was substantially different from those of similar social classes outside of convents. Idem, "Le célibat á la fin du Moyen Age:

les religieuses de Florence," *Annales: Economies Sociétés Civilisations* 27 (November–December 1972): 1344.

7. The entrance and death register of S. Jacopo di Ripoli is located in the Archivio di Stato of Florence. *Corporazioni Religiose Soppresse da Pietro Leopoldo e aggregate alle Montalve di Ripoli, S. Jacopo di Ripoli*, vol. 23. The register of S. Maria Annunziata delle Murate is located in the Special Collections of the Stanford University Library.

8. Young girls from somewhat lower socioeconomic strata entered convents as *converse* and performed much of the convents' manual labor.

9. Patrician dowries rose from ca. 1,000 florins in 1430 to ca. 15,000 scudi by mid-seventeenth century — roughly an eight-fold increase when adjusted for inflation. David Herlihy and Christiane Klapisch-Zuber, *Tuscans and Their Families: A Study of the Florentine Catasto of 1427* (New Haven, Conn.: Yale University Press, 1983), pp. 222–26; Robert Burr Litchfield, "Demographic Characteristics of Florentine Patrician Families: Sixteenth to Eighteenth Centuries," *Journal of Economic History* 29 (1969): 191–205.

10. Herlihy and Klapisch, *Tuscans*, p. 153. Since about half of the population was female and about two-thirds of those were over age 14, it was possible to arrive at an approximate percentage of the city's female religious.

11. Since in 1622 Florence had 26,309 women age 15 and over, female religious came close to 16 percent of the adult female population. Lorenzo del Panta, *Una traccia di storia demografica della Toscana* (Florence: Dipartimento Statistico-Matematico, Università degli Studi di Firenze, 1974), p. 44; and Karl Julius Beloch, *Bevölkerungsgeschichte Italiens*, 3 vols. (1937; rpt. Berlin, de Gruyter, 1965), 2: pp. 48–49.

12. Litchfield, "Characteristics." In the 1800s, the proportion of nuns in the city's total population had returned to about the 1427 level, but because the age structure of the population was less steep, nuns made up a smaller proportion of the adult female population.

13. Giuseppe Richa, *Notizie istoriche delle chiese fiorentine*, 4 vols. (Florence, 1756), 4: 300, 304. Richard Trexler, "Le célibat," p. 1340. Emilia Nesi, *Il diario della stamperia di Ripoli* (Florence, 1903), p. 9. Although the 1632 census reports 80 residents in the convent, the entrance and death register makes it clear that there could not have been more than 65.

14. The figure for 1461 comes from fol. 68r of an eighteenth-century copy of a late sixteenth-century convent chronicle. The document is being prepared for publication by Dr. Eliot Rowlands. I am grateful to him for showing me his transcription. Biblioteca Moreniana, Ms. 226, vol. 2, part 2, fols. 63r–89r, "Notizie estratte dal libro intitolato Cronache del Venerabile monastero di S. M. Annunziata delle Murate di Firenze, scritto da suor Justina Niccolini, nel di 31 gennaio 1597, e che esiste in detto monastero." The figure for 1494 is from Fra Benigno Raguseo, *Propheticae Solutiones* (1494), cited by Richa, II: 83. The 1552 figure is from the Florentine census; Pietro Battara, *La popolazione di Firenze alla metà del '500* (Florence, 1935), p. 20.

15. Niccolini, *Chronicle*, f. 67v, 69r; also Richa, *Chiese fiorentine*, p. 90.

16. Biblioteca Nazionale di Firenze, EB, 15, 2, Census of 1552. This figure does not distinguish between nuns and *converse*. If the gap between the census and the real figures is similar to that at S. Jacopo Ripoli, the population of the Murate may have been closer to 100.

17. Contrary to expectations, entrances did not occur more frequently on certain feast days of significance to the convent, the city, or female monastic institutions.

Professions, however, did cluster on certain days—most often All Saints' Day, the Purification of the Virgin, and the Annunciation.

18. A χ^2 statistic allows us to compare the observed monthly entrances at the convents with the entrances expected if there had been an even monthly distribution by measuring the difference between the two. At Ripoli $\chi^2 = 38.9$ for monthly entrances; with 11 degrees of freedom there is a probability of less than 1 in 1,000 of obtaining such a pattern by chance. At the Murate $\chi^2 = 60$ for monthly entrances in 1629–1737, with an even smaller probability of occurring by chance. The χ^2 declines by half in 1737–1806. (For the layperson in statistics seeking further elucidation of χ^2, see Roderick Floud, *An Introduction to Quantitative Methods for Historians* [Princeton, N.J.: Princeton University Press, 1973], pp. 130–33).

19. The variability of nomenclature is discussed by Trexler, "Les religieuses," pp. 1334–35. Some convents therefore kept track only of entrances but not veilings, or of veilings but not professions. The register of S. Jacopo Ripoli lists entrances from 1282, but dates of veiling only after 1530. These, but not entrance registrations, exist from 1657 to 1688; dates of profession exist for 1508–1687. The Murate recorded the entrance date as the date of veiling and sometimes added a date of profession in the first half of the eighteenth century and more regularly from the 1750s through 1780s.

20. Of 36 *converse* with known entrance and veiling dates, 20 were veiled within 2 weeks of entrance, another 7 in the third and fourth weeks, and the remaining 9 within 9 months.

21. The age at which *converse* entered convents also rose but at a slower pace because they had always entered later than nuns. At Ripoli the median age of entrance and profession for *converse* ranged between 16–18 and 17–22 respectively; at the Murate, median entrance age for *converse* ranged between 17–20. Because they were sent to convents to do manual labor, *converse* were of less use there as children or as young adolescents; to their parents, however, they may have been of greater use performing domestic labor, spinning, or helping with other crafts than the aristocratic girls who became nuns.

22. Leopold II, *Relazioni sul governo della Toscana*, ed. Arnaldo Salvestrini (Florence: Olschki, 1969), p. 217.

23. On the intent of these laws, see Osanna Fantozzi Micali and Piero Roselli, *Le soppressioni dei conventi a Firenze: Riuso e trasformazioni dal secolo XVII in poi* (Florence: L. E. F., 1980), p. 14.

24. Trexler, "Les religieuses," p. 1340.

25. Niccolini, "Chronicle," fols. 74v, 81r, 82r.

26. The dowries of 9 nuns are recorded for the years 1687–1699. They range mostly from 600 to 800 scudi plus gifts in kind. The one exception records that Sister Maria Teresa Federighi "gave 1,100 scudi, and this because she was exempt from all tasks, because she was unable to perform them."

27. All five *converse* who professed at Ripoli between 1687 and 1699 paid 300 scudi. Among 70 *converse* registered at Ripoli, several include their places of origin in villages near Florence. A few also mention the father's occupation—weaver, construction worker, dyer, etc.

28. Niccolini, "Chronicle," f. 89r.

29. The archbishop forbade more than two female religious from the same blood and lineage from being accepted in the same convent. Mansi, J. D. *Sacrorum Conci-*

liorum nova et amplissima collectio (Gratz, 1961; orig. Florence 1758–1598), 35: 263; cited in Trexler, "Les religieuses," p. 1341.

30. Sister Niccolini of the Murate tells us that in the fifteenth century, when the nuns moved to their permanent home, they "walled in [murarono] the door to the monastery, as they had done at the bridge, and it [the door] was not opened except to accept a girl to become a nun and then immediately it was closed again." Niccolini, "Chronicle," f. 65v.

31. Ibid., f. 85r.

32. Gabriella Zarri, "Monasteri femminili e città (secoli XV–XVIII)," *Storia d'Italia: Annali*, 9 (Turin: Einaudi, 1986), pp. 388–90.

33. Giovanni D. Mansi, *Sacrorum Conciliorum*, vol. 35, p. 263.

34. Benedetto Varchi, *Storia fiorentina* (Milan, 1803), 4: pp. 108–9. Cited in Trexler, "Les religieuses," p. 1342.

35. See Zarri, "Monasteri femminili," p. 371, 407.

36. Niccolini, "Chronicle," f. 83v.

37. Lorenzo del Panta, *Le epidemie nella storia demografica italiana (sec. XIV–XIX)* (Turin: Loescher, 1980); idem., "Cronologia e diffusione delle cristi di mortalità in Toscana dalla fine del XIV agli inizi del XIX secolo," *Ricerche Storiche* 7, 2 (1977): 293–342. Alfonso Corradi, *Annali delle epidemie occorse in Italia dalle prime memorie fino al 1850* (Bologna, publ. 1972; orig. 1865–1892), vols. 1–3.

38. Niccolini, *Cronaca*, f. 77r.

39. I have confined my analysis of expected mortalities to nuns because the number of *converse* was too small. Expected mortality figures were derived from a Kaplan-Meier survival curve, which is the most widely used method to estimate survival rates. The Kaplan-Meier method is helpful because it allows us to take into account both the age structure of the convent in every five-year period and "censored" observations, i.e. information about those individuals who survived at the end of the last period observed. Based on the "uncensored" data estimates are derived about the censored observations and these are taken into account in the final figures. See D. R. Cox and D. Oakes, *Analysis of Survival Data* (London: Chapman and Hall, 1984), pp. 84ff.

40. If there had been significantly large underlying changes in the pattern of mortality over time, χ^2 would have had a large value. At Ripoli, where we observed 40 five-year clusters, $\chi^2 = 88.59$, which with 39 degrees of freedom indicates a change in mortality patterns that is significant at the .001 level.

41. The value of χ^2 was 32.1, and with 27 degrees of freedom (from 28 five-year intervals) this is not significant because it is not much larger than the expected value of 27.

42. Barbara Harvey, *Living and Dying in England, 1100–1540: The Monastic Experience* (Oxford: Oxford University Press, 1993), pp. 130–32.

43. I am very grateful to Prof. Elissa Weaver for bringing this document to my attention and sending me a transcript of this passage.

44. Florence, Archivio di Stato, *Corporazioni religiose soppresse* 96, filza 12, cc. 129r–130r. "Ricordo" della scrivana suor Gabriella Angiola Baldovinetti, entry dated 1 October, 1633.

45. Elizabeth Santschi examined the mortalities of the nuns of San Daniele but only included data on nuns whose illness was reported. Based on this data, the mean age at death for 37 nuns born in 1600–1649 was 71.4; for 32 nuns born in 1650–1699 it was 69.7; and for 20 nuns born in 1700–1729 it was 69.4 years; the 70th percentile was

78 years and 76 years, for the first two cohorts. Elizabeth Santschi, "L'obituaire de San Daniele (1577–1804): étude Démographique," *Studi Veneziani* 13 (1971): 655–64.

46. The data are derived from Dante Zanetti's work on the Milanese patriciate. I have selected only married women who survived to age 15 and older. This minimum age is comparable to the entrance age into Florentine convents. As for marital status, there were almost no single women outside the convent, and those who went into the convent disappear from the family records and hence leave no data on age at death. This then leaves 209 married women age 15 and older whose ages at death are known. The data are taken from the genealogical appendix in idem, *La demografia del patriziato milanese nei secoli XVII, XVIII, XIX* (Pavia: Università di Pavia 1972).

47. Sigismund Peller calculated that there were between 19.4 and 20.2 maternal deaths per 1,000 deliveries among Europe's ruling families from the sixteenth to the eighteenth centuries. Idem, "Births and Deaths Among Europe's Ruling Families Since 1500," *Population in History: Essays in Historical Demography*, ed. D. V. Glass and D. E. C. Eversby (London: E. Arnold, 1965), p. 96. For efforts to isolate childbirth related mortality from other risks in historical populations, see Louis Henry, "Men's and Women's Mortality in the Past," *Population* 44, 1 (1989), pp. 177–201.

48. The nuns' extra longevity is estimated with 95 percent confidence to be between 2.7 and 10.1 years. The slight improvement in the ages at death of the Milanese women is not sufficiently large to be statistically significant. An analysis of variance (ANOVA) yields an F value = 0.26, with 2 and 134 degrees of freedom, p=.78.

49. Among British ducal families, ca. 1/4 of the daughters born between 1675–1724 never married and close to 1/5 of those who did remained childless; since the mean number of births per married women in that group was 4.5, the mean number of births for those who had children was about 5.5. By contrast, 30 percent of the Milanese women in our sample did not marry (mostly becoming nuns), but those who did marry and gave birth had an average of 8.3 children. The fertility of the Milanese patriciate was also much higher than that of the bourgeoisie of Geneva. See T. H. Hollingsworth, "A Demographic Study of the British Ducal Families," in *Population in History*, ed. Glass and Eversley, p. 372; Louis Henry, *Anciennes familles genevoises: Etude démographique XVI–XX siècles* (Paris: Presses Universitaires de France, 1956); Zanetti, *Patriziato Milanese*, pp. 149, 158–169.

50. At age 20 the expectation of life for women born into British peerage families in 1680–1729 was 35.4; for those born in 1730–1779 it was 44.2. For women of French ducal and peer families born in 1650–1799, expectation of life at 20 was 33.6; for the bourgeois women of Geneva expectation of life at age 20 rose from 36 in 1600–1649 to 44 in 1750–1799. The comparisons, based on the studies by Henry and Hollingsworth, are presented in Zanetti, *Patriziato Milanese*, p. 227. For Europe's ruling families, expectation of life for females at age 15 was 36.2 years in 1600–1699 and 39.9 in 1700–1799; S. Peller, "Births and Deaths Among Europe's Ruling Families Since 1500," *Population in History*, ed. Glass and Eversley, p. 98.

51. In the sixteenth and seventeenth centuries, the expectation of life among Jesuits (mostly Italian) was 34 at age 15 and 31.5 at age 20. This is roughly comparable to the expectation of life among British peers of the time. See Silvana Salvini, "La mortalità dei Gesuiti in Italia nei secoli XVI e XVII," *Quaderni del dipartimento statistico*, Università degli Studi di Firenze, 3 (1979): 15, 20. In the seventeenth and eighteenth centuries, the monks of St. Maur had an expectation of life at age 25 that ranged from

ca. 32.9 years to 35.8; H. Le Bras and D. Dinet, "Mortalité des laics et mortalité des religieux: les bénédictins de St. Maur aux XVIIᵉ siècles, *Population* 35, 1 (1980): 370. For the Benedictine monks at Canterbury, see John Hatcher, "Mortality in the XVth Century: Some New Evidence," *Economic History Review* 2nd ser. 39, 1 (1986): 28.

52. Le Bras and Dinet, "Mortalité des laics et mortalité des religieux," pp. 373–77.

53. For a recent study that notes the positive effect of female support groups on the survival rates of female cancer patients, see David Spiegel et al., "Effect of Psychosocial Treatment on Survival of Patients with Metastatic Breast Cancer." *The Lancet* (Oct. 14, 1986): 888–91.

7

Constructing the Female Self

Architectural Structures in Mary Wroth's *Urania*

Shannon Miller

WHEN BESS OF HARDWICK, Countess of Shrewsbury, began construction on her estate, Hardwick Hall, she assumed the position of an artistic creator. While there were some women visual artists in the period, and a few more women writers, as a woman builder Bess was more nearly unique. Work on Hardwick Hall began in 1590 immediately after — or perhaps a few weeks before — the death of Bess's husband; the end of a multiple-year legal battle with her husband had finally given her the resources to build one of England's most elaborate estates.[1] Her construction of Hardwick Hall powerfully illustrates the female appropriation of traditional male spheres, and spaces, for Bess's own purposes. In undertaking the building of an ideal manor house for herself and her second son, she asserts her financial independence from her estranged third husband.[2] The house loudly declares itself Elizabeth Shrewsbury's through her initials which are contained within the ornamental crests of the towers. Nor is this a subtle signature: ES is repeated three times on each of six towers. Further, Robert Smythson, the architect, skillfully proportioned the house, creating visual angles at which three separate towers align; certain views of the house, then, triple the view of Bess's initials. Smythson's proportions make this "the supreme triumph of Elizabethan architecture," while Bess's inscription of her initials onto the house makes it a noteworthy triumph for an early modern woman.[3] Bess of Hardwick also extended her identity as a builder into the interior decoration of Hardwick Hall. As Don Wayne has suggested, the portrait of Artemisia embroidered onto the estate's elaborate tapestries gestures to the ruler of Caria who constructed the first mausoleum for her husband.[4]

Yet as boldly as Bess of Hardwick may have declared her ownership over

Figure 1. Hardwick Hall, c. 1590, front entrance. The initials of Elizabeth Shrewsbury (Bess of Hardwick, Countess of Shrewsbury), who commissioned and may have designed the house, are repeated three times on each of the six towers. Certain angles of the house triple this view of her initials. Photo courtesy National Trust Photographic Library / Mike Williams.

this estate, her construction of this space relied upon the work of her architect, Robert Smythson, as well as that of multiple — male — workers.[5] Mark Girouard summarizes extant correspondence on the house's construction which details exactly what one would expect to find: male masons, male carvers, male ironworkers. Even existing records on the tapestries — in whose production Bess and other women may very well have been involved — suggest the prominent role of male embroiderers. Professionals — men — were employed for some portion of the tapestries, and Girouard has suggested that if Bess and her gentlewomen embroidered the smaller pieces, it was "perhaps with the aid of a professional to set out the design."[6] While the tapestries, embroideries, and statues within Hardwick Hall may have testified to a "discourse of feminine virtue" that began to appropriate traditional masculine authority over domestic space, Bess Hardwick nonetheless had to employ male labor in order to achieve her ideological, as well as her material, ends.[7]

Bess of Hardwick illustrates how one woman undertook the construction

Figure 2. Hardwick Hall, c. 1590. Tapestry panel of Artemisia with Pietas and Constancy. Photo courtesy National Trust Photographic Library.

of physical space by managing material production conventionally controlled by men. As Alice Friedman has shown, in undertaking a Palladian-style design which "openly defied [the] tradition" of the great hall by placing it at the center of a symmetrical plan, Bess was also re-designing architectural conventions in order to re-define the social and cultural expectations of a widow running an extensive domestic space. In "Architecture, Authority, and the Female Gaze: Planning and Representation in the Early Modern Country House," Friedman suggests how the conditions of a woman like Bess of Hardwick might have influenced her use of architectural space and resulted in "both a new form and a new meaning for the country house."[8] Like Bess, women in the Sidney family turn to architecture in physical, visual, and thematic forms to re-configure traditionally male-controlled spaces. Mary Sidney, after the death of her husband, commissioned a Palladian-style country house at Houghton Conquest in Bedfordshire. When "becom[ing] a builder" in 1619–1620, Mary Sidney opted for a compact design which fit her material needs as a wealthy widow who "had no family seat to call her own and no traditional ties of service and hospitality to maintain."[9] Like Bess of Hardwick, then, Mary Sidney employed but also redirected the conventions of architecture during the period in order to construct a space that suited her needs as a widowed aristocratic woman.

Friedman's analysis of Bess of Hardwick's and Mary Sidney's building plans suggests how gender inflects the designs of women who make spaces, here architectural. Bess' rather dramatic assertion of self as a female builder, and Mary Sidney's more modest use of Palladian architecture to create an architectural space appropriate for a dowager countess, provide a rich background against which to consider Mary Wroth's use of architectural motifs within her 1621 prose romance, *The Countesse of Mountgomeries Urania*. Written thirty years after Bess of Hardwick's construction of Hardwick Hall, and contemporaneous with Mary Sidney's commissioning the building of Houghton Conquest, the *Urania*'s architectural structures — both visual and thematic — serve Wroth as a strategy for negotiating female identity. Much like Bess of Hardwick's inscription of her initials on the crested towers of Hardwick Hall, Wroth's text employs such structures to provide an avenue for an expression of the female self. In the building of this text, as in Bess's construction of her estate, Wroth turns to spaces constructed by men — both architectural structures and literary traditions. Wroth employs these everyday structures to elucidate the interior self — the emotions, the concerns, the anguish — of the narrative's characters. Characters' movements through such structures — rooms, buildings, caves — reveal their emotional states in a text that highlights the difficulty, or inability, to access a modern conception of "interiority."

While architectural structures will mark Wroth's exploration of female subjectivity in the text, the frontispiece to Wroth's *Urania* offers the text's first and most visually prominent use of an architectural motif (see Figure 3). The frontispiece presents a detailed engraving of the central enchantment in Book 1. The reader enters the *Urania* through an architectural frame, an arch with a sharply angled perspective that opens onto an elaborate landscape dominated by two intricate buildings. As viewers of the engraving, we are visually directed by this framing arch to gaze upon the Throne of Love, the elaborate structure high on a hill which will be the site of the primary adventure of Book 1 of the romance. The Throne repeats many of the architectural traits of the framing arch — the base of the pillars, the shape of the cornice which is echoed by the roof of the Throne. This suggests the reader's simultaneous view of and our position within the Throne; the Throne, as the narrative will explain, represents the dominant emotion of love which structures the stories in the romance. Architecturally, then, the centrality of these internal emotions is announced from this beginning view of the text. As our eyes glance down onto the bridge at the bottom of the frontispiece, the engraving also spatially enacts

Figure 3. Frontispiece to Lady Mary Wroth, *The Countesse of Mountgomeries Urania* (London, 1621). By permission of the Huntington Library, San Marino, California.

for us the progression from Lust to Love to Constancy — the allegorical mean-ing of the three towers — which defines the hierarchy of love in Wroth's ro-mance. Like Bess of Hardwick, Wroth would have had to employ a male craftsman to convey this architectural vision into her text: Simon van de Passe engraved the frontispiece and may well have had Wroth's input. As Josephine Roberts argues, "The illustration for the title-page of the Urania was chosen by som[e]one very well-acquainted with the nature of the fiction" and the Throne of Love sequence.[10] However the subject for the frontispiece was selected, it highlights the thematic centrality of architectural building to the narrative of Wroth's *Urania*.

At a series of levels, then, architectural constructions resonate in and for the author of and the text of the *Urania* before we even enter the narrative. The vision of the frontispiece locates much of the story's narrative, and its emo-tional power, within the architectural structures that make up the Throne of Love sequence. Wroth's use of architecture to convey the particularities of her narrative matches with her own aunt's use of the construction of space to delineate one's social position. And Wroth explicitly draws upon a writing tradition within the Sidney family to announce herself as a builder of narrative and of scenes. The Corinthian pillars support an elaborate cornice emblazoned with the title of the romance, *The Countesse of Mountgomeries Urania*, along with Mary Wroth's literary genealogy: "Neece to the ever famous, and re-nowned Sr Phillips Sidney knight. . . . And to the most excellent Lady Mary Countess of Pembroke."[11]

The frontispiece consequently serves as an appropriate frame for our entry into the issues of women's literary production during the period. Wroth's gender, as well as her anomalous position as a woman writing and publishing during the early seventeenth century, becomes powerfully inscribed through the representation of interior space in the *Urania*. As we see here and within the romance itself, women's movement toward the "interior" of a physical structure serves as a metaphor for movement into the interior self. In an analogous fashion to the operation of the frontispiece, the narrative of the *Urania* repeatedly turns outward to physical, architectural structures in order to express aspects of Wroth's female characters rather than expressing "inward-ness." Wroth's text thus serves in part as a literary illustration of the new architectural emphasis in the early modern period on creating private spaces within houses for the well-to-do.[12] The construction of a sequence of rooms to which an individual could retire developed hand-in-hand with the creation of smaller private spaces in the Renaissance: closely guarded cabinets, alcoves, and closets. Whether architectural or decorative, these spaces allowed the self to remove from the public world, whether by hiding away one's things or oneself. These rooms, cabinets, and boxes provide a material analogue to the creation of psychological space in the Renaissance: "interiority," the creation of space for a self and for that self's private thoughts, accompanies the rise of privacy in the early modern period.[13]

But the *Urania* is also suggesting how differently these spaces function for men and women. Alan Stewart's work on the gendering of "closets" in the early modern period contrasts the male closet filled with "working papers," "a secret nonpublic transactive space between two men behind a locked door," with the use women made of their closets.[14] Though a woman's closet was "constructed as a place of utter privacy, of total withdrawal from the public sphere of the household . . . it simultaneously functions as a very public gesture of withdrawal, a very public sign of privacy."[15] In order to find a private space for self and thoughts, women's withdrawal into the physical interior space of their closets had to be publicly staged. Stewart's argument about the genuinely "secret nonpublic" space of the male closet grants such a space for privacy, even interiority, to men while suggesting its greater contestation, even its paradoxical existence, for women.[16]

Why does Wroth turn to the external world in order to express female interiority? More generally, what would make the female subject so hard to express? Theorists such as Francis Barker and Catherine Belsey have explored the historical development of subjectivity, the construction, in Belsey's terms, of a unified human subject who "affirm[s] a continuous and inviolable interiority as the essence of each person."[17] Both critics argue that this fiction of an autonomous human subject emerged in the later seventeenth century. Wroth's 1621 romance undoubtedly is struggling with the problem of expressing this "self," and the interior, private space accorded to the self.[18] And yet, as Belsey illustrates, the construction of subjectivity is a highly gendered act; the female subject faced significantly more barriers to the expression of a coherent self. While men were characterized by the unity attributed to a humanist subject, women were constantly defined as discontinuous. Their fluctuating authority in the family and their fluctuating rights in the legal sphere, for example, denied Renaissance female subjects a "single or stable place from which to define themselves as independent beings."[19]

Wroth negotiates this "single or stable place" from which to speak and write by repeatedly expressing the interiority of women through the external object. Yet these strategies simultaneously indicate the difficulty of, and the limits to, defining the female subject in terms other than those literally constructed by men — rooms, poetry, intricate buildings. In three episodes of the *Urania*, we see the female self articulated through male-built structures. In the opening scene of the romance, Urania's expression of her "heart" and "soul" is deflected onto a series of constructed spaces. In the Throne of Love, passage through an elaborate structure first metaphorizes but ultimately denies the "inward" movement into Wroth's characters. Finally, in the Hell of Deceit sequence, a glimpse offered of the self becomes a vision that threatens to fragment that self. And such problems of constructing a female "self" plague Wroth as well. Just as her female characters travel through rooms, structures, and buildings which serve as metaphors for the discovery of self, so too must Wroth, a writing female subject, negotiate the constructed artifice of the male literary tradition. Wroth herself passes through various "rooms" of tradition — previous writers, generic conventions — within her own narrative, rooms which can provide her with authority. In order to reach any room of her own, then, the female subject, both written in and writing the *Urania*, must move through male-authored spaces.

Whereas the *Urania*'s title page emphasizes Wroth's identity as a Sidney, the opening episode of the romance sustains an emphasis on the construction of a self through family and then through physical structures as it introduces us to Urania, the title character of the romance. Though raised as a shepherdess, Urania has just discovered that she is a foundling. Urania, "not being certaine of mine owne estate or birth," cannot "know my selfe."[20] While the family did not constitute women as independent selves or provide them with a "personal" identity, it did provide them with a stable cultural and social identification.[21] The patrilinear line emblematized in women's adoption of the "family" name serves as the most obvious example of this; Margaret More Roper, for example, is doubly inscribed by her name as the daughter of a More and the wife of a Roper. In a more macabre, if more powerful, illustration of the inscription of women into families, two deathbed paintings of the early seventeenth century, *Sir Thomas Aston at the Deathbed of his Wife* and *The Saltonstall Family*, picture a widower with both his dying and his future wife. Both women are given the same social identity: the wife of Aston or Saltonstall; their individual identities, meanwhile, become irrelevant in the dynastic terms of the portrait.[22] The assertion of a dynastic line also announces Wroth on the frontispiece of the *Urania*: as the "Daughter" of Robert and "Neece" of Philip and Mary Sidney, she is positioned within a family, here of well-known writers, which authorizes her identity as a writing subject.

The contrast with Wroth's character, Urania, could not be stronger; she is denied any position for the "self" that can be constituted through the family. Forced to construct this space outside of family lineage, Urania attempts to find a private place to "passe away her time more peaceably with lonelinesse" (2). As Catherine Belsey has suggested, the fictitious unified human subject is one that views "the mind [as] a place of retreat, defined by its difference from the exterior world."[23] Yet the interior space of Urania's mind becomes expressed not in opposition to but through the external world. Once family identity fails, she turns to other edifices for self-definition.

The opening of the narrative, then, creates a particular crisis about identity by combining the consequences of Urania's gender with the staging of Wroth's family affiliation one leaf before. As Urania follows "a little path which brought her to the further side of the plaine," she undertakes a journey which will substitute for knowledge of the self (1). Within the *Urania*, moving beyond complete "ignorance" of the self requires passage through delineated spaces, such as the cave upon which Urania stumbles. "Having attained the top, she saw under some hollow trees the entrie into the rocke: she fearing nothing but the continuance of her ignorance, went in" (2). The description of her entrance into, and her continuation through, the cave in a gradual unlayering process is a motif that marks Wroth's detailing of spaces throughout the *Urania*. Now, "Shee found a pretty roome, as if that stonie place had yet in pitie, given leave for such perfections to come into the heart as chiefest, and most beloved place, because most loving" (2). Urania's crisis over identity is displaced onto an unveiling of space. Upon Urania's entrance into the cave, passage through a sequence of architectural spaces becomes a strategy to reconstitute the "self" she has lost. Though this description is a classic example of the pathetic fallacy, the emotion attributed to this "pretty roome" actually describes the condition of the "heart" which Wroth has not narrated within the character of Urania. The "stonie" cave makes the "pretty roome" its "heart" or center to which the reader and Urania have access. Described as the "chiefest, and most beloved place, because most loving," this "pretty roome" is analogous to the interior of our heroine; Wroth expresses aspects of the human heart, but does so by moving into another space, another "roome." Thus, Urania's interiority is gestured at, but without ever entering or exposing the "heart" itself as Wroth deflects any inward movement within the "very soule" outward onto the "pretty roome" (1). Wroth thus successfully reorients the movement into one's heart which Orest Ranum has described as "invariably a sign of inwardness."[24] This "central symbol of intimacy" becomes expressible in the *Urania* only through the representation of exterior, architectural images.

Urania's movement into and through a sequence of rooms within the cave, then, becomes an allegory for movement into an elusive interior self. Just as Wroth's association with a line of Sidneys and writers sets the stage for Urania's loss of the knowledge of "my selfe," the movement towards an ineffable self becomes linked to writing. "[D]iscerning a little doore, which she putting from her, [Urania] passed through it into another roome, like the first in all proportion," where Urania discovers a sonnet on a table "which had

suffered it selfe patiently to receive the discovering of so much of it" (2). Just
as the "heart" lies within the floor-plan of this "stonie place," the poem has a
"self" contained within it that can be read and is "discovering" itself to Urania
and the reader. Wroth explicitly links the place and the poem through Urania's
response to the sonnet: "How well doe these words, *this place*, and all agree
with thy fortune?" (3; my emphasis). Thus, as she reads through the sonnet,
Urania continues the same search for the expression of an inner self, only now
within a new architectural construct. We see the same pun on "stanza," the
Italian word for room, that Donne uses in the "Canonization"; Urania moves
from "room" to "room" of the sonnet as she has previously moved through the
rooms of the cave. Once inside, Urania can continue to identify with the
"soule" she discovers in the sonnet. "[S]ure poore soule," she addresses
the poem, "thou wert heere appointed to spend thy daies, and these roomes
ordain'd to keepe thy tortures in" (3). This "soule" remains within the literary
architecture of the sonnet's stanzas just as it remained within the "stonie place"
of the cave.

Though we can get to the last room in the cave, or to the last stanza in the
poem, this process does not finally give us access to Urania's "inwardness." The
narrative continually deflects us from a description of Urania's "soule." These
external, physical structures, both the cave itself and the poem associated with
it, come to stand in for an ineffable, interior self. As Patricia Fumerton has
illustrated in her work on miniatures, sonnets, and rooms, the ever-receding
place of the "private" self cannot be reached: the Elizabethan subject "always
withheld for itself a 'secret' room, cabinet, case or other recess locked away. . . .
Or rather there never was any ultimate room, cabinet, or other *apart*ment of
privacy that could be locked away from the public; only a perpetual regress of
apartments."[25] The "self" which is displaced onto the description of the cave,
into the paper of the poem "it selfe," and then within the "poore soule" of the
sonnet, keeps slipping out of reach (2; 3). Fumerton's argument against a
unified subjectivity in the seventeenth century is quite convincing, yet it is an
argument which makes no distinction — as does Belsey — between the strategies each gender employed to construct such a "self." Wroth's romance suggests that while subjectivity is certainly problematic in the early modern period, female subjectivity is even more so. Her turn to male-constructed edifices
through which Wroth attempts to constitute a female subject implies a greater
stability of the male subject; as family portraits and the frontispiece of the
Countesse of Mountgomeries Urania declare, female subjects are defined through
patrilinear family structures. Wroth's strategy is to appropriate male structures
through which a female "self" can be identified, if not revealed. While cave
formations are linked with natural, even female, traits, the space into which

Urania enters quickly becomes an architectural construction, a sequence of carefully built "rooms," ones even compared to "ancient . . . Hermitages" (2); the necessary role of male builders that we saw in the construction of Hardwick House is implicit in these engineered rooms. This association of the cave with male-constructed spaces is reinforced by the authorship of the poem in which Urania finds a reflection of her suffering self. Perissus, a love-sick knight, has authored the poem, thus providing the expression of her interior state. Though the elusive self is never found, it can be gestured at through such male constructions.

This strategy of turning to male-authored spaces in order to articulate the female subject is repeated throughout the *Urania*. In the Throne of Love episode, Wroth employs more elaborate architectural images to describe the emotional state of her characters. This early episode describes pairs of lovers, including Urania, who are shipwrecked by a storm. Their emotional condition is revealed by perhaps the dominant architectural image in the romance: "Thus, on they went (but as in a Labyrinth without a thrid)" (47).[26] This highly elaborate architectural structure, the labyrinth, is tied to Daedalus, its creator, through the reference to Ariadne's thread, the device which allowed Theseus to escape the original labyrinth. "[T]ill they came within sight of a rare and admirable Pallace," the lovers' confusion and distraction are appropriately expressed by the labyrinth image (47). Wroth then substitutes one architectural motif for another as she employs the physical characteristics of the enchanted Throne of Love to describe emotions of love: "It was scituated on a Hill . . . all the Country besides humbly plaine, to shew the subjection to that powerfull dwelling" (47). As the land is dominated by the Throne of Love, so too do the lovers "shew the[ir] subjection" to the emotions of love. The emphasis on male-built spaces continues in a reference to the Throne's construction. The description of the edifice includes an account of the statue of Venus on the second of three buildings: it was "so richly adorn'd, as it might for rarenesse, and exquisitenesse have beene taken for the Goddesse her selfe, and have causd as strange an affection as the Image did to her maker, when he fell in love with his owne worke" (48). Here Wroth employs another myth — that of Pygmalion — to sustain a motif of male artists and architects. Though we will be told by the temple's priest that "Venus . . . hath built this" (48), we are initially presented with the work of the male craftsmen. Like Bess of Hardwick, Venus works through male sculptors, male builders, male artists.

As in the opening *Urania* sequence, the metaphorical use of architectural images soon becomes not only a description of an emotional state, here love, but a deflection of such interiority onto physical structures. The Throne of Love enchantment tests lovers in three towers. The first tower encases false lovers, while the second captures lovers of any kind. The third "can bee entred by none, till the valiantest Knight, with the loyallest Lady come together" (48–49). When they "open that gate" to the final tower of constancy, the enchantment will end. As in the initial cave sequence, Wroth aligns the inner states of female characters with physical structures more frequently than she uses such structures to describe male characters. Here, the male lovers become overwhelmed by the desire to pursue other goals and never enter the Throne. The condition of women's love, though, is revealed by their movement through the towers. On entering the building, as Mary Ellen Lamb has remarked, the women become literally confined by love.[27] Encased within the rooms of the Throne, their "interior" grief of love is externally manifested by the physical structure of the enchantment: "Thus were the women for their punishment, left prisoners in the throne of *Love*, which Throne and punishments are daily built in all humane hearts" (50). Like Urania's "pretty roome," the Throne becomes Wroth's mode of expressing the human heart itself. But "expression" never truly takes place since we never move into the "hearts" of these women; rather, the state of "inwardness" becomes unrepresentable, requiring this same deflection onto the architectural components of the Throne. Our movement into the "heart" is transformed into the description of an external image. Female subjectivity continues to recede farther and farther from "view," replaced by structures which dominate from the frontispiece on.

As the Throne of Love enchantment is lifted in the closing pages of Book 1, Pamphilia, "the loyallest Lady," and Amphilanthus, "the valiantest Knight," rescue the entrapped lovers. Pamphilia's passage through the Throne's interior rooms and into the final tower of constancy becomes a mode of revealing what Wroth conveys throughout the romance as the "essential" and defining aspect of Pamphilia's self: constancy. Elaine Beilen argues that Pamphilia "becomes" constancy in the resolution of Book 1.[28] But the *Urania* continues to locate such a "self" just beyond the characters. After passing through the first two towers, Pamphilia "made the Gate flie open to them, who passed to the last Tower, where *Constancy* stood holding the keyes, which Pamphilia tooke; at which instant *Constancy* vanished, as metamorphosing her self into her breast" (169). As with Urania's passage through the various "rooms" of the cave, Pamphilia's physical movement through architectural space comes to signify movement "into" human interiority. The final passage into Pamphilia's "breast" suggests that we are gaining access to her heart, to that sign of the ultimate space of interiority. Yet even this movement cannot finally expose, reveal, or describe Pamphilia's "heart" — the narrative stops us from this final entry, allowing us to see only the container of Pamphilia's heart, her breast. Though the narrative gestures to the final moment of revelation, it is —

again — "deferred [from] any arrival at innermost privacy."[29] Consistently, this act of deferral remains more resonant for female characters. It is women who are defined by architectural structures; the image of the Throne of Love is used to describe female hearts, and the "interior" condition of love revealed by the three towers applies primarily to women. Thus Amphilanthus — whose name means "lover of two" — can pass into the tower of constancy unaffected by its significance for women's hearts and their inner psychic "truths."

The difference between male and female "hearts," and the representation of what lies within, becomes the focus of the Hell of Deceit episode in Book 4. Here, Wroth at last offers the reader a glimpse of the interiority of the female self, but illustrates the danger in such exposure for the female self and, ultimately, for herself as a writer. In this episode, the only recently reconciled Pamphilia and Amphilanthus are separated while hunting. Individually, they come upon rock structures which open onto nightmarish images of the other encased within a cave structure. Again in this episode, interiority is expressed through actual structures and spaces which are progressively opened, their layers peeled back and exposed. Pamphilia peers into the Hell of Deceit, which physically opens up to allow her gradually to perceive the body of Amphilanthus: "Pamphilia adventured, and pulling hard at a ring or iron which appeared, opend the great stone, when a doore shewed entrance" (583). Pamphilia's passage through the stone entrance and then the door inside prepares us for an extensive process of exposure that continues until Amphilanthus's heart is revealed to her:

> . . . but within she might see a place like a Hell of flames and fire, and as if many walking and throwing pieces of men and women up and downe the flames, partly burnt, and they still stirring the fire, and more brought in, *and the longer she looked, the more she discernd*, yet all as in the hell of deceit, at last she saw Musalina sitting in a Chaire of Gold, a Crowne on her head, and Lucenia holding a sword, which Musalina tooke in her hand, and before them Amphilanthus was standing, with his heart ript open, and Pamphilia written in it, Musalina ready with the point of the sword to conclude all, by razing that name out, and so his heart as the wound to perish. (583; my emphasis)

Pamphilia must "discern" each of the layers of activity within the Hell of Deceit, a process of unlayering which Fumerton has detailed in descriptions of the miniature.[30] In this process, Pamphilia must also visually strip away the images of the two women whom Amphilanthus stands "before." At the heart of the scene, in the heart of Amphilanthus, Pamphilia finally discovers a verbal representation of her self — her name.[31] Earlier sequences in the romance suggest the link here between Pamphilia's "self" and her name: since she is defined in the text as constancy, who earlier "metamorphos[ed] her self into [Pamphilia's] breast" (169), her constant love for Amphilanthus is her identity. Here, she faces the erasure of her name from his heart. As she reads her name, so do we: both the character and the reader identify her sense of self as her inscription within his heart. In the first of a series of distinctions between Pamphilia's and Amphilanthus's visions, he sees "his name," but the text does not have us read "Amphilanthus" within her heart as we read Pamphilia's in his: "his heart ript open, and Pamphilia written in it" (583). Her entrance into this dream-like space consequently exceeds the earlier sequence — now the movement inward uncovers the interiority of Pamphilia's character. At last, the reader is shown the heart, that very symbol of "inwardness" deferred in Urania's cave and in the Throne of Love.

And yet this glimpse of the self proves to be fundamentally threatening. Images of dismemberment, "pieces of men and women" thrown about the cave, are present only in Pamphilia's vision (583). Maureen Quilligan suggests that "the dismembering tradition of the Petrarchan blazon may also be literalized in the bits and pieces of lovers' flesh being tossed about in the flames."[32] Nancy Vickers, in "Diana Described: Scattered Women and Scattered Rhyme," offers a cogent reading of fragmentation in Petrarchan verse, focusing on Petrarch's re-writing of the Actaeon myth: "If the speaker's 'self' (his text, his 'corpus') is to be unified, it would seem to require the repetition of [Laura's] dismembered image."[33] But, unlike Petrarch, Wroth is unable to construct such female unity by projecting the fear of fragmentation onto another (male) body. These "pieces" of men and women are part of the horror for Pamphilia: as this scene moves towards an expression of her autonomous and unified subjectivity, fracture, division, and literal dismemberment strew her visual path. Yet an even greater threat exists for the female subject and the expression of female interiority in this passage. At the moment Pamphilia sees her self within her own name inscribed in Amphilanthus's heart, "Musalina [is] ready with the point of the sword to conclude all, by razing that name out" (583). At the moment the female self is discovered, it is threatened with its own extinction, its literal erasure or "razing."

The threat to Pamphilia — Musalina's eradicating sword — is reinforced by Amphilanthus's complementary vision. His vision begins with a battle against a group of armed men; one of those killed by Amphilanthus is transformed into Pamphilia after he has slain the apparently threatening opponent. This body is then transported into the same cave which was the site of Pamphilia's vision; Amphilanthus attempts to regain her body from the cave much as Pamphilia pursued Amphilanthus. Unable initially to gain entrance, he vows that the cave "should be his monument, being the richest, her heart inclosing him, and there would he dye" (655). While in her vision "Amphilanthus was standing," Pamphilia's body is slain once before our and Amphilanthus's eyes, and then presented to our view in a sustained, and theatrically framed, anatomy of her body: "A Ring of iron hee then saw, which pulling hard, opened the stone; there did he perceive perfectly within it Pamphilia dead, lying within an arch, her breast open and in it his name made, in little flames burning like pretty lamps which made the letters, as if set round with diamonds, and so cleare it was, as hee distinctly saw the letters ingraven at the bottome in Characters of bloud" (655). As in the Urania episode, Pamphilia's heart is initially equated with this stone monument—interiority is yet again projected onto a cave transformed into a "monumental" space. Amphilanthus then gains entrance to the cave where Pamphilia's heart is exposed to view and his name is discernible there.

As in Pamphilia's complementary vision, the passage relies upon a series of unveilings, but the representation of the subjected lover differs dramatically. Pamphilia's dead body is immediately apparent to Amphilanthus. Nothing blocks his view of her heart—on which lies his name. What he must pass through is a description of an internal flaying of her body. Amphilanthus's heart was "ript open," a violent moment of exposure to be sure, but his experience of "reading" Pamphilia's body and heart is the sequential act of unlayering burning, encased, and finally engraved letters in "bloud." The flames give way to letters which appear as diamonds, and finally become "Characters of bloud" (655). Amphilanthus's name remains intact, unthreatened. No figure threatens to "raze" his name from her heart. The allegory implicit in this vision, buttressed by the imagery, assures us that Pamphilia will remain constant even in death: his name can never be stricken from hers. Consequently, his selfhood, as represented in this scene, is not threatened by exposure as is Pamphilia's.

In fact, the passage delves so deeply "into" her body that the fate of his "self" is offset in the scene by the unrelenting violence enacted onto her body. The aestheticizing of Pamphilia's body and the location of Amphilanthus's name within her heart highlights — rather than conceals — the violence of this act of engraving. And the violence of this flaying process complements the fate of her body in scenes previous to this vision of her heart. Amphilanthus has seen her "slaine, and by his hand" before the entrance into the Hell of Deceit, and then is shown her dead body: the amount of violence directed onto her body is much higher than what we see in her vision of him. She sees "her Deares Armour and Sword" and his dead horse, but never his dead body. Nor is the text explicit about Amphilanthus's future as he stands in Pamphilia's dream with Musalina ready to "raz[e] that name out, and so his heart as the wound to perish" (583); whether this threatens his life or only the love he has for Pamphilia remains unclear. Further, no images of dismemberment haunt his glimpse within the cave. The vision provided to Amphilanthus directs violence away from him, focusing it instead onto the receding layers of Pamphilia's body. Instead of scattering him, the text inverts the gender violence in Petrarch's technique. Fragmentation and violence are enacted onto the body and "self" of Pamphilia in order to protect him. Once again, he is protected from the violence to which Pamphilia is exposed in both scenes.

How do we explain the distinctions between what initially appear as parallel visions within this Book 4 episode? The multiplied acts of violence, as well as the more detailed exposure and division of Pamphilia's body and "self," resonate with Belsey's discussion of the inability of women to possess a unified and stable subjectivity. Consequently, the female character is subjected to a sight of her own violent end, even a view of her own dismemberment. If writing the female subject results in such visions, what is the effect on the female subject writing the text? This tableau of a dismembered, fragmented Pamphilia has powerful implications for Wroth, particularly since Pamphilia serves as a figure for Wroth throughout the *Urania*. Subjectivity and the act of writing are central in the romance for both characters and their creator. The rooms in which Urania and Pamphilia find themselves are often the same rooms of literary tradition through which Wroth herself had to pass. As Maureen Quilligan has discussed, the opening sequence of the romance illustrates Urania's passage through the tradition of Sir Philip Sidney's *Arcadia*. In addition to employing the Sidney family name on the frontispiece, Wroth is writing where her uncle left off: Urania is the first mentioned, though never seen, character in Philip Sidney's *Arcadia*.[34]

Yet Wroth also employs a technique of fragmenting her own influences. Her reliance on literary structures produced by men posed a significant quandary. By adapting such traditions or earlier texts, Wroth potentially could be absorbed by these structures, and her own attempts at writing "razed." Unlike her aunt, then, Wroth rejected translating male writers and turned instead to an original romance. But by turning away from a male tradition of writing, she threatened to fragment her authority, even lose the cultural position that allowed her to speak at all. The now famous publication history of the *Urania* illustrates how real the danger of dispensing with tradition was for a seventeenth-century woman writer. Lord Denny, upon the publication of *The Countesse of Mountgomeries Urania*, attacked Wroth in a poem as a "Hermaphrodite in show, in deed a monster," and in a prose addendum suggested that she "redeem the time with writing as large a volume of heavenly lays and holy love as you have of lascivious tales and amorous toyes; that at the last you may follow the example of your virtuous and learned aunt," the Countess of

Pembroke.[35] For Denny, when Wroth moved outside appropriate tradition — respectable women translated religious material — she transformed herself into a sexually incoherent beast, the hermaphrodite.[36]

Despite such cultural expectations about women's writing, Wroth nonetheless moved beyond appropriate female spaces and chose to pass through another powerful literary structure — Edmund Spenser's *The Faerie Queene*. Wroth employs central motifs from the Book 3 Busirane episode in her narrative. Busirane's enchanted space, where he binds and tortures Amoret, is variously described as a "Castle," a "house," a "secret den," and a "deepe dungeon." These distinct traits of Busirane's residence, along with the plot elements of the Busirane sequence, are divided between Wroth's Throne of Love and Hell of Deceit episodes. She adapts the architectural lay-out of Busirane's house to the three towers of the Throne of Love. Pamphilia moves through the towers much as Britomart passed through the House of Busirane: Britomart enters at the "Castle gate," moves into the "utmost rowme," into "the next roome," and finally penetrates "the inner roome" where Amoret is bound.[37] Pamphilia also ends the enchantment of the Throne of Love, passing through three towers which are a match for the three rooms in Busirane's house. In the Hell of Deceit episode, alternately, Wroth integrates the cave-like characteristics of Busirane's abode along with images evocative of the enchanter's possession of and violence toward Amoret. The words written at the entrance to the cave, "This no wonder's of much waight, / 'Tis the hell of deepe deceit," (656) recall the confusing instructions directed to Britomart and to the reader in the Busirane sequence. Told to "Be bold, Be bold," and then "Be not to Bold," the reader and the heroine are given interpretative guidelines, just as the poem or riddle presented to Pamphilia offers an inscription which guides her reading of the Hell of Deceit vision. Further, the "letters ingrauen at the bottome in Characters of bloud" which scar Pamphilia's heart are a re-imagining of Busirane's charms produced through Amoret's body.

Wroth thus establishes a conscious intertextuality between her two episodes and Spenser's poem. And yet her episodes fragment her source. Wroth separates the "castle" aspect of Busirane's abode from its cave-like or dungeon traits as she divides Spenser's episode between Books 1 and 4 of her own narrative. The resolution of the Throne of Love enchantment is significantly dilated, since she leaves it unreconciled through much of Book 1. This act of fragmentation is significantly extended in the Book 4 episode. While Scudamore is not allowed to see Amoret's torture at the hands of Busirane, the reader sees a single scene through the eyes of Britomart. Scudamore's visual access to Amoret might be blocked — since he is not allowed within Busirane's castle — but his perception of Amoret's experience is neither inverted, distinct, nor alternate to hers. Amphilanthus and Pamphilia, in contrast, experience opposed visions while physically separated. In every instance, Wroth produces spaces or gaps when rewriting Spenser's story line. Spenser may revise the original ending of Book 3, transforming the hermaphroditic union of Amoret and Scudamore into an unresolved story of separated lovers, but Wroth suggests a more fundamental distance in her fragmented version: the alternate visions that Amphilanthus and Pamphilia experience imply that men and women cannot share a single vision of the pains of love.

While Wroth's rewriting of the Busirane episode points towards her increasingly fragmented representation of the relationship between the sexes, this fragmentation of her "source" allows her to make the material her own. In reworking Spenser's scene, Wroth constructs a space for female creative power. The Hell of Deceit offers a structure through which the self is discovered. Yet this site is natural space — a cave — not constructed or overlaid by the (masculine) labor which characterized the "rooms" through which Urania first passed. More significantly, these visions have been created by an enchantress, Musalina. Wroth's re-writing of masculine tradition, then, transforms male-constructed spaces into sites of female creativity. Perissus's poem, in which Urania finds her "selfe," actually has been authored by Wroth herself. And, in both of the *Urania* episodes for which Spenser is a source, the creative force behind the structures becomes a woman. Venus builds the Throne of Love just as Musalina designs the visions of the Hell of Deceit. In perhaps her most significant revision, then, Wroth replaces the male creative force behind Spenser's original episode (Spenser and Busirane) with figures of creating women.

As we have seen in the Hell of Deceit, this very expression of self, this discovery of a space outside of constructions by men, also carries a threat within itself. Pamphilia's name and self, which are faced with erasure, have already illustrated such danger. In constructing a space for female subjectivity, Wroth also represents the potential division, even dismemberment, of the female subject. But, more significantly, she represents the potential for that same division in herself. Wroth is the creative power behind Musalina; as with "Perissus's" poem, she actually constructs the scene attributed to the enchantress. This figure of a powerful, creating woman simultaneously threatens to dismember another image of Wroth in the narrative: Pamphilia. Commentators on the *Urania* have unanimously agreed that Pamphilia is a figure for Mary Wroth within the romance, an interpretation buttressed by numerous biographical parallels between author and character. Wroth thus becomes both Musalina and Pamphilia, the figure Musalina attempts to erase. The act of writing, the act of expressing the female self, thus causes that very self to splinter into the figure of the writing woman who is punished and the figure of a woman who participates in, even constructs, this scene of violence. Wroth's attempts to create and express her position as an autonomous, speaking subject threaten to erase that very self constituted by the act of writing.

The Book 4 episode suggests the state of division Catherine Belsey identifies within the Renaissance female subject: while men of the period were gradually becoming defined as unified subjects, "single . . . stable" and "continuous," women, though "able to speak [and] to take up a subject-position in discourse[,] . . . were nonetheless enjoined to silence."[38] Yet Wroth's strategies for negotiating the demands of male tradition offer her a path, though treacherous, out of the silence that underlies Belsey's formulation. While women may have found a "place in discourse" within the domestic sphere,[39] Wroth employs domestic settings — interior space, buildings — as a strategy for establishing a public, publishing voice: in conjunction with the *Urania*, she published a full-length sonnet sequence and circulated in manuscript both a pastoral play and a continuation of the *Urania*.[40] Like Bess of Hardwick's public presentation of her estate with its visually resonating initials, the "construction" of domestic spaces offered strategies for women who wished to create. While Mary Wroth's strategy may recall the actions of the Countess of Shrewsbury, her use of such domestic spaces is biographically significant. As a self-identified Sidney, Wroth was aligned with a series of architectural spaces which had been used — even transformed — so that they constituted and consolidated family power: as Don Wayne has shown in *Pensurst*, Henry Sidney's modifications to the family estate valorized the Sidneys by fusing their virtue with the estate's pedigree.[41] And Mary Sidney's commission of Houghton Conquest evidences how the traditional manipulation of architectural space by members of the Sidney family was open to re-configurations by the women of the family. While Mary Sidney was "building" Houghton Conquest from 1619 to 1620, Mary Wroth turned to literary construction. Wroth's use of structures throughout the *Urania*, then, becomes a powerful (if self-threatening) strategy for the expression of female subjectivity, a strategy that appears to have been fashioned out of the everyday practices of the Sidney family.

Notes

1. Mark Girouard gives a fuller account of this story in *Robert Smythson and the Elizabethan Country House* (New Haven, Conn.: Yale University Press, 1983). See his chapter on Hardwick Hall, pp. 144–62.
2. Bess of Hardwick first rebuilt the Old Hall; she began this in 1587. Girouard argues that her anger at her third husband and her eldest son, who had sided with Lord

Shrewsbury, prompted her to make Hardwick "the dynastic seat of the Cavendish family, in favour of her second son, William" (*Robert Smythson*, p. 144).

3. Girouard, *Robert Smythson*, p. 146.

4. Don Wayne, "'A More Safe Survey': Social-Property Relations, Hegemony, and the Rhetoric of Country Life," in *Sounding of Things Done: Essays in Early Modern Literature in Honor of S. K. Heninger Jr.*, ed. Peter E. Medine and Joseph Wittreich (Newark: University of Delaware Press, 1997), p. 280.

5. Girouard's own comments reinforce the idea that Bess of Hardwick had to work through a male architect, although his remarks actively devalue her ideas while elevating Smythson's. Old Hardwick, built first, "gives the impression that Lady Shrewsbury acted as her own architect, for it has little of the drama or bold grouping of Worksop," built by Smythson. In describing Hardwick, Girouard goes farther: "Many of the idiosyncrasies of its planning are probably due to her; it was probably she who increased the height of the towers in the middle of building, and who ordered the corner colonnades to be abandoned. But one only has to compare the old with the new Hardwick to see how Smythson transformed her overbearing and somewhat crude preferences into a work of art" (*Robert Smythson*, p. 161).

6. Mark Girouard, *Hardwick Hall, Derbyshire: A History and Guide* (London: The National Trust, 1976), pp. 24–27.

7. Wayne, "Safe Survey," p. 28.

8. Alice T. Friedman, "Architecture, Authority, and the Female Gaze: Planning and Representation in the Early Modern Country House," *Assemblage* 18 (1992): 41–61, p. 50.

9. Ibid., p. 55.

10. Josephine Roberts, "Textual Introduction," *The First Part of the Countess of Montgomery's Urania*, ed. Josephine A. Roberts (Binghamton, N.Y: Center for Medieval and Early Renaissance Studies, 1995), p. cvi. Though this is not definitive evidence, other aristocratic authors, including the Countess of Pembroke, did provide direction in the composition of their frontispieces.

11. A number of critics have discussed the role of literary genealogy, including Maureen Quilligan in "The Constant Subject: Instability and Authority in Wroth's Urania Poems" (*Soliciting Interpretation: Literary Theory and Seventeenth-Century English Poetry*, ed. Elizabeth D. Harvey and Katharine Eisaman Maus [Chicago: University of Chicago Press, 1990] p. 307), and Mary Ellen Lamb in *Gender and Authorship in the Sidney Circle* [Madison: University of Wisconsin Press, 1990], pp. 149–50). Also see Maureen Quilligan's exploration of the role of the family romance as an enabling condition for Wroth in "Lady Mary Wroth: Female Authority and the Family Romance" (*Unfolded Tales: Essays on Renaissance Romance*, ed. George M. Logan and Gordon Teskey [Ithaca, N.Y.: Cornell University Press, 1989]).

12. Orest Ranum, "The Refuges of Intimacy," in *A History of Private Life*, ed. Philippe Ariès and George Duby, Vol. 3, *Passions of the Renaissance*, ed. Roger Chartier, trans. Arthur Goldhammer (Cambridge, Mass.: Belknap Press of Harvard University Press, 1989), p. 210.

13. For an extensive discussion of the shift in architecture and the use of decorative space, see Ranum, "The Refuges of Intimacy" in Ariès, *A History of Private Life: The Passions of the Renaissance*. Also see Mark Girouard's *Life in the English Country House: A Social and Architectural History* (New Haven, Conn.: Yale University Press, 1978).

Patricia Fumerton's *Cultural Aesthetics: Renaissance Literature and the Practice of Social Ornament* (Chicago: University of Chicago Press, 1991) explores the connection between the creation of these spaces and the rise of a modern notion of the self. In particular, see Chapters 3 and 4. Alan Stewart's article "The Early Modern Closet Discovered" offers a more specific reading of the use of closets in the early modern period (*Representations* 50 [Spring 1995]: 76–100).

14. Stewart, "The Early Modern Closet," p. 83.

15. Ibid., p. 81. Stewart argues that, in the process of physically retreating into their closets, women needed to publicly expose the self in order to express that self: "For when Lady Margaret goes into her closet, she does not merely withdraw to privacy, but rather she enacts that withdrawal publicly, and records it textually, indicating a space of secrecy outside the knowledge of the household" (81). Fumerton sees this process as occurring for both men and women. Her research is much more extensive, though Stewart's gender distinctions have interesting implications for Wroth's romance.

16. Stewart, "The Early Modern Closet," p. 83.

17. Catherine Belsey, *The Subject of Tragedy: Identity and Difference in Renaissance Drama* (London: Methuen, 1985), p. 40.

18. The construction of female subjectivity in Wroth's work, particularly her sonnets, has been the topic of numerous studies, including Jeff Masten's "'Shall I turne blabb?': Circulation, Gender, and Subjectivity in Mary Wroth's Sonnets," in *Reading Mary Wroth: Representing Alternatives in Early Modern England*, ed. Naomi J. Miller and Gary Waller (Knoxville: University of Tennessee Press, 1991) and Nona Fienberg's "Mary Wroth and the Invention of Female Poetic Subjectivity" in the same volume. These studies generally rely on the work of Francis Barker's *The Tremulous Private Body* (London: Methuen, 1984) and Catherine Belsey. Masten and Fienberg both emphasize the sonnet over the prose romance as the site of the growth of subjectivity.

19. Belsey, *The Subject of Tragedy*, pp. 149–50.

20. Mary Wroth, *The First Part of the Countess of Montgomery's Urania*, ed. Josephine Roberts (Binghamton, N.Y.: Center for Medieval and Early Renaissance Studies, 1995), p. 1. All subsequent references will be to this edition.

Maureen Quilligan suggests, in her reading of Urania's "echo" sonnet on the opening page of the romance, that "Wroth's use of Petrarchan discourse in which a female speaker laments her own lack of self-presence paradoxically works to insert that female into the generically well-defined position of the Petrarchan speaker" ("The Constant Subject," p. 312). Quilligan argues that Urania "is momentarily free to define her subject position by all its lacks" (p. 312). The echo sonnet serves as another attempt to reconstruct Urania's lost sense of self. I see that as primarily accomplished by Urania's passage through structure, while Quilligan reads the echo sonnet as creating some space for Urania's "self," however tenuous.

21. Catherine Belsey states that "In the family as in the state women had no single, unified, fixed position from which to speak" (*The Subject of Tragedy*, p. 160). But while the family may not have offered women such a subject position, it did offer them a cultural identity, as commentary on Wroth's use of her Sidney identity repeatedly emphasizes.

22. Catherine Belsey discusses these paintings in *The Subject of Tragedy*, pp. 149–52, and Jonathan Goldberg considers them in "Fatherly Authority: The Politics of

Stuart Family Images," in *Rewriting the Renaissance: The Discourses of Sexual Difference in Early Modern Europe*, ed. Margaret W. Ferguson, Maureen Quilligan, and Nancy Vickers (Chicago: University of Chicago Press, 1986), pp. 21–22.

23. Belsey, p. 35.

24. Ranum, p. 233.

25. Fumerton, p. 69.

26. As William Blissett has commented in "Caves, Labyrinths, and the *Faerie Queene*," it is very unusual for a labyrinth to be a natural formation (in *Unfolded Tales: Essays in the Renaissance Romance*, ed. George M. Logan and Gordon Teskey [Ithaca, N.Y.: Cornell University Press, 1989]).

27. Lamb, *Gendered Authorship*, p. 170.

28. Elaine Beilen, *Redeeming Eve: Women Writers of the English Renaissance* (Princeton, N.J.: Princeton University Press, 1987), p. 232.

29. Fumerton, *Cultural Aesthetics*, p. 74.

30. Fumerton's work discusses the sixteenth-century craze in miniatures, which re-occur frequently throughout Wroth's romance. One of the dominant motifs in recent criticism on Wroth is her purposeful anachronism: she is writing in a style, and clearly using styles, that were popular twenty years before. As should be clear, Fumerton's work on the layering of the miniature and the sonnet has greatly influenced my reading of Wroth's prose romance.

31. Joel Fineman's "Shakespeare's *Will*: The Temporality of Rape," *Representations* 20 (Fall 1987): 25–76 argues that William Shakespeare inscribes his own name into the text of *The Rape of Lucrece* through repeating M's and W's in a "cross-coupling orthographics" (50). He claims that "Shakespeare's person is itself marked out, and thereby subjectively constituted, by the literal chiasmus of MW" (51). A much more historically grounded study on the role of first names and their connection to subjectivity is clearly needed.

32. Maureen Quilligan, "Feminine Endings: The Sexual Politics of Sidney's and Spenser's Rhyming," in *The Renaissance Englishwoman in Print: Counterbalancing the Canon*, ed. Anne M. Haselkorn and Betty S. Travitsky (Amherst: University of Massachusetts Press, 1990), p. 321.

33. Nancy Vickers, "Diana Described: Scattered Women and Scattered Rhyme," in *Writing and Sexual Difference*, ed. Elizabeth Abel (Chicago: University of Chicago Press, 1980), p. 102.

34. See Quilligan, "Family Romance," pp. 259–61. Mary Ellen Lamb's *Gender and Authorship in the Sidney Circle* discusses the interplay among the numerous writers in the Sidney family.

35. Josephine Roberts, ed., *The Poems of Lady Mary Wroth* (Baton Rouge: Louisiana State University Press, 1983), pp. 33–34.

36. See Lamb, pp. 156–59 for a more extensive discussion of the sexual implications of this poem and Wroth's response.

37. Quilligan and Beilen have both remarked on the resemblance between the two Wroth episodes and Spenser's Busirane sequence. Quilligan suggests that Wroth's rewriting of the Busirane scene is a reversal of the aspects of the Spenser episode. While Pamphilia's half of this dream certainly is reversed in almost every way, the torture of the female continues in Amphilanthus's dream. My discussion of a "division" of Spenser's episode is thus an attempt to accommodate both halves of Wroth's Hell of Deceit.

38. Belsey, *The Subject of Tragedy*, p. 149.

39. Ibid., p. 193.

40. For Belsey, women find this "place in discourse" in the late seventeenth century, as the humanist construction of the self turns towards liberalism. See "Finding a Place" in *The Subject of Tragedy*.

41. Don Wayne, *Pensurst: The Semiotics of Place and the Poetics of History* (Madison: University of Wisconsin Press, 1984).

8

The Buck Basket, the Witch, and the Queen of Fairies

The Women's World of Shakespeare's Windsor

Richard Helgerson

IN 1607, just four years after his accession to the English throne, James I commissioned John Norden to produce a survey of "the honor of Windsor," the royal domain that included Windsor Castle and the surrounding forests. What we see in Norden's beautifully drawn and colored maps is the visual equivalent of a country house poem: an estate wholly amenable to the pleasure and possession of its proprietor. The most detailed of the maps is a perspective view of the royal manor house, Windsor Castle itself (Figure 1). The other sixteen maps show large or small parcels of the park and forest lands, all carefully delineating what most interested this sports-minded king: the opportunities the land afforded for hunting. The general map lists kinds of deer that can be found in each part of the domain, and other maps, like the map of Little Park (Figure 2), show some of those deer along with an occasional hunting dog. Seeing images like these, one might think of Gamage Copse in Ben Jonson's poem "To Penshurst," "That never fails to serve the seasoned deer," or of "the loud stag" in another of Jonson's country house poems, "oft rousèd for [King James's] sport."[1] In the closely related genres of estate survey and country house poem, the land and all its features belong to the lords who own it, both to the individual landlords and to their liege lord, the king — who was, of course, himself the direct owner under God of the honor of Windsor.

But look again at Norden's maps of Windsor Castle and Little Park. Over at the far right-hand side of each, crowded around the west end of the castle close, is a space that belongs neither to the king in the way that the rest of what we see on the map does nor to a genre like the estate survey or country house poem. Flaring out from the castle walls, dwarfed by castle and park, are the few

Figure 1. View of Windsor Castle, from John Norden's "Description of the Honor of Windsor," 1607. Harleian MS 3749. By permission of the British Library.

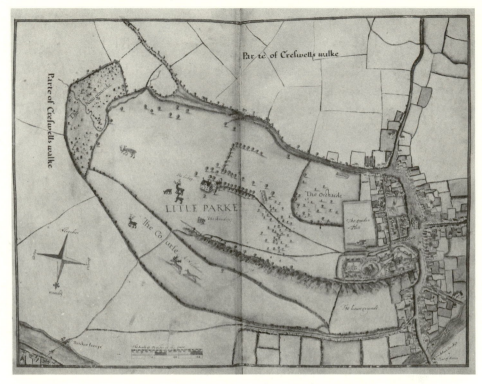

Figure 2. Little Park and the castle and town of Windsor, from John Norden's "Description of the Honor of Windsor," 1607. Harleian MS 3749. By permission of the British Library.

house-and-shop-lined streets of the town of Windsor — a borough town since 1277, with its own courts and responsibility for its own affairs, a town whose charter, and thus whose relative autonomy, had been renewed by King James in the first year of his reign. If Windsor Castle and Windsor Forest might suit a country house poem, the town of Windsor is a more likely subject for a play in the classical tradition of "new comedy," a play about the doings of urban dwellers of middling status. And, of course, there exists just such a play: Shakespeare's *Merry Wives of Windsor*.

Though it may seem a large jump from an estate survey like Norden's to a comedy like Shakespeare's, the first provides a surprisingly apt introduction to the second. For without the proximity of Windsor Castle the action of *Merry Wives* would be unthinkable. Shakespeare's play concerns not only the middle-class inhabitants of Windsor but, more importantly, their relation to their royal neighbor. The play features, however indirectly, both town and crown, both the burgher household and the royal state. In *The Merry Wives of Windsor*, the marginality we see on Norden's maps finds narrative and dramatic expression. But — and this has not been sufficiently noticed in discussions of the play — that marginality is also contested. As well as existing in relation to state and court, Shakespeare's Windsor provides a local and domestic alternative to the national power figured in Windsor Castle, though an alternative generated, as I will suggest, more by narrative accident and theatrical opportunism than by ideological design.[2]

History and Shakespeare's *Merry Wives*

The Merry Wives of Windsor has usually been read in terms of another, though closely connected, marginality: its marginal relation to Shakespeare's great sequence of chronicle history plays. Why this should be so is suggested by the title page of its first edition, the "bad" quarto of 1602: *A Most Pleasant and Excellent Conceited Comedy of Sir John Falstaff and the Merry Wives of Windsor*. Sir John Falstaff, as any Elizabethan playgoer would have known, was the famously dissolute companion of Prince Hal in Shakespeare's *Henry IV*. To bring him into a domestic comedy was to put that comedy and the world it represents in relation — however uncertain the nature of the relation — with the history plays and the world they represent. But if we take that world of history to be what both Shakespeare and the humanist historians of his generation took it to be — namely, the world of high politics, war, and monarchic government — the Windsor of Shakespeare's *Merry Wives* has still other relations to it.[3] The play's first speech mentions Star Chamber; the Privy Council comes up a few speeches later; and it is not long before we are hearing about the king and parliament. Nor is this casual intimacy with the leading institutions and persons of state power only a matter of the play's characters and setting. After telling us that this "pleasant and excellent conceited comedy" was written "by William Shakespeare," the title page continues, "As it hath been divers times acted by the right honorable my lord chamberlain's servants, before her majesty, and elsewhere." On at least one occasion, the court *was* just off-stage. The queen was a member of the audience.

    What brought this comic tale of jealousy, wit, and attempted seduction to the royal presence? Legend has it that Elizabeth was herself responsible. According to Nicholas Rowe, writing in 1709, more than a century after the play's first production, the queen "was so well pleased with that admirable character of Falstaff in the two parts of *Henry the Fourth* that she commanded

[Shakespeare] to continue it for one play more, and to show him in love."[4] More recently, and with considerably better evidence, another royal occasion has been proposed, the 1597 ceremony at which Lord Hunsdon, the lord chamberlain and patron of Shakespeare's company, was initiated into the Order of the Garter. Windsor was not only the "supremest place of the great English kings," but also "the Garter's royal seat."[5] The Chapel Royal at Windsor Castle was then, as it still is today, the chief gathering place of the Order, the place where the Garter Knights post their arms and have their stalls. A play set in Windsor, one whose final scene includes a blessing on Windsor Castle and "the several chairs of order," was thus neatly fitted for a Garter Feast.[6]

Or was it? What, after all, were the queen, the court, and the Garter Knights invited to see at their solemn banquet? Not a heroic history of knightly triumph, some piece of England's crusading and conquering past, but rather a comic tale of knightly defeat: the story of Sir John Falstaff's frustrated attempt to seduce two merry wives of Windsor and get his hands on their husbands' wealth. Was this in any sense the courtly audience's own defeat, as a history of knightly triumph would certainly have been felt to be their triumph? Probably not. Fat Jack Falstaff was hardly a figure with whom monarch or court or Garter Knights would have identified. Yet, in an odd way, such identification would not have been far wrong. Carnival king and lord of misrule in the First Part of *Henry IV*, drinking companion and surrogate father to the prince of Wales, Falstaff does represent the apex of royal power, even if only negatively. He stands for the king. No wonder that the *Merry Wives*'s Host of the Garter Inn should call him "an emperor — Caesar, Keiser, and Pheazar" (1.3.9–10) or that he should liken himself to Jove metamorphosed for love. Falstaff *is* an emperor of sorts, a mock-god descended from a mock-heaven. When he comes to Windsor, history comes with him.

Falstaff is not the only outsider in Shakespeare's Windsor. With him, he brings his page, Robin, and his followers, Bardolph, Pistol, and Nym. There too are Justice Shallow, his cousin Slender, and Slender's man Simple, all from the county of Gloucester; the Welsh parson, Hugh Evans; the French physician, Doctor Caius; some unnamed Germans, who never get on stage but who do steal the Host's horses; and Fenton, a gentleman and companion of "the wild Prince and Poins" (3.2.73). Though Windsor is as firmly and concretely realized as any dramatic setting Shakespeare ever created, it is nevertheless a place invaded by strangers. *Merry Wives* is about that invasion, about the relation between Windsor and its "others." The local and domestic are not only staged for the entertainment of a national audience, an audience that included the queen and the court, they are also engaged in a series of actions that involve a much broader national and even international community. That involvement has a double target: property and women's bodies. Falstaff pursues the wives and wealth of Windsor, while Slender, Caius, and Fenton compete for the love and fortune of one of Windsor's daughters. Look at the first of these plots and you see the local and domestic successfully repelling the invader. Look at the second and you see the invader — or at least one of the invaders — carrying off his desired prize. The Windsor wives, Mistress Ford and Mistress Page, utterly defeat the carnival king who seeks to woo them, but the Windsor daughter, Anne Page, happily gives herself to another courtly marauder.

Both actions are essential to Shakespeare's construction of English domesticity and English localism. If the local-*cum*-domestic can overcome the adulterous incursion of the outside world, its future will nevertheless be determined by marriage with an outsider. "Stand not amazed," says a Windsor neighbor to the parents whose own schemes for their daughter's wedding have been so thoroughly frustrated.

> Here is no remedy.
> In love the heavens themselves do guide the state.
> Money buys lands, and wives are sold by fate. (5.5.231–33)

The union of young Fenton and Mistress Anne Page is a wonder. Government and commerce may be ruled by reason; "wives are sold by fate." Though Anne's father protests that "the gentleman is of no having," that "he kept company with the wild Prince and Poins," that "he is of too high a region," that "he knows too much," and insists that "he shall not knit a knot in his fortunes with the finger of my substance" (3.2.71–75), his protests and insistences are of no avail. "What cannot be eschewed must be embraced" (5.5.237). Thus the play mystifies marriage and, with it, the transfer of Windsor wealth into courtier coffers. Fate and Shakespeare are on Fenton's side.

But they are not on Falstaff's — unless one reads Fenton and Falstaff as types of one another, as Falstaff himself seems to do when he finds consolation for his own defeat in Fenton's victory: "I am glad, though you have ta'en a special stand to strike at me, that [in the case of Fenton] your arrow hath glanced" (5.5.233–34). Falstaff and Fenton are mismatched twins — both companions of "the wild Prince and Poins," both prodigals who have wasted their substance in riotous living, both intent on repairing their decayed fortune with the wealth of Windsor, both convinced that the way to Windsor's wealth passes through the affections of its women. Fenton "smells April and May" (3.2.68–69); Falstaff more nearly resembles "a hodge-pudding . . . old, cold, withered, and of intolerable entrails" (5.5.151–54). But if these obvious differences lead to very different outcomes, Falstaff's story and Fenton's nevertheless remain contrasting versions of the same story, a story of the relation

between the local community and the court, between the middle-class household and the aristocratic state, between Windsor and history.

Watching this twice-told tale, different segments of Shakespeare's audience might have found different reasons for satisfaction. The court would
have applauded Fenton's victory; the town, Falstaff's defeat. But given the way
Shakespeare sets things up, both would in fact have applauded both. Falstaff is
such a preposterous lover, Fenton such an obviously attractive one, that any
outcome other than the one Shakespeare provides would have been shocking.
Yet the very characteristics that determine our response reveal the play's ideology most starkly. When the deck is so obviously stacked, we have a pretty good
idea where the playwright's sympathies lie—in this case with the prodigal
courtier.

More interesting because less clearly predetermined is the way the two
stories are told. The end of each may be obvious even from the beginning, but
the middle isn't. The pursuit of Anne Page spins off plot, subplot, counter-
plot, and by-plot at a vertiginous rate. We need not follow them all, but it is
worth pointing out how they sharpen the sense of Englishness, of the "domestic" in the most common Elizabethan usage—that is, the "home-grown," the
"not foreign." Though Slender and Caius are the rival candidates for Anne
Page's dowry and love, Shakespeare manages to substitute Evans for Slender in
the mock-duel with Caius, thus pitting the play's two prime abusers of "the
King's English" (1.4.5–6) —"*our* English" (3.1.77–78) —against one another.
Among Shakespeare's comedies, *Merry Wives* is not only uniquely English as a
simple fact of its setting; it also works at its Englishness, insists on it, makes it
fundamental to the definition of a domestic space that court and town can
share. That commonality underlies the easy acceptance by both audience and
characters of Fenton's eventual triumph: Anne Page is an English woman;
Fenton, an English man. Their union confirms the union of classes and conditions in a harmonious national state, while the noisy and aggressive confusion
that fills the middle of their story shows what that union is not.

But what then of the other story, the merry wives' rejection and humilia-
tion of Falstaff? If he too represents, though in a comically distorted way, the
king and the court, how is he undone? This, it seems to me, is where things get
most interesting. In the Fenton/Anne Page plot, the principals are largely kept
off stage and out of view. All the attention is given to the futile and misdirected
efforts of the losers. In the end, the lovers turn to their own uses an occasion
that others have prepared. But in the Falstaff plot the merry wives control the
action. They don't simply reject Falstaff. They punish him for his presumption.
And they do so with a series of devices that define them and their world with
extraordinary resonance, complexity, and precision.

In their response to Falstaff, the Windsor wives seize opportunistically on what comes to hand. And so does their author. First a buck basket, then an old woman's hat and gown, and finally a local legend. Each of these devices marks the intersection of the women's world of household and town and the playwright's world of literary kind and convention. And each suggests its own, quite different relation to court, state, and history. As is so often the case — the contrasting fates of Falstaff and Fenton have already supplied an example — Shakespeare teases his audience with ideological multiplicity. But that very multiplicity can suggest better than a more decided narrowing of options the full shape of a contested territory. Early modern domesticity is just such a territory, and the three humiliations of Falstaff have surprisingly much to say about it.

The Buck Basket

Consider the episode of the buck basket. No sooner has Falstaff appeared at Mistress Ford's house in response to her invitation than Mistress Page breaks in to announce that Master Ford, "with all the officers in Windsor," is on his way home "to search for a gentleman that he says is now in the house" (3.3.107–8). Feigning concern for Falstaff's safety, the two women cram him into a buck basket — a kind of laundry basket —, cover him with foul linen, and direct two of Mistress Ford's men to carry him "among the whitsters in Dachet Mead," where by prearrangement the men are to toss him into "the muddy ditch close by the Thames side" (3.3.14–16).

But why a buck basket? In this tale of attempted cuckolding, the name itself has a punning potential Shakespeare is quick to exploit. "Buck!" shouts the jealous Master Ford when he hears of the buck-washing. "I would I could wash myself in the buck! Buck, buck, buck! Ay, buck! I warrent you, buck — and of the season too, it shall appear" (3.3.157–59). But still more resonant than Ford's mistaken identification of himself as a buck-like horned beast is the physical fact of the basket — the physical fact and the material practices associated with it. There is of course the obvious utility of the buck basket as a container that is large enough to hold Falstaff and that can be plausibly carried out of the house. There is also the foul linen: "stinking clothes that fretted in their own grease" (3.5.113–14). A few lines earlier Falstaff had been bragging how his love — a knight's love — proved Mistress Ford "an absolute courtier," worthy to appear "in a semicircled farthingale" (3.3.62–64). The buck basket reverses that redressing. Stuffed in the basket with clothes dirty enough for buck-washing — that is, washing in a boiling alkaline lye — the court intruder himself gets redefined as filth in need of harsh cleansing.[7] And finally there is the gender and status specificity of buck-washing and other laundry work. The buck basket evokes a world of domestic labor, labor presided over by bourgeois wives and performed by servants, like the ones who carry Falstaff off, and by the lower class women who could be found at places like Datchet Mead working as laundresses and whitsters.

But the buck basket also evokes a world of story. Stories like this — stories of an adulterous lover interrupted by a jealous husband and hidden in some odd place — abound in those earlier genres of the domestic: the French fabliau and the Italian novella. Closest to this is the second story in Ser Giovanni's *Il Pecorone*, where the wife hides her lover under a pile of damp laundry. But in *Il Pecorone*, after the husband has completed his futile search and gone off, the wife locks the door, takes the lover from under the wet clothes, dries him by the fire, prepares him a lavish meal, and then leads him to the bedroom, where they spend the night "giving one another that pleasure each desired."[8] What a difference between this lover's fate and Falstaff's, between that night of pleasure and a hot, cramped, greasy, and frightening ride that ends in a muddy ditch!

Shakespeare's Windsor belongs in the company of the fabliau and novella, in a narrative tradition of elaborate and amusing sexual intrigue, but it reforms that tradition, playing deliberately against its most familiar expectations. Both Falstaff and Master Ford think they are in a story like *Il Pecorone*'s. The Windsor wives intend to show them their mistake. "We'll leave a proof, by that which we will do, / Wives may be merry, and yet honest too" (4.2.104–5). But they defend their honesty with much the same domestic prop that served the novella wife to conceal her vice. "This 'tis to be married!" exclaims the still deluded Ford when he learns how Falstaff evaded his search. "This 'tis to have linen and buck-baskets!" (3.5.142–43). A man's house may be his castle, as the familiar sixteenth-century saying had it; it was nevertheless a castle, like the "castle" of his wife's virtue, that she knew better than he and could better use to serve her own purposes.

At the furthest remove from the "public" realm of history and state power is the "private" domain of the domestic interior. And that domain belonged by fact, if not by right, to women. As Mistress Ford says to her husband, "Why, what have you to do . . . with buck-washing?" (3.3.154–56). If a woman chose to open her house, her buck basket, or her body to an outsider, there was little her husband could do to prevent her. "How many women," wrote Boccaccio in the work that followed his cuckold-filled *Decameron*, "have already dared, and dare day in and day out, to hide their lovers from their husband's eyes under baskets or in chests? How many have had them make their entrance silently, in the very same bed as their husbands lie in? . . . And, an even greater insult, there is an infinite number who dare to have their pleasure while their husbands are watching."[9]

So runs the paranoid male fantasy that governs fabliau, novella, and domestic drama alike. The genres that deal most concretely — some would say, most realistically — with the house and the local community are also the genres most obsessed with the crafty manipulation of domestic space by the women who inhabit it. What then are we to make of a play that uses the same female control of domestic space to correct this male fantasy in both its paranoid and its wishful versions? It may seem a long stretch to summon John Milton for an answer, but I can't help thinking of the famous sentence from *Eikonoklastes*: They in whom true virtue "dwell[s] eminently need not kings to make them happy but are architects of their own happiness and whether to themselves or others are not less than kings."[10] The merry wives' "honesty" provides the basis for just such an autonomy, an autonomy that is able not only to expel a licentious mock-king like Falstaff but also to cure the culturally induced jealousy of a domestic patriarch like Ford. "Pardon me, wife," says the chastened Ford, when much later he discovers the truth of the events he has so badly misunderstood. "Henceforth do what thou wilt" (4.4.6). "Do what thou wilt" — which was, not so incidentally, the motto of Rabelais's utopic Abbey of Thélème — might also be the motto of the republican bourgeois household, with of course the unspoken proviso that you must keep your virtue intact.[11]

But before we get to the patriarch's abdication, there is a second episode that significantly complicates this untroubled image of domestic virtue. And that episode is followed in turn by one that calls into question not the virtue of the female-dominated household, but rather its autonomy from royal government.

The Witch

Just as they played on anxieties concerning women's control of domestic space in their first punishment of Falstaff, so in their second Mistress Ford and Mistress Page play on the no less virulent fear of female society, the fear of what women do together. Again Falstaff is lured into the Ford house and again Mistress Page bursts in to announce the imminent and angry arrival of Master Ford. But this time, instead of being hidden in the buck basket, Falstaff is disguised as Mother Prat, Mistress Ford's maid's aunt, "the witch of Brainford" (4.2.98).

Again we may ask: Why this particular device? Like the buck basket, it has a double purpose. It gets Falstaff out of the house, but at the same time gets him punished. As the wives know it will, the appearance of the seeming Mother Prat provokes Ford's wrath, prompting him to beat the real Falstaff. Already Ford had expressed concern about the secret intimacy of his wife and Page's: "I think, if your husband's were dead, you two would marry" (3.2.14–15). And he feared their intimacy would prove his undoing: "Our revolted wives share damnation together" (3.2.39–40). Now the very mention of the old woman brings on another misogynistic tirade:

A witch, a quean, an old cozening quean! Have I not forbid her my house? She comes of errands, does she? We are simple men; we do not know what's brought to pass under the profession of fortune-telling. She works by charms, by spells, by th' figure; and such daubery as this is beyond our element—we know nothing. Come down, you witch, you hag, you. Come down, I say! (4.2.171–79)

What Ford dreads is a world of concerted and secret female power beyond the ken of men. And since, despite Mistress Ford's appeal, none of the other men standing by intervenes to stop his beating of the old woman, it seems likely they share at least enough of his fear to think his action appropriate.[12]

Fears of this sort were endemic to Elizabethan culture. They seep, for example, into *A Warning for Fair Women* (1599), a play based on the real-life murder of a London merchant by his wife and her lover that Shakespeare's company staged a couple of years after *The Merry Wives of Windsor*. Though pamphlet and chronicle accounts had presented the wife's gossip merely as an accessory to the murder, the play transforms her into a witch—a "cunning woman" expert in physic and fortune-telling—and makes her the murder's chief mover. *A Warning for Fair Women* thus does to this story what Ford's over-excited imagination would do to his own household: convert it into a scene of rebellious female enchantment. Nor are Ford's fears wholly misplaced. Falstaff's disguise does, after all, put Mistress Ford and Mistress Page into relation with a figure of occult female power. If they did not actually know the witch of Brainford, if she was not part of their circle of female acquaintance, why would her hat and gown be hanging in Mistress Ford's chamber and why would Ford have had to forbid her his house? In the same way that the buck basket evokes a world of domestic labor in which the Windsor wives are presumed to be actually engaged, the hat and gown evoke a world of witchcraft in which they are no less concretely involved.[13]

That Shakespeare should have linked witchcraft to small-town domestic life seems to me highly suggestive, for nowhere in Elizabethan England, with the obvious exception of religious observance, was state intervention in local and domestic affairs more intensely marked than in the prosecution of witchcraft. The royal government may not itself have been active in initiating such prosecutions, but without laws enacted early in Elizabeth's reign and strengthened early in James's, witchcraft would not have even been punishable in the royal courts.[14] The state established the framework within which witches could be treated as criminals. And, no less important, the witch became, for at least a few decades in the late sixteenth and early seventeenth centuries, one of the state's defining others — a signifying alterity that was put to dramatic use in two plays based on actual cases of witchcraft, as *A Warning for Fair Women* was based on an actual murder: Dekker, Rowley, and Ford's *Witch of Edmonton* (1621) and Thomas Heywood's *Late Lancashire Witches* (1634).

In *The Witch of Edmonton* suspicion of witchcraft, mounting in the minds of her neighbors to a certainty, fastens on the "poor, deformed, and ignorant" Mother Sawyer. Just as a band of these neighbors is about to attack and hang her, an unnamed "justice" intervenes. "Go, go," he says,

pray vex her not. She is a subject,
And you must not be judges of the law
To strike her as you please.[15]

"She is a subject." Here the witch is snatched from the hands of her unruly neighbors, saved from a purely local judgment, by a representative of the crown, who eventually judges her himself and sends her to execution. And, in *The Late Lancashire Witches*, at a comparable moment a gentleman turns to the newly arrested witches and asks, "Have you known so many of the devil's tricks and can be ignorant of that common feat of the old juggler; that is, to leave you all to the law, when you are once seized on by the talons of authority? I'll undertake," he continues, pointing to the officer standing by, "this little demigorgon constable, with these commonwealth characters upon his staff here, is able in spite of all your bugs-words to stave off the grand devil for doing any of you good till you come to his kingdom to him."[16] Not only does the state make witches subject, it also takes from them whatever autonomous strength and authority they may once have exercised. Through the witch, the state demonizes the local and domestic other, only to prove the demystifying power of its own "commonwealth characters."

But what would happen in a domestic world without the state? That is what Heywood imagines in still another of his domestic dramas, *The Wise Woman of Hogsdon* (1604). In the 1590s the prominent puritan divine William Perkins had preached that so-called "good" witches, those wise men and women who used their powers to heal and restore, were still more deserving of death than "bad" witches, for where the latter only destroyed the body, the former enslaved the soul.[17] And in 1604, the year of the play itself, parliament had increased the penalty for a second conviction of the practices most commonly associated with "cunning folk" from life imprisonment to death. Heywood's play takes a very different line. His wise woman is, to be sure, a fraud. The power of demystifying national drama is sufficient to see through this local charade. But, despite her transparent falsity and her well-documented lawlessness, the wise woman nevertheless presides over the comic resolution of the play's various domestic conflicts. The denouement takes place in her house, where all the characters have assembled, and under her supervision. And in the play's last words she is invited as the "chief guest" to the triple nuptial feast which her actions have made possible. The wise woman — "the witch, the beldam, the hag of Hogsdon," as she is called — thus functions as an alternative to the state. Think, for comparison, of Dekker's *Shoemaker's Holiday* (1599), where it is the king himself who appears in the last scene to resolve all problems and who is invited as chief guest to the shoemakers' feast, or think of those plays of domestic crime and witchcraft — *A Warning to Fair Women*, *The Witch of Edmonton*, or *The Late Lancashire Witches* — where a representative of the king's justice comes on in the fifth act to bring resolution and to mark closure. In the absence of such state action, the witch fills the void by supplying her own comic remedy.

How much of all this can we suppose to have been evoked by the disguise the Windsor wives choose for Falstaff? Certainly, the issues themselves — the fear of witchcraft and the use of state power in its suppression — were as pressing in the mid-1590s as they were in later decades when the Dekker and Heywood plays were produced.[18] But, still, this disguise seems like little more than a characteristic piece of theatrical opportunism on Shakespeare's part. Dressing Falstaff as the witch of Brainford, he could, as we have noticed, both get him out of the house and get him beaten, thus embarrassing the jealous Ford, humiliating the rapacious Falstaff, vindicating the witty wives, and maintaining the situation itself for a third and final round. Why should we insist on attaching broad cultural significance to what can be so satisfactorily explained as a brilliantly effective dramatic device? Because it is precisely in choices like these — choices of what works and what doesn't — that the richest meanings inhere. We have already seen how the equally opportunistic buck basket can serve as a powerful synecdoche for a whole range of literary and domestic relations. In a similar way, Falstaff's disguise connects Mistress Ford, Mistress Page, and the female community to which they belong to the illicit and mysterious world of wise women and witches, a world inscribed in both literature and social practice.

In Ford's beating of Falstaff, two actions are performed simultaneously: a man beats a woman, and two women secure the beating of a man. Ford beats (or at least thinks he beats) the witch of Brainford, and Mistresses Ford and Page secure the beating of Falstaff. In the fiction of the play, only the second "really" happens. But both are represented, and both are linked to the broader cultural and political concerns that we have seen associated with witchcraft. The domestic patriarch, worried about the "petty treason" threatened by his and Page's "revolted wives," exercises his authority on the body of the forbidden witch. Where he earlier imagined himself the cuckolded victim in a fabliau or novella, Ford here mistakes himself for a prototype of Master Generous, the deluded husband in *The Late Lancashire Witches*, whose wife and female friends have been consorting with devils. And Falstaff fears that his disguise will bring down on him not only Ford's beating but also the kind of state action that seized on Master Generous's wife: "But that my admirable dexterity of wit . . . delivered me, the knave constable had set me i' th' stocks, i' th' common stocks, for a witch" (4.5.117–20). But the "real" plot of *The Merry Wives of Windsor* is more like that of *The Wise Woman of Hogsdon*.[19] In both, women conspire to expose and reform wayward men. Though Mistress Ford and Mistress Page use no actual magic — the wise woman of Hogsdon uses none either — they do use the appearance of magic, or at least the appearance of a connection to a world of cunning folk and witches, a world, as Ford defines it, of fortune telling, charms, spells, and occult figures. And because the men who get corrected in *The Merry Wives of Windsor* are a carnival king, the comic representative of the court, and a domestic king, the patriarchal governor of the family, we can see shadowed in the women's successful action a reversal of the usual prosecution of local disorderliness by an ordering state. Here the local and the domestic, in the persons of Windsor's merry wives, take control.

The Queen of Fairies

And the women keep control — at least of the Falstaff plot — in the third and last of these episodes. But this episode takes a very different turn. After the success of their first and second schemes, the scheme of the buck basket and the scheme of the witch, Mistress Ford and Mistress Page decide to let their husbands in on what has been happening and to make Falstaff's third punishment a public shaming, for, as Mistress Ford puts it, "Methinks there would be no period to the jest, should he not be publicly shamed" (4.2.221–22). This impulse is deeply rooted in premodern English folk practices, in traditional rites of social control like the skimmington that is staged in Heywood's *Late Lancashire Witches*. And this particular punishment has a still more specific local resonance, based, as it is, on the "old tale" of "Herne the Hunter,/

Sometime a keeper here in Windsor Forest" (4.4.28–29). But as the performance develops, it takes on a generic aura well removed from local practices
and particularities. As numerous critics have remarked, the play of Herne the
Hunter is a masque, a complimentary entertainment of just the sort that
courtly poets were accustomed to staging for the queen. Suddenly, the world
of fabliau, farce, and domestic drama is transformed into a royal pageant.

The switch is signaled by a change in place, from the town of Windsor to
Windsor Park, from the burgher corporation to the royal domain. But there is
also a change in style from prose (*Merry Wives* has a higher proportion of prose
than any other Shakespeare play) to verse. So abrupt is this change that some
scholars have thought that in his rush to satisfy a royal command Shakespeare
simply stuck an earlier masque onto an ill-suited play. This seems an unlikely
and unnecessary supposition, but it does point to the marked change in direction represented by the final scene. Even the time of the play seems to change.
On the strength of Falstaff's presence and Fenton's supposed association with
"the wild prince and Poins," we imagine that *The Merry Wives of Windsor* takes
place in the early fifteenth-century reign of Henry IV. Yet the masque seems
clearly to address Queen Elizabeth and thus suddenly brings to play into the
present — where, of course, it has in fact always been.

But, more than addressing the queen, the masque of Herne the Hunter
puts her on stage, makes her the instrument of its reforming action. Presiding
over these forest solemnities is the "Queen of Fairies," incongruously played
by Mistress Quickly, the merry wives' gossip and fellow conspirator. In the
years following the publication of Spenser's *Faerie Queene*, it would have been
difficult to evoke the Fairy Queen without at least a suspicion that Elizabeth
might be meant. And when Pistol, in the role of Hobgoblin, says, "Our radi-
ant Queen hates sluts and sluttery" (5.5.46), the on-stage queen of fairies and
the off-stage queen of England seem equally implicated. As a result, the Fairy
Queen's punishment of Falstaff, her command that the fairies "Pinch him, and
burn him, and turn him about" and the song she sings as they do it — "Fie on
sinful fantasy!/Fie on lust and luxury!" (5.5.93–101) — is made to come as
much from the royal spectator of this play as from the fictional wives who are
presumed to have written the script. The local and the domestic are thus subsumed into the national, and women who just a few scenes ago were associated
with the witch of Brainford have suddenly acquired a more elevated ally.

That Queen Elizabeth was herself not always free from the taint of witchcraft has been shown by Leah Marcus and Louis Montrose, among others.[20]
Opposites are always in danger of collapsing into one another — particularly in
a case like this where the outlaw rebel and the lawgiving supreme magistrate
are both women. A fairy queen has, moreover, a relation to the occult that is at
least comparable to that of the wise woman or witch. But here difference seems

more significant than similarity. In *The Merry Wives of Windsor*, the local and the domestic, represented most tellingly by Mistress Ford and Mistress Page, are successively linked to contrary poles in the hierarchy of power, to the witch and to the queen. Both work to defeat the intruding Falstaff. The witch draws patriarchal fury down on him; the queen exposes his mock-kingship, his assumption of the lustful prerogatives of Jove, to the force of her more potent monarchy. But there is a great difference between being defeated by women in league with a neighboring wise woman and being defeated by women in league, if only metonymically, with the reigning monarch. In one case, the deeply and irremediably local expels the court-based outsider; in the other, the court itself overcomes a wayward pretender.

In moving from one to the other, Shakespeare takes his representation of local domesticity in a direction made familiar by his own comedies, so many of which end in a scene of recognition or reconciliation presided over by the ruler of whatever kingdom or dukedom the characters happen to find themselves in. But here an ending of this sort may come as a surprise. After all, this play — Shakespeare's only English comedy — has no onstage ruler, no king or duke, to dominate its final scene. But Shakespeare makes up for this lack by having the off-stage queen of England play that role. Perhaps this is what we should have expected from the play's setting in Windsor or from Shallow's opening threat to "make a Star-Chamber matter" of Falstaff's riots. Though Shallow's grievance quickly disappears from the play, the merry wives put his threat into effect for their own reasons and in their own way by haling Falstaff before the court of the Fairy Queen. Once again, as in the domestic dramas of murder and witchcraft, the national claims jurisdiction over the local. Like the witch of Edmonton, Falstaff is a subject and must submit to a royal judgment, a judgment that would come in another and still harsher form at the end of *Henry IV, Part 2*, where the newly crowned King Henry V brutally casts off the misleader of his youth. But in *The Merry Wives of Windsor* the wives themselves remain, as they insist, "the ministers" of Falstaff's correction (4.2.219). That fact gives a double aspect to even this final scene. The Fairy Queen's punishment of Falstaff is *both* the queen of England's correction of an errant knight, one who would have troubled the domestic peace of her common subjects, *and* the commons' rebuke of a mock-king and courtier. And in that second aspect, the domestic buck basket and the local witch are complemented rather than displaced by this midnight shaming ritual.

The last time we were offered a double impression of this sort, in the episode of the witch of Brainford, it was easy enough to see that the wives' chastisement of Falstaff really happened, while Ford's beating of the old woman only seemed to happen. Here things are less clear. What may, however, tip the hermeneutic scales in the direction of a reading that sees the court as the chief ideological beneficiary of the fairy masque is the way in which it is made the occasion not only of Falstaff's final defeat but also of Fenton's ultimate victory. It is during the masque that Fenton's rivals and their Windsor sponsors, including one of the merry wives, are frustrated in their marriage plans for "sweet Anne Page" and that Fenton himself is rewarded. And if we take— as I think there is good reason for doing—Falstaff and Fenton as versions of one another, we can see the defeat, in which both the local community and the queen participate, of the one as cover for the far more significant victory of the other. After wondering whether the "class dynamic" of *Merry Wives of Windsor* should be represented "as the victory of a bourgeois solidarity over the aristocratic court, as the reconciliation of the best of both bourgeois and aristocratic worlds, or as the consolidation of aristocratic power through a populist approach," Peter Erickson concluded that the third provides the most accurate account. "The play resolves class tension in a way that favors aristocratic interests."[21] I think he is right.

I also think Erickson is right in stressing the many connections between *Merry Wives* and Shakespeare's English history plays — not just the sharing of a handful of characters but also (and perhaps more important) the sharing of an emerging nationalist ideology of Englishness.[22] Shakespeare's English comedy is history by other means. Its "private" world of the domestic household and the small-town community is made to serve the purposes of a very "public" theatrical discourse. In this sense, Shakespeare and his audience, both the courtly audience and the public theater audience, may seem the ultimate intruders in domestic Windsor. But domestic Windsor was created to be invaded. Its women and its wealth, its very privacy, were produced for appropriation — Fenton's appropriation and ours. But along the way to that preordained culmination some odd things happen with a buck basket and an old woman's hat and gown, things that threaten to undermine and reverse the court's otherwise easy victory. As Queen Elizabeth watched *The Merry Wives of Windsor*, she was seeing an expression not only of the royal power she represented — power that both disrupts and orders the local and domestic — but also of an alternative to such power, the expression of a local and domestic and female authority that stood for a significantly different England than the one based on patriarchy and royal dynastic succession over which she, as a woman, incongruously ruled.

Notes

1. *Ben Jonson*, ed. C. H. Herford, Percy Simpson, and Evelyn Simpson, 11 vols. (Oxford: Clarendon Press, 1925–52), 8: 94, 97. For a fuller discussion of the relation of estate survey to country house poem, see Richard Helgerson, "Nation or Estate?:

Ideological Conflict in the Early Modern Mapping of England," *Cartographica* 31 (1994): 68–74. I here paraphrase a couple of sentences from this article.

2. Three recent essays have usefully addressed the local specificities of Shakespeare's Windsor: Leah S. Marcus, "Levelling Shakespeare: Local Customs and Local Texts," *Shakespeare Quarterly* 42 (1991): 168–78; Arthur F. Kinney, "Textual Signs in *The Merry Wives of Windsor*," *Yearbook of English Studies* 23 (1993): 206–34; and Rosemary Kegl, "'The Adoption of Abominable Terms': The Insults that Shape Windsor's Middle Class," *ELH* 61 (1994): 253–78. Marcus's essay has been reprinted in her *Unediting the Renaissance: Shakespeare, Marlowe, Milton* (New York: Routledge, 1996), pp. 68–100, and Kegl's in her *The Rhetoric of Concealment: Figuring Gender and Class in Renaissance Literature* (Ithaca, N.Y.: Cornell University Press, 1994), pp. 77–125. Both Marcus and Kinney are much concerned with textual differences between the quarto and folio versions of *Merry Wives*. Like all modern editions, the editions I have used in writing this essay, including the one from which I quote (see note 6 below), are based on the 1623 folio, a text that, in the words of one recent editor, "has a close connection with the first performance of the play." See the "Textual Note" on *Merry Wives* in *The Norton Shakespeare*, ed. Stephen Greenblatt et al. (New York: Norton, 1997), p. 1231.

3. I discuss humanist historiography in relation to another play set in a small English town, the anonymous *Arden of Faversham* (1591), in "Murder in Faversham: Holinshed's Impertinent History" in *The Historical Imagination in Early Modern Britain*, ed. Donald R. Kelley and David Harris Sacks (Cambridge: Cambridge University Press, 1997), pp. 133–158.

4. Quoted by H. J. Oliver in his introduction to the Arden edition of *Merry Wives* (London: Methuen, 1971), p. xlv.

5. From Michael Drayton's *Poly-Olbion*, quoted in William Green, *Shakespeare's Merry Wives of Windsor* (Princeton, N.J.: Princeton University Press, 1962), p. 7. Green develops the argument for *Merry Wives* as "Shakespeare's Garter play" that was first proposed by Leslie Hotson in *Shakespeare Versus Shallow* (Boston: Little, Brown, 1931). For a further elaboration of this argument, one that adventures an implausibly grand thesis, see Giorgio Melchiori, *Shakespeare's Garter Plays*: Edward III *to* Merry Wives of Windsor (Newark: University of Delaware Press, 1994). The critical implications of the relation of Shakespeare's play to the Garter feast have recently been explored by Leslie S. Katz, "*The Merry Wives of Windsor*: Sharing the Queen's Holiday," *Representations* 51 (1995): 77–93.

6. *Merry Wives* 5.5.60. Act, scene, and line references are from *The Riverside Shakespeare*, ed. G. Blakemore Evans (Boston: Houghton Mifflin, 1974). In quoting from this edition, I have expanded some contractions and occasionally altered punctuation.

7. For a description of buck-washing, see Gervase Markham, *Countrey Contentments, or the English Huswife* (London: R. Jackson, 1623), sig. Z4–Aa1. Materials collected by Lena Cowen Orlin in *Elizabethan Households: An Anthology* (Washington, D.C.: Folger Shakespeare Library, 1995), pp. 53–54, nicely evoke the world of Elizabethan laundering.

8. "Si dierono insieme quel piacere che l'una parte e l'altra volse." Ser Giovanni, *Il Pecorone*, ed. Enzo Esposito (Ravenna: Longo, 1974), p. 29.

9. Boccaccio's *Corbaccio*, quoted by John Hines, *The Fabliau in English* (London: Longman, 1993), p. 234.

10. *Complete Prose Works of John Milton*, ed. Don M. Wolfe et al., 8 vols. (New Haven, Conn.: Yale University Press, 1953–82), 3: 542. Such thinking is still current. As an example, consider Charles Murray, the conservative advocate for the abolition of welfare, who was recently quoted as arguing that such abolition "is needed to reverse the nation's spiraling rates of out-of-wedlock births," which, according to Murray, "portend the rise of a white underclass and an authoritarian state" — the implication being that the antidote to a strong and intrusive state is an orderly and self-sufficient citizenry, orderly and self-sufficient especially in their domestic lives (*New York Times*, April 22, 1994).

11. For a reading of *Merry Wives* that emphasizes "a communal harmony not dependent on the sovereign," see Carol Thomas Neely, "Constructing Female Sexuality in the Renaissance: Stratford, London, Windsor, Vienna," in *Feminism and Psychoanalysis*, ed. Richard Feldstein and Judith Roof (Ithaca, N.Y.: Cornell University Press, 1989), pp. 209–229. Similarly, R. S. White argues that "just as the town is seen as a backwater under seige from the London court and Europe, so also can it be seen, in Elizabethan terms, as a bulwark of 'traditional' values which were being threatened in the late sixteenth century by the increasing dominance of London, and even by the threat posed by Queen Elizabeth marrying a foreigner in a diplomatically arranged marriage." See White's book, *The Merry Wives of Windsor* (New York: Harvester Wheatsheaf, 1991), p. 14. The dangerous empowerment of virtuous women that gets represented in *Merry Wives* may have found a quick answer in Henry Porter's *The Two Angry Women of Abington* (1598), in which patriarchal order is celebrated and female unruliness exposed.

12. One version of this fear has been discussed by Nancy Cotton, "Castrating (W)itches: Impotence and Magic in *The Merry Wives of Windsor,*" *Shakespeare Quarterly* 38 (1987): 320–26.

13. One set of associations is suggested by the name twice used for the old woman in the 1602 quarto of *Merry Wives*: "Gillian of Brainford." The name may come from Robert Copland's *Gyl of Braintfords Testament* (c. 1560), but it had considerable currency in the 1590s. In addition to allusions by Thomas Nashe and John Harington, there seems to have been a now lost play by Thomas Dowton and Samuel Rowley called *Friar Fox and Gillian of Brainford* (1598). But of still greater interest is the name's recurrence in Thomas Dekker and John Webster's *Westward Ho* (1607), where Mistress Tenterhook exclaims, "I doubt that old hag Gillian of Brainford has bewitched me." In this and other citizen comedies of the early seventeenth century, Brainford is a place where wives go to "make merry," thus suggesting the continued linking of witchcraft, Brainford, and female independence that we find in *Merry Wives*. See *The Dramatic Works of Thomas Dekker*, ed. Fredson Bowers, 4 vols. (Cambridge: Cambridge University Press, 1953–62), 2.379 and 364.

14. The first statute against witchcraft was enacted in 1542 but was repealed in 1547, along with the other newly defined felonies of Henry VIII's reign. It was revived in 1563 and remained in force throughout the Elizabethan period. Bishop John Jewel is often thought to have prompted the 1563 reenactment. Preaching before the queen in 1560, Jewel remarked that "witches and sorcerers within these few last years are marvelously increased within this your grace's realm" and argued strongly for state intervention. "Your grace's subjects pine away even unto death, their color fadeth, their flesh rotteth, their speech is benumbed, their senses are bereft. Wherefore, your poor sub-

jects' most humble petition unto your highness is that the laws touching such malefac-
tors may be put in due execution. For the shoal of them is great, their doings horrible,
their malice intolerable, the examples most miserable. And I pray God they never
practice further than upon the subject." Witchcraft menaces the monarch directly. This
had long been the principal — often the only — reason royal governments had for concerning themselves with it. Jewel plays on such traditional fears to enforce his argument. But that argument has a novel emphasis. Now, in this post-Reformation and
post-Marian era of radically changing social and religious values, the government must
also intervene to protect subjects from the effects of their own disorderly cultural
practices. Enlightened by the godly ministers of the new religion, the crown must order
and control the country. See George Lyman Kittredge, *Witchcraft in Old and New
England* (Cambridge, Mass.: Harvard University Press, 1929), p. 252.

15. William Rowley, Thomas Dekker, and John Ford, *The Witch of Edmonton*
(4.1.65–6) in *Three Jacobean Witchcraft Plays*, ed. Peter Corbin and Douglas Sedge
(Manchester: Manchester University Press, 1986), p. 187.

16. Thomas Heywood and Richard Brome, *The Late Lancashire Witches*, ed. by
Laird H. Barber (New York: Garland, 1979), p. 213. This claim that a duly constituted
officer of the state could resist witchcraft had been made earlier by no less an authority
than King James himself. In his *Daemonologie* (Edinburgh: Robert Waldegrave, 1597),
James argues that where a "private person," apprehending a witch, would be unable to
keep her from escaping or "doing hurt," "if on the other part, their apprehending and
detention be by the lawful magistrate . . . their power is then no greater than before that
ever they meddled with their master [Satan]. For where God begins justly to strike by
his lawful lieutenant, it is not in the Devil's power to defraud or bereave him of the
office or effect of his powerful and revenging scepter" (pp. 50–51).

17. William Perkins, *A Discourse of the Damned Art of Witchcraft* (Cambridge:
Cantrel Legge, 1608), sigs. L7–M1v and Q8–R1.

18. Still earlier, in 1579, there was a case in Windsor itself where witches were
reported to "have made away and brought to their deaths by certain pictures of wax
certain persons," a matter of particular concern to the lords of the Privy Council because
similar devices had, so it was charged, been "intended to the destruction of her majesty's person." *Acts of the Privy Council*, ed. John Roche Dasent, new series, vol. 11
(London: Her Majesty's Stationery Office, 1895), p. 22.

19. As Jean E. Howard argues in a paper delivered at a conference on "Material
London, ca. 1600" (Folger Shakespeare Library, March 1995), the other play in which
Brainford figures prominently and in which Brainford's witch gets at least a passing
allusion, Dekker and Webster's *Westward Ho*, achieves a similar reformation of way-
ward men by the agency of their apparently revolted wives. On this pattern in *The Wise
Woman of Hogsdon*, see Howard's *The Stage and Social Struggle in Early Modern England*
(London: Routledge, 1994), pp. 73–92.

20. Leah S. Marcus, *Puzzling Shakespeare: Local Reading and Its Discontents*
(Berkeley: University of California Press, 1988), pp. 51–105, and Louis Adrian Mon-
trose, "'Shaping Fantasies': Figurations of Gender and Power in Elizabethan Culture,"
Representations 2 (1983): 61–94. Helen Hackett offers a careful discussion of these
issues in *Virgin Mother, Maiden Queen: Elizabeth I and the Cult of the Virgin Mary* (New
York: St. Martin's Press, 1995), pp. 163–197 and 235–41.

21. Peter Erickson, "The Order of the Garter, the Cult of Elizabeth, and Class-

Gender Tension in *The Merry Wives of Windsor*" in *Shakespeare Reproduced*, ed. by Jean Howard and Marion O'Connor (New York: Methuen, 1987): 124.

22. I pursue the connection between *Merry Wives* and Shakespeare's history plays in "Language Lessons: Linguistic Colonialism, Linguistic Postcolonialism, and the Early Modern English Nation," *Yale Journal of Criticism* (forthcoming).

9

Three Ways to be Invisible in the Renaissance

Sex, Reputation, and Stitchery

Lena Cowen Orlin

IN JOHN FORD'S *'Tis Pity She's a Whore*, Annabella has just had her first sexual experience — with her own brother —, has pledged herself to him, and has received her maid Putana's bawdy congratulations when her father Florio unexpectedly approaches. He calls from *"within"* (off-stage), "Daughter Annabella." In a chaos of emotion, she is certain of only one thing, which is that Florio must not know what has taken place. "O me, my father!" Annabella cries. "Here sir!" she calls out in response to him, while whispering frantically to Putana, "Reach my work." Still offstage, he inquires ominously, "What are you doing?" But, with her needlework in hand, Annabella is prepared: "So: let him come now." Florio sees the answer to his question when he enters and finds her "hard at work." "That's well," he comments approvingly, "you lose no time" (2.1.49–52).[1]

The prescriptive literature of early modern England is full of admonitions that women should "lose no time." Edmund Tilney advises the woman "not to sit always ydle, but to spende hir time in some profitable exercise, as with hir needle" (1568). It is understood that idleness makes easy work for the devil. The ideal wife represented by Robert Snawsel recounts that sometimes "Satan suggesteth euill motions in my heart . . . so that often I thinke better of my selfe than I ought," and then "I may neglect to worke with my hands" (1631).[2] For Snawsel, needlework is a talisman of virtue — as also, evidently, for Florio.

But Annabella seems less interested in stilling her transgressive thoughts by means of her busy hands than in striking a recognized pose of virtuous industry. Further, with eyes dropped to her work, she can avoid a potentially betraying eye contact with her father. The effect is that of another quasi-magical property of needlework, one that may be the first meaning of needlework on the English stage. In *'Tis Pity* stitchery functions less as a charm than as a cloak, a cloak that obscures, that wraps Annabella in irreproachable activity, that shields her from the penetrating gaze of her father, and that disguises her subversive intents. For Annabella to say, "Reach my work . . . So" is as much as for Oberon to announce, "I am invisible." She is rendered impervious to scrutiny and to suspicion.

This essay is concerned with constructs of invisibility outside the world of ghosts and fairies, in the everyday world of early modern English men and women. It outlines a cultural ideology of the everyday occupation of needlework and, specifically, the role needlework played in maintaining the invisibility of women in early modern society. The sources for representations of needlework are, first, didactic literatures and, then, stage plays. A guiding issue is whether, to cite an important author on the subject, there is evidence of subversiveness in the stitch.

Recent attempts to understand the force of patriarchy and the construction of the feminine have focused on the frequent admonition that women should be "chaste, silent, and obedient." Considerable attention has been paid to the constraint of silence. In this, however, there has been largely overlooked such a correlative as that issued by Vives in *The Instruction of a Christen Woman* (1529): "hit were better to be at home within, and unknowen to other folkes. And in company to holde her tonge demurely. And let fewe se her," as well as "none at al here her."[3] The exhortations for women to "keep home"—repeated by Henry Smith and William Gouge and William Whately and a host of other preachers and moralists—were exhortations for women, and especially married women, to make themselves invisible to the larger world.

For those who were married, this was more than just a matter of prescription. The doctrine of the "feme covert" denied wives a legal presence or visibility, any prerogative of legal action, and all rights to own, contract, or transfer property. While this was a legal fiction, especially for women of privilege, the construct had its own cultural force. Prevailing analogies were, as Amy Louise Erickson has said, "contemptuous": the "feme covert" shared "the weakenesse and debilities" of "outlaws, prisoners, infants, 'men unlettered' and 'ideots out of their right minde'" (according to Henry Finch in 1627). To T. E., "Euery Feme Couert is quodammodo an infant," lacking power "euen in that which is most her owne" (1632).[4] For the purposes of this paper, I would emphasize not T. E.'s analogy with infancy but instead the ruling metaphor of England's Anglo-Norman legal terminology, the "cover." The *femme* was supposed to be *couverte* at marriage, as if during the ceremony she assumed a cloak that rendered her invisible to the law courts and to public action. This is how Francis Bacon saw the circumstance of the female, in his memorial tribute to Elizabeth I: "the reigns of women are commonly obscured by marriage; their praises and actions passing to the credit of their husbands; whereas those that continue unmarried have their glory entire and proper to themselves." In choosing not to marry, Elizabeth chose not to don the marital cloak of invisibility.[5]

Invisibility was a theme to which Bacon returned more than once. Notably, he applied it to men as well as to women — with a difference:

Certainly the ablest of men that ever were have had all an openness and frankness of dealing; and a name of certainty and veracity; but they were like horses well-managed; for they could tell passing well when to stop or turn; and at such times when they thought the case indeed required dissimulation, if then they used it, it came to pass that the former opinion spread abroad of their good name and clearness of dealing made them almost invisible.[6]

The difference, in Bacon's telling, would seem to be that the invisibility of women in early modern England was an enforced invisibility, while that of men was an object of desire and of profitable utility. Men achieved invisibility by cultivating a reputation for honesty.

Both the coerced invisibility of gender and the achieved invisibility of reputation were enmeshed in cultural notions of virtue. The invisibility that allowed a man to pass unexamined was a function of his "fame," in the Renaissance sense. For women, in the first instance, virtue moved in the other direction: when in Richard Brome's *The Queen and the Concubine* a countryman remarks of the unjustly exiled queen that "she is an unknown woman," his fellow replies quickly, "And therefore a good woman," because "those that are well known" — i.e., those who are not publicly invisible — "are e'en bad enough" (p. 57). But just as it was possible for men to establish their good names, so it was possible for women to make virtue visible.

Stitchery was a principal strategy for doing so. As Rozsika Parker has pointed out in her excellent work on *The Subversive Stitch: Embroidery and the Making of the Feminine*, needlework has been the means not only of "educating women into the feminine ideal," but also of "proving that they have attained it." Parker identifies the essence of the "proof" with the pose of the stitcher: "Eyes lowered, head bent, shoulders hunched — the position signifies repression and subjugation." Perhaps because her argument seeks the subversive in the stitch, Parker continues that "the embroiderer's silence, her concentration also suggests a self-containment, a kind of autonomy."[7] But I would emphasize instead that it suggests a self-abnegation. All evidences are that for early modern viewers the woman disappeared into her work. Needlework signified as a badge of virtue, and its practice enabled a woman to achieve an invisibility that

Figure 1. Jan van der Straet, "Celebrated Roman Women," 1513. Stitching women are often shown in groups of three, whether to emphasize the stages of their lives, as in Shakespeare's *Coriolanus*, or the ranked status of their pursuits, as in this print. The lady of the household seems to do decorative work, perhaps a cushion cover; her companion has a more practical task, either sewing or mending a household cloth or garment; and the servant in the background employs a distaff. Folger Shakespeare Library Art Box S895 no. 13. By permission of the Folger Shakespeare Library.

in this respect paralleled that of the man of good fame. To the invisibilities of gender and reputation, then, must be added this third form, an invisibility of behavior.

There are reasons for the cultural power of needlework besides its mandate of the submissive pose and the downcast eyes, important as these alone were. For one thing, "needlework," writ large, performed as a universal signifier, an occupational topos for women across all class boundaries (see Figure 1). At the lowest stratum of society the family of clothworking activities involved spinning, with its inevitable referrents to the distaff as the mark of the gender. Vives creates a long and distinguished genealogy for work with wool and flax, which he terms "two craftes yet lefte of that olde innocent worlde, both profitable and kepers of temperance" (sig. C3^v). His improbable catalogue of spinners includes the noblest of ancient Greeks, Romans, Macedonians, and Persians, down to the Spanish queen Isabella, and every woman he cites is reported to have demonstrated her chastity, wisdom, honesty, and industry in pursuing the craft (sigs. C4^r–D1^r). Although several contemporary authors emphasize that even gentlewomen should know how to spin and weave,[8] the needlework generally practiced in the higher social strata was decorative. For embroidery, as Parker has indicated, "Every conceivable surface became a site . . . sheets, valences and coverlets, table carpets, cupboard carpets, cushions for benches and chairs, coifs, stomachers, sleeves, handkerchiefs, bags, hawking gear, needlecases, book covers, book marks, book cushions, shoes, gloves, and aprons"[9] (see Figure 2).

Fancy stitchery was a matter of "rare deuises and inuentions," according to the author of an early pattern book, and in this it merited the attention of gentle, noble, even royal women.[10] John Taylor enthuses that any object can be translated to matter for the needle: "There's nothing neere at hand, or farthest sought,/But with the Needle may be shap'd and wrought" (1631). Taylor also offers some sense of the complexity of the business of fine embroidery, with its many difficulties of choice. Even when the larger issue of the object is decided, there still remains each color to select, and, as Taylor is particular to detail in a mock-Homeric list, the myriad kinds of stitch to consider:

For Tent-worke, Raisd-worke, Laid-worke, Frost-worke, Net-worke,
Most curious Purles, or rare Italian Cutworke,
Fine Ferne-stitch, Finny-stitch, New-stitch, and Chain-stitch,
Braue Bred-stitch, Fisher-stitch, Irish-stitch, and Queen-stitch,
The Spanish-stitch, Rosemary-stitch, and Mowse-stitch,
The smarting Whip-stitch, Back-stitch, & the Crosse-stitch,
All these are good, and these we must allow,
And these are every where in practise now.[11]

Figure 2. New Testament / Book of Psalms. The binding of these companion volumes, which were meant to be carried by a woman for easy consultation, was probably embroidered by their user (who would also have tooled the fore-edges of each book). As in this example, the New Testament and Book of Psalms were often bound together, dos-à-dos, with one or the other book facing up depending on the way the book was held. This New Testament was printed in 1609, the Psalms in 1610. Folger Shakespeare Library STC 2907. By permission of the Folger Shakespeare Library.

Parker argues that embroidery is not "mindless" and merely "decorative," as it has so often been characterized, because of the many choices called for and because "embroiderers do transform materials to produce sense — whole ranges of meanings." But even that obsessive needlewoman Mary Stuart emphasized the importance of "the diversity of colours" because, as she told Cecil's agent, they "[made] the work seem less tedious."[12] So much of the process was repetitious and mechanical.

That needlework was a matter of following patterns was in fact a critical aspect of its ideological appeal. Women may have been endlessly inventive in their choices of stitch and of color, but these were freedoms generally pursued within the constraints of the range of subjects available for copying. In the sixteenth century, women used bestiaries and illustrated Bibles (usually printed on the Continent); in the seventeenth century, sheets of purpose-designed prints sold in London bookstalls.[13] The corpus of images is in many respects reminiscent of the small canon of approved literature for women. Thomas Salter condemned undirected reading for women, because they might learn ballads, songs, sonnets, and other provocative literatures. He insisted that their bibliographies should be confined to "examples and lives of godly and vertuous ladies . . . out of the holy Scripture, and other histories." Needlework was easily directed along similar moral lines by the most popular pattern illustrations. In surviving pieces of work the themes are sufficiently redundant to demonstrate that women did follow the available patterns, most often from hoary Old Testament stories (see Figure 3).[14]

At the same time, if needlework was essentially tedious, there followed the danger (to ideologues) that it was insufficiently occupying. The hazard did not pass unaddressed by the moralists. As Parker has perceptively pointed out, stitchery provided a unique, legitimate, and potentially subversive occasion for women to gather in a group.[15] A popular Renaissance model, however, was the image of a household of women bent over their needlework, following selected patterns, while the lady of the house read aloud the histories of virtuous women, themselves described as behavioral "patterns." Communal reading presumably prevented thoughts from wandering or tongues from wagging on inappropriate lines.

As this image would suggest, early moderns themselves clearly saw needlework as an instrument for the control of women. Henricus Cornelius Agrippa von Nettesheim, writing for a royal female patron in *The Nobilitie of Woman Kynde* (1542), observes:

For anon as a woman is borne euen from her infancy, she is kept at home in ydelnes, & as thoughe she were vnmete for any hygher busynesse, she is p[er]mitted to know no

Figure 3. This pillow cover is one of a set of four from the early seventeenth century with designs clearly taken from printed biblical illustrations. Each has four scenes depicting in sequence the stories of Adam and Eve, Noah, Isaac, and Jacob. This cover, the second in the set, shows in its upper left-hand section the image of Adam delving and Eve spinning — an important and familiar emblem of the gender construct that prevailed in the early modern period, and a reminder of the way clothworking activities were implicated in that construct. Victoria and Albert Museum, T.116–1928. By permission of the Victoria and Albert Museum.

farther, than her nedle and her threede. . . . the women being subdewed as it were by
force of armes, are constrained to giue place to men, and to obeye theyr subdewers, not
by no naturall, no diuyne necessitie or reason, but by custome, education, fortune, and
a certayne tyrannicall occasion.[16]

Agrippa recognizes the larger irony that sets "needlework" in supposed opposition to "idleness" rather than, as it rightly was for his audience of privileged women, an occupation *of* idleness. The busy-ness of fancy stitchery was a
cultural myth, intended to suggest to women of status that their practice of
embroidery was in some sense comparable to (and as valuable as) the professional and profit-making pursuits of men. Even the term "needlework," so
often shortened just to "work" in the language of the time, was collusive in this
cultural construct. It implied a priority interest in the product, when in fact
that which was necessary to the gender hierarchy was the process.[17] The practice of needlework served to keep leisured women in their place, out of the
public sphere, functionally invisible.

    A century later, this view of needlework as an instrument of oppression
still obtained. The author of *The Woman's Sharp Revenge* (1640), adopting a
female persona, observes that

lest we should be made able to vindicate our own injuries, we are set only to the Needle,
to prick our fingers, or else to the Wheel to spin a fair thread for our own undoing, or
perchance to some more dirty and debased drudgery. If we be taught to read, they then
confine us within the compass of our Mother Tongue, and that limit we are not suffered
to pass. . . . And thus if we be weak by Nature, they strive to make us more weak by our
Nurture; and if in degree of place low, they strive by their policy to keep us more under.[18]

The juxtaposition of the practice of stitchery and the normal limits on learning
is significant. As Thomas Salter remarks complacently, "how far more convenient the Distaffe and Spindle, Nedle and Thimble were for them with a good
and honest reputation, then the skill of well using a penne, or writyng a loftie
vearce with diffame and dishonour, if in the same there be more erudition then
vertue."[19]

    The exceptional women who achieved learning in the period were praised
for it, as marvels of their sex. But, as Parker has rightly pointed out, in each
instance this praise "was invariably accompanied by words of admiration for
her skill with a needle,"[20] in a gesture to refeminize her. Like Salter, the author
of *The Necessarie, Fit and Convenient Education of a Yong Gentlewoman* emphasizes that use of the needle and the spindle purchases "the name and reputation
of graue and honest matrons" rather than the "vncertaine report" of reading
and writing.[21] Even queens seemed to need the "cover" of the practice of
stitchery, for Catherine of Aragon, Mary Tudor, and Elizabeth Tudor were

frequently described at their needles, as a way of normalizing these most visible of women.

This paradigm returns us to the thesis that launched this argument, that stitchery was the behavioral badge of virtue that rendered women unsusceptible of ill report, the "cover" that approximated that of a man's earned reputation. But if we revisit Bacon's remarks on men going "almost invisible," we will note that he writes of the way that reputation could be (and certainly was) exploited: "at such times when they thought the case indeed required dissimulation, if then they used it, it came to pass that the former opinion spread abroad of their good name and clearness of dealing made them almost invisible."[22] Luke, in Massinger's *City Madam*, puts the case even more crudely: "Have money and good clothes,/And you may pass invisible" (2.1.100–101) — to any illicit purpose.

The prescriptive literature for women is so single-mindedly devoted to the propagation of needlework as the ideal female occupation that it seems incapable of entertaining the question now to be addressed: did the "cover" of stitchery offer women a similar means of deceit? Did, they, too, have access to a desired (rather than coerced) invisibility, one that suited their individual agendas rather than cultural imperatives? *'Tis Pity She's a Whore* alone suggests that this might be the case, with Annabella throwing up a screen of industry to hide behind. Notably, however, *'Tis Pity* takes us out of the world of prescription and theory and into a world of practice. Admittedly, it is practice as *represented* on the English stage, but we will beg the issue of representation for the moment, to investigate the evidence that stage plays provide in the matter of the ideology of needlework. There are so many sewing scenes in Elizabethan and Jacobean drama — twenty-one are consulted here — that it is unarguably apparent that needlework played a significant and signifying role in early modern culture.

The stitchery of the stage often conforms to the stitchery of the didactic literature. "When women embroider," summarizes Parker, "it is seen not as art, but entirely as the expression of femininity,"[23] and in many plays needlework serves, as it does for the moralists, merely as a gender marker: in *Gallathea* (2.4.10–11), in *The Taming of the Shrew* (2.1.25), in *A Midsummer Night's Dream* (3.2.203–9), in *Othello* (4.1.187–88). The link between needlework and virtuous industry is frequently made. In *Eastward Ho*, stitchery is stage shorthand to establish character: the unassuming Mildred is first seen *"sewing,"* while her idle, ambitious sister Gertrude displays *"a French head attire"* with her *"citizen's gown"* (1.2.0sd). Gertrude comes to repent the fact that she has "scorned" Mildred's status-appropriate "velvet cap" and has been "proud and lascivious" rather than modest and industrious (5.5.174–77). Sewing scenes are often strategically employed in the interest of heightened dramatic contrast, to establish a woman's impregnable purity just before it is assailed or before she encounters some other form of jeopardy. Hamlet's antic disposition is displayed to Ophelia in her moment of greatest innocence, "as I was sewing in my closet" (2.1.74). In *A Knack to Know an Honest Man*, Annetta and Lucida are seated at their needlework when Sempronio approaches with a chest of gold and an immoral proposition (ll. 683–85). In this instance, the women's virtuous occupation is a perfect predictor of the moral resistance that they will be able to summon. There is no fissure between behavior and character.

Only in *All Fools*, *1 Edward IV*, *The Launching of the Mary*, *The Shoemaker's Holiday*, *The Wisdom of Doctor Dodypoll*, and *A Woman Is a Weathercock* does a woman sit alone to sew (about which more follows, below). Elsewhere, however, the group scenes of the moralists are the rule. The generational subtext of *Coriolanus*, *James IV*, and *A Knack to Know an Honest Man* accommodates the popular notion that stitchery is a craft passed down among women, in these cases from mother to daughter. Needlework is also taught in the girls' schools displayed in *Law Tricks*, *The Wit of a Woman*, and *The Queen and the Concubine*. In the last of these plays, needlework is a saving skill for the queen Eulalia, who has been unjustly exiled by her husband. She is visited by an allegorical character identified as her Genius, who gives her first the gift of healing and then the inspiration to teach "Handy-Works and Literature" in the countryside (p. 47). When Eulalia announces that she is skilled in the use of the needle, the loom, the spinning wheel, the frame, the net-pin, and bobbins, countrymen are eager to send their children to learn (p. 76). Eventually, Eulalia has occasion to demonstrate to her estranged husband how she has lived respectably, without begging, and she "*Shews her works, and makes a brave description of Pieces: As Sale-work, Day-work, Night-work, wrought Night-caps, Coyfs, Stomachers*" (p. 110).[24] Eulalia plays to the prescriptive theme of Vives and Taylor (among others) that needlework is a fit occupation even for queens. So also for the title character in *Campaspe* (4.2.13–15), for Queen Katherine in *Henry VIII* (3.1.osd, 24, 74–76), and for Elizabeth I in *If You Know Not Me* (xvi. 1191).

A Knack to Know an Honest Man, *The Launching of the Mary*, *Law Tricks*, *Pericles*, *The Shoemaker's Holiday*, and *The Wise Woman of Hogsdon* share with *The Queen and the Concubine* the theme of a woman temporarily abandoned by a man; for each heroine, needlework is a means of earning a living while maintaining both chastity and reputation. The theme is explored at greatest length in *The Launching of the Mary*, where Dorotea Constance, left alone while her husband is at sea, "*shewes her worke*" to the audience, explaining, "here's the thinge / that shall supply my wants, & keepe the bed / of holy wedlocke still immaculate." Her attempted seducer, Captain Fitz John, comes upon her as she stitches, giving her the opportunity to drive home yet again the message that is familiar to us from the moralizing literature: needlework, she tells him, preserves her "honour" as well as her "substance" (ll. 2583–84, 2599). She recognizes with some pain that her solitary diligence has made her invisible: "not once frequented, visited, or seene" (l. 700).

All indications are that the theatrical presentation of sewing scenes was often highly conventionalized, "patterned," in accord with the prescriptive tracts. As it is described in *A Midsummer Night's Dream*, so it is staged in *All Fools*, *Coriolanus*, *1 Edward IV*, *Henry VIII*, *James IV*, *A Knack to Know an Honest Man*, *The Launching of the Mary*, *Law Tricks*, *Monsieur D'Olive*, *The Shoemaker's Holiday*, *The Wisdom of Doctor Dodypoll*, and *A Woman Is a Weathercock*: female characters sit to sew. Stage directions so often refer to stools and chairs that the visual formula was undoubtedly followed in other sewing scenes that go undescribed. There is also a remarkably high incidence of sewing pursued during a lapse in the dialogue, accompanied by an unscripted song, as is similarly suggested in *Dream*, to which there is a leap of association in *Othello*, and for which there are explicit directions in *All Fools*, *Henry VIII*, *James IV*, *Law Tricks*, and *Sir Gyles Goosecappe*.[25] Thus, sewers were often presented on the early English stage as if in tableaux, with the stage action frozen to display the ideologically satisfying picture of women seated, heads bent, fingers moving rhythmically.[26]

The essence of the tableau is, unarguably, a visual image. The nature of the theatrical medium is, after all, to make visible, and the display of stitching women on stage might at first glance seem to work against the prevailing ethos of needlework off stage. But, by making visual *objects* of them, the living emblem in fact renders the component parts static, etiolated, and ethically inoperative. The effect is most easily demonstrated in *Monsieur D'Olive*, where a scene opens with the stage direction "*Enter Phillip [the Duke]. Gveaq[uin, the Duchess]. Ieronnime [her lady-in-waiting]. & Mygeron [a courtier]. Gveaq. & Iero. sit down to worke*" (p. 209). The women do not take part in the action of the scene until its end; through a long exchange, they speak not a word. Their silent attendance might prove distracting were it not for the needlework, which gives them a pretext and a context. It also constitutes their entire meaning. In a scene in which D'Olive remembers living in humble "obscuritie" far from court, "As private as I had King Giris Ring / And could haue gone invisible" (pp. 211–12), needlework makes it possible for these women to be present on stage but functionally invisible.

Another way of putting it is that women in sewing scenes signify allegorically or ideologically as well as (or rather than) characterologically. Their tableaux interrupt the plot in the manner of dumb shows and masques. Sempronio, for example, glosses the image in *A Knack to Know an Honest Man*. "Yonder sits chastitie at beauties feete," he says of Lucida and Annetta, who have entered "*with their worke in their handes*" (ll. 660–61, 677). A similar effect is achieved in *Coriolanus*, when the intrusion of Valeria upon the sewing session of Virgilia and Volumnia and the insistent association of needle-work with gender identification suggests an iconographic representation of "woman" in the three stages of her life: maid, wife, widow. In *Law Tricks*, through the contrast between an aging and divorced Countess and her young student-embroiderers, needlework is the ruling metaphor of a *memento mori*.

So far, the themes of the stage and of the moralizing page cohere. In a series of plays, however, the very tableau-effect of the standard sewing scene, which seems so much a product of the prevailing ideology, finally works at cross purposes to that ideology. Stitchery is subverted to imperil female char-acters rather than to shield them. In these cases, the sewing scene is exploited as a plot device, a mechanism to display chaste women not only to the eyes of the audience but also to those of "lewd and lustie" male characters. For plot purposes, it is important that these female characters be exposed to view while alone, and, at the outset, stitchery is a way of making them publicly visible without impugning their private virtue. But then the plot advances to reveal that stitchery is an ineffective cloak of moral invisibility.

The Wise Woman of Hogsdon's Luce, for example, sits "*in a Goldsmith's shop, at worke upon a lac'd Handkercher*." She tells the apprentice, Joseph, that "I doe not love to sit thus publikely," but needs must. Immediately thereafter Boyster enters and propositions her. Similarly, in *1 Edward IV*, Jane Shore occupies herself with needlework while supervising the apprentices in her husband's goldsmith's shop (p. 63). Essentially, she is put on exhibit for the king, who thereafter determines to make her his mistress and who takes her away to court. In *The Shoemaker's Holiday*, Hammon observes Jane alone "*in a sempster's shop, working*" and, knowing she is "chaste," resorts to the strategy of telling her that her husband has died in France in order to woo her (12.0sd). In *The Rape of Lucrece*, Collatine wins the wager of the husbands by displaying his wife Lucrece, and the scene that awakens Tarquin's fatal lust is that in which she reads to her maids as they sew (ll. 1573–96). Because their display puts them at risk, stitchery is in fact complicit in these characters' jeopardy.

Three great theatrical set pieces on needlework together suggest the range of meanings that attached to stitchery on the stage. At one extreme is *James IV*, which employs the tableau-effect to a moralizing purpose: a woman under sexual assault is displayed in all her chaste industry, and her occupation is sufficient to establish her character and indicate her response. Ida, who has attracted the persistent attention of the Scottish King James IV, is shown with her mother the Countess of Arran, *"in their porch, sitting at work"* and listening to *"A song."* They are interrupted by Eustace, who delivers letters to which the Countess attends. He engages Ida in a suggestive discussion of her needlework: "Say that your needle now were Cupid's sting." But, with "I'll prick no hearts, I'll prick upon my work," Ida states the position she will take throughout, as she resists the king's seductions and remains as virtuous as her work shows her to be (2.1.0sd–71). This is stage stitchery that reflects the prevailing myths and assumptions of the didactic literature.

In *Sir Gyles Goosecappe*, however, the mood is comic and there is more scope for transgressive irreverence. As has been suggested, the staged practice of needlework is strictly gendered, and *Goosecappe* establishes the norm early on: *"Enter Wynnefred, Anabell, with their sowing workes and sing"* (2.1.16sd). Thus, when a male character is shown stitching, as Goosecappe later is, he becomes a recurrent object of fun. The joke is prolonged with detailed descriptions of his craftsmanship: "He will make you flyes and wormes, of all sortes most liuely, and is now working a whole bed embrodred, with nothing but glowe wormes; whose lightes a has so perfectly done, that you may goe to bed in the chamber, doe anything in the Chamber, without a Candle" (2.1.328–41). The reference to chamber work keeps the gender jest alive, as does Eugenia's later attempt to re-gender Goosecappe by pointing to the "pretie worke he weares in his boote-hose" (5.1.50–51). For Hippolita, his sewing is still "a more gentlewoman-like qualitie I assure you." Penelope laughingly tells him that "you neede neuer marrie, you are both husband and wife your selfe" (5.1.81–84). The prolonged conceit of Goosecappe's stitchery as an inversion of the gender order concludes palliatively, when Goosecappe must divest himself of his "work" in order to produce a sonnet.

The third set piece on stitchery, while as irreverent as that of *Sir Gyles Goosecappe*, is also an ethical inversion of *James IV*, and it advances our notion of the transgressive capacity of the sewing scene. The women at work in *The Atheist's Tragedy* are the bawd Cataplasma and the courtesan Soquette. In a parody of the needlework schools of, for example, *The Wit of a Woman*, Cataplasma "examines" Soquette's work and finds "the leaves o' the plum tree falling off, the gum issuing out o' the perished joints, and the branches some of 'em dead and some rotten, and yet but a young plum tree." Soquette's work is symptomatic of her own state of moral decay. Sebastian's subsequent "moralizing" on "this gentlewoman's needlework" is so bawdy that for Languebeau the effect is pornographic: "The very contemplation o' the thing makes the spirit of the flesh begin to wriggle in my blood." He asks Cataplasma's permission for Soquette to "leave her work" and join him for what he euphemistically terms "honest recreation" (4.1osd–85). While Soquette's behavior as a needleworker is unexceptionable, that behavior is not morally predictive. With *The Atheist's Tragedy* we pass out of the world of emblems and exempla and into a world of subversion and double entendres.

Indeed, for every Virgilia, for whom needlework is stage shorthand to establish virtue and industry, there is a Volumnia, for whom needlework cannot adequately encompass character, ambition, or motivation. In other words, the deliberate misdirection of *'Tis Pity*'s Annabella is not unique. Other characters, too, adopt needlework as a cloaking device, in overt attempts to purchase invisibility. For them, stitchery is not a virtuous end but a transgressive means.

Sometimes the strategic use of needlework is sympathetic, as is the case with Mary Fitzallard in *The Roaring Girl*. She and her betrothed, Sebastian Wengrave, have been separated by the disapproval of Sebastian's father. Moll's means of re-establishing surreptitious contact is to come to his house shielded from possible identification, innocuously *"disguised like a sempster, with a case for bands"* (1.1.0sd). Over sartorial "bands" the two unfortunate lovers discuss their relational "bonds," their contractual vows, and Sebastian outlines his scheme to outfox his father. Needlework is similarly an element of a forgivable fraud practiced by the frustrated lovers of *The Wisdom of Doctor Dodypoll*. There, the Earl of Lassingbergh poses as a "mercinary painter" to gain access to the household of Lucilia's father. The two are *"discouered"* on stage, he *"(like a Painter) painting Lucilia, who sits working on a piece of Cushion worke,"* both in postures so irreproachably decorous that they and their secret agenda are rendered invisible to the household (1.1.2–4). In *The Wit of a Woman*, the women of Balia's girls' school are more occupied with their marital plots and stratagems than with their tutelage in needlework. After a private conference, they return to "worke" "lest we be mist to long" (sig. F2ʳ). As the comedy moves towards its approved end of multiple matches, stitchery is a behavior the women adopt to divert suspicion rather than a skill they pursue to produce a product.

The humor of *The Launching of the Mary* is somewhat darker. Mary Sparke and Isabell Nutt, seamen's wives like Dorotea Constance, scorn Dorotea for "euer workinge." While Dorotea keeps herself at home, Mary and Isabell range widely. They carry handbaskets as a pretext for doing so, but Dorotea recognizes that while the baskets are "needfull," their use of them is "needles." An entire scene is devoted to exposing the contents of the counterfeit needlewomen's baskets: a brick bat wrapped in a clean napkin instead of silk cloth, three or four pieces of painted cloth instead of children's caps and sleeves. By focusing on difference, on the active contrast between the honest Dorotea and the duplicitous Mary and Isabell, *The Launching of the Mary*

engages the gap between behavior and being. The impedimenta of the seam-
stress are no guarantees of her virtue.

In *A Woman Is a Weather-Cocke*, stitchery is used deliberately to entrap.
The suggestively named Mistris Wagtaile has discovered herself to be pregnant
and has identified a patsy, the aptly named Sir Abraham Ninnie. Pendant helps
Wagtaile snare Ninnie by bringing him to observe her where she has posed
alone, as if grieving, *"with worke sowing a purse."* Knowing that Ninnie is watching, she pretends to reveal that she suffers from a secret love for him. Because
Ninnie swears he has never slept with her, Wagtaile also explains for his over-
hearing that she conceived while *dreaming* of lying with him. In a final parox-
ysm of feigned despair, she blows into the purse that she has been stitching,
asks Pendant to "Beare him this purse fil'd with my latest [i.e., last] breath,"
and then *"Offers to stab"* herself. At this Ninnie steps forward to rescue her and
accept responsibility for the unborn child. Pendant has already aphorized that
"euerie woman has a Sprindge to catch a Wood-cocke." Wagtaile has several
"sprindges," but needlework is a critical one in entrapping the foolish knight
(4.3.1–4, 92–95).

As suggested by *The Atheist's Tragedy*, *The Launching of the Mary*, *The
Roaring Girl*, *The Wisdom of Doctor Dodypoll*, *The Wit of a Woman*, *A Woman Is
a Weather-Cock*, and *'Tis Pity She's a Whore*, the process of needlework was
more likely to be subversive than was its product. There *was* a historical exception to this rule, in the work of Mary Stuart (who may have been disingenuous
in protesting the tedium of embroidery to an agent of Elizabeth I). She famously sent her proposed husband, the duke of Norfolk, a treasonous embroidered emblem: a hand pruning a vine, with the motto *"Virescit Vulnere Virtus"*
("Virtue flourishes by wounding"). As Margaret Swain renders the message:
"the unfruitful branch of the royal house (Elizabeth) was to be cut down; the
fruitful branch (Mary) would be left to flourish and bear more fruit." Mary
dispatched similarly dangerous emblematic messages to Norfolk's son and to
his daughter-in-law.[27]

This is not the only counter-argument that history poses to the meanings
of stitchery as shown on stage. The fact is that while Sir Gyles Goosecappe was
a figure of fun within the confines of theatrical convention, the needle did not
always unman a male employer, nor was it exclusively the province of women.
Fine embroidery in early modern Europe was a highly professionalized skill,
and many of the surviving examples of needlework — by definition, often those
which are the most meticulous, ornate, and valuable — were the handiwork of
male careerists. (Men were called "embroiderers"; women, "needleworkers.")
Further, while it is true that there were many ideological reasons for attention
to be focused on the process of amateur needlework, there were also many

private reasons for householders and housewives to value the product, its decorative impact, and the status that elegant work conferred.[28] Similarly, the author of *A Woman's Sharp Revenge* may have rightly understood needlework to be an instrument of oppression, but nonetheless many women enjoyed the craft, found creative release in its pursuit, and were proud of their skill. To return to a point that was deferred earlier, staged sewing scenes were, admittedly, matters of artistic representation.

What this paper has outlined is less historical practice than cultural myth about the role of stitchery in gender construction, patriarchy, and domestic ideology.[29] On this subject, there is one last point to make, and it is a point to which only representation, perhaps, can easily lead us. The moralist Thomas Salter opined that "I wishe our maiden wholie to refrain from the use of musicke; and seeyng that *under the coverture of vertue*, it openeth the dore to many vices, she ought so muche the more to be regarded, by how muche more the daunger is greate, and lesse apparent" (emphasis added).[30] Although no moralist would go so far as to make a similar suggestion for needlework, playwrights did, as has been shown. They demonstrated an active awareness that women's virtuous pursuits could offer "coverture" for vice.

Such an awareness will inevitably have its consequences, and these too are implied in a contemporary stageplay. In *All Fools*, Cornelio is an irrationally, extravagantly jealous husband. His wife Gazetta is virtuous by all accounts, and, indeed, as if to reassure us on this point, she is first shown "*sewing.*" But, as she "*sits and sings sewing*," Cornelio interrogates her on the meanings of her embroidered flowers, accuses her of employing the "darkest language" in her work, and finally concludes: "This were a pretty present for some friend,/ Some gallant courtier, as for Dariotto,/One that adores you" (2.1.236–38). So perverse is Cornelio's obsession that Gazetta's very badge of virtue is turned against her, her chaste stitchery translated into a love token for her supposed suitor. For Cornelio, even needlework is insufficient to prove Gazetta's honesty. A household page recognizes that Gazetta may suppose "her innocence a sufficient shield against [his] jealous accusations" (3.1.170–71), but it is not.[31]

Cornelio recognizes that conditioned behavior is no guarantor of virtue, and so, finally, did playwrights, moralists, and the author of *The Woman's Sharp Revenge*. Even the exigencies of law, of moral prescription, and of social convention, when joined to behavior modification, could not wholly stifle women's wit, wisdom, shrewishness, and wantonness. This understanding informs the transparency of the stratagems of the stitching women of *The Atheist's Tragedy*, *The Launching of the Mary*, *The Roaring Girl*, *The Wisdom of Doctor Dodypoll*, *The Wit of a Woman*, *A Woman Is a Weather-Cock*, and *'Tis Pity*

She's a Whore. Early modern English women were always suspect. For them, there was no way to be invisible in the Renaissance.

Appendix: Plays Cited

Those asterisked include important sewing scenes.

The Atheist's Tragedy [1611], ed. Irving Ribner. The Revels Plays. Cambridge, Mass.: Harvard University Press, 1964.

*Brome, Richard. *The Queen and the Concubine* [1635]. In *The Dramatic Works of Richard Brome*, 2: 111–30. London: John Pearson, 1873.

*Chapman, George. *All Fools* [1599], ed. Frank Manley. Regents Renaissance Drama. Lincoln: University of Nebraska Press, 1968.

*Chapman, George. *Monsieur D'Olive* [1606]. In *The Comedies and Tragedies of George Chapman*, 1: 187–252. London: John Pearson, 1873.

*Chapman, George. *Sir Gyles Goosecappe. Knight* [1606], ed. John F. Hennedy. In *The Plays of George Chapman: The Tragedies with Sir Gyles Goosecappe*, ed. Allan Holaday, pp. 711–802. Cambridge: D. S. Brewer, 1987.

*Chapman, George, Ben Jonson, and John Marston. *Eastward Ho* [1604], ed. R.W. Van Fossen. The Revels Plays. Manchester: Manchester University Press, 1979.

*Day, John. *Law Tricks* [1608], ed. John Crow and W. W. Greg. Malone Society Reprints. Oxford: The Malone Society, 1950.

*Dekker, Thomas. *The Shoemaker's Holiday* [1599], ed. R. L. Smallwood and Stanley Wells. The Revels Plays. Manchester: Manchester University Press, 1979.

*Dekker, Thomas and Thomas Middleton. *The Roaring Girl* [1611], ed. Paul Mulholland. The Revels Plays. Manchester: Manchester University Press, 1987.

*Field, Nathaniel. *A Woman Is a Weathercock* [1611]. In *The Plays of Nathan Field*, ed. William Perry, pp. 55–139. Austin: University of Texas Press, 1950.

*Ford, John. *'Tis Pity She's a Whore* [1633], ed. Brian Morris. The New Mermaids. London: Ernest Benn, 1968.

*Greene, Robert. *The Scottish History of James the Fourth* [1594], ed. Norman Sanders. The Revels Plays. London: Methuen, 1970.

Heywood, Thomas. *If You Know Not Me, You Know Nobody* [1605], ed. Madeleine Doran. Malone Society Reprints. Oxford: The Malone Society, 1935.

*Heywood, Thomas. *King Edward the Fourth, Part One* [1599]. In *The Dramatic Works of Thomas Heywood*, ed. R. H. Shepherd, 1: 1–90. London: John Pearson, 1874.

*Heywood, Thomas. *The Rape of Lucrece* [1608], ed. Allan Holladay. Urbana: University of Illinois Press, 1950.

*Heywood, Thomas. *The Wise Woman of Hogsdon* [1604], ed. Michael H. Leonard. Renaissance Drama: A Collection of Critical Editions. New York: Garland, 1980.

A Knack to Know an Honest Man [1596], ed. H. De Vocht. Malone Society Reprints. Oxford: The Malone Society, 1910.

Lyly, John. *Campaspe* [1584], ed. G. K. Hunter. In *"Campaspe" and "Sappho and Phao"*, ed. G. K. Hunter and David Bevington. The Revels Plays. Manchester: Manchester University Press, 1991.

Lyly, John. *Gallathea* [1585]. In *"Gallathea" and "Midas"*, ed. Anne Begor Lancashire. Regents Renaissance Drama. Lincoln: University of Nebraska Press, 1969.

Massinger, Philip. *The City Madam* [1632], ed. Cyrus Hoy. Regents Renaissance Drama. Lincoln: University of Nebraska Press, 1964.

*Mountfort, Walter. *The Launching of the Mary* [1632], ed. John Henry Walter. Malone Society Reprints. Oxford: The Malone Society, 1933.

Shakespeare, William. *A Midsummer Night's Dream* [1596], ed. G. Blakemore Evans. In *The Riverside Shakespeare*, pp. 217–49. Boston: Houghton Mifflin, 1974.

Shakespeare, William. *Pericles, Prince of Tyre* [1608], ed. G. Blakemore Evans. In *The Riverside Shakespeare*, pp. 1479–1516. Boston: Houghton Mifflin, 1974.

Shakespeare, William. *The Taming of the Shrew* [1594], ed. G. Blakemore Evans. In *The Riverside Shakespeare*, pp. 106–42. Boston: Houghton Mifflin, 1974.

*Shakespeare, William. *The Tragedy of Coriolanus* [1608], ed. G. Blakemore Evans. In *The Riverside Shakespeare*, pp. 1392–1440. Boston: Houghton Mifflin, 1974.

Shakespeare, William. *The Tragedy of Hamlet, Prince of Denmark* [1601], ed. G. Blakemore Evans. In *The Riverside Shakespeare*, pp. 1135–97. Boston: Houghton Mifflin, 1974.

Shakespeare, William. *The Tragedy of Othello, the Moor of Venice* [1604], ed. G. Blakemore Evans. In *The Riverside Shakespeare*, pp. 1198–1248. Boston: Houghton Mifflin, 1974.

*Shakespeare, William and John Fletcher. *The Famous History of the Life of Henry VIII* [1613], ed. G. Blakemore Evans. In *The Riverside Shakespeare*, pp. 976–1018. Boston: Houghton Mifflin, 1974.

The Wisdom of Doctor Dodypoll [1600], ed. M. N. Matson. Renaissance Drama: A Collection of Critical Editions. New York: Garland, 1980.

The Wit of a Woman [1604], ed. W. W. Greg. Malone Society Reprints. Oxford: The Malone Society, 1913.

Notes

An early version of this paper was circulated in a seminar on "Shakespeare and the Recovery of Women's History" at the World Shakespeare Congress in Los Angeles in 1996. I thank the members of that seminar and especially its leaders, Linda Woodbridge and Juliet Fleming. The University of Maryland, Baltimore County provided assistance in securing illustrations and permissions. I am also grateful for the generosity of Leslie Thomson, without whose invaluable database of early modern stage directions this argument could not have been pursued; for the collegiality of Carole Levin, with whom I have been fortunate to exchange work and good discussion; for the saving suggestions of Peter Stallybrass; and for the gentle but prudent editorial interventions of Paddy Fumerton and Simon Hunt.

    1. For the editions of plays consulted, see the appendix.

    2. Edmund Tilney, *A Brief and Pleasant Discourse of Duties in Marriage, Called the Flower of Friendship* (London, 1568), sig. E4^r. Robert Snawsel, *Looking-Glass for Maried Folkes* (London, 1610), sig. B1^v. On this subject see also John Taylor, *The Needles Excellency* (London, 1639), p. 4; and Richard Brathwait, *The English Gentlewoman* (London, 1631), sig. H1^r.

    3. Joannes Ludovicus Vives, *Instruction of a Christen Woman*, trans. R. Hyrd (London, 1529), sig. E2^v.

4. Amy Louise Erickson, *Women and Property in Early Modern England* (London: Routledge, 1993), p. 100. See also pp. 24–25, 229. T.E., *The Lawes Resolutions of Women's Rights* (London, 1632), sig. K7ʳ.

5. Francis Bacon, *In Felicem Memoriam Elizabethae Angliae Reginae*, translated as "On the Fortunate Memory of Elizabeth Queen of England," in *The Works of Francis Bacon*, ed. James Spedding, Robert Leslie Ellis, and Douglas Denon Heath, new ed., 14 vols. (London: Longman, 1857–74), 6: 310.

6. Cited by F. G. Bailey, *The Prevalence of Deceit* (Ithaca, N.Y.: Cornell University Press, 1991), p. 27.

7. Rozsika Parker, *The Subversive Stitch: Embroidery and the Making of the Feminine* (New York: Routledge, 1984), pp. iv and 10 (compare also the variant in the caption to figure 5). Although I take a different line from Parker and it is useful to clarify my stance by distinguishing it from hers, I am enormously indebted to her for her foundational work in this area.

8. See also Thomas Salter, *The Mirrhor of Modestie* (1579), ed. John Payne Collier (London: privately printed, 1866): "I wishe our maiden, not onely to learne all maner of nedle woorke meete for a maiden, but also all that whiche belongeth to the Distaffe and Spindle; not thinkyng it unseemely to any, of what estate or degree so ever, seeyng that *Augustus Caesar*, prince and monarche of the worlde, was willyng to have his daughter and niece skilfull in the same" (pp. 27–28). Compare also the very similar statement in *The Necessarie, Fit and Convenient Education of a Yong Gentlewoman* (London, 1598), sigs. 14ʳ⁻ᵛ.

9. Parker, p. 69.

10. Federico di Vinciolo, *New and Singular Patternes and Workes of Linens*, trans. [A. Poyntz] (London, 1591), sig. A3ʳ.

11. On stitches, see Lu Emily Pearson, *Elizabethans at Home* (Stanford, Calif.: Stanford University Press, 1957), p. 210; and Margaret Swain, *The Needlework of Mary Queen of Scots* (New York: Van Nostrand Reinhold, 1973), pp. 30–31.

12. Parker, p. 6. For Mary, see *The Calendar of the Manuscripts of the . . . Marquis of Salisbury . . . at Hatfield House* (London: Her Majesty's Stationery Office, 1883), vol. 1, p. 400, item 1279 (26 February 1569).

13. Parker cites Bernard Salamon, Jost Ammon, and Gerard de Jode as the most important sixteenth-century illustrators, pp. 96–97.

14. Salter, p. 11. See Parker on the possible meanings of the stories represented, pp. 12 and 96.

15. Parker emphasizes that stitchery authorized such gatherings. Women did not feel "they were neglecting their families, wasting time or betraying their husbands by maintaining independent social bonds" (pp. 14–15).

16. Henricus Cornelius Agrippa von Nettesheim, *A Treatise of the Nobilitie and Excellencye of Woman Kynde*, trans. David Clapham (London, 1542), sigs. F8ᵛ and G1ᵛ. A character in Chapman's *Sir Gyles Goosecappe* aptly uses spinning as a metaphor for this manipulation of women: "we will turne her, and winde her, and make her so plyant that we will drawe her through a wedding ring yfaith" (1.4.148–50).

17. Again, Parker has a different reading: "Although to some extent an appropriate term, it ['work'] tends to confirm the stereotypical notion that patience and perseverance go into embroidery—but little else. Moreover, the term was engendered by an ideology of femininity as service and selflessness and the insistence that women work for others, not for themselves" (p. 6).

18. *The Woman's Sharp Revenge* (1640), excerpted in *Half Humankind: Contexts and Texts of the Controversy about Women in England, 1540–1640*, ed. Katherine Usher Henderson and Barbara F. McManus (Urbana: University of Illinois Press, 1985), pp. 313–14.

19. Salter, p. 20, is echoed closely in *The Necessarie, Fit and Convenient Education of a Yong Gentlewoman*, sig. G2ʳ.

20. Parker, p. 74.

21. *The Necessarie, Fit and Convenient Education of a Yong Gentlewoman*, sig. G2ʳ.

22. Bailey, *The Prevalence of Deceit*, p. 27.

23. Parker, p. 5.

24. Eulalia may be an intriguing allusion to Catherine of Aragon, who brought lace-making skills to Bedfordshire following her divorce by Henry VIII. Of course, with Eulalia's validation through the display of her work, the parallel fails.

25. See also *Coriolanus*, where Volumnia asks the grieving Virgilia, "I pray you, daughter, sing, or express yourself in a more comfortable sort" (1.3.1–2).

26. The tableau effect is heightened in a scene like that which opens *The Wisdom of Doctor Dodypoll*, where a "curtain" is drawn to "discover" the Earl of Lassingbergh painting Lucilia, "who sits working on a piece of Cushion worke" (1.1.0sd).

27. See Swain, pp. 75, 78, 87.

28. This is an argument that Parker makes, passim.

29, The theme of cultural myth versus historical practice marks my ongoing research in early modern private life; see also "Women on the Threshold" in *Shakespeare Studies* 25 (1997): 50–58.

30. Salter, p. 25; and compare *The Necessarie, Fit and Conuenient Education of a Yong Gentlewoman*: "Our gentlewoman then shall abstaine wholly from vsing musicke: and seing that *vnder the honest couerture of vertue* it openeth the gate to many vices, by vs it ought to be the more auoided, because the danger is great and lesse apparant" (sig. H6ᵛ; emphasis added).

31. Editor Frank Manley emphasizes that the main plot of *All Fools* was from Terence but that the Cornelio/Gazetta plot is native, "Chapman's own" (p. xvi).

10

Household Chastisements

Gender, Authority, and "Domestic Violence"

Frances E. Dolan

RECENTLY A NUMBER OF CRITICS have described sixteenth- and seventeenth-century English culture as a "culture of violence." Those who do so tend to assume that such a culture is invariably dialectical: Francis Barker, for instance, discusses "the dialectical relation between the coercive violence of the authorities on the one hand, and the various forces which attempt to oppose, block or mitigate that violence on the other."[1] The evidence that early modern England was a "culture of violence" comes most obviously, then, in its reliance on public whippings, mutilations, burnings, hangings, and beheadings to punish crime and maintain order, and in the occasional violent rebellions against state power. In such a culture, violence is not inevitably transgressive; it can assert authority or impose discipline as well as betray a lack of control.[2] If violence is a pervasive means of wielding power, preserving order, controlling behavior, and resolving conflicts, then it must extend beyond the scaffold to less visible sites, such as the household, in which relations are less clearly or stably dialectical, violence takes on a subtler range of meanings, and the line between acceptable and unacceptable, everyday and transgressive violence must constantly be negotiated and redrawn.

The decorums shaping household discipline in early modern England, and distinguishing between its legitimate and illegitimate manifestations, suggest that many members of the domestic culture of violence were multiply positioned. The violence that subordinates learn, for instance, is not inevitably, as in Barker's dynamic, turned against their oppressors; instead, a person who is the victim of violence in one location, or in relation to one person or group, may strive for dominance elsewhere (especially where the odds are better). Because of the wife and mistress's contradictory position in the early modern household — as both her husband's partner and his subordinate — I will scrutinize her relation to the culture of domestic violence in early modern England, hoping thereby to problematize the sharp dichotomy between the dominant and the subordinate, the violent and the victims. I am most interested here in the processes by which early modern culture attempted to distinguish between acceptable and unacceptable forms, targets, and occasions of violence in the household. Under what conditions were women licensed to discipline others? I am less interested in evidence of the extent to which women actually harmed, coerced, or threatened others than in a range of representations, including books on personal conduct, ballads, and plays such as *The Taming of the Shrew*, in which women's verbal and physical domination of others is constructed positively.

If, as Derek Cohen argues, "acts of violence belong to patriarchy as surely as fathers do," the violence in patriarchal households is not perpetrated only by fathers.[3] While marriage was widely represented in the early modern period as a struggle for dominance in which violence was, according to Joy Wiltenburg, "the fundamental arbiter," wives were not imagined to be violent only when resisting their husbands, despite the fact that such violent resistance was feared and frequently represented.[4] Elsewhere I have examined the disparity between assize court records, which tend to depict women more often as the victims of domestic *murder* than its perpetrators, and legal statutes, pamphlets, plays, and ballads, which invert this pattern by depicting women as the dangerous, rather than endangered, murderers of their intimates.[5] This sharp opposition — between the representation of women as casualties in court records and as killers in a range of legal and literary representations — collapses when the focus shifts from murder to non-lethal forms of violence. So does the sharp opposition between court records and other kinds of evidence. Prosecution rates are an unreliable gauge of the extent of any kind of legally prohibited conduct; they are even less helpful in assessing acceptable conduct. Non-lethal physical and verbal abuse is difficult to document through legal records because, for the most part, it was not illegal; as a result, it is impossible to quantify how common or how severe domestic violence was in the early modern period. Indeed, "domestic violence" seems an inadequate category for describing a whole range of behaviors, some of which were considered transgressive at the time and many others of which were not. The category elides the very distinctions that gave meaning to the use of physical force in early modern households, and obscures the rules by which that force was applied.

Those forms of violence that were censured in the early modern period as transgressive or disorderly, and were therefore scrutinized and regulated, are the most visible now. Legal records, and subsequent scholarship, focus on those assaults by subordinate women against their social superiors which can be understood as acts of resistance — for instance, the transgressive speech of "scolds" and "witches." Verbal or physical assaults on one's social *inferiors* left few traces precisely because they were not seen as transgressive. Furthermore, men's and women's non-criminal uses of violence were not of particular interest to those who documented sensational crimes. Obscured because it is assumed to be acceptable and unremarkable, non-lethal violence against acceptable targets (that is, obvious subordinates) tends to appear in comedies rather than tragedies, in subplots rather than mainplots, in folktales, ballads, and jokes, and woven through the prescriptions in books on personal conduct. In the absence of any unmediated access to what actually happened in early modern households, such discourses offer valuable insight into the available constructions of acceptable modes of domestic discipline. Such constructions, while not necessarily descriptions of lived experience, would have informed that experience, shaping its conditions of possibility.

The Taming of the Shrew provides a useful focus because it is increasingly labelled a "problem" comedy, in part because many readers and viewers find the taming process so disturbing. But where is the violence in the households the play depicts? If asked, most students of the play will focus on the relationship between Katharine and Petruchio, then immediately become confused. For the most expected form of domestic violence — wife-beating — does *not* occur here. Yet in looking for Petruchio to hit Katharine, and being unsettlingly disappointed that he does not, it is easy to miss the other forms of violence through which they negotiate their relationship, as well as the most prominent kind of violence in the play — the beating of servants by both masters and mistresses.

The shrew-taming tradition, which includes jokes, ballads, stories, and plays such as *The Taming of the Shrew*, and which thrives throughout the early modern period, assumes a gendered domestic hierarchy — man in charge, woman his subordinate — which is overturned by the shrew and righted by her tamer. The tradition is organized around a double standard for domestic violence. The shrews in folktales and ballads routinely encroach on their husbands' authority and usurp their power by beating, as well as scolding, them. The frequent pun on "baiting" and "beating" reinforces this association; in *The Winter's Tale*, for instance, Leontes calls Paulina "a callat [scold]/Of boundless tongue, who late hath beat her husband,/And now baits me" (2.3.91–93).[6] The "patient" husbands whose laments are recorded in ballads often complain about their wives' violence: in "The Patient Husband and the Scolding Wife" (c. 1660–80), the husband complains that his wife broke his nose with a ladle and beat him until he "bepist" himself; in "The Cruel Shrew:

Or, The Patient Man's Woe" (c. 1600–50), the husband describes how his wife "takes up a cudgel's end,/and breaks my head full sore."[7] In striking the first (and only) blow in her conflict with her husband, Katharine is thus typical of the physically and verbally abusive "shrew." Although this tradition depicts shrews as initiating, even monopolizing, domestic violence, it also suggests that the shrew's self-assertions, no matter how angry and violent, are temporary.[8]

The patient husband can regain his appropriate mastery through his own show of violence, a violence provoked and justified by his wife's conduct. Although some husbands lament their inability to rise to the challenge — the husband in "My Wife Will Be My Master" (c. 1640), for instance, regrets that he is not "a lusty man, and able for to baste" his wife — most husbands in these stories respond to their wives' insults and blows with maximum force.[9] The most famous example of this is the lengthy verse tale *A Merry Jest of a Shrewd and Curst Wife Lapped in Morel's Skin* (c. 1550), often considered a source for *The Taming of the Shrew*, in which a husband locks his wife in the cellar, beats her senseless with rods, then wraps her raw, bleeding body in a salted horsehide until she submits to him. As this example shows, the husband's violence — depicted as discipline more than as retaliation — is excessive. This is hardly a prescription for actual conduct, especially since most wives would not have survived such treatment. What interests me here is the double standard governing the violence in the shrew-taming tradition: women's violence is depicted as disorderly and transgressive; men's violence is depicted as a legitimate way of restoring the order that women have overturned. Violence thus seems to be a masculine prerogative that shrews usurp; when they insist on wearing the breeches, they also seize the rod.

But outside the supposedly comic shrew-taming tradition the gendering of domestic violence is considerably more complicated. Men's use of violence was not always endorsed, nor was women's use of violence always censured or ridiculed. During this period, as various scholars have shown, men's use of violence in the household was being questioned and monitored. Wife-beating had an ambiguous status in the early modern culture of violence precisely because of the wife's double position as an "authoritative mistress who is also a subjected wife."[10] Although a wife's misbehavior might sometimes require that she be treated like a child, that is, beaten, in most cases "that small disparity which . . . is betwixt man and wife," according to divine William Gouge, "permitteth not so high a power in an husband, and so low a servitude in a wife, as for him to beate her."[11] Wife-beating was not illegal, and within limits — that is, if it did not kill, maim, or make too much noise — neighbors and courts did not intervene to stop it. Yet prescriptive texts urged men not to abuse their right to "correct" and discipline their wives, not because it was immoral or unfair, but because it was counterproductive.[12]

While the comic tradition of violent spousal antagonism rollicked on, prescriptive literature articulated an emergent sense that the household, at least for husband and wife, should not be a site of physical contests. William Gouge even goes so far as to argue that a particularly recalcitrant wife who will not respond to "forceable meanes" other than beating, which might include being "restrained of liberty, [and] denied such things as she most affecteth," should be handed over to a magistrate to be beaten so that "shee may feare the Magistrate, and feele his hand, rather then her husbands."[13] Although William Whately argues that "even blows," when they are provoked, deserved, and judiciously administered as a last resort, "may well stand with the dearest kindnesses of matrimony," blows and marriage were increasingly being viewed as incompatible.[14] It is impossible to tell whether men were actually hitting their wives less frequently or less hard. But prescriptive literature was constructing wife-beating as a failure of control, a lapse in good household government. Although violence became a less acceptable solution to spousal strife, if not a less common one, the alternative, offered in *The Taming of the Shrew* as well as in prescriptions for domestic conduct, is not a nonviolent household. Instead, a happy ending involves ingenious forms of coercion which can be called "policy" rather than "force" and the redirection of both spouses' violence away from one another and toward more acceptable, that is, unambiguously subordinate, targets.

The focus on Petruchio's methods of taming Katherine, as well as the assumption that domestic violence is always and only enacted by husbands against wives, can obscure who hits whom and why in the play. As I have mentioned, Petruchio never strikes Katharine, despite the fact that she strikes him. Yet, as part of his "politic" regime for taming her, he relies on physical violence, directed at those near her and enacted before her eyes. The first instance of violence we see in the play occurs when Petruchio wrings Grumio's ears (1.2.). At the wedding, Petruchio cuffs the priest and throws winesops in the sexton's face (3.2). We hear that on their way home, he beats Grumio because Katharine's horse stumbled (4.1); once at home, he kicks, strikes, and throws food at his servants (4.1). Many critics emphasize that Petruchio's violence "is not aimed at Kate."[15] But whether we believe that Petruchio routinely acts this way, or that this is a performance in which he and his servants collaborate (a favorite justification of his conduct by critics, for which there is little evidence), he directs his violence at his subordinates — at those over whom he has power — to remind Katharine that she, too, is his subordinate and that he could beat her if he chose. At the wedding, we are told that

Katharine "trembled and shook" (3.2.157); when Petruchio abuses his servants, she intervenes to stop or reprimand him (4.1). She responds as if the violence *is* "aimed at" and threatening to her.

Just as Petruchio simultaneously espouses a "politic regime" that distinguishes him from other shrew-tamers and engages in extremely violent behavior, so Katharine is simultaneously tamed and domineering. Katharine, like Petruchio, uses violence to assert mastery over those to whom she feels superior. She threatens to hit Hortensio on the head with a three-legged stool (1.1.64–65); she ties up Bianca and strikes her; she breaks Hortensio's/Litio's head with the lute; and she strikes Petruchio (2.1). Petruchio's servants assume that Katharine will be violent toward them. Grumio warns Curtis that he will "soon feel" their new mistress's hand, "she being now at hand" (4.1.22–23). Indeed, later at Petruchio's house, Katharine beats Grumio for refusing to feed her (4.2).

Katharine's violence toward characters other than Petruchio is not necessarily, or not only, "shrewish." That is, it is not invariably depicted as something she must learn not to do. For if the blow she strikes at Petruchio allies her to the shrew tradition, some of her other outbursts place her in the tradition of spirited English lasses or, as Petruchio says admiringly, "lusty wench[es]" (2.1.156). In this tradition, in which women's violence is celebrated as helpful and fun, women assault others (usually men) in the interests of English nationalism, sexual probity, and social order. In the ballad "Couragious Betty of Chick-Lane," Betty beats up two tailors who "provoke" her — "She bang'd 'em, and bruis'd 'em, and bitterly us'd 'em" — thus reforming them; in "The Coy Cook-Maid," the far from coy maid brains, kicks, and threatens her Irish, Welsh, Spanish, French, and Dutch suitors, holding out for the poor English tailor, to whom she submits.[16] Long Meg of Westminster, and Moll Frith, the Roaring Girl, dress as men and use violence to defend themselves and other "good women" and to triumph over and humiliate men by being better fighters. But Moll Frith never marries, and Long Meg refuses to hit her husband, even in self-defense. When her husband decides to "try her manhood" by arming her with a staff and cudgeling her, she simply bows her head, drops to her knees, and submits to the beating. When her husband asks why she doesn't fight back, she replies: "Husband . . . whatsoever I have done to others, it behoveth me to be obedient towards you; and never shall it be said, though I can swinge a knave that wrongs me, that Long *Meg* shall be her husband's master: and therefore use me as you please."[17] Long Meg expressly distinguishes herself from shrews here, both by assuming that her husband is not "a knave that wrongs her," despite his cudgel, and by asserting that she does not want to master him. In all of these cases, women vent their spleen only against those who have no authority over them, and who are stout antagonists rather than dependents; the spectacle is therefore entertaining rather than threatening. In the last scene of *The Taming of the Shrew*, Petruchio urges Katharine to play the role of lusty wench in her verbal sparring match with the widow: "To her, Kate!" (5.2.33).

But Katharine is not only a "lusty wench," but a wife and mistress; her characterization participates in yet another discourse constructing women's violence positively. Prescriptive texts on personal conduct suggest that, under certain circumstances, women's use of violence was acceptable and unremarkable. In those relations in which women had authority — over servants and children, for instance — they were licensed to use violence. In fact, they were empowered to use violence to the same extent that they were construed as inappropriate targets of it. William Gouge's claim, for instance, that "God hath not ranked wives among those in the family who are to be corrected" depends upon the assumption that God has ranked others, children and servants, "among those in the family who are to be corrected."[18] The distinction made between wife-beating and servant-beating relied on the assumption that servants (like children, but unlike wives) were unambiguously subordinate to their masters. Even as prescriptive literature censured blows between spouses as disorderly, it defended the corporal punishment of servants as crucial to the maintenance of order. As Dod and Cleaver argue: "God hath put the rod of correction in the hands of the Governors of the family, by punishments to save them from destruction which, if the bridle were let loose unto them, they would run unto"; "household chastisement is agreeable to God's will, [as] is evident out of the Proverbs."[19] The wife asserts and maintains her status as "a joynt governour of the family" by administering "correction," especially corporal punishment.[20] To see women only as victims or resisters is to ignore those locations and relations in which women had authority; it also oversimplifies women's position in the household. While the household was an arena in which women were subordinate, it was also the arena in which they could most readily and legitimately exercise authority. Thus it was not just masculinity that was associated with violence — usurped by the shrew, then reasserted in the taming — but authority.

If some evidence suggests that the household was a dangerous place for women, in which they could be starved, overworked, sexually preyed upon, or beaten with little recourse, other kinds of evidence depict the household as a place in which women were dangerously powerful and likely to injure others. Assize court records, for instance, cast women in significant roles as the murderers of children and servants, who were more likely than any other members of the household to be murdered by family members. According to J. A.

Sharpe, women constituted 7% of those accused of non-domestic killing, but 42% of those accused of killing a relative, and 41% of those accused of killing servants or apprentices, in Essex assizes, 1560–1709; women also figured importantly in prosecutions for the murder of children, especially newborns.[21] The high acquittal rate for murders of servants suggests a reluctance to punish discipline that gets out of hand, that is, to criminalize household chastisement. Of 44 persons accused at these assizes of killing servants or apprentices, only 5 were found guilty (3 men, 2 women).[22] While these assize records would seem to suggest that women were more likely to murder their servants or their children than anyone else, they also represent only those outbreaks of violence in the family that ended in death, and that were discovered and prosecuted. As J. S. Cockburn has argued, "the true dimensions of domestic violence in earlier times are irretrievably lost behind a veil of domestic privacy, societal reticence and the common-law doctrine which sanctioned the 'moderate' correction of wives, children and servants by heads of households."[23] This veil was designed to protect the authority and privacy of *male* heads of household; but it also obscures the role of women in correcting servants and children.

Advice on running households and governing families often confers on women not only the right but the responsibility to use force. This is especially clear in instructions on parenting, which assume that mothers will shirk their obligation to discipline their children. Both parents were obligated to "beat into their childrens heads the lessons which they teach them." As Gouge explains, "correction is as physicke to purge out much corruption which lurketh in children, and as a salve to heale many wounds and sores made by their folly."[24] Children must be rigorously disciplined because they are corrupted by original sin, evil from birth; even when their bodies are small, their wills are great: "If this sparkle be suffered to increase, it will rage over, and burne downe the whole house." Only vigilant instruction and correction will shape them into virtuous people, "For wee are changed and become good, not by birth, but by Education."[25] In order to fulfill their obligations, parents must learn to govern their affections: "There is more neede in these dayes, to teach and admonish [parents] not to love them [their children] too much, then to perswade them to love them."[26] Parents offend not in disciplining children but in loving them too tenderly. Since "over-much lenitie is very great crueltie," good parents should "dissemble and hide their love."[27]

Mothers were assumed to be most likely to "cocker" their children by refraining from "correction." Mothers are "so farre from performing this dutie themselves, as they are much offended with their husbands if they doe it"; some coddling mothers even enjoin schoolmasters and tutors not to correct their children.[28] As Mary Beth Rose has argued, the threat offered by the overindulgent mother is that she encourages too close an attachment between herself and her child, preventing him from developing independence.²⁹ By sternly disciplining her child, a mother wields one kind of power, which associates her with the father as a household governor, while mitigating another, perhaps more threatening kind of influence, which allies her with the child in love. One particularly extreme statement describes how the good mother "holds not [the father's] hand from due strokes, but bares their [the children's] skins with delight, to his fatherly stripes."³⁰

The writers of books on parenting and household government recognize the danger of those "unnaturall parents" who beat their children "too sorely: so as the childe is lamed, or some way so hurt as he shall feele it as long as he liveth."³¹ One pamphlet, for instance, *Strange and Lamentable News from Dullidg-Wells; or, the Cruel and Barbarous Father* (1678), describes a father who cudgels and stomps his twelve-year-old son to death, then claims the child was kicked by a horse. The author of the pamphlet insists that "it was the too excessive Correction of his Father, that brought him to his end."³² Parents who killed their children and masters who lamed or killed servants or apprentices might face criminal charges. Obviously, it was assumed that discipline could be distinguished from injury, that there was a meaningful difference between "correction" and "excessive correction." But cases of "excessive correction" turned murderous do not figure importantly either in court records or in pamphlet accounts of notorious murder; even less is made of beatings that did not end in death or permanent injury. While writers such as Gouge and Dod and Cleaver acknowledge the possibility of overly severe or brutal discipline of children (and servants), they do not dwell on it.

Instead, they insist that the problem is parents, especially mothers, who are unwilling to assert their authority and to use appropriate forms of correction. In an amazing rhetorical displacement, Dod and Cleaver depict the refusal to discipline children as a kind of murder. Lenient parents "make graves for their owne children, and burie them quicke without all compassion, and thinke they doe well in it." Foolishly, "while the parent layeth his hand upon his childs mouth, to keepe away the colde winde, he presseth it downe so hard, that he strangleth him therewith." "Thus many a father and mother in the world, have killed their deare ones by their inordinate love and cockering of them, and thus many poore infants must still be murthered, because parents will not be warned."³³ According to surviving court records, our only, if inadequate, witnesses, most poor murdered infants in this period were illegitimate newborns killed or fatally neglected by their mothers (and perhaps fathers, although legal statutes and prosecutions were less interested in them), who hoped to avoid disgrace, poverty, and criminal prosecution for bastardy. Most murdered children were the victims of their parents' or employers' violence. Yet Dod and Cleaver suggest just the opposite, that parents murder their children by neglecting to discipline them.

Although household chastisement was an obligation, it was not a license to lash out in anger. Instead, domestic discipline was expected to operate within carefully delineated rules.[34] Parents and employers should always punish in response to a particular fault, rather than out of anger; they should be sure that they are punishing the right party and that the punishment suits the crime, the age, and the temper of the offender; they should consider whether the mistake was intentional or accidental; and they should not disgrace the servant or child in front of others. The offender should know why he or she is being punished. Conduct books even describe a gendered decorum of domestic violence: "And as it is not comely or beseeming, that the wife should take upon her to rule and correct the men-servants; so likewise, it is not comely or meete, that the husband should meddle with the punishing or chastising of the maide-servants"; "for a mans nature scorneth and disdaineth to be beaten of a woman, and a maids nature is corrupted with the stripes of a man." The assumption here is that discipline can only become unseemly when the dominant and submissive roles are played by people of different genders. This gendered etiquette for beating licenses women to inflict corporal punishment, yet assumes that they, like men, should follow a complex set of rules so that this violence will support gender and class hierarchies, rather than upsetting them. Gouge proposes an exception to the gendered division of the labor of beating, however: "if a maid should wax stout, and mannish, and turne against her Mistresse, she being weake, sickly, with child, or otherwise unable to master her maid, the Master may and must beat downe her stoutnesse and rebellion."[35] That is, if a maid-servant acts like a man, she may appropriately be treated like one.

Because disciplinary violence was as much about authority and obedience, class and status, as it was about gender, an escape into female separatism did not necessarily mean an escape from violence, unless it was also a movement away from relations of dominance and submission. In convents, for instance, the Abbess was supposed to act as both Mistress and Mother, that is, with both severity and affection. Alexia Gray's translation of the rule of St. Benedict advises that the Abbess "punish with bodyly punishment and blowes the stubborne hardharted and disobedient, so soone as ever they have offended." The Abbess may employ "bodyly Chastisement" when excommunication fails, but only she can license others to do so: it is "not lawfull for any to excommunicate or stricke the Sisters, excepting her onely to whom the authoritie is given by the Abbesse."[36] All of the sisters may, however, chastise children under sixteen years. Again, the issue is that peers may not hit peers or subordinates their superiors.[37]

Striking a subordinate counts as a transgression only when it disregards the rules. Yet such indecorous acts of "household chastisement," those that are marked as exceptional rather than everyday, are most likely to be represented, especially on the stage. While there may have been more physical scuffles on stage than those registered in dialogue or stage directions, textual references to non-lethal violence against family members (including servants) are extremely rare. Those kinds of violence that were probably the norm in early modern households, or were, at the very least, propounded as normative and legitimate — disciplinary beatings administered by parents and masters or mistresses — emerge into the visibility of the stage only under unusual circumstances. The earnest, moderate "correction" described in conduct books does not appear on stage, nor is it sung about in ballads. Instead, characters who beat their subordinates are usually tyrannical men or women who abuse their authority, striking out in anger, with neither justification nor discretion. I shall focus on representations of violent mothers and mistresses here. In *The Comedy of Errors*, which includes a great deal of slapstick violence, most of it directed at servants, the first violence mentioned (although not enacted before us) is that which Dromio of Ephesus reports he has received from his mistress, Adriana, because he served her cold meat; this is also the first reference to Adriana, who is introduced simultaneously as mistress and as violent chastiser (1.2.46–47, 65). In *A Chaste Maid in Cheapside*, Maudlin drags her daughter Moll by the hair because she will not cooperate in her parents' marriage plans for her; an observer calls Maudlin a "cruel mother." In *Volpone*, Nano suspects that Lady Politic Would-Be will "beat her woman," because cosmetics cannot compensate for her red nose.[38] In these instances, which occur in comedies, the enacted or expected violence marks the women as foolish, shrewish, and unworthy of the power they have.

Comic associations among female authority, vanity, and violence were not limited to the stage or the street. They also provided a rich resource for defaming powerful women, informing, for instance, gossip circulated about Queen Elizabeth. The infamous "scandal letter" addressed by Mary Stuart to Queen Elizabeth attempts to anger Elizabeth by depicting her as a shrew in these familiar terms — as simultaneously vicious and ridiculous. In this letter, which some biographers have used uncritically despite its provenance, Mary attributes to the Countess of Shrewsbury the claim that Elizabeth swore at and beat her ladies in waiting, going so far as to break one woman's finger and to stab another's hand. Carolly Erickson dimly recognizes that the Elizabeth depicted in this letter is a type, "more suited to the stalls of fishwives or the squabbling of prostitutes in the stews than to the queen's privy chamber," yet she bases her own depiction of the aging Elizabeth on this letter nonetheless: "Flowers in her hair, round oaths on her lips, she stormed through her apartments, slapping and stabbing at her women when they displeased her and demanding to be told how beautiful she was."[39] The depiction compels belief because it is so familiar; the conjunction of vanity and violence readily discredits even the most powerful woman's claims to authority. The "scandal letter" is useful in this context, I think, because it suggests how inaccessible to us women's actual domestic conduct was, even under exceptional circumstances; the available terms in which to represent women's exercise of authority are so limited that this undated letter, with its claims to inside knowledge, is determined just as much by literary convention as are dramatic representations.

Shakespeare's depiction of Cleopatra offers an extended example of the conditions under which women's use of disciplinary violence emerges into visibility, and, especially, of how suspicion of female power can blur the distinctions among fishwives, prostitutes, and queens. Cleopatra drags a messenger who bears bad tidings (that Antony has married Octavia) by the hair, striking him, and warning: "Thou shalt be whipped with wire and stewed in brine, / Smarting in lingering pickle!" (2.5.66–67). She even draws a knife and threatens to kill him. But Cleopatra immediately repents her action:

These hands do lack nobility, that they strike
A meaner than myself, since I myself
Have given myself the cause. (2.5.83–85)

While it would be acceptable for a queen to strike one meaner than herself, she may not do so without a good reason; furthermore, the knife marks clearly the shift from discipline (however excessive) to tyrannical assault. Cleopatra's abuse of the messenger contributes to the depiction of her in the play as passionate, irrational, uncontrolled — and "tawny" (1.1.6).

This episode in *Antony and Cleopatra* suggests that assaults on subordinates were likely to be represented as transgressive when they were attributed not only to women but to those racially marked as "other." *Othello* should also be considered in this context. The drama relatively rarely depicts husbands hitting their wives. Yet we do see Othello slap Desdemona; the text suggests that this action shocks her — "I have not deserved this" — and Lodovico, who protests that "this would not be believed in Venice" (4.1.244–45). One reason it is so startling that Othello slaps Desdemona, and in front of witnesses, is that his doing so indicates that he has lost control. Her offense is unclear, to her and to others, and his public display of his inability to master his feelings and his wife is unseemly. Just as prescriptive texts such as sermons and conduct books

Figure 1. From "Halfe a dozen of Good Wives: All for a Penny," *Roxburghe Ballads* I,
152–53. By permission of the British Library. This same woodcut also illustrates another Roxburghe Ballad, "The Patient Husband and Scolding Wife." On the right, the
woman raising her stick is in the typical position of the shrew—armed and above her
husband. While this image is a common one, the norm the shrew inverts—the husband
"on top"—is rarely represented. Images of men wielding sticks over their wives are
extremely rare, especially in comic contexts such as this one.

increasingly discouraged wife-beating, so those few plays that depict a husband hitting his wife suggest that his act demonstrates his failure rather than
hers.[40] In *Othello*, the racial difference between husband and wife exacerbates
the inappropriateness of his action, since the legitimacy of domestic violence
was determined as much or more by the status relation between the two parties
as by the severity of the violence. For a sixteenth- or seventeenth-century
audience, I think, it would not be clear that Othello has the right to beat
Desdemona, not only because she is his wife and thus not unambiguously his
inferior, but also because she is white and he is black.

    Taken together, these few instances suggest that the "household chastise-
ments" urged upon masters, mistresses, and parents, and operating according
to carefully delineated rules, did not provide much of interest to watch or

Figure 2. From "Anne Wallen's Lamentation, For the Murthering of Her Husband John Wallen," *Pepys Ballads* I, 124. By permission of the Pepys Library, Magdalene College, Cambridge. This is the most extreme depiction of the "woman on top." The details indicating a domestic setting are typical of woodcuts of domestic murders.

discuss. Those beatings represented on the stage, in both comedies and trag-edies, are depicted as transgressive, illicit, objectionable. They are also often attributed to women and, in those two Shakespearean cases that occur in trag-edies, associated with a Moor and an Egyptian. The woodcuts illustrating bal-lads, broadsides, and pamphlets similarly tend to depict inversions and trans-gressions — women beating or killing their husbands — far more frequently than normative kinds of violence, such as the disciplining of servants (see Figures 1 and 2). Indeed, it is almost impossible to find visual representations of acceptable forms of "household chastisement." It is as if acceptable forms of violence within the household are invisible; they cannot be brought into view — in pictures or on the stage or even in gossip — unless they break the rules or depart from the norm.

But then there is *The Taming of the Shrew*, which, given the paucity of dramatic and visual representations of domestic violence, seems fraught with incident. As I have mentioned, the play is not as violent as some shrew-taming stories, such as *A Merry Jest* or even *Punch and Judy*. Nor is it that *Shrew* is more violent than, say, *Titus Andronicus*, with its mutilations and murders, or than the many plays preceding and succeeding it in which body parts (a tongue, a finger, a hand, a heart, etc.) become crucial props.[41] What distinguishes *Shrew*, I think, is that its violence is so mundane: it does not kill or maim; it does not require poisoned crucifixes, Bibles, or portraits, or any of the other ingenious methods of tragedy; whatever disorder it creates is temporary; and it takes place at home and among intimates.

In *The Taming of the Shrew*, we begin with the familiar spectacle of a woman who abuses authority — Katharine binding and striking her younger sister — and then watch the process by which she learns the complex etiquette for domestic violence. Obviously, Petruchio teaches other husbands how to tame their unruly wives. Under his instruction, Katharine also learns not only how to be an obedient wife, but how to use violence to assert dominance in more socially acceptable ways. Although many critics argue that, as actress Fiona Shaw puts it, "Petruchio abuses a servant to teach her that the abuse of servants isn't right," I would argue that Petruchio inducts Katharine into a more complex moral universe and network of power relations than this.[42] This is especially clear in *The Taming of a Shrew*, in which the violence progresses differently. In this "alternate version" of the play, printed in 1594, the first violent act we witness is Ferando (the husband and master, or Petruchio figure) beating his servants in front of Kate; as a stage direction explains, "He beates them all."[43] Kate's first act of violence is not to beat her tutor, her suitor, or her sister (none of whom she ever hits in this version), but to beat her husband's servant, *after* she has watched him do so repeatedly. In this version of the play, she observes and emulates violence toward servants as an acceptable form of unruliness, which purports to maintain rather than disrupt household order.

Throughout *The Taming of the Shrew*, Katharine attempts to instruct others in obedience and subordination by means of both physical violence (from torturing her sister to "swingeing" Bianca and the widow "soundly forth unto their husbands" [5.2.108]) and of assertive speech (from her first complaint to her father to her final sermon to other wives). What Katharine learns is not to be less aggressive, but to redirect her violence toward more appropriate targets; that Bianca becomes an acceptable target by the end of the play — a "breeching scholar" — suggests how the balance of power has shifted between the sisters. When Katharine uses violence to dominate servants and other women rather than to resist her father and husband, her conduct is presented as acceptable, even admirable.

While it is true that Katharine often resorts to violence "because of provo-

cation or intimidation resulting from her status as a woman," as Coppèlia
Kahn has argued, she also acts out of an empowerment resulting from her
status as a *gentle*woman.[44] She acts simultaneously out of gender subordination and class (or age) privilege. It is not just that class is displaced onto
gender, as Lynda Boose has brilliantly argued, but also that attention to gender
alone can obscure conflicts of class in which Katharine is a privileged participant. Richard Burt argues that "Petruchio and Kate become emotionally closer
whenever Petruchio enables Kate to redirect the aggression he directs at her at
another victim"; Burt identifies other women as the "socially acceptable target
of aggression" for Katharine.[45] In her violent outbursts, then, Katharine ex-
hibits "the simultaneous recognition of [her] own oppression and a will-to-
power" that Kim Hall identifies in some women's writings; she also participates in the dramatic representation of "aggressive female characters [who]
manipulate and coerce other female characters" to which Douglas Bruster has
recently drawn attention.[46] As Hall's and Bruster's work makes clear, women
become acceptable targets of violence especially when they are marked as
inferior to or weaker than the women who dominate them. In the taming
process, however, Petruchio does not simply teach Katharine to look for female scapegoats; instead, he instructs her to look down the social scale. In her
first bout with Petruchio, she imperiously advises him that she is not one of his
subordinates: "Go, fool, and whom thou keep'st command" (2.1.250). Marriage, however, transforms her into one whom he keeps and therefore can
command. But it also confers on her more authority than she exercised before.
After the wedding, at the same time that Petruchio demonstrates that Katharine cannot do as she pleases, and that she cannot command him, he also
suggests that she look elsewhere for the pleasures of domination, to those who
should "attend" on her: "*They* shall go forward, Kate, at thy command. — /
Obey the bride, you that attend on her" (3.2.211–12, my emphasis).

Just as the pivotal scene in Katharine's submission is the sun and moon
exchange (4.5), the turning point in her assumption of command is the scene
in which she hits Grumio because he refuses her request for food, teases her,
and "triumph[s] upon . . . [her] misery" (4.3.34). At this moment in Petruchio's household, Katharine's relation both to him and to the servants is
uncertain. Grumio acts as if he is Petruchio's ally here, empowered to thwart
and discipline Katharine; throughout the play, Grumio has been a disorderly
figure — from the violent confusion of his first exchange with Petruchio, to his
conspiracy with Petruchio in tormenting the tailor and Katharine, to his imitation of Petruchio in beating a fellow servant, Curtis. When Katharine beats a
male servant in anger, she reveals that she has not yet resigned herself to her
position as wife, that she is still not in control of her anger. But she also

demonstrates that she is learning more acceptable targets for her anger, and that she is testing out domestic authority on Petruchio's model. Indeed, Grumio, who has violated class hierarchy throughout the play, "knocking" Petruchio, tormenting Katharine, and hitting a fellow servant, becomes a more obedient and less raucous servant, and therefore less visible, as Katharine submits to taming. This slap does, then, seem to discipline him.

Katharine not only shifts the targets of her aggression, she also shifts her tactics; this exchange with Grumio is also pivotal in that process. Throughout *The Taming of the Shrew*, physical and verbal violence are complexly interconnected. Katharine's speech is presented as abusive, disorderly, and wounding; when Hortensio enters pilloried in the lute, he conflates Katharine's verbal and physical assaults: "And with that word she struck me on the head" (2.1.149). This commingling of physical injury and discursive harm is not unique to the "shrew." Grumio warns that Petruchio can use rhetorical figures to "disfigure" Katharine (1.2.105–7). Grumio himself uses violence to command attention. Asking Curtis to lend him his ear, he then cuffs him: "This cuff was but to knock at your ear and beseech listening" (4.1.46–47). Even in the play's last scene, words can wound: Katharine complains of the Widow's "mean meaning" and Petruchio remarks that jests about shrewish wives can "glance away from" him and "maim" the other two husbands "outright" (5.2.61–62). As Katharine learns to entreat and beseech, then, it is not surprising that she employs physical force to command her audience's attention, dragging in Bianca and the Widow "as prisoners of her womanly persuasion" (5.2.124). The focus has shifted from overt physical violence (slapping and cuffing) to less injurious coercion (dragging and pushing) and to discursive domination (the longest speech in the play, as many critics have remarked). In relation to more acceptable targets and by means of more acceptable tactics, Katharine still dominates others.

I am *not* arguing here that Katharine and Petruchio are "equals" in the culture of domestic violence. He clearly has the upper hand, because he controls Katharine's access to material resources (like food), he is stronger, he has more lines, he addresses the audience directly and when he is alone (we never see Katharine alone), and, as the husband, he is assumed to be the one who should be "on top." Indeed, he rewards Katharine's submission to him by authorizing her to domineer over others. Furthermore, in early modern England, men and women use different forms of violence, choose different targets, and act violently in different contexts. Gender shapes how the culture perceives and responds to their violence. All of the representations I have discussed, from conduct books to plays, are to some extent prescriptive, instructing men and women in these complexly gendered decorums of violence.

With the exception of Mary Stuart's "scandal letter," all of the evidence I have used was written by men. While I can demonstrate a range of representations of women's violence, I cannot show the extent of women's violence, how women felt about resorting to violence, or the reactions of subordinate women to the household chastisements inflicted on them by other women. It has not been my goal to prove that women were actually violent; I have assumed that sometimes they were. What has interested me here are those circumstances under which women's violence was not demonized or criminalized. In the early modern evidence that survives, women are not only represented as victims, or as murdering those who abuse or oppress them—which I sometimes find quite satisfying, even if these representations invariably conclude with the women's executions. Women are also represented as chastising their inferiors. I do not wish just to create a new category for women in the household; it is not particularly revolutionary to suggest that in addition to being the victims or murderers of men, they might be the victims or murderers of other women. Instead, I hope to contribute to efforts to demonstrate how complex relationships within the household were, and how inseparably intertwined are the categories of class, gender, race, sexuality, authority, and violence as they conflict and overlap to position co-habitants in the household.[47]

Obviously, I join others in trying to render visible forms of violence that many of the most-studied representations, such as Shakespeare's plays, occlude; but I have tried to avoid the rhetoric of indignant discovery that often gets in the way of that project. To be too shocked by representations of domestic violence in the early modern period is to obscure how very familiar that violence is. It can be hard to recognize in the surviving evidence precisely because it was so pervasive and assumed; we ignore it in those instances—between parents and children, masters and servants—in which it was most accepted and legitimate. The rhetoric of indignant discovery also conceals the ways that a reader's own investments and assumptions can blind him or her to certain kinds of violence. As Linda Gordon has argued about her work on the history of family violence in America: "Defending women against male violence is so urgent that we fear women's loss of status as deserving, political 'victims' if we acknowledge women's own aggressions." In the last decade or so, this reluctance, and a practical concern about diverting scarce funds away from battered women, has created deep divisions between researchers and activists focusing on "domestic violence," which is usually construed as synonymous with wife abuse, and those who define their topic as "family violence," to include attention to women's aggression as well as their victimization.[48] While I agree with those who focus on battered women that men's violence causes more harm and is therefore a more pressing social problem, I also think that the reluctance to scrutinize women's violence obstructs the project of understanding everyday life in the past and of improving it now. It is too easy to draw sharp lines between innocent victims and evil perpetrators, and to side with the former. Inhabitants of a culture of violence participate in and perpetuate it in ways that blur those distinctions. If we refuse to see that, then we collude in reproducing such a culture.

The double position of the wife in the early modern culture of domestic violence troubles the satisfying prospect of resistance, and muddies the reassuring distinction between victims and aggressors, insisting on a less comfortable category of analysis — complicity — and a less self-righteous stance for the critic. Finally, the rhetoric of indignant discovery insists on the difference between "then" and "now" in too self-congratulating a way, obscuring the enduring familiarity of domestic violence.

Notes

1. Francis Barker, *The Culture of Violence: Essays on Tragedy and History* (Chicago: University of Chicago Press, 1993), p. 189.

2. Susan Dwyer Amussen, "Punishment, Discipline, and Power: The Social Meanings of Violence in Early Modern England," *Journal of British Studies* 34, 1 (1995): 1–34.

3. Derek Cohen, *Shakespeare's Culture of Violence* (New York: St. Martin's, 1993), p. 1. The assumption that men were the only or the primary disciplinarians in households is widely shared.

4. Joy Wiltenburg, *Disorderly Women and Female Power in the Street Literature of Early Modern England and Germany* (Charlottesville: University of Virginia Press, 1992), p. 137.

5. Frances E. Dolan, *Dangerous Familiars: Representations of Domestic Crime in England, 1550–1700* (Ithaca, N.Y.: Cornell University Press, 1994).

6. Citations of all Shakespeare plays other than *The Taming of the Shrew* are from *The Complete Works of Shakespeare*, ed. David Bevington, 4th ed. (New York: Harper Collins, 1994).

7. *Roxburghe Ballads*, vols. 1–3 ed. William Chappell; vols. 4–9 ed. J. Woodfall Ebsworth (Hertford: Ballad Society, 1872–99), rpt. 9 vols. (New York: AMS, 1966), 7: 182–84, 1: 94–98.

8. On the shrew-taming tradition, see Lynda E. Boose, "Scolding Brides and Bridling Scolds: Taming the Woman's Unruly Member," *Shakespeare Quarterly* 42, 2 (1991): 179–213; Valerie Wayne, "Refashioning the Shrew," *Shakespeare Studies* 17 (1985): 159–87; Wiltenburg, *Disorderly Women*; and Linda Woodbridge, *Women and the English Renaissance: Literature and the Nature of Womankind, 1540–1620* (Urbana: University of Illinois Press, 1984).

9. *Roxburghe Ballads* 7: 188–89.

10. Catherine Belsey, *The Subject of Tragedy: Identity and Difference in Renaissance Drama* (London: Methuen, 1985), p. 154. See also, among many others, Lena Cowen

Orlin, *Private Matters and Public Culture in Post-Reformation England* (Ithaca, N.Y.: Cornell University Press, 1994), pp. 98–104. While the wife's double position has been much discussed, her relation to the complex dynamics of domestic discipline has not.

11. William Gouge, *Of Domesticall Duties: Eight Treatises* (London, 1634), p. 395. Modernized and standardized versions of many of the primary texts discussed here are included in William Shakespeare, *The Taming of the Shrew: Texts and Contexts*, ed. Frances E. Dolan (Boston: Bedford Books, 1996); references to the play will be to David Bevington's edition, included in that volume.

12. On changing attitudes toward domestic violence, see Susan Dwyer Amussen, " 'Being stirred to much unquietness': Violence and Domestic Violence in Early Modern England," *Journal of Women's History* 6.2 (1994): 70–89; Emily Detmer, "Civilizing Subordination: Domestic Violence and *The Taming of the Shrew*," *Shakespeare Quarterly* 48, 3 (1997): 273–94; Anthony Fletcher, *Gender, Sex, and Subordination in England 1500–1800* (New Haven and London: Yale University Press, 1995), chaps. 10 and 11; Laura Gowing, *Domestic Dangers: Women, Words, and Sex in Early Modern London* (Oxford: Clarendon Press, 1996), chap. 6; and Margaret Hunt, "Wife Beating, Domesticity and Women's Independence in Eighteenth-Century London," *Gender and History* 4.1 (1992): 10–33.

13. Gouge, *Of Domesticall Duties*, p. 397.

14. William Whately, *A Bride-Bush* (London, 1623), p. 108.

15. Wayne, "Refashioning the Shrew," p. 171.

16. *Roxburghe Ballads* 3: 641–44; 3: 627–30.

17. *The Life of Long Meg of Westminster* (London, 1635) rpt. in *Old Book Collectors Miscellany*, ed. Charles Hindley (London: Reeves and Turner, 1871), 2: 36.

18. Gouge, *Of Domesticall Duties*, p. 395.

19. John Dod and Robert Cleaver, *A Godly Forme of Household Government* (London, 1612), sigs. D5ᵛ, D4ᵛ.

20. Gouge, *Of Domesticall Duties*, p. 395.

21. J. A. Sharpe, "Domestic Homicide in Early Modern England," *The Historical Journal* 24, 1 (1981): 29–48, esp. pp. 37, 36; J. S. Cockburn, "Patterns of Violence in English Society: Homicide in Kent, 1560–1985," *Past and Present* 130 (February 1991): 70–106, esp. pp. 95–97.

22. Sharpe, "Domestic Homicide," pp. 38–39.

23. Cockburn, "Patterns of Violence," pp. 93–95.

24. Gouge, *Of Domesticall Duties*, pp. 549, 553.

25. Dod and Cleaver, *A Godly Forme of Household Government*, sig. T. On pedagogical violence, see Rebecca Bushnell, *A Culture of Teaching: Early Modern Humanism in Theory and Practice* (Ithaca, N.Y.: Cornell University Press, 1996).

26. Dod and Cleaver, *A Godly Forme of Household Government*, sig. Tᵛ.

27. Gouge, *Of Domesticall Duties*, p. 553; Dod and Cleaver, *A Godly Forme of Household Government*, sig. T.

28. Gouge, *Of Domesticall Duties*, p. 557; cf. Dod and Cleaver, *A Godly Forme of Household Government*, sigs. T2ᵛ–T3.

29. Mary Beth Rose, "Where Are the Mothers in Shakespeare? Options for Gender Representation in the English Renaissance," *Shakespeare Quarterly* 42, 3 (1991): 291–314, esp. p. 301.

30. Daniel Rogers, *Matrimonial Honor* (London, 1642), p. 299. I would like to

thank Marilyn Luecke for this reference. On the complexity of the mother's position, see her "The Reproduction of Culture and the Culture of Reproduction in Elizabeth Clinton's *The Countess of Lincolnes Nurserie*," in *Women, Writing, and Culture in Early Modern Britain*, ed. Mary Elizabeth Burke, Jane Donawerth, Linda Dove, and Karen Nelson (Syracuse, N.Y.: Syracuse University Press, forthcoming).

31. Gouge, *Of Domesticall Duties*, p. 558.

32. *Strange and Lamentable News from Dullidg-Wells; or, the Cruel and Barbarous Father* (London, 1678), sig. A3ᵛ.

33. Dod and Cleaver, *A Godly Forme of Household Government*, sig. S8ᵛ.

34. Amussen, " 'Being Stirred', " p. 82, and "Punishment," pp. 12–18.

35. Dod and Cleaver, *A Godly Forme of Household Government*, sig. Aa3ᵛ; Gouge, *Of Domesticall Duties*, p. 672; cf. Henry Smith, *A Preparative to Marriage* (London, 1591), p. 25. See Fletcher, *Gender, Sex, and Subordination*, p. 216, for a discussion of how Pepys delegated the beating of a female servant to his wife in accord with such advice.

36. *The Rule of the Most Blissed Father Saint Benedict, Patriarke of All Munkes*, trans. Alexia Gray (Gant, 1632), sigs. Bᵛ–B2, Dᵛ, G2–G2ᵛ.

37. On why servants should not hit their fellows, see Thomas Carter, *Carters Christian Common Wealth; or, Domesticall Dutyes Deciphered* (London, 1627), sigs. S4–S5.

38. Thomas Middleton, *A Chaste Maid in Cheapside* (5.1.26); Ben Jonson, *Volpone* (3.2.46–47), both in *Drama of the English Renaissance II: The Stuart Period*, ed. Russell A. Fraser and Norman Rabkin (New York and London: Macmillan, 1976). Amy Richlin's discussion of Ovid's *Ars Amatoria* suggests a classical precedent for this conjunction of cosmetics use and violence toward servants: "Ovid . . . suggests that it isn't nice for a woman to scratch the face of her *ornatrix* (hairdresser) with her fingernails or to stick hairpins in her arms, causing the servant to curse the head she works on (3.239–42). The late first-century A.D. satirist Juvenal picks up the same motif (6.487–507), in the context of the flogging of slaves by bored mistresses." Amy Richlin, "Making Up a Woman: The Face of Roman Gender," *Off with Her Head! The Denial of Women's Identity in Myth, Religion, and Culture*, ed. Howard Eilberg-Schwartz and Wendy Doniger (Berkeley: University of California Press, 1995), p. 193.

39. Carolly Erickson, *The First Elizabeth* (New York: Summit, 1983), pp. 264, 262; cf. p. 329; Christopher Hibbert, *The Virgin Queen: The Personal History of Elizabeth I* (London: Viking, 1990), p. 122; David N. Durant, *Bess of Hardwick: Portrait of an Elizabethan Dynast* (London: Weidenfeld and Nicolson, 1977), pp. 128–35.

40. In her work-in-progress on Mary Wroth's *Urania*, Mary Elizabeth Burke lists some other plays in which a tyrannical husband beats his wife.

41. For a tongue, see *The Spanish Tragedy*; a finger, *The Changeling*; a hand, *The Duchess of Malfi*; a heart, *'Tis Pity She's a Whore*.

42. Carol Rutter, *Clamorous Voices: Shakespeare's Women Today* (London: Women's Press, 1988), p. 18. In her recent essay on the play, Natasha Korda also emphasizes an educational process, in this case one in which Petruchio "seeks to educate Kate in her new role as a consumer of household cates" (Natasha Korda, "Household Kates: Domesticating Commodities in *The Taming of the Shrew*," *Shakespeare Quarterly* 47, 2 [1996]: 109–31, esp. p. 112). As I do here, Korda emphasizes the authority conferred on the housewife in prescriptive literature, and in the play, but she focuses on the authority to oversee and manage status objects, rather than to discipline servants.

43. *A Pleasant Conceited History, Called The Taming of a Shrew*, ed. Graham Holder-

ness and Bryan Loughrey (Lanham, Md.,: Barnes and Noble, 1992), sig. D3. Compared to *The Shrew*, *A Shrew* also makes it more clear that, in the "wager scene," Kate "brings her sisters forth by force . . . thrusting [them] before her." *The Taming of a Shrew* was published in 1594; *The Taming of the Shrew* was not published until 1623, in Shakespeare's First Folio. Critics have long debated the relationship between the two versions. See Graham Holderness, "Introduction," to his facsimile edition, p. 34; Brian Morris, "Introduction," *The Taming of the Shrew*, by William Shakespeare, ed. Morris (London: Methuen, 1981), pp. 12–50.

44. Coppèlia Kahn, *Man's Estate: Masculine Identity in Shakespeare* (Berkeley: University of California Press, 1981), pp. 104–18, p. 108.

45. Lynda Boose, "*The Taming of the Shrew*, Good Husbandry, and Enclosure," in *Shakespeare Reread: The Texts in New Contexts*, ed. Russ McDonald (Ithaca, N.Y.: Cornell University Press, 1994), pp. 193–225; Richard A. Burt, "Charisma, Coercion, and Comic Form in *The Taming of the Shrew*," *Criticism* 26, 4 (1984): 295–311, esp. pp. 299, 302.

46. Kim F. Hall, "'I Rather Would Wish to Be a Black-Moor': Beauty, Race, and Rank in Lady Mary Wroth's *Urania*," in *Women, "Race," and Writing in the Early Modern Period*, ed. Margo Hendricks and Patricia Parker (London and New York: Routledge, 1994), pp. 178–94, esp. p. 180; Douglas Bruster, "Female-Female Eroticism and the Early Modern Stage," *Renaissance Drama* n.s. 24 (1993): 1–32, esp. p. 14.

47. On the importance of using gender in tension with other categories of analysis and systems of difference, see Hall, "'I Rather Would Wish to Be a Black-Moor'"; Dympna C. Callaghan, "Re-Reading Elizabeth Cary's *The Tragedie of Mariam, Faire Queene of Jewry*"; and Ania Loomba, "The Color of Patriarchy: Critical Difference, Cultural Difference, and Renaissance Drama," all in *Women, "Race," and Writing in the Early Modern Period*, ed. Margo Hendricks and Patricia Parker (London and New York: Routledge, 1994).

48. Linda Gordon, "Family Violence, Feminism, and Social Control," *Feminist Studies* 12.3 (1986): pp. 453–78, esp. p. 458; see also *Current Controversies on Family Violence*, ed. Richard J. Gelles and Donileen R. Loseke (Newbury Park, Calif.: Sage, 1993).

PART III

EVERYDAY
TRANSGRESSIONS

11

Money and the
Regulation of Desire

The Prostitute and the Marketplace in
Seventeenth-Century Holland

Ann Jensen Adams

In 1654 Gerard Terborch created an image of prostitution whose exquisite portrayal belies its subject (Berlin, Staatliche Museum, Dahlem, Figure 1).[1] Seated in a lavishly appointed interior, a soldier raises his hand—and may proffer a coin—to an expensively dressed young woman, whose profile is outlined by a bed richly draped in red.[2] A slightly older women, a procuress seated between them, is preoccupied with the glass of wine she silently sips. The latter's presence and activity dispel any doubt about the nature of the encounter. Rather than responding to the gesture or accepting money—much less soliciting either—the object of the soldier's attention stands impassively, almost demurely, her face hidden from our view. The artist provides us with little indication of whether she will accept or reject the offer—although presumably if she and her partner have maneuvered the comely young soldier this far into their rooms they will not let him escape without turning a profit. The soldier communicates with the woman wordlessly, almost respectfully. His emotions, too, remain opaque. The lust apparently driving the exchange—desire for money by the women, and desire for sexual satisfaction by the man—can be inferred only from these few clues to its subject rather than from its representation.

Terborch's painting contrasts dramatically with both earlier and contemporaneous representations of sexual encounters, which customarily depict one or both parties with their passions out of control. Gerard van Honthorst, for example, shows a lusty soldier fondling the generous breasts of a young woman, whose fingers in turn grasp a symbolically enflamed candle (c. 1621, Herzog Anton Ulrich-Museum, Braunschweig, Figure 2).[3] In a painting by

Figure 1. Gerard Terborch, *"The Paternal Admonition"*, c. 1654. Staatliche Museum, Dahlem, Berlin. Photo, S. J. Gudlaugsson, *Gerhard Ter Borch* (The Hague: Martinus Nijhoff, 1959), p. 268.

Figure 2. Gerard van Honthorst, *The Soldier and the Maid*, c. 1621. Herzog Anton Ulrich-Museum, Braunschweig. Photo, E. de Jongh et al., *Die Sprach der Bilder* (Braunschweig: Herzog Anton Ulrich-Museum, 1978), p. 90.

Jacob Duck dating from the 1650s, both a prostitute and her visitor sleep off their drink and sex, while an avaricious procuress picks the pocket of her hapless client.[4] Were it not for the transaction implied by the gesture and the context of the glass of wine, and the stunningly sensual white satin dress and black stole of the young woman — a marked contrast to the sober black dresses and white collars worn by women in the artist's portraits — Terborch's image brings to mind nothing so much as a courtly exchange between a lady and her gallant.[5]

Indeed, Terborch portrayed this encounter with such subtlety that by the eighteenth century its subject had been forgotten. Believing that it depicted instead two loving parents instructing their devoted daughter to chastity, an eighteenth-century engraver inscribed his reproduction with the title the "Paternal Admonition," a misinterpretation repeated into our century.[6] Even after its subject was recognized, Terborch's enigmatic treatment of his theme has been used to define the characteristics of late seventeenth-century Dutch genre painting. In his *Principles of Art History*, published in 1915, Heinrich Wölfflin wrote,

. . . the purpose of the baroque is not to be unclear, but to make clarity look like an accidental by-product . . . Everyone knows Terborch's picture, the *Paternal Admonishment*. The title does not fit the picture, but in any case, the point of the representation lies in what the seated male figure is saying to the standing girl, or rather in how she takes the speech. But just here the artist leaves us in the lurch. The girl, who with her white satin dress already forms, as light tone, the chief center of attraction, remains with averted face. This is a representational possibility which only the baroque knows.[7]

In 1984 a major survey of Dutch painting still described Terborch's genre images of women in quiet interiors as "to be interpreted in any way the viewer likes."[8]

Twentieth-century art historians have traditionally based their explanations of the enigmatic quality of such exquisite yet elusive paintings upon one of two assumptions. Either they describe these works as created exclusively for visual delight,[9] or they argue that such paintings hide their symbolic content, usually a moralizing message.[10] Some scholars split the difference and celebrate these works for making instruction palatable through delight. But the precise outlines of that instruction remain unclear. A painting such as Terborch's does not appear to condemn the encounter between the two figures. No negative consequences for either party seem to be articulated. Indeed, it describes sin as positively inviting. But surely this and similar paintings do not publicly condone the practices they describe.

My purpose here is not to propose a new "interpretation" of the image.

Both its visual beauty and its association with prostitution seem to me clear. Nor do I discuss the image as a reflection of social conditions, for, in spite of its lovingly observed detail, the painting is far from illustrating the characteristic poverty of prostitutes working in seventeenth-century Holland. Rather, my interest here is in the cultural work of this image — the function in the cultural imagination of a painting of an elegantly dressed prostitute being propositioned by a well-mannered soldier — and in identifying the contemporary issues that may have lent themselves to this theme and its singular treatment.

This painting is only one of the more subtle of the literally hundreds of Dutch seventeenth-century images of men and women over-indulging in sensual experiences: drinking, making music, and exchanging money for sex. Jan Steen's many representations of dissolute households, which depict the chaos that can result from unbridled sensual dissipation, are more characteristic treatments of these themes (c. 1668, Wellington Museum, London, Figure 3).[11] Although unusual, Terborch's vision, once produced, seems to have captured the imagination of its audience, for it was reproduced in at least twenty-seven copies, partial copies, and imitations over the subsequent two centuries.[12]

In contrast to the near obsession of visual culture with sexuality and prostitution suggested by these and countless similar images, these seem not to have been such pressing social issues. Birth records indicate that there was no notable rise in illicit sex during the seventeenth century. On the contrary, while we have no reliable records for earlier periods, illegitimate births in the seventeenth century hovered around one percent, dramatically lower than in the eighteenth and subsequent centuries.[13] While there was a shift in the moral and legal status of prostitution in some seventeenth-century Dutch cities, the traffic in extra-marital sexual encounters remained relatively unchanged. Following Aristotle, from the Middle Ages through the late sixteenth century prostitutes were considered a necessary evil, an outlet for male passions which, if not discharged in this directed manner, would otherwise disrupt the social order. This view continued to be voiced through the seventeenth and into the eighteenth centuries. In his *Modest Defense of Publick Stews*, published in 1724, Bernard de Mandeville wrote, "If courtesans and strumpets were to be prosecuted with as much rigor as some silly people would have it, . . . what locks and bars would be sufficient to preserve the honor of our wives and daughters? . . . Some men would grow outrageous, and ravishing would become a common crime."[14] Many cities supported licensed brothels. Men were warned not so much to avoid prostitutes as to beware of their inherent propensity to thievery.

The Reformation brought about complex changes in attitudes toward sexual desire, and by extension toward prostitution. While older views of

Figure 3. Jan Steen, *The Dissolute Household*, c. 1668. Board of Trustees of the Victoria and Albert Museum, exhibited at the Wellington Museum, London. Photo, P. C. Sutton et al., *Masters of Seventeenth-Century Dutch Genre Painting* (Philadelphia: Philadelphia Museum of Art, 1984), Plate 85.

women continued to be circulated, the Reformation placed a new valuation on marriage and the pleasures of sex between a man and his wife, as pictured by Frans Hals in his affecting marriage portrait of Stephanus Geraerdts and his bride Isabelle Coymans (c. 1650–52, Antwerp, Koninklijk Museum voor Schone Kunsten; Paris, Private Collection, Figure 4).[15] This new attitude toward sexuality within marriage was accompanied by a corresponding intensification of moral and legal prohibitions against sexuality outside marriage, specifically, adultery and prostitution. These prohibitions were disseminated in texts ranging from sermons to popular literature, and apparently in some visual imagery as well.

Figure 4. Left: Frans Hals, *Stephanus Geraerdts*, c. 1650–52. Koninklijk Museum voor Schone Kunsten, Antwerp. Right: Frans Hals, *Isabelle Coymans*, c. 1650–52. Private collection, Paris. Photos, S. Slive, *Frans Hals* (London: Royal Academy of Arts, 1989), pp. 324, 325.

After the Republic was established at the end of the sixteenth century, many Dutch cities passed ordinances prohibiting prostitution in an attempt to eliminate it completely. The Hague, for example, enacted an ordinance in 1595 specifying that anyone found keeping a brothel would be publicly flogged.[16] The effect of these regulations on social practices, however, seems to have been minimal. It has been estimated that the number of prostitutes working in Amsterdam in 1680 hovered around 1000.[17] Most cities turned a blind eye through lax enforcement of their laws. While prostitutes and those who housed them were sometimes fined, flogged, condemned to a stint in the public pillory, sent to the Spinhuis (woman's house of correction) for a year to two, or temporarily banished, the high number of repeat offenders indicates that these measures were completely ineffective in stopping the trade.[18] Clients, too, faced fines, but frequently these went into the pockets of the sheriff who conveniently looked the other way.[19] Published guides to well-known prostitutes and brothels even appeared, from the probably imaginative *Spiegel der Vermaarde Courtisanen* (*Mirror of the Most Celebrated Courtesans*) of 1630 to *'t Amsterdamsche Hoerdom*, published in 1681. Thinly veiled as a warning against Amsterdam's red-light district, the latter is a detailed and apparently reliable guide to the sexual practices of the city's underworld. While its legal status changed, then, prostitution as an activity was hardly disturbed.[20] The only apparent effect of these laws was to make prostitution less visible.[21] Large male-owned brothels were for the most part broken up. Young prostitutes set up house on their own or with one or two other women. Frequently she sought the mentorship of an experienced older woman, who rented her a room for her encounters and might lend her money for the clothing which — like that worn in Terborch's painting — might be worth more than she could afford on her own. Women were forbidden to solicit on the streets or keep their doors open. They sought their clients instead in the many inns and music halls of cities both large and small, and returned with them to their rented rooms. An evening's entertainment consisted of drink, sometimes music, and the satisfaction of sexual desire. Indeed, the sexual service of the woman herself was usually the least expensive aspect of the evening. One seventeenth-century visitor to Amsterdam noted that while he spent only three gulden for the woman, the wine for the evening totaled twelve. (Rental of her bed was two gulden extra.)

Court documents indicate that cities were in fact less concerned about sex than about the disorder accompanying its practices, particularly drunken citizens disturbing the peace. Men were hauled before church councils with much more frequency for drink and the ensuing rowdiness than for visiting a prostitute.[22] Complaints about prostitutes were voiced primarily when they themselves disturbed city peace by accosting men in the street or by soliciting on church porches on Sunday.[23] Cities seem to have been more concerned by unruly passions in the public sphere than by sexual practices in the private.

Such observations suggest, then, that Terboch's painting may not, in essence, be about sexual morality at all, but that it and similar works may have served another cultural function. I would like to offer here that Terborch's painting is not about sex but about money; not so much about morality in the personal sphere as about economic practice in the public one. Specifically, I suggest that Terborch's image expresses confidence in the power of money to regulate even the most unregulatable of passions in the breasts of the most unruly classes of society: female prostitutes and male mercenary soldiers. My interest here, however, is not in its subject per se but in the potential cultural work of such a subject. I will argue that such an image could provide a site, at a safe psychic remove from the immediate life of its (male) viewers, for considering a pressing issue: the fear that money, circulating in the marketplace, would generate increasing lust for money, goods, and services; and that this might cause the economy to spin out of control, even to collapse, and bring to an end the dramatic prosperity that was enjoyed in the Republic. The quiet dignity of Terborch's figures, the lack of passion even in some of society's most potentially unruly classes and occupations, could reassure the viewer that the exchange of money itself had the potential to regulate the very passions that engendered its circulation.[24]

The odds are high that the soldier is a foreign mercenary.[25] The Netherlands was the first country in Europe to raise and support a standing army. This had dramatically increased the number of soldiers garrisoned in the country over the course of the century. The Republic's army more than doubled from 50,000 men in the 1630s to around 110,000 by the 1670s.[26] Like prostitutes, then, mercenary soldiers were a familiar aspect of Dutch life.

Terborch depicts an encounter in one sense between social equals (Figure 1).[27] Whether a camp follower or an urban harlot, an impecunious foot soldier or a trained cavalryman, both the prostitute and the mercenary sold their bodies for very low pay.[28] Both were similarly marginal figures in society, yet they provided services that kept society in order. As I noted, prostitutes were traditionally viewed as a necessary outlet for men, keeping them from seducing virtuous women and disrupting society. The duty of the mercenary was to maintain the peace within the country and defend the nation from threats from without.

Although instruments of social control themselves, the prostitute and the mercenary were at the same time traditionally believed to be among the most unruly classes of society. They were considered men and women close to their natural state; the passions of both threatened to break loose at any moment, subverting social stability. Traditional beliefs about the unruly nature of female sexuality run like a red thread through both Dutch texts and images. Similarly, the mercenary was potentially lawless as well. In the Middle Ages, soldiers had been drawn from the upper classes. They had fought out of a sense of loyalty to their prince, and in the hope of gaining honor through a noble title and economic profit through plunder. Mercenaries, on the other hand, worked not out of loyalty and for honor but simply for pay. Such men labored at the fringes of society outside the aristocratic ethos of war.[29] Moreover, mercenaries in a standing army were positively feared, because when unpaid or simply bored they could scourge the countryside even of the nation that had hired them.[30] According to a biographer writing in 1691, Descartes had joined the Dutch army "to study the various customs of man in their most natural state."[31]

Soldiers and prostitutes were linked not only conceptually but also in practice. Soldiers in a standing army spent a great deal of time doing almost nothing except drinking, gambling, . . . and passing the time with women. Every army had a "tail" of women who provided a variety of services from cooking and washing to sex. In 1629, for example, there were 289 women for 1043 soldiers in the Walloon *tercio* of Count Hennin.[32] Men with wives and children were thought to be more expensive and more fearful in battle. Governments across Europe, therefore, attempted to limit the number of married men in service. It was thus thought necessary to provide sexual outlets for these single, idle, potentially dangerous men. Most commanders agreed that each company of 200 men required between four and eight prostitutes.[33] (The overworked women would have had to entertain multiple clients each night to provide soldiers with more than one visit per month.) In contrast to the strict moral codes operating elsewhere in the society, a military man could enjoy sex with a woman without marrying her. While encounters between mercenaries and prostitutes might be immoral, they were expected and frequently provided for.

The subject of Terborch's image, then, is particularly freighted—one where natural desire on both sides, in theory at least, might run wild. The image, however, could not picture a greater degree of control. Far from the bawdy encounter of a mercenary and a camp-follower or peasant girl in a country inn, Terborch's image appears almost respectable. We see a richly-dressed, demure and apparently urbane young woman—identifiable as suspiciously licentious only by her lavish dress and the female companion preoccupied with a drink—standing before an equally agreeable soldier offering her a coin. What, then, is the viewer supposed to think? Why this focus on sex and money? Why is such a potentially disordered subject so tranquil? If prostitution itself was not an important social issue, what contemporary cultural question made possible this theme and its treatment?

In formal terms, the soldier's raised hand, perhaps holding a coin, is a focal point for the beginning and end of an imaginary circle begun by the soldier's gesture and running through the woman's body to be completed by his own. Together, the poses of the soldier and the prostitute frame another alarming source of social disorder, drink, here engrossing the procuress. Situated at the center of the image, the soldier's gesture thereby defines and structures the relationship between the mercenary, the prostitute, and the procuress. I suggest that this and similar images provided an imaginative site for the consideration of an issue that was central to Dutch seventeenth-century society — not sex or even sensual dissipation, but desire. And desire of a particular sort: the desire for money, goods, and services that drove the emerging market and capital economies in the Northern Netherlands. In this image, however, far from generating unbridled passions, money appears to turn even a confrontation between a prostitute and a mercenary soldier into controlled and ordered chivalry. Coin exchanged in a social setting apparently regulates internal passions.

There was nothing new in imagining social relations through money and sex. A longstanding northern tradition of images equated sex for money with economic desire. Mercenary marriage had been a prominent theme of sixteenth-century prints and paintings that satirized avaricious young beauties who married wealthy, withered old men.[34] Quentin Massy's scheming young woman, for example, passes her victim's purse to a waiting fool (Figure 5). Avarice was itself traditionally represented as a woman, from, for example, a print by Pieter Breughel in the sixteenth century, where a blind women jealously guards a hoard in her lap while reaching for more in the filling chest beside her (designed 1556), to a seventeenth-century painting by Gerard van Honthorst where a shriveled old hag greedily examines a coin.[35] La Belle Angloise in *Spiegel der Vermaarde Courtisanen* mentioned above suggestively invites, "Where gold begins, / Virtue is but air."

In the seventeenth century, negative associations of monetary greed with female sexuality were supplemented by positive images employing women in metaphors for economic prosperity. The leading Dutch poet Joost van den Vondel, for example, wrote a poem celebrating the glories of Holland's mercantile activities. In it he portrays the profits of shipping through the female gender of ships and their often female figureheads, and describes their lucratively loaded bellies through the metaphor of pregnancy:

Where she [shipping] comes into fashion, or sticks out her bosom,
Every village becomes a city, every shipowner a lord.[36]

Figure 5. Quentin Massys, *Ill-Matched Lovers*, c. 1520–25. National Gallery of Art, Washington, D.C. Photo, J. O. Hand and M. Wolff, *Early Netherlandish Painting* (Washington, D.C.: National Gallery of Art/New York: Cambridge University Press, 1987), p. 147.

The Dutch original for "comes into fashion," *"in zwange raeckt"* is a pun on "to make pregnant". (This in spite of Vondel's having experienced at first hand the grief that speculation could bring; the poet had lost his shirt in ventures at the Amsterdam Stock Exchange.)

Texts not only describe the economy in female terms, they also describe prostitution in economic terms: *Het Leven en Bedryf van de Hedendaagse Haagsche en Amsterdamsche Zaletjuffers* (*The Life and Trade of Present-Day Hague and Amsterdam Salon Misses*) is an anthology of women whose behaviors run the gamut of illicit sex, from courtesans, common whores, and procuresses to adulterous wives. Even more pointed was the *De Beurs der Vrouwen* (*Stock Exchange of Women*) in which each of the vices traditionally associated with women, including those who engaged in extramarital sex, each take a column in their "Bourse" as if her activity was a commodity for which she served as broker.

Attitudes toward money and the marketplace changed dramatically in seventeenth-century Holland, and it is this change that made possible — even necessary — a redefinition of prostitution, if only in the imaginative sphere. Formerly associated with peasants and farmers of the countryside, or disreputable moneylenders, a flourishing marketplace had became an essential metaphor for the international trade and capital speculation in Amsterdam, Holland's major urban center. Caspar Barlaeus opened his inaugural address for the new Amsterdam Atheneum not by speaking of the secluded world of intellectual pursuits, but by praising Amsterdam as "the most flourishing trade center of all Europe . . . to which the desire to buy and sell drives here from all corners of the world. The immense amount of merchandise [here] strikes the spectator dumb." In his description of the visit to the city in 1638 of Marie de Médici, Barlaeus equated "the quality of her blood and that of her ancestors" with "the greatness of this city in trade."[37]

The monetary exchange and credit that made possible this thriving market moved in the seventeenth century from the remote domain of usurers — social outcasts — to a central position in Dutch society. No longer marginal activities, exchange and credit structured fundamental social relationships over a broad spectrum of society.[38] Seventeenth-century Holland had become the economic capital of Europe not through the production of raw materials but through the circulation of capital and goods through buying and selling. English merchants, for example, complained that it was cheaper to export raw materials to Holland, and to import finished goods, than to produce them at home.

This shift from a subsistence economy to a capital economy of surplus necessitated a radical reshifting of values, for, in order for such an economy to flourish, money had to circulate. Specifically, goods and services had to be bought and sold. In the sixteenth century, John Calvin had vehemently condemned the purchase of luxuries: "Those who sail to distant places are no longer content with home comforts but bring back with them unknown luxuries. . . . It too often happens that riches bring self-indulgence, and superfluity of pleasures produces flabbiness as we can see in wealthy regions and cities (where there are merchants)."[39] Seventeenth-century Holland viewed consumption differently. In his plan for the city of Utrecht in 1664, burgomaster Henrick Moreelse wrote: "We must attract more customers through increased consumption; we can best do this by establishing well-run, attractive and choice economic opportunities for powerful and wealthy individuals; this will renew and comfort our increasingly exhausted trades- and craftsmen; from this originates the improvement of all public and private income."[40]

This economic machine, the circulation of goods and capital, was made possible by the troublesome passion of desire. While avarice, the hoarding of goods or capital which took them out of circulation, continued to be condemned, the desire that fueled its circulation was now an essential component of the new economic and social order. And, to make matters worse, this took place in a marketplace not controlled by reason but governed by Fortuna (or predestination — depending on one's religious persuasion). The Dutch were acutely aware that unregulated desire of men who gave themselves over to Dame Fortune could produce economic disaster. By the mid-1630s, for example, speculation in tulip futures had gotten completely out of hand. It was satirized in such images as Roemer Visscher's emblem of a pair of tulips entitled "A fool and his money are soon parted" in his *Sinne-poppen* first published in Amsterdam in 1614, and an engraving entitled *Flora's Geks-kap* (*Flora's fool's cap*) of 1637 by Pieter Nolpe. The future on one Semper Augustus tulip bulb, for example, was sold for 4,600 gulden, a coach, and a dapple-gray pair of horses worth 2,000 gulden more — over four times the cost of Rembrandt's *Nightwatch*, or more than eight times the annual income for the manager of a prosperous delftware workshop.[41] Scores were ruined when the value of contracts plummeted, and the States of Holland decreed that all agreements contracted after the planting of 1636 would be paid at 3 1/2 percent of their face value.[42]

Sixteenth-century men like Pieter Brueghel viewed economic exchange as all-out warfare, a literal battle between the mercenary troops of monetary exchange, as pictured in his engraving of the *Battle of the Piggy-Banks and Strong-Boxes* (c. 1558–67, Figure 6). Seventeenth-century textual descriptions of the Amsterdam Bourse, established in 1611, picture a place that was equally frightening. One foreign observer noted how men offered their hands to confirm a price with such speed that the proceedings degenerated into frenetic hand slapping. "Hands redden from the blows," he wrote, "handshakes are followed by shouting, insults, impudence, pushing and shoving." The typical speculator "chews his nails, pulls his fingers, closes his eyes, takes four paces, and four times talks to himself, raises his hand to his cheek as if he has a toothache and all this accomplished by a mysterious coughing."[43] This could not be farther, however, from the painted depictions of the institution by Dutchmen, such as those by Job Berckheyde and by Emanuel de Witte (Figure 7). Similarly, in his University address praising Amsterdam's markets mentioned above, Caspar Barlaeus praised merchants' "respect for the laws, the obedience of the residents, their composure, and first and foremost, their desire for order." It is as if the Dutch needed to picture their economic relations reassuringly as ordered and controlled, even as they were fueled by desire at the mercy of fortune.

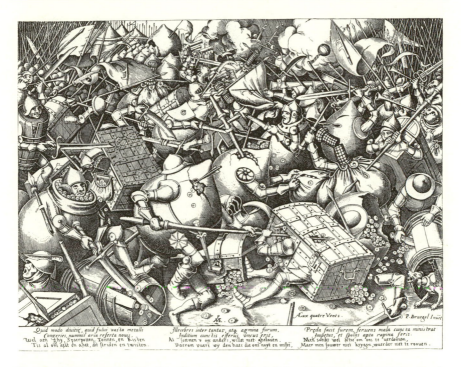

Quid modo diuitiæ, quid fuluis vasta metalli
Congeries, nummi arca referta nouis.
Wel arm, Ghy Spaerpotten, Tointen, en Kisten
Tis al om geltt en goett, dit striden en twisten.

Illecebris inter tantas, atq, agmina furum,
Inditum cunctis efferuit, Oncus erit.
Ai siruen v oec anders, willen niet ghelouen.
Datrom vuert wy den hals die ons neyt en misst,

Præda facit furem, feruens mala cuncta ministrat
Impetus, et spolijs apta rapina feris.
Mich soekkt wel alste om ons te 'uerdoouen,
Maer men souwer niet krygen wanrder niet te roouen.

Á̆.E . Ó.   *Aux quatre Vents.*   *P. Bruegel Inuet*

Figure 6. Pieter van der Heyden after Pieter Brueghel the elder, *Battle of the Piggy-Banks and Strong-Boxes*, c. 1558–67, engraving. Photo, A. Klein, *Graphic Worlds of Peter Bruegel the Elder* (New York: Dover, 1963), p. 147.

There was no end to moralizing proverbs about money. And there was an unending stream of texts promoting temperance, the production of restraint by sheer will. At the same time, the Dutch began to be dimly aware that money and economic exchange itself might be self-regulating. In the Netherlands, desire for money properly administered had been used to discipline no less than the unruly mercenary. Among the important organizational innovations of the army made by Prince Maurits of Orange was the regular — and for a soldier high — pay received by the troops in his employ.[44] The result was that mercenaries working for the Republic were dramatically better behaved than their counterparts elsewhere. Their passions now were kept in line not by intangible honor, loyalty, and occasional sex, but by contracts guaranteeing tangible and regular coin.

The uncertainties of the marketplace of course, were another matter. By the eighteenth century in England, thinkers like Adam Smith would produce a systematic economic theory where individual passions, redefined as interests,

Figure 7. Emanuel de Witte, *The Courtyard of the Amsterdam Stock Exchange*, 1653. Museum Boymans-van Beuningen, Rotterdam. Photo, M. Westermann, *A Worldly Art: The Dutch Republic, 1585–1718* (Englewood Cliffs, N.J.: Prentice-Hall, 1996), p. 24.

were regulated by the marketplace itself.[45] Most contemporary analyses of the conceptual relation of sexual desire and the economy begin with the eighteenth century.[46] But the first large-scale and broadly accessible capital market had been established in seventeenth-century Holland. Dutch beliefs about and attitudes toward this market have been frustratingly elusive, however, because the Dutch remained silent on the subject. With the exception of one unsystematic plea for a free-market economy by Pieter and Johan de la Court, seventeenth-century Dutchmen produced no economic texts of note.[47] Indeed, economic theory abroad was stimulated precisely by Dutch success at home — produced by thinkers in rival countries trying to understand exactly how the Dutch had accomplished their economic miracle. The Dutch themselves were too busy making money to theorize about it. Moreover, theirs was an intuitive enterprise, one functioning on only dimly articulated concepts and justifications for its activities.

While texts are lacking, images such as Terborch's, I suggest, address some of the issues that concerned Dutch men and women about their new economic enterprise. The potential function of the image as opposed to the text for the culture is implied, moreover, by the painting itself. Not only is the painting an object to be desired and consumed through vision, but its subject is not touch, as might be expected, but sight. Specifically, the mercenary is propositioning the woman and looking. Moreover, for the viewer, the image draws attention to itself in the beauty of its painted surface. Vision was considered a more potent sense than touch in seventeenth-century Holland. In religious practice, for example, the worshipper obtained the Eucharist not through the mouth, but through the eyes.[48] Vision was also the most dangerous sense. In an emblem book of 1644 Johan de Brune defined "the eyes as the cause of love," while in his description and guide to Amsterdam of 1663 Philip von Zesen claimed that certain taverns and playhouses of Amsterdam (the kinds of places in which prostitutes found their clients) were called "Dool-hof" (The Maze) "because there the senses go astray and the eyes do dote."[49]

I suggest, then, that these images provided the site lacking in texts for the exploration of ideas about the marketplace at home. Terborch's image does not suggest why economic exchange regulates desire but seems to propose that the activities of the market itself could be self-regulating. The image itself seems intended to inspire reflection on its subject by its viewer as he or she empathizes with the meditative state of the three figures portrayed.

Outside social boundaries, the prostitute and the mercenary help to reconfigure them, for the image would have been understood by its seventeenth-century viewer in tension with developing boundaries between the domestic and the economic spheres. While many businesses and trades remained tied to the physical space of the house, the boundary between living and working spaces was increasingly delineated and jealously guarded. Gerrit Ludens locates a silk-manufacturer in his study, while his wife is holding the emblems of her domesticity; his pose is open to the world, hers self-enclosed (1656, Boreel Family Foundation, Figure 8). Contemporary authors, too, insisted upon a clear distinction between the locations and activities appropriate to a wife and to her husband. Popular moralist Jacob Cats admonished that

Figure 8. Gerrit Ludens, *Portrait of a Man, Portrait of a Woman*, 1656. Boreel Family Foundation / Stichting Familie fonds Boreel. Photo, E. de Jongh, *Portretten van echt en trouw* (Zwolle: Uitgeverij Waanders, 1986), p. 177.

The husband must be on the street to practice his trade
The wife must stay at home to be in the kitchen
The diligent practice of street wisdom may in the man be praised
But with the delicate wife, there should be quiet and steady ways.
So you, industrious husband, go to earn your living
While you, O young wife, attend to your household.[50]

Like her raucous sisters, Terborch's prostitute transgresses those boundaries, transforming the domestic interior into a public place of business. By crossing these boundaries she helps to reinforce them. The mercenary, on the other hand, turns the desire that circulates money to non-productive ends. Rather than investing it in a public arena of commodities, he invests in the private arena of sensual satisfaction. He too defines the boundaries between public and private gendered spaces by crossing them — in the opposite direction.

In closing, we might ask why Terborch may have selected money and mercenaries as his theme in the first place. Mercenaries, their female companions, and money would have had particular and personal associations for Gerard Terborch, associations that may have lent themselves to his imaging of this theme through both. On the eastern border of the Northern Netherlands, Terborch's native Zwolle had housed soldiers at the conclusion of the Twelve Years Truce in 1621. Indeed, soldiers were the subject of his first childhood sketches as well as of his earliest surviving painting, haunting images of a cavalry man viewed from the rear.[51] His adopted city of Deventer had been the staging ground for German mercenaries in the winter of 1629 when they were discharged after the siege of 's-Hertogenbosch.[52] Mercenaries returned to peacetime duty and idleness in 1654, the year to which the painting is dated, with the conclusion of the Treaty of Westminster that ended the first Anglo-Dutch war. In the mid-1650s when Terborch was creating the image, Deventer was in fact agitating for provincial control of the mercenary army stationed within its borders, a protest that led in 1657 to near civil war. Terborch would have been particularly aware of economic issues as well, for he was related by marriage to the *muntmeester* of Deventer. Shortly after 1650, the mints underwent increased and controversial regulation.

Terborch's painting, still called the *"Paternal Admonition"* but now in quotes, is situated at the shift in social attitudes toward both money and desire. Unlike the activities of the prostitute and mercenary soldier who provided regulation for society through their actions from without, money ordered social relations psychologically, from within. The imaginative theme of prostitution is thus here used as a site for the formulation of new attitudes toward economic exchange — exchange which in real life of course took place primarily between men. Terborch's painting, then, served as a safely removed site for the exploration of men's attitudes toward their own behaviors in entirely different and evolving economic spheres.

Notes

This essay was first presented at a session of the *1993 Berkshire Conference on the History of Women*, Vassar College. I am grateful to the participants of that seminar, to Paddy Fumerton and Simon Hunt, and to anonymous reviewers of this volume, for their helpful comments and questions. Finally, thanks must go to Steve Brown of the University of California at Santa Barbara's Artworks office, who produced the photographic material for this essay with his characteristic care, speed, and skill.

1. The painting survives in two autograph versions, in Amsterdam and in Berlin: canvas, 71 x 73 cm., Amsterdam, Rijksmuseum, inv. no. A404; canvas, 70 x 60 cm.; Berlin, Gemäldegalerie, Staatliche Museen Preussischer Kulturbesitz, no. 791. C. Hofstede de Groot, *Beschreibendes und kritisches Verzeichnis der Werke der hervorragendsten holländischen Maler des XVII. Jahrhunderts* (Erlingen and Paris, 1908–27) 5 (1912): nos. 186, 187; S. J. Gudlaugsson, *Gerard ter Borch*, 2 vols. (The Hague: Mouton, 1959–60) 1: 97–98, pls. 110-I, 110-II; 2: 116–117, nos. 110-I, 110-II. *Gerard Ter Borch. Zwolle 1617–Deventer 1681*, exh. cat. (The Hague, Mauritshuis, Koninklijk Kabinet van Schilderijen, and Landesmuseum, Münster, 1974), 31 and no. 32; Jan Kelch in *Masters of Seventeenth-Century Dutch Genre Painting*, Peter C. Sutton et al., exh. cat. (Philadelphia: Philadelphia Museum of Art, 1984), no. 9 with additional bibliography. Following Hofstede de Groot, Gudlaugsson and Kelch argue that the Amsterdam work is the earlier of the two.

2. Alison McNeil Kettering, "Ter Borch's Ladies in Satin," *Art History* 16 (1993): 95–124, esp. p. 116 n. 5, observes that there is no trace of a coin in the Amsterdam version, that the Berlin painting is apparently rubbed in that area, and that the copy by Caspar Netscher made of the Berlin painting shortly after it was created shows no coin.

3. R. Klessman et al., *Die Sprache der Bilder*, exh. cat. (Braunschweig, Anton Ulrich-Museum, 1978), no. 15; E. de Jongh, *tot Lering en Vermaak*, exh. cat. (Amsterdam: Rijksmuseum, 1976), no. 28; H. Braun, *Gerard und Willem van Honthorst*, Ph.D. dissertation (Gottingen, 1966), 81–83, 150–52; E. de Jongh, *Rembrandt en zijn tijd*, exh. cat. (Brussels, Musées Royaux d'Art et d'Histoire, 1971), 175–76.

4. Sutton et al., *Masters*, no. 30. To draw examples almost at random, others range from the woodcut by Lucas van Leyden, *A Tavern Scene*, 1518–1520, with the banderolle, "Pay attention to which way the wind blows," Ellen S. Jacobwitz and Stephanie Loeb Stepanek, *The Prints of Lucas van Leyden & His Contemporaries*, exh. cat. (National Gallery of Art, Washington D.C., 1983), no. 72; to Adriaen van Ostade, *Tavern Interior*, 1674, Staatliche Kunstsammlungen, Dresden, Gemäldegalerie Alter Meister, illus. Christoper Brown, *Images of a Golden Past: Dutch Genre Painting of the 17th Century* (New York: Abbeville, 1984), p. 185.

5. Terborch's sister Gesina had been fond of such courtly themes, reproducing them in great numbers in her drawing album. See *Drawings from the Ter Borch Studio Estate*, ed. Alison M. Kettering (The Hague: Staatsuitgeverij, 1988). It was also the theme of such romantic pastoral narratives as Granida and Dalfino, popular in painting,

poetry, and the theater. See *Het Gedroomde Land. Pastorale schilderkunst in de Gouden Eeuw*, Peter van den Brink et al., exh. cat. (Central Museum Utrecht, 1993). See also Kettering, *Drawing*.

6. Johan-Gerog Wille engraved the painting in 1765 under the title "L'instruction Paternelle"; see Vivian Lee Atwater, *A Catalogue and Analysis of Eighteenth-Century French Prints After Netherlandish Baroque Paintings*, 3 vols., Ph.D. dissertation (University of Washington, 1988), 2: 179. W. Drost, *Barockmalerei in den germanischen Ländern* [Handbuch der Kunstwissenschaft] (Potsdam: Wildpark-Potsdam, 1926), p. 187, was apparently the first scholar to identify the setting as a bordello.

7. Heinrich Wölfflin, *Principles of Art History*, trans. M. D. Hottinger of *Kunstgeschichtliche Grundbegriffe* [1915] (New York: Dover, 1950), p. 206.

8. Bob Haak, *The Golden Age: Dutch Painters of the Seventeenth Century* (New York, H. N. Abrams, 1984), p. 399, apparently following the arguments of Eddy de Jongh on the poly-interpretability of Dutch painting. See the latter's comments in De Jongh, *Rembrandt*, p. 145.

9. Svetlana Alpers, *The Art of Describing: Dutch Art in the Seventeenth Century* (Chicago: University of Chicago Press, 1983). On the basis of a reading of Philips Angel, Eric Jan Sluijter has argued that artists sought to delight viewers in order to sell paintings. See his "Didactic and Disguised Meanings? Several Seventeenth-Century Texts on Painting and the Iconological Approach to Northern Dutch Paintings of this Period," *Art in History/History in Art: Studies in Seventeenth-Century Dutch Culture*, ed. David Freedberg and Jan de Vries (Santa Monica, Calif.: Getty Center for the History of Art and the Humanities, 1991), pp. 175–207.

10. De Jongh, *Rembrandt*, or idem, De Jongh, *tot Lering*, and the author's subsequent publications; see now his cautionary remarks in "Some Notes on Interpretation," in *Art in History*, pp. 118–36. In an unpublished lecture, "The Sexual Economy of Genre Painting," delivered at the symposium held in London in 1984 in conjunction with the exhibition *Masters of Seventeenth-Century Dutch Genre Painting*, Simon Schama noted that many Dutch genre paintings obviously link sex and money, and argued that they express concern about female sexuality upsetting the economic sphere. I am grateful to Allison Kettering for the reference.

11. Nanette Salomon, "Jan Steen's Formulation of the Dissolute Household, Sources and Meanings," *Holländische Genremalerei im 17. Jahrhundert: Symposium Berlin 1984*, ed. Henning Bock and Thomas W. Gaehtgens (Berlin: Mann, 1987), pp. 315–344.

12. In addition to the autograph canvases in Amsterdam and Berlin, the Berlin canvas was reproduced by Terborch's pupil Caspar Netscher in 1655 (Gotha Museum, cat. 1890, no. 298; Gudlaugsson, *Gerard Ter Borch*, 1: no. 110-IIa), illus. pl. XII, fig. 1). Netscher studied with Terborch from about 1654 in Deventer. The date inscribed on Netscher's copy provides the basis for the date of Terborch's two canvases. Gudlaugsson lists additional copies, including a mezzotint by Wallerant Vaillant (1623–1677; mezzotint not in Hollstein, vol. 31), engravings by J. C. Bendorp (1767–1849) and W. Unger (1775–1855), and a lithograph by C. Wildt. The Berlin version was engraved by J. G. Wille, see note 6 above.

13. The data for the seventeenth century are sparse, and are based upon the records of baptized children. Nonetheless, the differences between the seventeenth and eighteenth centuries is striking. Around 1700 in both Rotterdam and Maassluis fewer than 1 percent of baptized children were illegitimate, according to Donald Haks,

Huwelijk en gezin in Holland in de 17de en 18de eeuw (Assen: HES, 1982), p. 102. D. J. Noordam found similar statistics for Barendrecht and Huizen. See his "Lust, last en pleizier; Vier eeuwen seksualiteit in Nederland," in *Een kind onder het hart; Verloskunde, volksgeloof, gezin, seksualiteit en moraal vroeger en nu*, ed. R. E. Kistemaker (Amsterdam: Amsterdams Historisch Museum/Meulenhoff Informatief 1987), pp. 127–70, esp. p. 137. For comparison of these statistics with later periods, see Jan Kok, "The Moral Nation: Illegitimacy and Bridal Pregnancy in the Netherlands from 1600 to the Present," *Economic and Social History in the Netherlands* 2 (1990): 7–35, esp. 9–10 and graph fig. 1, who notes that in Rotterdam the percentages doubled in the 1730s, an increase that accelerated after 1780.

14. Bernard de Mandeville, *A Modest Defence of Publick Stews* (London, 1724), cited by Richard I. Cook, "The Great Leviathan of Lechery: Mandeville's *Modest Defence of Publick Stews*" in *Mandeville Studies*, ed. Irwin Primer (The Hague: Martinus Nijhoff, 1975), pp. 95–96.

15. Eric Fuchs, *Sexual Desire and Love: Origins and History of the Christian Ethic of Sexuality and Marriage*, trans. Marsha Daigle (Cambridge: James Clarke, 1983), pp. 157–63. Seymour Slive, *Frans Hals*, 3 vols. (London: Phaidon, 1970/1974), 3: nos. 188, 189; Seymour Slive, *Frans Hals*, exh. cat. (London, Royal Academy of Arts and Brussels: Ludion, 1989), nos. 68, 69.

16. N. Wiltens and P. Scheltus, *Kerkelyk Plakaatboek*, 2 vols. (The Hague, 1722–35) 1: 720; for ordinances against brothel-keepers in other places, see A. Hallema, "Rechterlijke maatstaven ten aanzien van de morele integriteit in het verleden," *Verslagen en mededeelingen van de vereeniging tot uitgaaf der bronnen van het Oud-Vaderladsche recht* 12 (1962): 410. Both cited by A. T. van Deursen, *Plain Lives in a Golden Age: Popular Culture, Religion, and Society in Seventeenth-Century Holland* (Cambridge: Cambridge University Press, 1991), p. 345 ns. 4, 5; J. G. W. F. Bik, *Vijf eeuwen medisch leven in een Hollandse stad* (Assen: Van Gorcum, 1955), p. 436. The artist Pieter Codde and a maid with whom he had a sexual encounter did spend a night in shackles, see Slive, *Frans Hals* (1989), p. 257.

17. Sjoerd Faber, *Strafrechtspleging en Criminaliteit te Amsterdam 1680–1811. De nieuwe menslievendheid* (Arnhem: Gouda Quint, 1983), p. 78. In the same year, 1680, thirty-one pimps and procuresses were also arrested.

18. For a colorful account of a particularly hardened woman, Jannetje Hendricx, see Simon Schama, *The Embarrassment of Riches: An Interpretation of Dutch Culture in the Golden Age* (New York: Knopf, 1987), pp. 477–78.

19. Until 1593 in Gouda, the wages of the servants of the bailiff were based on this extra income. See Van Deursen, *Plain Lives*, p. 345, n. 9.

20. Particularly with increased wealth and mobility—and increased poverty on the part of single women—the profession flourished, as is clear from documents from Enkhuizen, Dordrecht, Haarlem, Overveen, Voorburg just outside of The Hague, and of course Amsterdam. See Van Deursen, *Plain Lives*, p. 345, ns. 10–16. Lotte van der Pol has comprehensively delineated the life of Amsterdam prostitutes and brothels from a vast array of documents from the seventeenth and eighteenth centuries. See her *Het Amsterdams Hoerdom: Prostitutie in de zeventiende en achtiende eeuw* (Amsterdam, Wereldbibliotheek, 1996).

21. On prostitution see Lotte C. van de Pol, *Het Amsterdams Hoerdom*. Idem, "Van Speelhuis naar Bordeel? Veranderingen in de organisatie van de prostitute in Amsterdam in de tweede helft van de 18de eeuw," *Documentatie-Blad Werkgroep Achttiende*

Eeuw (1985): 65–66, 157–71; idem, "Voor- en buitenechtelijke seksualiteit in de vroeg-moderne tijd," *Het Westers gezin in historisch en vergelijkend perspektief* [Heerlen: Open Universiteit] 4 (1986): 261–89; idem, "Vrowencriminaliteit in Amsterdam in de tweede helft van de 17e eeuw," *Tijdschrift voor Criminologie* 29 (1987): 148–55.

22. For a long list of men who were charged for drunkenness see Van Deursen, *Plain Lives*, p. 345, n. 33.

23. Sir William Brereton reported of his visit to Amsterdam in June 1634 that "About nine hour we passed Harlemmer Port and came into a fair street, wherein of late swarmed the most impudent whores I have heard of who would if they saw a stranger come into the middle of the street unto him, pull him by the coat and invite him into their house," *Travels in Holland* . . . [1634–35] (London: Printed for the Chetham Society, 1844), p. 55.

24. For an excellent discussion of possible political contexts of this work see Richard Helgerson, "Soldiers and Enigmatic Girls: The Politics of Dutch Domestic Realism, 1650–1672," in *Representations* 58 (Spring 1997): 49–87. On p. 83, n. 4, he kindly cites this unpublished essay, which was brought to his attention after writing his own. There was an apparent miscommunication concerning my argument, however: he writes that I assert Terborch's image is "about" "the submission of unruly women and potentially threatening men to the mercantile regime controlled by the governing burghers." My argument is, however, almost the reverse. I here suggest that the image is actually not "about" its currently understood subject, prostitution, but serves instead as a psychic site for a resolution of anxieties about the potential dangers of the circula-tion of money in general, and specifically for the kinds of activities in which the viewer himself might be engaged.

25. It is highly unlikely that a member of the militia of one of the Netherlands' cites, a *schutter*, would be depicted propositioning a prostitute. While no doubt they numbered among these women's visitors, the shooting companies were comprised of some of the cities' leading citizens and served almost as emblems of city identity and pride. Mercenary forces, on the other hand, were made up to a large extent of peasants and foreigners, Scots, English, French, and especially German. Identifying either the company or nationality of a soldier is at this point not possible, because soldiers did not wear regular uniforms until the end of the century. They identified each other with a feather, scarf, or sash of the same color, causing no small amount of confusion in the heat of battle. See Geoffrey Parker, *The Army of Flanders and the Spanish Road, 1567–1659* (Cambridge: Cambridge University Press, 1972), pp. 164–65, and idem, "The Military Revolution, 1560–1600 — a Myth?" *Journal of Modern History*, 48 (1976): 195–214, esp. p. 196.

26. F. J. G. Ten Raa and F. de Bas, *Het Staatsche leger, 1568–1795*, 6 vols. (Breda: Koninklijke Militaire Academie, 1911–18), vol. 1, cited by Parker, "Military Revolu-tion," p. 206.

27. The angry soldier and the seductive prostitute were sometimes paired by artists in representations of the emotions. See for example Willem van Mieris's pair in the Gemäldegalerie, Kunsthistorisches Museum, Vienna, and discussion in Peter Hecht, *De Hollandse fijn schilders: Van Gerard Dou tot Adriaen van der Werff*, exh. cat. Amsterdam, Rijksmuseum (1989), nos. 19–20, illus.

28. A prostitute made about 2 gulden per encounter; a soldier in 1623 from eleven to fifteen gulden (pikemen made more than musketeers).

29. Repeating Machiavelli's remarks, Pieter de la Court contemptuously de-

scribed mercenaries as battling for hours without killing anyone ("die uuren naaeen sloegen, zonder iemand te dooden"); *Politike Discoursen handelende in ses onderscheide boeken van steeden, landen, oorlogen, kerken, regeeringen en zeeden* (Leiden, 1662), 3: ch. 17, p. 236. He observed that mercenaries fought only for pay, while citizens who took up arms were defending their fatherland.

30. For the representation in art of mercenary violence see Jane Susannah Fishman, *Boerenverdriet: Violence Between Peasants and Soldiers in Early Modern Netherlands Art*, Ph. D. dissertation, University of California, Berkeley, 1979 (Ann Arbor, Mich., UMI Research Press, 1982), and Keith P. F. Moxey, *Peasants, Warriors, and Wives. Popular Imagery in the Reformation* (Chicago: University of Chicago Press, 1989), pp. 67–100.

31. Adrien Baillet, *Vie de Monsieur Descartes (1691)* (Paris: Table Ronde, 1946), pp. 23 ff.

32. Parker, *Army of Flanders*, p. 289, Appendix I.

33. Ibid., p. 175, with references.

34. Larry Silver, *The Paintings of Quinten Massys, with Catalogue Raisonné* (Montclair, N.J.: Allanheld and Schram, 1984), no. 35, pl. 129; idem, "The Ill-Matched Pair of Quinten Massys," *Studies in the History of Art* 4 (1972): 104–23; John Oliver Hand and Martha Wolff, *Early Netherlandish Painting* (Washington, D.C.: National Gallery of Art; and New York: Cambridge University Press, 1987), 145–50, color illus. See also Alison Stewart, *Unequal Lovers: A Study of Unequal Couples in Northern Art* (New York: Abaris Books, 1979).

35. Gerard van Honthorst, *Old Woman Examining Coins by Lantern Light (Avarice)*, ? 1653; Richard Judson, *Gerrit van Honthorst: A Discussion of His Position in Dutch Art* (The Hague: Nijhoff, 1959), cat. 157, illus. as "Allegory of Sight."

36. Joost van den Vondel, "Hymnus, ofte Lof-Gesangh, over de Wijd-Beroemde Scheeps-Vaert der Vereenighde Nederlanden: Aenden Goed-Jonstigen Aens-chouwer," in *Werken*, Lennep/Unger, II: 287–300, esp. 289, lines 63–64, "Waer sy in zwange raeckt, oft uyt-steeckt hare borst,/Werd yder Drop een Stadt, elck Reeder een Vorst."

37. Caspar Barlaeus, *Medicea Hospes, sive Descriptio Publicae Gratulationis, qua Serenissimam Augustissimamque Reginam, Mariam de Medicis, excepit Senatus Populusque Amstelodamensis; Marie de Medicis entrant dan Amsterdam: Blyde Inkomst der allerdoorluchtighste Konininne, Marie de Medicis* (t'Amsterdam, 1638), preface.

38. Investment was open to a broad spectrum of society. Government bonds at mid-century for example were sold in amounts ranging from a mere 50 florins to 39,750.

39. John Calvin, *Commentary on Isaiah*, 2: 12, 16.

40. Literally, "In order to attract more customers, principally through the opening of well-run, attractive and choice occasions for powerful and wealthy people, for the renewal and comfort of our increasingly exhausted trades- and craftsmen, (through) an increase of consumption; from this originates the improvement of all public and private income." "Om aen te locken een meerder toevloet van Menschen, voornamentlyck door 't openen van bequame, vermaeckelycke ende heerlycke gelegentheden voor machtige ende rycke luyden, tot verquickinge ende soulagement van onse meer ende meer vervallende Neeringhs- ende Ambacktsluyden, vermeerderinghe van Consumptie, ende daer uyt spruytende verbeteringe van alle publycke ende privé incomsten." Henrick Moreelse, *Copye van de deductie geëxhibeert by de Heere Borgermeester Moreelse, in*

het collegie van de Vroedtschap der Stadt Utrecht: den xxiijen Januarij 1664, raeckende de verbeteringe ende het nodigh uytleggen der selver stadt (Utrecht, 1664), p. 64, cited by E. Taverne, *In 't land van belofte: in de nieue stadt. Ideaal en werkelijkheid van de stadsuitleg in de Republiek (1580–1680)* (Maarssen: Gary Schwartz, 1978), p. 252. I am indebted to Harrie Vanderstapen for help with this translation.

41. John Michael Montias, *Artists and Artisans in Delft* (Princeton, N.J.: Princeton University Press, 1982), p. 112.

42. Charles MacKay, *The Tulipomania, Memoirs of Extraordinary Popular Delusions and the Madness of Crowds*, (London: National Illustrated Library, 1852) 1: 89–97; N. W. Posthumus, "The Tulip Mania in Holland in the Years 1636 and 1637," *Journal of Economic and Business History* 1, 4 (1929): 434–66; E. H. Krelage, *Bloemenspeculatie in Nederland* (Amsterdam: P.N. van Kampen Zoon, 1942).

43. Joseph de la Vega, *Confusion de Confusiones*, 1688, in *Portions Descriptive of the Amsterdam Stock Exchange*, ed. H. Kellenbenz (Boston, 1957), cited by Schama, *Embarrassment*, p. 349.

44. "In the wars of Europe these last four score years and upwards . . . we find that the Estates of the United Provinces have paid their armies better than any other prince or state; this makes the mercenary soldier run to their service and capacities them to make great levies in a very short time," wrote the admiring Sir James Turner in 1687, *Pallas Armata* (London, 1687), 198, cited by Parker, "Military Revolution," p. 213; see also Charles R. Boxer, *The Dutch Seaborne Empire: 1600–1800* (New York: Knopf, 1965), p. 4.

45. Albert O. Hirschman, *The Passions and the Interests: Political Arguments for Capitalism Before its Triumph* (Princeton, N.J.: Princeton University Press, 1977).

46. Thomas W. Laqueur, "Sexual Desire and the Market Economy During the Industrial Revolution," in *Discourses of Sexuality: From Aristotle to AIDS*, ed. Domna C. Stanton (Ann Arbor: University of Michigan Press, 1992), pp. 185–215.

47. Pieter de la Court and Johan de la Court, *Consideratien en Exempelen van Staat; omtrent de Fundamenten van allerley Regeringe* [Considerations and Examples of State Concerning the Foundations of all Kinds of Government] (Amsterdam, 1660); for a discussion of the economic thought of Pieter and Johan de la Court see Th. van Tijn, "Pieter de la Court, zijn leven en zijn economische denkbeelden," *Tijdschrift voor geschiedenis* 69 (1956): 304–70, and E. H. Kossmann, *Politieke theorie in het zeventiende-eeuwse Nederland*, in series *Verhandelingen der Koninklijke Nederlandse Akademie van Wetenschappen. Letterkunde* n s 67, 2 (Amsterdam, 1969): 30, 37.

48. Calvin argued that the spirit of Christ was actually present in the Eucharist, which was to be apprehended visually, Letter Calvin 25 Feb. 1547, in Johannis *Calvini Opera* . . ., (Brunsvigae: C. A. Schwetschke, 1863–1900 [New York: Johnson Reprint Corp., 1964]), 12, col. 482. I am deeply grateful to Brian Gerrish for this citation.

49. Philipp von Zesen, *Beschreibung der Stadt Amsterdam* (Amsterdam, 1664), p. 190.

50. Jacob Cats, *Houwelick, dat is de gantsche gelegentheyt des echten-staets*, *Vrouwe* (Middleburg, 1625), p. 317.

51. Gudlaugsson, *Gerard Ter Borch*, drawing illus. 175, painting in two versions cat. nos. 1, 2; Kettering, *Drawings*, pt. 1, 92, no. GJr1.

52. Algemeen Rijksarchief, The Hague, Staten van Holland, Res. Holland, 1629, 221, cited by Van Deursen, *Plain Lives*, p. 30.

12

Reorganizing Knowledge

A Feminist Scholar's Everyday Relation to the Florentine Past

Stephanie H Jed

IN HIS STUDY *The Writing of History*, Michel de Certeau invokes the moment in which historians question the relation between their fields of research and the spaces in which they come to know about the past: "Interrupting their erudite perambulations around the rooms of the National Archives, for a moment they detach themselves from the monumental studies that will place them among their peers, and walking out into the street, they ask, 'What in God's name is this business? What about the bizarre relation I am keeping with current society. . . ? . . . no thought or reading is capable of effacing the *specificity* of the place, the origin of my speech, or the area in which I am researching. . . . my way of speaking, my patois, represents my relation to a given place.'"[1] In this passage, de Certeau theorizes history's precarious balancing act "between a past that is its object and a present that is the place of its practice" and finds that our current historical projects are a "symptom" of past organizations of knowledge, while "history endlessly finds the present in its object."[2] He underscores the importance of bringing into the play of historical research the "I" of the researcher whose particular relation to the places in which s/he comes to know is always represented in her scholarly discourse. And, in my understanding of his text, de Certeau paves the way for a radical practice of literary/historical research which would rethink actual organizations of knowledge — in libraries and archives — through the symptomology of our current projects and questions.

In the case of this essay, current questions of how we come to know about Lorenzino de' Medici's assassination, in 1537, of Alessandro de' Medici, duke of Florence, lead to the various sites in which knowledge of this event, theories of state, and erudite and bibliographic discourses have met "my way of speaking," thinking, and writing about the Florentine past: sixteenth-century histo-riography and diplomatic archives, the history of libraries and erudite so-cieties, and feminist reflections on taxonomies. The value of this approach will lie, it is my hope, not in the presentation of my own personal reflections and associations (for this would surely be solipsistic and incommensurate with my interest in historical knowledge as a product of social relations), but rather in the attempt to move away from an argumentative/descriptive rhetoric about the past (which obfuscates the "I" of the researcher) towards a practice of actually reorganizing knowledge by means of citation, translation, collage, and imitation — all rhetorical techniques in which a socially constructed "I" in the present identifies with language from the past.

Like feminists in many other fields, I am interested in historicizing and situating ourselves on de Certeau's high wire stretched, for our sublime "per-ambulations," between the "objects" of our knowledge and the spaces in which we work. With Donna Haraway, Joan Scott, Dorothy Smith, Chandra Mohanty, and others, I understand the experience of these movements, not as the origin of knowledge, but as a series of practices of looking for, listening to, stumbling across, handling, compiling, and transcribing texts — practices which situate us in particular social relations and produce our visions, identi-ties, and interpretations.[3]

Furetière, in his *Dictionnaire* of 1690, defined the space of libraries as crisscrossed by a rhetoric of sameness. A library, he wrote, is "a Compilation of several works of the same nature or of Authors who have compiled all that can be [compiled] on the same subject."[4] Similarly, the *Dictionnaire* of the Aca-démie Française (1694) defined a library as holding "Collections and Com-pilations of works of like nature."[5]

Caught in such a library of sameness is the image of Lorenzino de' Medici, whose story emerged almost as a compilation of several stories of tyrannicide of like nature. The sixteenth-century humanistic historiography which can-onized his narrative placed him in a tradition of repetition and sameness which went back to the story of the first tyrant-slayers (Harmodius and Aristo-geiton) represented by Thucydides.[6] In the early sixteenth century, the learned man needed such a tradition of sameness to guide him in an ever more chaotic and indecipherable forest of knowledge; he needed instruments that would maintain a semblance of sameness in the labyrinths of diversity. Thus, in the same years in which Lorenzino plunged his dagger into the neck of the duke, the first modern catalogues were born.[7]

On the night of January 6, 1537, Lorenzino de' Medici devised an elabo-rate ambush against his cousin Alessandro de' Medici, duke of Florence. Ales-sandro reportedly had a weakness for insulting noblewomen and climbing convent walls. Lorenzino, capitalizing on this weakness, lured Alessandro into his bedroom and persuaded him to wait there unarmed; a woman, Lorenzino said, had agreed to satisfy Alessandro's lust for her on that very night. Alessandro waited for Lorenzino to bring back the woman. Instead, Lorenzino came back with his henchman Scoroncolo and together they assaulted the duke. Lorenzino, in order to muffle Alessandro's screams during the attack, put his hand in Alessandro's mouth. Alessandro then clamped his teeth down on Lorenzino's hand so hard that he nearly bit off his thumb. Blood gushed from Lorenzino's hand so fast as to force him to seek medical treatment in Bologna before notifying key people in Florence of what he had done. Lorenzino's melancholy, his brooding over books, and his resemblance to Brutus were important facts in the construction of this humanistic narrative.[8]

These facts, indeed, were instrumental in constructing the space of a library which would hold such historians as Herodotus, Thucydides, Livy, Valerius Maximus, Suetonius, Tacitus; their sixteenth-century avatars Machiavelli, Benedetto Varchi, Paolo Giovio, Filippo de' Nerli, Iacopo Nardi, Bernardo Segni; and the nineteenth-century and twentieth-century scholars attracted, for different historical reasons, to the problematic of tyrannicide. However, the compiling and collecting activities through which the "facts" about Lorenzino were organized with reference to this tradition are generally left unexamined.

What does it mean to come to know of this event in our own particular historical moment and place in the United States, the greatest exporter of violence in the world, the greatest exporter of arms and images of violence?[9] Calling all cataloguers! Calling all cataloguers! How would it work to take the story of Lorenzino out of the humanistic section of the library and put it under the classification "attraction and desire," the attraction and desire in the story, the attraction and desire of scholars to transmit the story, my own attraction and desire, for example, to reorganize the way in which the subjection of women is built into the formula for liberty? What would happen if we made "attraction and desire" visible as a taxonomic category, a new call number which organizes the readership and proliferation of this narrative? Already, details of Alessandro's lust and the sexual nature of Lorenzino's assault permeate the atmosphere in which we come to know about this incident in history; these details organize the environment in which scholars debate about whether or not Lorenzino was an authentic tyrant-slayer — that is, a patriotic citizen — or a pathological murderer. But these details are not enough to help us understand the way in which the subjection of women is built into the formula for freedom — nor the constructedness of that "subjection" and the formula. If we look, on the other hand, at the history of scholarly attraction to this subject, a different history emerges.

Filippo Strozzi (1489–1538), a humanist scholar and capitalist grain magnate, was attracted to Lorenzino and his deed and to examples of Brutus-like behavior in historiography. According to historiographic accounts, when Strozzi learned that Lorenzino had slain the duke, he hailed Lorenzino as the "new Brutus"[10] — a great Althusserian moment in history, a moment in which the force of attraction persuades us that Lorenzino was a great champion of liberty and an authentic tyrant-slayer in the tradition of Brutus. The figure of Brutus indeed is prominent in the organization of knowledge about Lorenzino.

But Strozzi was not the first scholar or the last to be attracted to the historiographic myth of Brutus. Delio Cantimori (1901–1966), an important Italian historian, revealed an ambivalent attraction to Brutus in his early essays written when he was an enthusiastic adherent of fascism. In 1927, he wrote that Girolamo Olgiati, a Milanese scholar of Latin who assassinated the duke Galeazzo Maria, was inspired by his attraction to Brutus: "Desire for political freedom, love of the fatherland, of the city, hatred of the tyrant, enthusiasm for Brutus, Sallust, study of the philosophers — all of it bookish and not ripened in life — was enough for Olgiati."[11] Brutus was not enough, however, for another tyrant-slayer, the Florentine Pier Paolo Boscoli, who attempted in 1512 to take the lives of Giulio, Giovanni and Giuliano de' Medici. Unlike Olgiati, Boscoli rejected the myth of Brutus's heroism as deceptive in the last minutes before his execution.[12]

The fascist Cantimori shared his attraction to the figure of Boscoli with a circle of erudites who gathered in Florence in the 1840s in the study of Gian Pietro Vieusseux and who published the text of Boscoli's confession. This circle of erudites founded the *Archivio Storico Italiano*, a journal which aspired to construct a "national" archive from the sources of Florentine archives and libraries. In the inaugural issue of this journal, Filippo Luigi Polidori, referred to as the "negro" of this erudite circle to mark his duties as secretary and scribe, transcribed and published Boscoli's confession. This publication of 1842, which served as a source for the construction of the Italian nation and for the interpretation of Cantimori's fascist Italy, also preserved something of these complex social attractions and hierarchies.

Gino Capponi, considered the most fascinating, passionate and erudite of the *Archivio Storico Italiano* group, also depended on Polidori's transcribing activity to write about Boscoli and his own ambivalent attraction to Brutus: "There were two conspirators," he wrote in his *History of the Florentine Republic*," but my heart goes out to the first, Pier Paolo Boscoli, a man of great intelligence and literary sensibility, who explained in his last hours the temper of his soul, how his mind's error was covered over by a refinement of feeling. Classical and pagan ideas had invaded the mind of the poor young man, a sincere Christian, such that he asked his dear ones to take Brutus from his head, because he wanted to die as a Christian. History can draw a great and vital lesson regarding the interior life and feeling of men in that singular age from the sad story and words of those unhappy youths."[13]

In June of 1826, Marco Pieri, "the angry, most erudite, most academic, celibate whining 50-year-old"[14] of the Florentine group, wrote of a French feminist historian, novelist and political theorist, Hortense Allart: "I found my young French literata to have given birth three days earlier to a beautiful baby boy whom she named Marcus Brutus. And I made my visits more frequent, so that an entire day didn't pass without my seeing her."[15] Perhaps inspired by the baby boy's name, Guglielmo Libri, in the days after Allart gave birth, "would visit her every evening to converse near her bed about Roman history which he knew by heart."[16] Indeed, the boy's name became a center of play for the Florentine erudites. Niccolò Tommaseo, in a letter to Gino Capponi of August 13, 1834 (from Paris), mentions the boy's father: "I saw the father of Marcus. He resembles Cicero somewhat, but not in his style."[17] Allart's scholarly commitment to writing a history of Florence was always tempered by her dedication to Brutus. In her letter to Capponi of July 18, 1837, Allart wrote of Italian unity as an enterprise for the likes of Brutus: "You dream of unity; do you despair of virtue, like Brutus?"[18] It is difficult to distinguish here between the erudites' attraction to Brutus and their desire for Allart, between Allart's dedication to her son and her dedication to her writing. Some of these difficulties must be inscribed somewhere in the atmosphere of the library in which we come to know about Lorenzino.

The erudites were mercilessly cruel, writing to each other about their fears of Allart's sexuality. Tommaseo and Capponi exchanged letters about the shape of her nose.[19] Tommaseo imagined her to be constantly propositioning him.[20] Capponi was afraid of his fondness for her, writing: "I have been fond of her, as you know, for 13 years, because she is fundamentally good and has noble parts . . . I have never touched her, nor would I touch a finger. And she already knows that for me it would be impossible, physically impossible. And I have told her so, and written, thousands of times, how and why. She is too good to be [my] prostitute; as my wife, may God protect me from it. And it is necessary for me to imagine women in one of the two roles. I have never liked it any other way: I have never known how to be gallant and my too many sins are, without exception, those of an angel or a pig, a pig not disguised as a decent man."[21]

What seems to have been most painful for these dedicated scholars was Allart's erudition and the agility and enthusiasm with which she crossed over boundaries of fiction, erudition, and feminism. Tommaseo complained that she worked simultaneously on her history of Florence and her 1836 work *La femme et la démocratie de nos temps*.[22] Capponi wrote: "Poor thing, I have almost lost the patience even to discuss with her and write to her, which I used to enjoy so much. She has grown so old in specious reasoning that, at least for me, there is no woman left in her. And . . . she has taken to defending all of the infamies and making from them a social system."[23] All of this translates neatly into modern scholarly assertions such as "Gino Capponi wrote 'the very first modern history of Florence.'"[24] Still, the subjection of Allart's scholarship achieves a different inflection in our scholarly atmosphere — is, indeed, constructed differently — imprinting a different social space for knowing in the library.

Now Gino Capponi himself wrote in the preface to his classic, first modern history of Florence published in 1875: "Allart . . . published in 1843 a compendium [600 pages!!] of the History of the Florentine Republic, which in many respects is the best of all that have been attempted so far. Alessandro Carraresi translated it, but some things were too much for us Italians, others weren't enough. So I started to make some mental notes, then to cut some passages of the French text and lengthen others. In this way, little by little, I found myself with all of the thought inside my History of Florence."[25] Allart's history is today unknown, although Capponi appropriated the organization of her history almost to the chapter and, in many places, did nothing more than translate her words into Italian.

At first, I was sure I identified with Lorenzino. But of course! I too, after all, was a lover of liberty and wanted, with Lorenzino, to be victorious over Alessandro's tyranny. Then, I worried that maybe after all, under the cloak of political righteousness, I too was a tyrant. I wanted people to feel and think in ways completely identical to my own. Soon I realized that I was being tricked into identifying with one or the other or even with both. The organization of historical knowledge led me to affirm these traditional understandings of "liberty" and "tyranny" and discouraged me from questioning how the subjection of women was constructed in these political categories; from developing a diversity of other identifications; and from exploring the space in which such identifications are constructed, in which such identifications help to construct me as a scholar.

There is a very somber section of the library organized around the category "state." In this section, we might find Arcangela Tarabotti (1604–1652), a Venetian political theorist forced to become a nun, hovering in the atmosphere, hoping to reorganize our understanding of the concept "reason of state." She organizes her political analysis not around the logic of power, but rather around the suffering of daughters, deceived by their fathers into believing that the convent will be a sort of pleasure palace; this deceit takes place at an age in which children's trust in their parents and the world is total. The tyranny of Nero and Diocletian cannot compare with the tyranny of fathers raging against innocent, defenseless daughters who feel only "the most tender affection for their persecutors." Men condemn the power of the tyrant in theory, but then they support a reason of state which makes the father's tyranny one of its mainstays.[26]

For Tarabotti, the reason of State is not the "neutral" knowledge necessary for founding, conserving, and expanding a political domain, but rather the actively deceptive efforts of noble fathers to conserve their wealth and class at the expense of their daughters' servitude. She writes: "If you believe that the large number of daughters threatens the reason of State, because if they all married, the nobility would increase and the noble families would become impoverished with the disbursement of so many dowries, take up the company given to you by God without greed for money. And since you buy wives as slaves, it would be more decent for you to shell out the gold, than for the wives to pay to buy their masters."[27] Tarabotti overturns the terms of western political discourse by situating the state concretely in the private ledger books of noble families.

Now a state archive is a "private" and "practical" affair. The state archive's taxonomy conserves the internal memory of that institution, the particular interests of those who categorized and inventoried, their specific historical vicissitudes. This private and practical memory, conserved in the history of categories and classifications, "permeates" the environment of the archive and produces the historicity of our research.[28] For the year in which Lorenzino finished off the Duke, the state archive of Milan conserves, under the rubric "Chancery of the State," the internal memory of Charles V's Italian administration; its categories and classifications for the year 1537 thus constitute one important locality of writing in which we come to know about Lorenzino.

Knowledge is vagabond. Scholars, books, and other text-bearing objects are constantly involved in intense peregrinations about the social world, escaping the specific rules, conventions, and hierarchies within which they were produced.[29] And so, toward the middle of the reign of Ronald Reagan, Stephanie Jed of San Diego visited Milan. She had just completed a seminar in paleography at the Newberry Library and was full of excitement and trepidation about what she might find among the sixteenth-century records of diplomatic correspondence about the assassination of the duke Alessandro de' Medici by his cousin Lorenzino. What she already "knew" about the act she had learned in humanistic historiography. How it is that she came to "know" what it is she "knew" was already a quiet question lingering around the margins of the struggle between liberty and tyranny. She wanted precisely to get to the margins to understand the canonization of a particular humanistic vision and its heroes.

What she found in Milan, thanks to the fact that an incisive and generous archivist, Maria Bortolotti, was in the process of reorganizing the very documents pertaining to Lorenzino, was a series of letters about Lorenzino addressed to the governor of Milan and "originally" filed under the category "Cancelleria dello stato." This category, conserving part of the private and practical memory of the Archivio di Stato of Milan, permeates the airy, luminous, and relaxed reading room with a bright and varied history of literacy and new writing subjects. But once Jed started to transcribe the documents, it became clear that a different taxonomic category of "literacy" might reorganize knowledge about these documents: as new writing subjects acquired the power to write, this power was subsumed under the power over writing represented by the imperial bureaucracy.[30] The letters filed in this category which refer to Lorenzino are written by a wide range of writers of different occupations—diplomats, spies, military commanders—from different sociocultural backgrounds, who mark in their writing various local inflections of Italian and Spanish, various types of handwriting, and various degrees of literacy. There are several letters written in cipher and deciphered upon receipt in the Milanese chancery. Sometimes, letters appear to be dictated or even composed by scribes, sometimes they are "autographs." In some cases, where the signatory has not written the letter, the contrast between the unwieldy signature and the semi-professional writing of the scribe points to the discontinuous relation between power and writing in this period.[31]

Bortolotti's reordering was but the last in a long series of reorganizations of knowledge about the Milanese chancery. The correspondence of the Milanese chancery had been repeatedly renamed, dismembered, and reordered according to taxonomies of "logic," chronology, and subject matter. I want to focus on one moment at the end of the nineteenth century, when this kind of archival work—the ordering and reordering of inventories, files, and catalogues—had come to a halt in Milan. Historian Raponi noted, "This was not a period of inertia, but a rich and intense period of methodological disorientation, or, if you will, a period of methodological empiricism, which was reflected in a sort of eclectic productivity."[32]

This intense period of disorientation must have permeated the atmosphere of the archive on the day in which I became intensely attracted to a particular document, the letter of Giovanni Antonio, "called the tailor," employed by the emperor to oversee the activities of the post in Bologna and to write to him about anyone significant who passed by. On January 9, 1537, two and a half days after Lorenzino's deed, this "tailor" wrote a letter in great haste and excitement to Charles V's governor in Milan, telling him that Lorenzino had just passed through Bologna: "He was wounded and it seems that he was fleeing from Florence and he left with the greatest fear . . . and I think I heard that said messer Lorenzo. And I think I heard, as I said, that he has killed the lord duke of Florence, and so, hearing this news which is of greatest importance to his imperial majesty, I thought of sending this mail to you, most revered excellency, only for this news."[33] Giovanni "the tailor" was in such a hurry to send this news to Caracciolo that he seems not to have waited for the ink to dry. The signs of this haste are the particles of sixteenth-century sand which stuck to the ink and that are still there today on the paper.

A certain vertigo sets in as one realizes that "sand" and "ink" may also be categories of knowing which permeate the atmosphere in which we come to know. For Jed (and here I am imitating and making a collage of Joan Scott's words), witnessing the sixteenth-century sand sparkling in the ink in the bright large reading room was an event. It marked what in one kind of reading we would call a coming to consciousness of herself, a recognition of something about her identity heretofore unexamined.

Another kind of reading, closer to Jed's preoccupation with understanding knowledge as constituted within a social environment, sees in this event the compelling emergence of a new political subject and his local situation, a new taxonomic category for the visions and the heroes and the knowledge of the "state." Jed presents this displacement as a clarifying moment, after which she wants to write about the atmosphere in which we come to know. The properties of the medium through which the visible appears — here, the sixteenth-century sand, whose shiny, sparkling qualities produce a vertigo of the visible — make any claim to transparency impossible. Instead, the sparkling light permits a vision beyond the visible, a vision that tries to grasp the varying rhetorics which permeate archives, libraries, department meetings, lunches at the Stanford Humanities Center, and which contain the fantastic projections that are the basis for political identification. In this version of the story, political consciousness and power originate, not in a presumedly unmediated experience of presumedly real documents, but out of an apprehension of the moving, differencing properties of the representational medium — the motion of light in ink.[34]

Jed was moved by the possibilities offered by these graphic expressions to affirm a different "reality" than the "reality" or "reason" of state within which these documents were framed. My attraction to the categories of "sand" and "ink" was not an unmediated attraction between me and the sand and the ink. Rather, I think, it was an attraction enabled by the methodological disorientation and empiricism and productivity which brought archival work to a halt at the end of the nineteenth century and which still permeated the atmosphere of the archive. Breathing the air of this late nineteenth-century methodological empiricism in the bright airy reading room of the archive, I might have started to breathe the ideas of a late nineteenth-century feminist political theorist, Anna Maria Mozzoni (1837–1920), whose ideas about empiricism, taxonomies, humanism, the state, and the subjection of women were already influencing my own.

What I am trying to work out in my research is this: we cannot understand the constructedness of the sixteenth-century subjection of women in the formula for freedom, if we don't study the different taxonomic organizations of the places in which we come to know about such "freedom"; these taxonomies, charging the atmosphere with attraction, at some level rub off on the researcher. Anna Maria Mozzoni was attuned to this issue of how republican thought, in the sixteenth and seventeenth centuries, constructed the subjection of women; she located the beginning of feminism in the years in which Lorenzino plunged the dagger in Alessandro's neck; she cited Tarabotti as one of her foremothers in the areas of feminist political theory; she translated John Stuart Mill's essay on The Subjection of Women;[35] she, along with Irene Silverblatt, understood that "state formation" could not account for the subjection of women; but that rather, the very concept of the subjection of women in states was still "another resurrection" of Western taxonomies which have divided culture from economy, private from public, women from the state. Such divisions, Silverblatt and Mozzoni agree, have "sapped women of their historical souls." We therefore need to "rethink the categories we use to grasp historical process."[36] In her work *La donna e i suoi rapporti sociali* (1864), an extended critique of the new Civil Code then being proposed and discussed in Parliament, Mozzoni explicitly connected taxonomic activities to a politics of intolerance. She wrote: "The most excruciating injustices to devastate humankind and the most enormous philosophic errors were born from the mania for classifications. Classifications have created prejudices; prejudices, in their turn, have generated outcasts and slaves. Prejudices have led to contempt for the slave and have given rise to false and unfair biases against differently colored races, biases which unluckily persist even among many whose profession it is to understand justice. From classifications and prejudices, deep hatreds were born and lasting international conflicts, as if the person who lives on one bank of a river or on one side of a mountain differs essentially from the person who inhabits the other bank or the other slope."[37] But what if we start from the rhetorics implicit in our activities of compiling, transcribing, collecting which crisscross both sides of the slope? Would different categories like "literacy," "ink" and "sand," enable us to bridge current gaps between, say, the Italian Renaissance, Chicano Studies and feminist theory? Would the atmosphere in which we think and know begin to change?

From Mozzoni's point of view, it is possible to understand all existing categories for knowing as part of "a systemic deformation"[38] — that is, every component of the "system" is itself a "deformation"; terms, theories, traditions, concepts, institutions, ideologies all form part of a taxonomic code which convinces people to leave the categories of knowledge intact, a code which educates women in terms of introspection and psychology,[39] a code which would need to be completely rewritten for women (and other untolerated groups) to take their place as social subjects in the new democracy.

At the heart of the "systemic deformation" which produced the political inertia of women was the ideology of the feudal family which persisted in the new Civil Code of Italy. According to Mozzoni, this new Civil Code deleted the very existence of women from the representation of society. What then was the status of women scholars in the national libraries and archives which would form part of that Civil Code? To democrats like Mazzini who theorized that "woman" and her "rights" did indeed exist in the kingdom of familial duty, Mozzoni responded that the family represented not a kingdom but a non-place for women, a space inhabited not by humans but by burdens and obligations: "Say no more that the woman is made for the family, that the family is her kingdom and her empire! . . . In the family, in the city, wherever, her existence is in terms of burdens and obligations; excepting these [burdens and obligations], she does not exist in any place."[40] What would these burdens and obligations mean in terms of the compiling, transcribing, and collecting activities she enacts in the course of her scholarly work? To think of scholarship as implicated in a national politics and taxonomy requires a radical rethinking of women's nonplace in places of knowing and the burdens and obligations which mark such a spatial configuration. Mozzoni herself, after her death, lived on in the state archive on a police list of wanted persons; her crime was that of raising the taxonomic consciousness of Italian women.[41]

It is important to note the special place Mozzoni reserves for literary and historical example in the taxonomies of intolerance. On several occasions, coupling literature with philanthropy, she notes with antipathy that literature provides a poor example for women's struggles. In particular, women who have acquired privilege through intellectual and literary work have little to offer in the field of women's struggles, because they do not combat privilege as yet another "systemic deformation," and they tend to see class privilege as something one chooses rather than as something which conditions one's choices.[42] And intellectuals in general are complicit with lawmakers in their obsequiousness towards examples from tradition. "The voice of Cicero and Tribonian," wrote Mozzoni, "sounds louder to the ear of the Italian Senate than public opinion, the cry of philosophy, and the unanimous vote of a whole century and a whole nation."[43] And intellectuals (and in this case, she refers specifically to male intellectuals) reinforce this deafness to the present by burying themselves in literary and historical examples: "Isn't it laughable," Mozzoni asks, "that the scholar discusses the laws of Lycurgus and the Twelve Tables, and then knows nothing about which institutions more or less safeguard his person and his property? Isn't it irrational that he speaks about the wars of the Titans and then is a complete stranger to the upheavals that produced Italian liberty and to the thousands of those who, on the field, from prisons, and in exile prepared the way for our current cultural state?"[44]

The repetition of examples from the past, Mozzoni suggested, was the cause of continued intolerance in the present; over the course of time, past examples of slavery and feudalism have gathered force as a stone gathers moss, until the "force of example" has acquired the force of law. For this reason, Mozzoni claimed, citing examples from the past, contrary to every truism about history we have been taught, has never served any purpose at all. To think that the example of history could be useful was "to pretend that a people could free itself from foreign domination by dint of legal demonstrations."[45]

As Cattaneo observed, Mozzoni was one of those women who took the risk of expressing new insights derived from her compilation, transcription, and collection of the "dust of the laws."[46] One of those insights was that systems of knowledge contributed to the production of a politics of prejudice in post-unification Italy and that it was important to refigure such systems. As we become more self-conscious about our own activities of collecting and compiling and transcribing and categorizing, imaginary spaces based on tolerance of difference may emerge, spaces organized according to the acts and relations by which we come to know.

In any case, to make such activities and their reckoning visible helps us to understand the construction of our political identities and social relations as scholars. History is full of self-consciousness about collecting and compiling. François de La Croix du Maine, the author of an imaginary Bibliothèque of 1584, wrote that his own "real" library consisted of "800 volumes of Memoirs and diverse Collections, written by my hand and otherwise, and all of my invention or sought by myself, and extracts from all the books that I have read until this day, of which the number is infinite."[47] La Croix du Maine (according to Chartier) actually calculated his compilation activities. He wrote "three hours per day, and he figures that if in one hour he filled one sheet of paper of over one hundred lines, his yearly production was some one thousand sheets."[48]

La Croix du Maine had a passion for counting his transcriptions, and I am passionate about understanding how it is we come to know through our acts of transcription; how our sheets of writing become a social space from which new configurations of knowledge emerge. Giovanni "the tailor" dried his ink, consolidating his knowledge with sixteenth-century sand; he has encouraged me to situate my own compilations in the places and times in which I come to know. Tarabotti was a bold defender of anachronism, and one has the impression that she nibbled here and there in the books she read, looking for the right words and phrases to fit her original arguments of political theory.[49] Her mixing up of different historical moments and eclectic reading practices have given me the courage to come out to myself about my own historical designs and risky reading habits. Allart had a passion for both feminism and erudition; she maintained an erudite passion for Florentine history and the Florentine erudites even in the face of their mostly misogynistic consideration of her, and she drew strength for this erudition from her feminist politics and writings. Mozzoni had the measure of skepticism we all need to understand the taxonomies in which we are all caught.

Although my own yearly production of notes, letters, and memos is probably somewhat less than 1000 sheets, my identification with compilers of knowledge like La Croix du Maine, Giovanni the tailor, Tarabotti, Allart, and Mozzoni remains fierce and unflinching; they inform my own reorderings of knowledge about Lorenzino and Allessandro. And they give me a tangible sense of my identity as a scholar and of the love I bear for compiling bits of knowledge in new configurations and alliances.

When I started reading about the great bibliomaniac Antonio Magliabechi (1633–1714), I began to realize that much of this project is concerned with identifications. Magliabechi was the State librarian to Cosimo III, the grand duke of Tuscany, and his own private library of 30,000 volumes was joined, in 1861, with the private library of King Victor Emanuel to become the Biblioteca nazionale of Florence. Magliabechi was the focal point of an extensive correspondence with intellectuals from all over the Italian peninsula, intellectuals who wrote to him, hoping to break free of the Counter-Reformation dogmas of knowing which weighed so heavily in their own peripheral locales; they hoped to break their intellectual isolation and to reorganize knowledge as a collective process, as a "literary republic" with Florence as its historiographic capital.[50]

By virtue of their questions and requests, their descriptions and laments, Magliabechi's correspondents traced the first configurations of an Italian national culture. In my own research dreams, I become one of those correspondents from the periphery; I dream of retracing the beginnings of a future national past; a past in which foundational stories of liberty, tyranny are organized according to a different vision. My unwillingness to accept the subjection of women as an inevitability even in history leads me to look for those writers from the past who help us create new configurations of political knowledge, whose social imagination might also include us in a process of change.

Notes

This essay is a first presentation of research completed as a Marta Stutton Weeks Fellow at the Stanford Humanities Center (1994–95). I would like to acknowledge here the warm and supportive intellectual environment created by the staff and directors of the Center, Gwen Lorraine, Sue Dambrau, Susan Sebbard, Wanda Corn, and Charles Junkerman. I would like to thank all the fellows for their suggestions, feedback, and daily conviviality, and in particular, Hilary Schor, Hilton Obenzinger, Clifton Crais, Renée Romano, Joss Marsh, Ericka Miller, David Palumbo-Liu, Martin Bloomer, and my fellow-traveler Eduardo García. Mary Jane Parrine, Curator of Romance Languages at the Stanford Library, extended her intellectual support from the beginning to the end of my stay at Stanford. I was fortunate to encounter once again Armando Petrucci as a Visiting Professor of Italian at Stanford in the fall quarter. His pointers, suggestions, and supportive responses at the beginning of my research were, as always, indispensable in the planning of my research itinerary. I want to thank Patricia Parker for her inspiration and support in this project and Karen Offen for her generous reading and comments on this essay in its early stages. I want to express my general indebtedness, in this research into our scholarly environments, to the work of the Società italiana delle storiche, in particular the book they published entitled *discutendo di storia: Soggettività, ricerca, biografia* (Turin: Roseberg and Sellier, 1990). But most important, I would like to acknowledge Paolo Valesio, who mentored and directed my first research on problems of "liberty" and "tyranny" and whose figure as a scholar and poet returns now to inspire this more experimental turn in my research.

1. Michel de Certeau, *The Writing of History*, trans. Tom Conley (New York: Columbia University Press, 1988), p. 56.

2. Ibid., p. 36.

3. Donna Haraway, "Situated Knowledges: The Science Question in Feminism and the Privilege of Partial Perspective," in *Simians, Cyborgs, and Women: The Reinvention of Nature* (New York: Routledge, 1991), pp. 183– 201; Joan Scott, "The Evidence of Experience," *Critical Inquiry* 17, 4 (Summer 1991): 773–97; Dorothy E. Smith, *The Conceptual Practices of Power: A Feminist Sociology of Knowledge* (Boston: Northeastern University Press, 1990); Chandra Talpade Mohanty, "Cartographies of Struggle: Third World Women and the Politics of Feminism" in *Third World Women and the Politics of Feminism*, ed. Chandra Mohanty, Ann Russo, and Lourdes Torres, (Bloomington: Indiana University Press, 1991), pp. 1– 47.

4. Roger Chartier, *The Order of Books*, trans. Lydia G. Cochrane (Stanford, Calif.: Stanford University Press, 1994), p. 65.

5. Ibid., p. 66. Of course, as was pointed out to me by a reader of this essay, these "definitions" were at variance with what we know of the wildly eclectic libraries of such figures as John Dee or Pico.

6. Thucydides, *The Peloponnesian War*, trans. Charles Forster Smith (Cambridge, Mass.: Harvard University Press, 1952), 6.54.

7. Mario Rosa, "I depositi del sapere: Biblioteche, Accademie, Archivi" in *La memoria del sapere: Forme di conservazione e strutture organizzative dall'antichità a oggi*, ed. Pietro Rossi, (Bari: Laterza, 1988), p. 171.

8. This narrative represents a digest of material from the following sixteenth-century historians: Paolo Giovio, *La istoria del suo tempo*, trans. (into Tuscan) Lodovico Domenichi (Florence: Torrentini, 1550–52), book 38; Iacopo Nardi, *Istorie della città di Firenze*, ed. Agenore Gelli, 2 vols. (Florence: Le Monnier, 1858), 2: book 10; Filippo de' Nerli, *Commentarj de' fatti civili occorsi dentro la città di Firenze* (Trieste: Colombo Coen Tipi Editore, 1859), book 12; Bernardo Segni, *Storie fiorentine*, 3 vols. (Milan: Società Tipografica de' Classici Italiani, 1805), 2: book 7; Benedetto Varchi, *Storia fiorentina*, 5 vols. (Milan: Società Tipografica de' Classici Italiani, 1803–4), 5: book 15.

9. The source of this "fact" is Eduardo Galeano, who was visiting Stanford in spring 1995. It should also be noted that I aspire toward the historiographic style he uses in his trilogy *Memories of Fire* (although, of course, I cannot hope to achieve his level of artistic monument).

10. Joyce G. Bromfield, *De Lorenzino de Médicis a Lorenzaccio: étude d'un thème historique* (Paris: Marcel Didier, 1972), p. 21.

11. Delio Cantimori, "Il caso del Boscoli e la vita del Rinascimento," *Giornale Critico della Filosfia Italiana* 4 (1927): 249 (translation mine).

12. Ibid.; p. 250; Luca della Robbia, "Recitazione del caso di Pietro Paolo Boscoli e di Agostino Capponi . . . l'anno MDXIII," ed. Filippo Polidori, *Archivio storico italiano* 1st ser. 1 (1842): 290.

13. Gino Capponi, *Storia della repubblica di Firenze* (Firenze: Barbéra, 1875), vol. 2, pp. 311–12: "ma l'affetto di chi legge si ferma sul primo, il quale essendo di molto ingegno e di buone lettere, spiegava nelle ultime sue ore un tempra d'animo dove l'errore della mente veniva coperto dalla squisitezza del sentire. . . . Il povero giovane, cristiano sincero, aveva la mente pure invasata delle idee classiche e pagane, onde a que' suoi cari chiedeva che gli cavassero dalla testa Bruto, perchè egli voleva morire da cristiano. Grande e vivo insegamento circa alla vita interiore ed al sentire degli uomini in quella età singolare può trarre l'istoria dal mesto racconto e dalle parole di quei giovani infelici."

14. Ernesto Sestan, *La Firenze di Vieusseux e di Capponi*, ed. Giovanni Spadolini (Florence: Olschki, 1986), p. 121 n. 57.

15. Ibid.: "Trovai quella mia giovane letterata francese puerpera di tre giorni, e madre di un bel maschio, al quale ella pose il nome di Marcus Brutus; e spesseggiai le mie visite tanto, che non correva un'intera giornata senza ch'io la vedessi."

16. Hortense Allart de Méritens, *Lettere inedite a Gino Capponi*, ed. Petre Ciureanu (Genoa: Tolozzi e C., 1961), p. xi.

17. Ibid., p. xlvi: "ho veduto il padre di Marcus, e somiglia un po' a Cicerone, ma non nello stile . . ."

18. Ibid., lettera 48, p. 85: "Vous songiez à l'unité; désespérez-vous de la vertu, comme Brutus?"

19. Ibid., pp. lxi, lxiii.

20. Ibid., pp. xlvi, lvi, lvii.

21. Ibid., p. lxix and Sestan, *La Firenze*, p. 122 n. 57: "Ed io che le voglio bene, come sapete, da 13 anni in qua, perchè di fondo è buona e ha nobili parti, . . . io non le ho toccato mai, né toccherei, un dito. E già la lo sa, ch'e' mi sarebbe impossibile, impossibile fisicamente; e glie ne ho dette le mille volte, e scritto, il come e il perchè. Per meretrice la vale troppo; per moglie, Dio ne guardi; ed io le donne bisogna che una delle due cose me le figuri o figurassi. Né altro modo mi piacque: galante non seppi essere mai, ed i miei troppi peccati sono, senza eccezione tutti, di angelo o di porco; di porco non travestito da uomo civile."

22. Ibid., p. xlvi.

23. Ibid., pp. lxix–lxx: "Con lei, poveretta, ho quasi perduto la pazienza anche per discorrervi e scriverle, che prima piuttosto mi piaceva. Ma la s'è tanto invecchiata nel sofisma, che almeno per me, di donna non v'è più nulla. E . . . la s'è messa a difendere tutte le infamie, ed a farne sistema sociale."

24. Sestan, *La Firenze*, p. 136.

25. Gino Capponi, *Storia della Repubblica di Firenze* (Florence: G. Barbèra, 1875), pp. v–vi: "Allart . . . mandò alle stampe nel 1843 un ristretto della Storia della Repubblica Fiorentina, che per molti rispetti è il migliore di quanti se ne abbiano tentati fin qui. Di questo Libro il signore Alessandro Carraresi negli anni seguenti aveva compito una traduzione: ma in esso alcune cose erano di troppo per noi Italiani, altre non bastavano. Mi posi a farvi così a mente alcune note, poi a ristringere alcuni brani del testo francese, altri ad allargare: così a poco a poco mi trovai con tutto il pensiero dentro alla Storia di Firenze."

26. Ginevra Conti Odorisio, *Storia dell'idea femminista in Italia* (Turin: Edizioni RAI Radiotelevisione Italiana, 1980), pp. 42–43.

27. Francesca Medioli, *L' "Inferno monacale" di Arcangela Tarabotti* (Turin: Rosenberg and Sellier, 1990), p. 93: "Se stimate pregiudicar la multiplicità delle figliole alla Ragion di Stato, poi ché, se tutte si maritassero, crescerebbe in troppo numero la nobiltà et impoverirebber le case col sborso di tante doti, pigliate la compagnia dattavi da Dio senz'avidità di danaro. Già a comprar schiave, come voi fatte le mogli, saria più decente che voi sborsaste l'oro, non elle, per comprar patrone." For an interpretation of Tarabotti's critique of the dowry system, see the important dissertation by Jutta Sperling (Stanford, 1995).

28. Mario Rosa, "I depositi," p. 183.

29. Here I am imitating and making a collage of Roger Chartier's words, pp. viii, x.

30. See Armando Petrucci, "Pouvoir d'écriture, pouvoir sur l'écriture dans la Renaissance italienne," *Annales ESC* 4 (1988): 823–24.

31. Ibid.

32. Nicola Raponi. "Per la storia dell'Archivio di Stato di Milano: Erudizione e cultura nell'*Annuario* del Fumi (1909–1919)." *Rassegna degli Archivi di Stato* 31, 2 (1971): 316.

33. Cancelleria dello Stato di Milano, Archivio di Stato of Milan, folder 20, folio 208: "era ferite e mi pare che se ne fugiva da fiorenza e se ne andava cum grandissima paura . . . e me pare de intendere che ditto messer Lorenzo, E me pare de intendere como ho ditte che ha morto il signor ducha di fiorenza e cosi intendende tal nova, la

quale e di grandissima importanza a la maesta cesarea me parse de espedire questa posta
solamente per tal nova . . ."

34. Scott, "The Evidence," p. 794.

35. John Stuart Mill, *La servitù delle donne*, trans. Anna Maria Mozzoni (Milan:
Felice Legros, 1870).

36. Irene Silverblatt, "Interpreting Women in States: New Feminist Ethnohisto-
ries" in *Gender at the Crossroads of Knowledge: Feminist Anthropology in the Postmodern
Era*, ed. Micaela di Leonardo (Berkeley: University of California Press, 1991), p. 156.

37. Anna Maria Mozzoni, *La liberazione della donna*, ed. Franca Pieroni Bortolotti
(Milano: Mazzotta, 1975), p. 67: "Dalla manía delle classificazioni nacquero le più
strazianti ingiustizie che hanno desolato l'umana progenie, e gli errori più cubitali della
filosofia. Le classificazioni crearono i pregiudizii; i pregiudizzi a loro volta generarono i
Paria e gli Iloti; consigliarono lo sprezzo dello schiavo; suggerirono false ed inique
prevenzioni sulle diverse razze colorate, che sgraziatamente perdurano presso molti che
fanno anche professione d'intendersi di giustizia. Dalle classificazioni donde i pregiudizii, nacquero gli odii profondi, e le lunghe ire internazionali, quasi l'uomo che abita
l'altra sponda di un fiume, o l'altro versante di una montagna, essenzialmente differisca
dall'uomo che abita la prima sponda ed il primo versante."

38. Ibid., p. 41: "una viziatura di sistema."

39. Franca Pieroni Bortolotti, *Alle origini del movimento femminile in Italia, 1848–
1892* (Turin: Einaudi, 1963), p. 57.

40. Anna Maria Mozzoni, *La donna e i suoi rapporti sociali* (Milan: Tipografia
sociale, 1864), p. 214: "Non dite più che la donna è fatta per la famiglia; che nella
famiglia è il suo regno ed il suo impero! . . . Ella esiste nella famiglia, nella città e
dovunque in faccia ai pesi ed ai doveri; da questi all'infuori ella non esiste in nessun
luogo."

41. Mozzoni, *Liberazione*, p. 25.

42. Bortolotti, *Alle origini*, p. 63.

43. Ibid., p. 76: "la voce di Cicerone e di Triboniano suon[a] piú alto all'orecchio
dell'italico senato che non l'opinione pubblica, il grido della filosofia, il voto unanime di
tutto un secolo e di tutta una nazione."

44. Ibid., p. 63: "Non è egli risibile che lo scolaro discuta le leggi di Licurgo e le
dodici tavole, e poi non sappia da quali istitutioni è piú o meno tutelata la sua persona e
la sua proprietà? Non è egli fuor di ragione che vi parli delle guerre dei Titani e poi
sia completamente straniero ai rivolgimenti che produssero la libertà italiana e alle
miglia[ia] di coloro che sul campo come dalle prigioni all'esilio prepararono l'attual
civiltà."

45. Ibid., p. 63: "pretendere che un popolo si sbarazzi da uno straniero dominio a
furia di legali dimostrazioni."

46. Carlo Cattaneo, *Opere edite ed inedite*, ed. A. Bertani, 7 vols. (Firenze: Le
Monnier, 1883), 1: p. 358. Cited by Bortolotti, *Alle origini*, p. 53.

47. Chartier, pp. 77–8.

48. Ibid., p. 78.

49. Medioli, p. 146–7.

50. See the introduction of Amedeo Quondam and Michele Rak to their edition
of *Lettere dal Regno ad Antonio Magliabechi* (Naples: Guida, 1978).

13

"The Catastrophe Is a Nuptial"

Love's Labor's Lost, Tactics, Everyday Life

Richard Corum

I always thought marriage was one step away from death.
— Sandra Bullock, *The Late Show with David Letterman*,
12:10 A.M., Friday, July 25, 1995

In such conditions, the *heterogeneous* elements, at least as such, find themselves subjected to a *de facto* censorship. . . . They cannot be kept within the field of consideration.
— Georges Bataille, *Visions of Excess*, 1

"IN THE EIGHTEENTH CENTURY," Michel de Certeau writes, "the ideology of the Enlightenment claimed that the book was capable of reforming society, that educational popularization could transform manners and customs, that an elite's products could, if they were sufficiently widespread, remodel a whole nation."[2] This ideological program's long-term effect on Shakespeare's plays — their appropriation and dissemination as a "book" — was to move these plays from the margins of the culture to its center where, remade as "an elite's products," they were called upon (through various modalities: in-, re-, trans-, con-) to "form" a heterogeneous public.[3] In this location, Shakespeare's comedies, deployed as one of several dominant homogenizing technologies, staged festive or problematic models of gender/sex conflicts resolved by love/marriage, and did so to inculcate heteronormativity, gender inequality, homosociality, and class difference, among other practices, into everyday life.[4] For this scheme *Loues Labors lost* long posed a problem. It leaves us, Stephen Booth notes, with the "feeling that [it] has not come out right"[5]: "The wooing doth not end like an old play; / Jack hath not Jill" (5.2.864–65).[6] Moreover, encountered in contexts where "coming out right" was a signal marker of social stability, such "not coming out right" generated powerful anxieties. So it is not

surprising that we may read this play's critical/performative history as a collection of middle-class discourses engaged, however consciously, in assigning
blame for *LLL*'s failure, and/or in erasing it.

For the first two hundred-plus years of the play's post-folio life, failure
was attributed to Shakespeare's inexperience: too many puns and obscure
jokes; a trivial plot; his first play.[7] When Shakespeare gravitated close enough
to the culture's center that appearances had to be saved, *LLL*'s infelicities were
reattributed first to its historical referents, Henri of Navarre and Marguerite de
Valois,[8] then, after a further rise in Shakespeare's stature in the 1920s, to the
putative source of the play's allegedly affected language, Lyly's euphuistic
style,[9] and, a decade later, to members of Raleigh's alleged "School of Night"
and/or participants in the Martin Marprelate controversy.[10] In the decades
following the Second World War, when the middle classes no longer needed to
use *LLL* as stick to beat this or that upper-class cultural formation via Elizabethan or Shakespearean surrogates, these classes attributed *LLL*'s failure to
aristocratic practices which various internal elements continued to ape, and
turned the play's satiric energies against one or another alleged aristocratic infection: homosocial coteries of men, rhetorical verbiage, brittle wit, heartless
mockery, fancy, independent women, sterile imagination, artifice — anything,
that is, which seemed to be denying these classes access to their utopias and
which could be scapegoated onto their predecessors in power, a King and
three Lords, who will do penance for "a year and a day."[11] Finally, given the
momentum generated by such recuperative endeavors, it was but a short step
from the last of these ideological appropriations of *LLL* to a recasting of noble
penance into an educational program whereby King and Lords grow up and
prove everyday middle-class life (its values, ordinary speech, heteronormativity, fertility, etc.) preferable to aristocratic excess: "As the [final] songs are
sung, Time seems to pass . . . and, as the seasons change, *the lovers prove
inseparable*. Armado's last words, 'You that way; we this way' (V.2. 920),
announce, then, only a qualified separation, for his show has already conducted the stage and theatre audiences through a year and a day to *the true,
comic end of the action*. The owl and the cuckoo assure us that the labour of love
will not be very long lost" (my emphasis).[12] Because Comedy and St. Paul
(powerful bulwarks of bourgeois culture) insist that four allegedly immature
men must mature and marry, there will be proper middle-class heroes, there
will be a proper comedic ending, there will be everyday bourgeois life as the
middle classes envision it, and *LLL*, finally "coming out right," will realize itself
as a proper festive comedy — its failed ending, jests, and sport disappearing; its
difference from the lost play, *Loves Labor's Won*, reduced to the infinitesimal.

So successful was this long-evolving middle-class appropriation of *LLL* as a dominant ideological instrument (a process in which the primary critical task proved to be ascertaining *where* to aim the play's aggressivity), that it is difficult now to reconstruct the functions such an ungeneric comedy may have had in the 1590's other than (as above) to implement one or another form of anti-aristocratic or anti-adolescent scapegoating. As a way, however, of offering a new analysis of several early modern functions of this play's difference, we may entertain the distinction de Certeau makes between *strategy* and *tactic*. That is, if the cultural appropriations of *LLL* itemized above are recognized as *strategies* — "A strategy assumes a place that can be circumscribed as *proper* (*propre*) and thus serve as the basis for generating relations with an exterior distinct from it" — then we may ask how *LLL* may have performed in its own time (and how it may be retheorized in our time) as a *tactic*:

> I call a "tactic," on the other hand, a calculus which cannot count on a "proper" (a spatial or institutional localization), nor thus on a borderline distinguishing the other as a visible totality. The place of a tactic belongs to the other. A tactic insinuates itself into the other's place, fragmentarily, without taking it over in its entirety, without being able to keep it at a distance. It has at its disposal no base where it can capitalize on its advantages, prepare its expansions, and secure independence with respect to circumstances. The "proper" is a victory of space over time. On the contrary, because it does not have a place, a tactic depends on time — it is always on the watch for opportunities that must be seized "on the wing." . . . It must constantly manipulate events in order to turn them into "opportunities." Many everyday practices . . . are tactical in character. And so are, more generally, many "ways of operating": victories of the "weak" over the "strong" (whether the strength be that of powerful people or the violence of things or of an imposed order, etc.), clever tricks, knowing how to get away with things . . . maneuvers, polymorphic simulations, joyful discoveries.[13]

Rather than encouraging us to go on constructing *LLL* in our time as a passive bearer of dominant cultural strategies, de Certeau's distinction allows us to reperceive this play as an active maker of cultural difference in its own time, as well as reperceiving Shakespearean theatre itself as an "everyday practice [of making] . . . tactical in character."[14] It also allows us to recast the characters Shakespeare gives dramatic agency — Berowne, the French Princess, Moth, and Costard, among others — as tacticians whose "maneuvers, polymorphic simulations, joyful discoveries" allow them to "seize" opportunities "on the wing" and "get away with things." And it allows us as well to rerepresent *LLL* as a Shakespearean tactic which, despite obvious strategic overcodings, enables its everyday audiences to reappropriate comedy for their own uses and pleasures.

But by what methodology, it may be asked, is it possible to generate a radically new assessment of the tactical potentialities of a play that has consistently been read as a failed, and recuperated as a strategic, ideological instrument? One answer is to turn to the resources of a discourse — psychoanalysis — which offers techniques for analyzing those everyday tactics (slip of tongue, joke, hysteria, defense mechanism, dream, fantasy, symptom, etc.) at play within all strategic behavior. Thus, if dominant codes have long given us access to the strategic functionalities of appropriated, "Shakespearean" comedy, discourses like Lacanian psychoanalysis and de Certeau's socio-materialism may provide access to comedic tactics which of necessity will be temporary, largely invisible, and, in the main, unrecorded and unrepresented because — as emergent everyday practices — they did not (and do not) conform to strategic, and thus *proper*, comedic formulae or ends.[15] There is this gain: *LLL*, seen for the first time (in our time) as a staging of tactics, will be recognized as a more interesting cultural document than the submissive instrument of dominant strategy it has been; moreover, its strategically perceived "failed" ending will prove, tactically speaking, its chief success.[16]

To collate the appropriative arguments that have reduced *LLL* to a strategic instrument is to produce the following abstract: the King of Navarre and his attendant Lords, Berowne, Dumaine, and Longaville, are narcissistically self-enclosed boys who fear women; don't know how to woo, speak, or love properly; and worse, write sonnets, forswear oaths, and thus face the prospect of losing their love's labors unless they perform sufficient penance for their errors to get themselves, after a year and a day, to the requisite socially inscribed goal: marriage to their Jills. In short, a moral: young men must give up prophylactic defense mechanisms constructed to protect the interiority of their male selves (and its architectural extension, their all-male court) from the contamination, disintegration, pain, and death that would be caused, they fear, by contact with the female body — its earth, fluids, and fluxes — which they take to be grotesque if not lethal. And they must marry.[17]

From a tactical perspective, however, *LLL* functions quite otherwise. Consider the situation of its eight young aristocrats (*four* young men and *four* young women to insure that we contemplate, not individual actions, but those of a species). The old King of Navarre has just died, and this death instantiates an unspoken demand with respect to the young men: "Now you must grow up, become men, get married, be King and courtiers in fact as well as in name." The young men know this, and the King of France knows this; hence the embassy France sends to Navarre composed of his daughter, three ladies in waiting, and a parallel unspoken demand: "Now you, too, must grow up, become women, get married, be Queen and Ladies in fact as well as in name." If we ask what mode of agency Shakespeare is representing on stage, it is clear that these young persons' desires at this transitional moment of the father's death are no doubt divided between a powerful urge, as children, to obey the law of the father, *and* a powerful urge, as emergent adolescents, *not* to obey this law, a conflict which, in this play, takes as its compromise formation a desire *not* to obey the law of the father, but not to obey in such a way that non-compliance will nonetheless appear to be—will be masked as—compliance. So if we ask—"Why does the expected comedic ending fail to occur in this play?"—the answer, read tactically, is that these eight young people do not want it to take place. Their loves' labor is lost because the young men and women desire this labor to be lost. Not only do these Jacks not get their Jills, they do not want to get them, nor do these Jills want to be got. Perceiving that "The catastrophe [in the sense both of disaster and of comedic denouement] is a nuptial," and seeing themselves about to be cast in a strategic comedy in which they do not wish to participate, they choose to fail, they intend to fail, and, in the end, they do fail, and they do so by pursuing activities that, conventionally (and strategically) speaking, should guarantee success, but, tactically speaking, prevent "catastrophe." What is particularly brilliant about their use of tactics, moreover, is that they defeat their wooing with all the tools of Cupid's trade ("A tactic insinuates itself into the other's place . . . without taking it over in its entirety, without being able to keep it at a distance"). Thus, the men do *everything* Renaissance lovers do: sonnets, flirtatious battles of wit, broken vows, courtly pastimes, witty repartee, melancholic swooning, jeweled bribes, excessive flattery, Muscovite masque, sexual innuendoes, pageant of nine worthies. Despite setbacks, they never give up. They bemoan their "failures," and they vow to do whatever they can do in the future to make up for what they haven't done right in the past. So, they win when they fail, and they win again when they accomplish their "failure" in such a way that it will be impossible for anyone in authority to identify them as the intentional rather than the immature cause of their failure, since they will be seen as having done their very best to succeed at courtship and marriage.

Wooing to fail at wooing is not, of course, the only tactic these young men use. Consider the opening scene of the play. Navarre and his colleagues do not (as is commonly assumed) get together and vow to maintain three years of self-imposed academic isolation in serious imitation of Platonic or French neo-Platonic models, a solitude that is only *then* interrupted by the arrival of women and desire. Rather, they have previously received notice that an embassy of French women is about to arrive. They understand what this embassy portends. And, knowing these things, they *then* get together and construct a male-only enclave. They are then *surprised* when Berowne *remembers* that the women are coming, and *solve* the problem they have engineered (vowing to see and speak to no women in the face of the arrival of women they must see and speak to) by deciding to meet the women in a field adjacent to the Navarre's court. The "first" action, and the vows constituting this action are intentionally constructed, that is, as *impossible* (and thus as tactical) enterprises, and the men know this; but they engage in these tactics (which they dress up as strategies necessary for the salvific eternalization of their classical bodies, minds, and homosociality) in order purposefully to send a signal (by instituting an all-male academy, lodging the women in the field, failing to entertain them at court) that they are not in, and, despite whatever will seem to be the case in the future, are not going to be in, the matrimonial business — a signal that is received and reciprocated by the four young women. In other words, at the outset of this play, both parties conspire *not* to succeed at the task assigned them by their respective fathers, and it is clear that one motive the young men have for *not* entertaining the visiting French women at court is to keep these women and themselves out of a space that was constituted by and which to a large extent remains the domain of the dead father's desire/demand/law. They understand, that is, the need to maintain distance from this paternal space and its implicit gaze, if only to insure that the guilts, anxieties, obsessions, melancholies, and paranoias which tend to occur in such a domain will not be sufficiently energized outdoors to prevent them from seizing this post-paternal opportunity to differ and defer.

It is useful to note how this tactical evasion of paternal (and generic) law differs from strategy. As de Certeau's distinction indicates, the eight adolescents' evasion of adult eventualities does not proceed from a center of cultural power (a court); it is not planned in its entirety ahead of time; and it generates the numerous problematics attendant upon the *not proper*. That is, a tactical evasion of "catastrophe" is improvisational for both parties, neither the young men nor young women knowing in any certain way exactly what the other party is doing or what they themselves will do next. This evasion is also inescapably excessive, not to mention inconsistent except as a consistent use of tactic disguised as conventional strategy. As a result, it is constantly open to misinterpretation, and thus is almost never free of uncertainty, anger, pain, and embarrassment. Egos are very much at stake. At any time, failure, however strongly desired, is capable of being perceived by self and others as nothing but failure, just as the tactics independently engaged in by both parties are capable of being seen by the other party as hypocrisy, insult, neglect, condescension, arrogance or whatever. Thus, the duration of this play's action is not simply a function of the time it takes eight young men and women to foreclose successfully the possibility of precipitate "arranged" marriages; rather, narrative duration is a function as well of the time it takes them to appear to be submitting to parental demand, as well as to negotiate a complicit evasion of catastrophe which cannot be regarded as either party's sole responsibility, nor played out in such a way that it will constitute a real loss or failure for either party.

Once it is possible to read part of this play from a tactical perspective, it is possible to read all of it in such a fashion. And to see just how far these four young men go out of their way to fail is to juxtapose what we see them do against what they would do were they intent upon success. (i) Berowne, were he seriously in pursuit of love and its consequences, would speak to Rosaline in person instead of writing a sonnet, and worse, sending it via a messenger.[18] (ii) Instead of sticking together, as a gang of four men wooing a gang of four women, Berowne and his colleagues would end the ritualistic "square dance" we see taking place on stage and woo in private (as Costard tries to do, and Don Armado does, with Jaquenetta). (iii) Instead of masking themselves during their Muscovite entertainment (5.2.157ff) and wooing masked women according to their favors, they would woo face to face. In other words, it's not that these young men immaturely and mistakenly woo "the sign of she"; it is that, as wooers, they intentionally become signs of he (as the women become signs of she) to be in a position to (mis)woo signs of she.[19] (iv) Instead of intentionally proliferating a discourse of witty idealization which distances them from actual persons, bodies, and feelings ("O queen of queens, how far dost thou excel" [4.3.36]), or an equally witty discourse of bawdy innuendo which turns social intercourse wholly to the sexual body ("Did not I dance with you in Brabant once?" [2.1.113]), these young men would speak their own speech to the objects of their desire.[20] (v) Rather than fetishize the woman's eyes, hair, etc., they would get past, as it were, the blazon. (vi) Instead of distancing themselves from their love objects by sublimating these objects into the heavens as "stars," they would (to alter Donne's phrase) "go to bodies" and look for violet-covered banks upon which to recline. And (vii) rather than accept rejection, they would endeavor "to convert the ladies' striking refusal into a conventional acceptance" in the fashion of lovers throughout the canon who encounter such obstacles.[21] In short, when the men are not engaged in preposterous "infantile" *overshootings* of their objects, keeping the young women at an excessively idealized distance, they engage in equally preposterously "adult" *undershootings* of these objects, maintaining an excessive closeness of physical proximity sufficient to drive the woman away.

But what of other features of this play, particularly the pageant in which five lesser-classed men present themselves to their betters as legendary worthies (5.2.485ff)? Though this pageant is an overdetermined event in the structure of the play, it constructs a strikingly visible analogy for the argument I take as fundamental to *LLL*: Costard, Nathaniel, Holofernes, Moth, and Armado are to the roles they have engaged to act (Pompey, Alexander,

Judas Maccabaeus, Hercules, Hector) what Navarre, Berowne, Dumaine, and Longaville would be to the role paternal law is demanding they play (husbands). Like their subordinates heroized, the noble young men, married, would be cast in parts beyond their desire to perform, a matrimonial part, moreover, which would put them out of that part, adolescence, in which they have just been cast, which they enjoy, and which they desire to go on playing. The pageant's on-stage function, then, is to convey to the women (and to us) — and, due to the men's forceful interventions, is *made* to convey — the principal reasons why the young men do not want to marry after a day or so of adolescence.[22]

Another significance of this pageant is that it constructs a visible but untenable version of the paternal demand the young men are resisting. As the law/death-of-the-fathers commands the four males to "Be men!" and the four females to "Be women!," so the "law" of the pageant commands Costard and his associates to "Be legendary heroes!" (or, alternatively, to "Be brilliant actors!"). But if the pageant fails (and the noble youths ensure that it does), then the resulting parental imperative ("Be what you do not desire to be and therefore in a sense can't be!") becomes identical to the theatrical demand on their subordinates — "Be what you are not and cannot be!" — a demand that is legitimately resistible because, impossible to obey, it becomes tyrannical by definition. In short, the play's "failure" to produce young men as husbands is anticipated and explained by the pageant's failure to produce Nathaniel as Alexander, etc.[23]

In this context, it is clear that one of the play's most frequently quoted sentences has frequently been misread — that is, the Princess's observation (reacting to a claim that the pageant of the worthies will fail) that "Their form confounded makes most form in mirth/When great things laboring perish in their birth" (5.2.517–8). Usually taken as articulating the central thrust of *LLL*'s satiric action, these lines are glossed in the major editions (as in Kerrigan's) as "The ruin of *great things* . . . creates more *mirth* than anything else could" (227). In such readings, the phrase, *great things*, refers to the pageant and the pretensions of its lower-class performers. But to read this way is, I suggest, to miss the larger point. The "great things laboring" that "perish in their birth" in this play, and quite specifically in this pageant of worthies, are a pantheon of cultural signifiers — Pompey, Hector, Judas Maccabaeus, Hercules, Alexander — and the *dominant* social formation these heroes epitomize, namely, that humanistic, homosocial, patriarchal ideological legacy that is being handed down through these exemplars (as through the dominant form of marriage) to these adolescents. Given, then, that it is precisely this cultural legacy which they are tactically subverting, surely the eventuality which would provide *them* with the most *mirth* (and the most release from their anxieties) would be to see *great things* like Hercules and Alexander *perish*, not to mention seeing those *labors* perish which the cultural formation symbolized by Hercules uses to contain subversive individuals like themselves. For the young men to patronize (and deconstruct) a pageant in which a nine-fold epitome of the regime of the father self-deflates is to entertain themselves, *and* to justify the loss of their love's labor — i.e., the loss, not of their labor to love the young women, but of their labor to love the heroic "fathers," the desire/law of these fathers, and the roles (particularly the matrimonial role) this desire/law demands of them. The pageant is one of several opportunities, then, by which these adolescents realign their desire by making this desire, to a greater extent, *their* desire rather than the desire of the paternal other. Moreover, this pageant allows them to raise and answer a question: "If no one can live up to these models, and if trying to do so makes one a ridiculous failure, then why try, given that such roles are clearly not worth the trouble of living up to anyway?"

Strategic readings of *LLL* tend to pit the events of the play's last two hundred-plus lines — Marcade's entrance, the men's proposals, the women's refusals, the men's year-and-a-day vows, Armado's reentry, the songs of cuckoo and owl — against the play's remainder. It is in these sobering activities, we are told, that prior expenditures of time and energy are judged as waste and converted into the suburbs of maturity. And it is in this textual space that strategy (in de Certeau's terms) has been seen to "assume a place that can be circumscribed as *proper* (*propre*) and thus serve as the basis for generating relations [of power] with an exterior distinct from it." How, then, does tactic insinuate itself in these closing activities, and how does it prevent a victory of *proper* ideological space over adolescent time, or a victory of the *proper* over *LLL* itself?

One popular way of reading the fifth act arrival of Marcade's news of the King of France's death is that this eruption of death/reality into a world of fantasy, game, and pastime shocks four young men out of their affectations, teaches them humility, subjects them to the law of the father, and aims their truant desires toward a matrimonial target via the penitential demands placed on them by young women standing in as surrogates for an absent cultural mother. Perhaps. But in a play where interruption is a fundamental structuring device,[24] Marcade's entrance is, I suggest, precisely what enables the desire of all eight adolescents *not* to marry. Narrative sequence, to be sure, encourages one to think that Marcade's news *causes* the men to proffer sincere marriage proposals, but it is more likely, I suggest, that the men seize this opportunity to make the expected/demanded proposals (what the dead fathers, not to mention many members of an audience, expect) because they know that this is by far the most *inappropriate* moment they could choose to do so, and thus the moment when such proposals would be the most likely to fail. Marcade's entrance, then, allows the men to do the expected, paternally-demanded strategic thing, but prevents this "right" thing from succeeding, since it allows the men to make their most "sincere" move at the very point when such a move has the least chance of success. France's death, far from creating desires for maturity, creates, as does old Navarre's, an opportunity to differ and defer that eight adolescents seize "on the wing."

Nevertheless, rejected, the young men do swear new vows that, if honored, will, in effect, force them to offer the women a pageant of four worthies for a year and a day. The Princess instructs Navarre to go "To some forlorn and naked hermitage" (5.2.786), and he vows performance: "If this, or more than this, I would deny/ . . . The sudden hand of death close up mine eye!" (5.2.803–5). Told to use his "wit/To enforce the painéd impotent to smile" (5.2.841–4), Berowne likewise vows obedience: "befall what will befall/I'll jest a twelvemonth in an hospital" (5.2.860–1). Thus the vow, slighted in the past, reasserts itself in an allegedly workable form, and the young men, seeming at last to have thrown away their "idle scorns" (5.2.855), appear to be proving that the longstanding "developmental" reading of the play is accurate. But since every earlier vow these young men make has been forsworn — since they have rejected every other chance to cast themselves as "Worthies" — why assume now that these final vows will not succumb to tactical evasion as surely as their predecessors did? A newly crowned Renaissance King is likely to vacate throne, power, courtiers, and public presence to spend a forlorn year in solitary confinement? Berowne (who passionately vowed, one act earlier, that anyone who saw Rosaline would, "like a rude and savage man of Inde," bow "his vasal head . . . and kiss the base ground with obedient breast," but who in fact did no such thing himself) is going to give up his freedom and place at court for a year and a day to entertain groaning wretches? To satisfy the law/demand of the father (mediated parodically through the women) the men must make these vows, but surely it is clear by this point in the play that as soon as the women return to France the men will seize whatever opportunity avails itself to forswear these oaths as thoroughly as any they made in the past. It is also clear that the women impose penances they know the men will not, in fact cannot, fulfill, and that they do so not just to evade nuptial catastrophe themselves, but to enjoy being able to hear at some future point that another set of "great [vows] laboring [have] perish[ed] in their birth." The women, that is, understand (and help the play's audiences recognize) that strategic vows tactically "confounded make most form in mirth."

It is similarly conventional to read Armado's closing affirmations — "For mine own part, I breathe free breath. I have seen the day of wrong through the little hole of discretion, and I will right myself like a soldier," and "I am a votary; I have vowed to Jacquenetta to hold the plough for her sweet love three year" (5.2.713–15, 872–74) — as symbolic of the marital consummation the young men should *not* be avoiding, and thus a yardstick against which to find them lacking. However, if we recognize that Shakespeare's representation of Armado presents the urgency of an adult man "who spends time only to make time, whose desires brook no deferral," and whose "body of desire cannot wait [because] it is unfree, impelled, lacking in the interior space of lack inhabited by the will," we will see that unlike the adolescents in *LLL*, who possess a "body capable of deferral and lack," Armado and Jaquenetta are among those who impatient consummate-or-fail narrative requires the closure that only nuptial catastrophe — its dutiful sacrifice, its "little hole of discretion," its "ploughing," its lack of subjectivity, freedom, and vitality — seems capable of providing.[25] In short, Armado and Jacquenetta are a precise figuration of one sort of so-called adult maturity the adolescents are subversively resisting, and, although Armado and Jacquenetta presumably find it worthwhile to cast themselves in the roles of yet two more mythic worthies, King Cophetua and the Beggar Maid, it is nonetheless clear that their culture's repertoire of adult erotic roles is no more viable than its adult heroic roles.

The play's closing songs have also been taken as sentimentally satisfying proleptic substitutes for the plot's absence nuptials, but to take them this way is to ignore that these songs are deeply embedded in this play's warring forces of signification. It would be more accurate to see that two unmarried men — a verbose pedant, Holofernes, and a sycophantic curate, Nathaniel — sing a cuckoo-owl "dialogue" that functions, not to conduct "theatre audiences through a year and a day to the true, comic end of the action,"[26] but to debate, among other possibilities, which are worse, the inevitable side-effects of premature and/or arranged marriages, or the residues of such marriages later in life. *Ver* (Holofernes) represents such marriages as an exceptionally bad deal for men, given that the energies of youth's spring will lead inescapably to the adultery and cuckoldry mocked by the cuckoo: "When Dasies pied, and Violets blew,/ . . . Do paint the Medowes with delight./The Cuckow then on euerie tree/Mocks married men, for thus sings he,/Cuckow./Cuckow, cuckow: O, word of feare,/Vnpleasing to a married eare" (Folio, ll. 2860–68). In short, spring nuptials cast young men in the role of horned beasts, a form as grotesque as the page Moth is in his Hercules costume, or Armado is in his "worldly traveler" affectations. In reply, Nathaniel, as *Heims* (winter), argues caution on the grounds that the wintry residue of marriages lacking love is little more than tedium and/or depression: "When all aloud the winde doth blow,/And coffing drownes the Parsons saw:/And birds sit brooding in the snow,/And Marian's nose lookes red and raw . . . /Then nightly sings the staring Owle,/Tu-whit to-who:/A merry note,/While greasie Ione [Joan] doth keele the pot" (Folio, ll. 2888–96). A loveless marriage's wintry catastrophe, we understand, is relieved solely by a merry note from outside the house which painfully reminds those in the house of what should be but isn't taking place *inside* the house, namely, to-whoing and to-whitting: that is, wooing ("to-who"—i.e., *to woo*) and copulating ("tu-whit"—i.e., *to it*, or *to't*).[27] In listening to this "debate" we are not asked to decide which is worse, spring's adulteries or winter's aftereffects, but to recognize the fear—held by men and women alike—that the pleasures of matrimony will be quickly and permanently lost in these sorts of traditional marriages, and to recognize as well that women who are denied a viable, independent adolescence will most likely flower in youth's spring as wives cuckolding husbands, and decline in winter's age to raw, red-nosed Marians and "greasy," disempowered and dispirited Joans who have been left to "keel" (i.e., stir) their unused and undesired "pots."[28]

It would be a mistake, however, to equate Holofernes and Nathaniel with the young men for and to whom they present this dialogue, since to speak of Holofernes is to speak, in both psychoanalytic and rhetorical terms, not only of repetition—"coelo, the sky, the welkin, the heaven" (4.2.5)—but of pointless repetition. Holofernes and Nathaniel, that is, represent what adult life is like if it lacks that *repetition with significant difference* which is the hallmark of the adolescence that is being constructed in *LLL*. As men who clearly did not enjoy a significant adolescence themselves, Holofernes and Nathaniel have become such petrified practitioners of marital delaying tactics that the only sex they seem now to engage in is a tedious and grandiose *multiplication* of words, innuendoes, and fantasies. Thus, in much the same way that Armado's and Jaquenetta's precipitate flight into nuptial consummation brackets the adolescent youths' behavior at one adult extreme, Holofernes's and Nathaniel's permanent avoidance of matrimony does likewise at the other. To realize, then, that Holofernes and Nathaniel are repetitively defending against, and paralyzed by, what Armado and Jaquenetta race toward—i.e., "the Parsons saw"— is to see why eight adolescents are negotiating an indefinite space of time prior to nuptials in order to make their erotic/sexual/marital relationships something more, or less, or other than submission to or rebellion against strategic ideological impositions.

Up to this point I have been arguing that the understanding of *LLL* we get if we read it tactically is radically opposed to the meanings produced by reading it strategically. Though this argument is clearly not complete, it is necessary at this point to turn to a number of larger questions: why Shake-speare staged such warring forces of signification in a French *mise en scène*, in a *comedy*, and in virtually invisible fashion? First, there is, I suggest, an English royal citation. Throughout her reign, Queen Elizabeth, if not also her suitors, wooed in order to fail at wooing's formal consummation, and did so perhaps most spectacularly a decade prior to *LLL* with the duc du Alençon, the young-est son of Catherine de Medici, and Henri of Navarre's brother-in-law. For many of her subjects, Elizabeth's negotiations with Alençon seemed to aim solely at imposing Catholic rule over herself and England; however, the ob-vious necessity was to see that Elizabeth and Alençon were tactically defeating, by means of sonnets, tokens, masks, and pageants of excessive wooing, the strategic matrimonial goal each had to pursue. To keep peace with Catherine de Medici, both Elizabeth and Alençon had to woo as "sincerely" as possible, and had to do so for considerably longer than a year and a day. For Eliza-beth not so to woo most likely would have meant an unwanted conflict with France at the time England was already supporting an expensive war against Spain in the Netherlands.[29]

There is also, I suggest, a powerful (and, in relation to this play, an as yet unnoticed) aristocratic citation. In 1590 Lord Burghley determined that his seventeen-year-old ward, Henry Wriothesley, third Earl of Southampton (and Shakespeare's patron at the time *LLL* most likely was written), would marry his granddaughter, Lady Elizabeth Vere, daughter of the Earl of Oxford. While seeming to acquiesce to Burghley's insistence as well as to his mother's and his grandfather's persuasions that he honor this arranged marriage, South-ampton in fact tactically resisted, in part by gaining "a further respitt of one yere to answere resolute in respect of his yonge years"; however, at the end of this "respitt of one yere" (echoing the play's "year and a day"), Southampton refused and was forced to pay Burghley 5,000 pounds to extricate himself from a "vow" Burghley had unilaterally made for him.[30]

Most immediate to the play's dramatic action, however, is the French royal citation. Despite a long-standing claim that the action of this play refer-ences an embassy which Marguerite de Valois (hereafter Margot), her mother Catherine de Medici, and their famous bevy of ladies-in-waiting known as "l'escadron volant" conducted to Nérac in 1578 to negotiate with Henri of Na-varre, Margot's estranged husband, in fact it does not.[31] *LLL* refers not to an actual meeting which took place years *after* Henri's and Margot's marriage in 1572 (he at 26, she at 19), but, I suggest, to an *imaginary* meeting that should have taken place *prior to* their wedding, but did not. For audiences in the 1590s enjoying the advantage of historical hindsight, the question that makes the point is, "What would happen *next* in the play if Navarre and the Princess of

France did *not* resist matrimony and history repeated itself?" As every Elizabethan knew, what would happen if history repeated itself on Shakespeare's
stage, as it did on the stage of Marlowe's probably earlier *Massacre at Paris*,
would be a repeat performance of massacre, forced conversion, incarceration,
renewal of religious civil war, and a long and disastrous marriage.[32]

In these citational contexts, answers to why Shakespeare stages a Navarre
and a Princess who desire to lose their love's labors seem obvious. Given that
Queen Elizabeth and Southampton were always already in its audience, *LLL*
retroactively applauds their tactical resistance to entering into arranged dynastic marriages by celebrating Elizabeth's ability to insinuate tactical maneuvers
into the place of wooing, and by praising and justifying Southampton's tactical
victory as a relatively weak ward over Burghley's strength. And, as importantly,
LLL prevents, in fiction at least, a disaster that had happened in another,
historical place from happening again *in this place*, an outcome which satisfies at
least one definition of comedy. That is, if the adolescents we see on stage retroactively fail to institute Elizabeth's and Southampton's tactics within the normative activities of Henri's and Margot's past, the historical trajectory originat-
ing in the law/demand of parents, guardian, and tradition would once again
lead to catastrophe.[33] *LLL* is designed in part, then, not to repeat history by
pushing stage versions of Margot and Henri once again into a nuptial that had
been a catastrophe, nor to stage a Navarre liberating himself from a dominant
social order's strategic ambush in some impossibly utopian fashion; rather, it is
designed to demonstrate how fictionally improved surrogates could successfully engage (as Elizabeth and Southampton engaged) in innovating practical
modes of tactical resistance *within* such an order — a lesson Essex tragically, and
Southampton expensively, forgot seven or eight years after *LLL* was written
when both replaced tactical resistance with open rebellion.[34]

The royal citations also explain why *LLL* stages resistance to matrimony
in virtually invisible fashion. By providing its audiences with a vicarious experience of the tactical skills needed to keep such a wasteful history as Margot's and
Henri's from repeating itself — skills that, by definition, have to be invisible if
they are to be tactical and successful — *LLL* teaches these audiences the considerable value of being able to resignify such tactical events retroactively if not to
deconstruct them while they are taking place. *LLL* does this by offering its
audience a chain of signifiers that seems to be moving directly toward comedy's obvious generic destination, but a chain that inexplicably ends up at an
altogether different destination instead, and does so because the visible chain
of signifiers was in fact part of another, invisible chain all along. How valuable
such knowledge can be is made pointedly clear if we again consider Elizabeth's
and Alençon's wooing. Had John Stubbs been able to resignify this wooing

deconstructively as it was taking place, or retroactively after the fact, and had he understood that it was about Elizabeth's maintaining power rather than securing a foreign royal husband, he would not have lost to the Queen's executioner the hand that penned his attack on her love's labors in 1579; instead, he would have understood that these labors had always already been designed to be lost.

Again, however, the context immediately relevant is the French one, and the speculative question to ask is, "What can one imagine going through Henri's head five days after his spectacular arranged wedding to Margot in 1572?" The most likely answer is that Henri was painfully recognizing that what had looked at the time like a marriage capable of cementing peace between Catholics and Huguenots was in fact, retroactively resignified, a Catholic ambush designed by Henri III and his mother, Catherine de Medici, to obliterate the core of the Huguenots, and force Navarre and his cousin Condé to convert to Catholicism. The point, then, is that if *prior to* his marriage Henri had been able to read the chain of exceptionally visible signifiers that seemed to be leading through his marriage to a Huguenot-Catholic peace other than, or more than, or less than he in fact did, and thus had recognized that these signifiers were part of a virtually invisible chain that led through this marriage to bloody slaughter, he no doubt would willingly have *lost* all of his love's labor.[35] Thus for Shakespeare to design *LLL* to take fictive representatives of Henri and Margot back to a better French future than the tragic one their real life doubles experienced via a more intelligent imaginary past, in which a Navarre resists and a Princess of France says "No," teaches theater audiences to use tactics to subvert strategic containment as well as the considerable value of reading the tactics of powerful others retroactively if not deconstructively *in the first place*.

Staging an eminently sane evasion of a nuptial that proved catastrophic for Henri and his Huguenot followers in order to celebrate Queen and patron, and instruct English theater audiences goes a long way in explaining why *LLL* takes the form it does, but to understand the larger tasks *LLL* was designed to perform requires asking how it relates to early modern everyday life, a question which raises the complex issue of how everyday life itself is to be signified. The argument, "The catastrophe is a nuptial," must be contextualized, not just in terms of Queen Elizabeth, Southampton, Henri, and Margot, — "the actors" (to use de Certeau's terms) "who possess proper names and social blazons" — nor of 'secondary characters" like Burghley, Montagu, and Stubbs who crowd into the historical accounts, but also in terms of the "countless thousands" of persons who make up "the mass of the audience" whose desires Shakespeare did not neglect.[36]

At present two rival ways of theorizing everyday life seem to be shaping social histories of early modern England (roughly 1450–1700): (i) the conviction that throughout this period everyday life was a relatively homogeneous organic affair, ambivalently viewed sometimes as peaceful security, sometimes as tedious routine, but in any case surviving relatively unchanged throughout the period despite being punctuated on an everyday basis by heterogeneous deviations from a dominant everyday norm — positive ones like weddings and festivals, as well as negative, transgressive ones like food riots, rebellions, murder and war. And (ii), the conviction that, despite some of the features itemized above, early modern everyday life was a social construction that came to be fundamentally and irreversibly altered in form and content over the course of the period in question. As is well known, Lawrence Stone is notorious for arguing (and for the way he argued) the latter view, an argument infected, his detractors imply, by America, German psychoanalysis, and French theory — particularly Foucault's. Stone's detractors and opponents — most notably, Alan Macfarlane — take the former (and, in their minds, the pure, English) position.[37] What makes Stone scandalous (rather than, admittedly, merely at times overstated and underevidenced) in the eyes of these opponents is that (a) he maps the fundamental social changes he sees in early modern English history as a function precisely of those heterogeneous ruptures which his opponents marginalize as relatively ineffectual deviations, and that (b), rather than reading the facts drawn from statistical studies of wills, diaries, and parish records from a strategic perspective, he retroactively resignifies these facts from an emergent perspective in terms (as we shall see below) of quality, or adequacy. So, where Macfarlane limits analysis to dominant chains of signifiers, Stone extends analysis to the chains of signifiers that emerged from within such dominant chains and in time replaced them. What is chiefly at stake, then, between these rival modes of historiography is the role played (properly? improperly?) by (i) the heterogeneous ruptures/deviations that transform/punctuate everyday life, (ii) the emergent theoretical discourses Stone uses to rupture the dominant discourses of his opponents, and (iii) the equally heterogeneous ruptures his problematizing of adequacy makes in discourses that take quality as a given. In short, whereas something like Macfarlane's historiographical method is homologous with the traditional readings of *LLL*, a version of Stone's is homologous with the analysis presented above.

The subject of this historiographical debate most immediately relevant to *LLL* is the way various forms of adolescence functioned in early modern England.[38] Keith Thomas's "Age and Authority in Early Modern England" details the facts. At the beginning of the early modern period the gap between child and adult (i.e., between puberty and marriage) was minimal. This does not mean that formal categories of youth (ages 7–14 for men, 6–12 for women) and adolescence (14–21 for men, 12–19 for women) did not exist; rather it means that fourteen-year-old male, and twelve-year-old female youths routinely took on full adult roles, adolescence regularly being foreclosed. By the end of the period, however, this minimal gap between puberty and the assumption of adult roles had considerably expanded, 28 becoming the average male age for marriage, and 24/26 the average end of apprenticeships. Thus, a roughly 2–7 year period in which youth might be continued as adolescence gradually stretched to a 7–14 year period in which adolescence became increasingly inevitable—a change of considerable magnitude since more than half the population of England at this time was under 28.[39]

At issue is the relation this lengthening period of adolescence had to everyday social life: that is, how did English society utilize the increasingly massive pool of energies it was diverting away from childhood, yet was preventing for increasingly longer periods of time from being channeled into adulthood, and what effect did the energies of these progressively older, more numerous, and more powerful adolescents have on English society? Did these energies, as Stone's schema maintains, produce new modes of family and marriage that significantly rewrote everyday English life? Or, as Stone's opponents insist, did they go either smoothly into longer and more complex, but still rather traditional, preparations for adulthood, or roughly into transgressive waste activities, but in either case maintaining the forms of self, family, and marriage that characterized everyday life from the outset? For Stone's opponents, for whom the phenomenon of adolescence was unitary except for deviations, everyday life contained adolescent energies irrespective of duration, ensuring that adolescence would take roughly the same forms and serve the same functions throughout the period. For Stone's followers, however, for whom adolescents became less and less a homogeneous group, these energies not only took residual, dominant, and transgressive forms, but also emergent ones that over time restructured everyday life as it had been lived.[40]

What are the larger consequences of Stone's opponents' position? By arguing that early modern adolescence was in the main an extension of youth, and thus a phenomenon similarly prior to, less valuable than, and prefatory to adulthood no matter how long it lasted, social historians like Macfarlane, and historians of adolescence like Ilana Ben-Amos, *assume*, however unconsciously, that, despite negative deviations, the core of English society was relatively, and relatively equally, *adequate* throughout the early modern period, so that adolescence, whatever its duration, remained a series of relatively inflexible steps that youths took to enter this relatively unchanging, yet positive, status quo. Moreover, arranged marriages were equally adequate, given that they were the formal means whereby adolescents entered this adequate status quo by becoming one, not with a spouse, but with the dominant social order itself.[41] In such a social order there would be no legitimate reasons for youths to employ *tactics*; and, should they do so, such tactics would be regarded as nothing more than transgressive deviations (as would the tactical reading of *LLL* offered above).[42] In this model, then, comedy celebrates successful completion of a culturally constructed drive towards oneness with a homogeneous social order—one reason why, for Macfarlane, literature is irrelevant to the writing of history, since it either repeats the status quo or subverts its unitary adequacy.[43] From this perspective, the young men in *LLL* deviate as much from their proper cultural roles as *LLL* deviates from its proper generic role.

For Stone's perspective, such a view of adolescence (not to mention of marriage, literature, and social history), falls "like that of a hagiography . . . into the platitude of repetition" (to borrow a sentence from de Certeau[44]) and does so because it ignores several crucial socio-historical realities: (i) that, at the beginning of the early modern period, the dominant core of everyday English social life was *by no means adequate* in the eyes of powerful oppositional constituencies that should not be written off as negative deviations; (ii) that adolescence, a relation of power, not a thing or a duration, must be understood as being "constituted not substantively but oppositionally, not by *what* it is, but *where* it is and *how* it operates"; and (iii) that history is not an account just of a subject's interpellation, but also of the breakdowns in this process that open "up the possibility of a derailment from within."[45] From Stone's perspective, then, the increased duration of adolescence that made a variety of *adolescences* possible was not just a lengthier way of entering an adequate adult status quo (despite dominant attempts that adolescence should be no more than this), but one of the sites where social institutions regarded as inadequate (e.g., arranged marriages) were remodeled through increasingly sophisticated employment of tactics. Thus, whereas arranged marriages had worked successfully, and virtually across the board, as a means of reproducing the dominant social order by reproducing dominant property owners, and whereas this primarily economic form of marriage, though it did not need to do so, occasionally produced affectionate husband-spouse relationships and viable affective families, the desire that increasingly came to shape marriages throughout the period—particularly emergent adolescent ones that chose not to reproduce the self-perpetuating socioeconomic oligarchies of the past—was a desire to produce *something other*. And although this "something other" took a variety of forms, one particularly popular one was the one Stone terms the companionate marriage—that is, a reconfiguration of marriage *as a relation to an individual person* (i.e., a love marriage) instead of a relation through a generic type to the dominant social order. Indeed, a new sense of what constituted an adequate marriage, not to mention an adequate family and society — generated by a new sense of what were adequate *relations of power* in all three formations — gradually but fundamentally emerged as the basis of a new everyday life, as did an enabling sense of what constituted an adequate sense of self.[46]

At the outset of the period the dominant (though not, of course, the only) sense of self was a self who occupied a specific, known role cast for it by a relatively fixed social structure (Moth, Armado, and Holofernes trying to fill roles as Worthies when they aren't filling their page, monarcho, and pedant roles[47]) — a social structure that was paternalistic at the top (Armado as *Cophetua*), deferential at the bottom (Jacquenetta as Beggar Maid), and content to repeat the past (Armado *as* Cophetua, etc.). Increasingly throughout the period, however, a concept of an individual self relatively separable from such fixed identity-roles emerged within these older roles (as the commoners do from their failed "Worthy" roles), but not wholly independent of these roles (Navarre and his courtiers in their "lover" roles). That this tactical sense of individuality (which had first emerged decades earlier[48]) became increasingly separable from the extremely hierarchical paternalistic/deferential relations of power meant that strong adolescents had something like the opportunity, however slight, to create relatively new roles for themselves in a relatively changing dynamic social process, the future forms of which could not be foreclosed. One result was that an increasing number of adolescents moved from various *object* positions of the past (youth, wife, boy, servant, etc.) to new authoritative *subject* positions, and did so *without becoming dominant adults*. In *LLL*, for example, the Princess, in contrast to her historical predecessor, is able to be the subject, "I," of the predicate, "do not want to marry you" instead of being the object of royal/maternal law, "We command you to marry Henri."[49] This shift from object to subject positions also meant that vows, like those the young men make, though they could not be broken, could be negotiated and reconfigured. Clearly this relatively flexible relation between self and social identity-role did not erase the former relatively fixed self-identical dominant relation, nor did it work the same way for everyone, nor was it absent at the beginning of the period; rather, it was a choice increasingly made by masses of strong adolescents who, tired of being youths or adolescents per se, seized the opportunity to make new meanings. From this perspective, the adolescents in *LLL*, alienated from dominant role-identities, can be seen as tactically exploiting their object positions to prevent further interpellation, and to mask such prevention. In short, Stone's model, unlike his opponents', allows us to resignify *LLL* retroactively, and thus to see, not just the chain of signifiers that leads (in Zizek's terms) to "the empty, homogeneous time of continuity," but also the chain that creates "the 'filled' time of discontinuity."[50]

If, in *LLL*, Shakespeare is staging a version of an emerging process whereby subject-positioned adolescents tactically prevent their energies being appropriated by/for an inadequate status quo, then what we deconstructively see as the play unfolds (or retroactively when it is over) is that, with few if any models to identify with, with much improvisation, with considerable potential for mischance and embarrassment, with no encouragement from the dominant culture of which they are a part, and with all the difficulty of having to proceed without discussion and by means almost solely of action, eight youths are roughing out that new cultural construct, that new range of fictionalities and narrativities, that freedom and *différance*, which we now designate as significant *adolescence*. That is, the "contraceptive" tactics eight strong adolescents engage in to defer the inevitable "catastrophe" of dynastic marriages (and whatever "adult" eventualities may follow in the wake of such marriages) provide an early modern blueprint for a way of configuring power that prevents everyday "adult" history from repeating itself, an innovation that for four hundred years made these adolescents and this play vulnerable to accusations of being frivolous, trivial, unproductive, immature, hysterical, affected failures. If one were grudging, one would say, then, that it is the emergence of strong adolescence that writes *LLL*'s "failed" ending; however, the energy, tonalities, sophisticated obliquities, and historical contingencies of this play encourage us to take the wider view and see that the strong adolescence it figures helped rewrite everyday life itself by "ending" at least one of its failures. So, if analyzing *LLL* has long been a matter of deciding where to aim its aggressivities, and if in the past these have been aimed at one or another aspect of the play itself, an emergent reading of *LLL* lets us see that Shakespeare aimed them at the inadequacies of early modern adult everyday life itself.

At the outset of early modern English social life there was no place, no practice, no writing constitutive of popular professional public theater; however, by the end of the sixteenth century such a place, such practices, and such writing had come to exist because a critical mass of strong adolescent energies, diverted from flowing "naturally" into the dominant order, flowed instead into the creation of such a place, practices, and writing. Moreover, given that this theater's repertoire of plays was, in the main, a collection of retroactive deconstructive resignifications of power relations characteristic of the dominant past and present, it is clear why early modern theater existed "on the wing" (in several senses) as a site of continual *différance*, and that plays such as *LLL* restaged historical events like the 1572 marriage of Henri and Margot to announce "victories of the 'weak' over the 'strong'"—victories, that is, of innovative adolescents over adult law/demand/desire. That is, by staging retroactive resignifications of everyday adult life's institutions and practices for adolescent audiences (i.e., audiences who resisted identifying with, or fully

with, dominant adult roles — in short, virtually everyone who attended theater[51]), popular public theater constituted itself as one of several strong "adolescent" formations emerging within, and tactically rewriting, everyday life.

What, then, can protect *LLL*'s "not coming out right" from centuries of
de facto censorship and/or misappropriation? What can keep it from being
interpellated into yet one more variation of the symbolic order it was designed
subversively to resignify? The answer is nothing less, of course, than an equally
aggressive reappropriation of *LLL* powerful enough to keep its heterogeneous
differences and deferrals "within the field of consideration," and thereby to
keep the play itself from being cast, despite its extraordinary tactical resis-
tances, among the comedic Worthies entombed in bourgeois cultures' pan-
theons of fame.

Notes

A shorter version of this paper was presented at "The Culture of Class" at the
University of California, Santa Barbara, in April, 1992. I would like to thank Peter
Stallybrass and Patricia Fumerton for responding to its argument in provocatively
helpful fashion.

1. Georges Bataille, *Visions of Excess: Selected Writings, 1927–1939*, trans. A. Stoekl
(Minneapolis: University of Minnesota Press, 1985), p. 141.

2. *The Practice of Everyday Life* (Berkeley: University of California Press, 1984),
p. 166.

3. The *heterogeneous/homogeneous* distinction is Georges Bataille's, "The Psychological Structure of Fascism," *Visions of Excess*, pp. 137–60. For discussions of this appropriative history, see, among others: Jonathan Dollimore and Alan Sinfield, "History
and ideology: the instance of *Henry V*," in *Alternative Shakespeares*, ed. John Drakakis
(London and New York: Methuen, 1985); Gary Taylor, *Reinventing Shakespeare: A
Cultural History from the Restoration to the Present* (New York and Oxford: Oxford
University Press, 1989); Margreta de Grazia, *Shakespeare Verbatim: The Reproduction
of Authenticity and the 1790 Apparatus* (Oxford: Clarendon Press, 1991); and Hugh
Grady, *The Modernist Shakespeare: Critical Texts in a Material World* (Oxford: Claren-
don Press, 1991).

4. The debt to Michel Foucault's analyses of the constructedness, not to mention
the ideological power of socio-political institutions, apparatuses, practices, and discourses is obvious. Particularly relevant is the "Marriage" section of *The Care of the Self*,
the third volume of *The History of Sexuality*, trans. Robert Hurley (Harmondsworth:
Penguin, 1990). The discourse of dominant, residual, and emergent forms of power (to
which transgressive has been added) is Raymond Williams's, *Marxism and Language*
(Oxford: Oxford University Press, 1977), pp. 121–27.

5. *King Lear, Macbeth, Indefinition, and Tragedy* (New Haven, Conn.: Yale University Press, 1983), p. 76. Also see: David Bevington, "'Jack hath not Jill': Failed
Courtship in Lyly and Shakespeare," *Shakespeare Survey* 42 (1990): pp. 1–13.

6. All citations to *Loues Labors lost* are from Alfred Harbage's revised Penguin edition, *Love's Labor's Lost* (Harmondsworth, 1973), except the songs of the cuckoo and owl which have been transcribed verbatim (except for the long 's') from *The Norton Facsimile of The First Folio of Shakespeare*, ed. Charlton Hinman (New York: Norton, 1968), p. 162. The title used in the body of this paper is taken from the first Quarto's title page: *A Pleasant Conceited Comedie Called, Loues Labors lost* (London: W. W., 1598).

7. For example, by Pope, who "found the comic scenes so generally barren," writes the Arden editor, Richard David, "that he cut whole pages of them out of his text, printing them at the page-foot for those curious archaeologists who might wish to see what blunders Shakespeare made before he learnt his business" (*Love's Labor's Lost* [London: Methuen, 1951]), p. xiii. For the stage history, see Nancy Lenz Harvey and Anna Kirwan Carey, *Love's Labor's Lost: An Annotated Bibliography* (New York: Garland, 1984), pp. xii–xiii; and Miriam Gilbert, *Love's Labour's Lost* (Manchester and New York: Manchester University Press, 1993).

8. Sir Sidney Lee, "A New Study of *Love's Labour's Lost*," *Gentleman's Magazine* 249 (1880): 447–458.

9. O. J. Campbell, "*Love's Labor's Lost* Restudied," in *Studies in Shakespeare, Milton, and Donne*. University of Michigan Publications in Language and Literature 1 (1925): rpt. New York: Haskell House, 1964, pp. 3–45; and E. K. Chambers, *Shakespeare: A Survey* (New York: Oxford University Press, 1926).

10. The principal advocates of this position were Muriel C. Bradbrook, *The School of Night: A Study of the Literary Relationships of Sir Walter Raleigh* (Cambridge: Cambridge University Press, 1936), and Frances A. Yates, *A Study of Love's Labor's Lost* (London: Cambridge University Press, 1936). For a rebuttal, see David Young, "Recent Studies in Elizabethan and Jacobean Drama," *Studies in English Literature* 16 (1976): 344.

11. Of those arguing a moral and/or satiric reading, the following are representative: Bobbyann Roesen, "Love's Labour's Lost," *Shakespeare Quarterly* 4 (1953): 411–26; Northrop Frye, *A Natural Perspective: The Development of Shakespearean Comedy and Romance* (New York: Columbia University Press, 1965); E. M. W. Tillyard, *Shakespeare's Early Comedies* (London: Chatto and Windus, 1966); Thomas M. Greene, "*Love's Labor's Lost*: The Grace of Society," *Shakespeare Quarterly* 12 (1971): 315–28; Leslie Fiedler, *The Stranger in Shakespeare* (New York: Stein and Day, 1972); Terence Hawkes, *Shakespeare's Talking Animals: Language and Drama in Society* (London: Edward Arnold, 1973); Malcolm Evans, "Mercury Versus Apollo: A Reading of *Love's Labor's Lost*," *Shakespeare Quarterly* 26 (1975): 113–27; Louis Adrian Montrose, "Sport by sport o'erthrown': *Love's Labor's Lost* and the Politics of Play," *Texas Studies in Language and Literature* 18 (1977): 528–52; Peter B. Erickson, "The Failure of Relationship Between Men and Women in *Love's Labor's Lost*," *Women's Studies* 9 (1981): 65–81; Richard Wheeler, *Shakespeare's Development and the Problem Comedies* (Berkeley: University of California Press, 1981); Carol Thomas Neely, *Broken Nuptials in Shakespeare's Plays* (New Haven and London: Yale University Press, 1985); and Meredith Anne Skura, *Shakespeare: The Actor and the Purposes of Playing* (Chicago and London: University of Chicago Press, 1994). For a useful compendium, see *Love's Labor's Lost: Critical Essays*, ed. Felicia Hardison Londré (New York: Garland, 1992).

12. The New Penguin *Love's Labor's Lost*, ed. John Kerrigan (London: Penguin, 1982), pp. 36, 24. Kerrigan's redemptive version of the play is indebted to C. L. Barber's

Shakespeare's Festive Comedy: A Study of Dramatic Form and Its Relation to Social Custom (Princeton, N.J.: Princeton University Press, 1959); and William C. Carroll's *The Great Feast of Language in Love's Labor's Lost* (Princeton, N.J.: Princeton University Press, 1976).

13. De Certeau, *The Practice of Everyday Life*, p. xix.

14. The *bearer/maker* distinction is Laura Mulvey's, "Visual Pleasure and Narrative Cinema," *Screen* 16 (1975).

15. For an alternative Lacanian analysis of this play, see Carolyn Asp, "*Love's Labour's Lost*: Language and the Deferral of Desire," *Literature and Psychoanalysis* 35 (1989): 1–21.

16. In proposing this argument I rely silently on Gilles Deleuze and Félix Guattari's distinction between *arborescent* and *rhizomatic*, as well as Deleuze's analysis of *minoritarian* literature. For the former, see *A Thousand Plateaus: Capitalism and Schizophrenia*, trans. Brian Massumi (Minneapolis: University of Minnesota Press, 1987); for the latter, *Kafka: Toward a Minor Literature*, trans. Dana Polan (Minneapolis: University of Minnesota Press, 1986).

17. Underlying this "developmental" formula is Bakhtin's distinction between the ideal *classical* body and the *grotesque* body. For an analysis of this distinction and its temporal implications in relation to the *preposterous* sodomitical body, see Patricia Parker, "Preposterous Reversals: *Love's Labor's Lost*," *Modern Language Quarterly* 54 (1993): 435–82.

18. Except in cases like Spenser's recuperation, early modern sonnets were figures of failure, and, as many have argued, served to defend *against* erotic success. See Mark Breitenberg, "The Anatomy of Masculine Desire in *Love's Labor's Lost*," *Shakespeare Quarterly* 43 (1992): 430–49, and Nancy Vickers, "Diana Described: Scattered Women and Scattered Rhyme," *Critical Inquiry* 8 (1981): 265–79.

19. On the constructedness of gender roles and the ways we "act out" the signs we make of ourselves, see Judith Butler, *Gender Trouble: Feminism and the Subversion of Identity* (New York and London: Routledge, 1990).

20. This "speech of their own" is not a matter of "russet yeas and honest kersey noes" any more than it is a matter of "Taffeta phrases, silken terms precise, / Three-piled hyperboles, spruce affection," and the like (5.2. 414, 407–8), since the former undershoots the young men's everyday speech (they do not speak in the fashion of "homespun," "wollen" cloth) just as much as the latter overshoots it. For "dance" as a euphemism for "fornicate" see Frankie Rubenstein, *A Dictionary of Shakespeare's Sexual Puns and their Significance* (London: Macmillan, 1984), p. 70.

21. This point is Keir Elam's, *Shakespeare's Universe of Discourse: Language-Games in the Comedies* (Cambridge: Cambridge University Press, 1984), p. 71.

22. If we vary slightly a brilliant insight of Alice Miller's, we can say that these adolescent males have "no other way of telling [their thoughts and desires] other than the ones [they] actually use," which, at this moment in time, is the pageant of the nine worthies. See *The Drama of the Gifted Child* (New York: Basic Books, 1981), p. 77.

23. Note that most *LLL* criticism aims this "Be what you are not and cannot be" demand, in amplified form, at the noble characters ("Grow up and be proper dominant adults") and at the play itself ("Be a proper comedy").

24. Old Navarre's death interrupts the young men's adolescence, the French women interrupt the all-male academy, Armado's morning walk interrupts Costard and

Jaquenetta's love-making, each eavesdropping sonneteer interrupts another, etc. On interruptions in *Love's Labor's Lost*, see Joseph Chaney, "Promises, Promises: *Love's Labor's Lost* and the end of Shakespearean Comedy," *Criticism* 35 (1993): 51.

25. For the language cited above and access to an analogue — Chaucer's *Parliament of Fowls* — that has played little if any significant part in discussions of *LLL*, I am indebted to Louise Fradenburg's *City, Marriage, Tournament* (Madison: University of Wisconsin Press, 1991), p. 126.

26. Kerrigan, *Love's Labor's Lost*, p. 36.

27. For evidence supporting these glosses, see Herbert A. Ellis, *Shakespeare's Lusty Punning in "Love's Labor's Lost,"* Studies in English Literature 81 (The Hague: Mouton, 1973), pp. 198–200, particularly the parallel cited from Lyly's *Endimion*.

28. For the "pot"/vagina substitution, see Gordon Williams, *A Dictionary of Sexual Language and Imagery in Shakespearean and Stuart Literature* (London: Athlone Press, 1994), 2: 1079. For the masturbatory sense of "keeling a pot," one may read between the lines of the *OED*, **keel**, v, 1.b: "To cool (a hot or boiling liquid) by stirring," and 2.a: "To make less violent, eager, or ardent; to assuage, mitigate, lessen." For the sense of a sexual body and its desire grown frigid, see 4. *fig.* "To grow cold, in feeling, etc.; to become less violent, fervid, or ardent, to 'cool down'." If these readings seem farfetched it is important to remember that they *are* farfetched if these chains of lyric signifiers are read strategically. Such a sense will be quite different from the tactical sense they have when read as part of an emergent chain of signifiers. For an argument that they celebrate daily events of country life, see Barber, *Shakespeare's Festive Comedy*, pp. 113, 118; for one arguing that "the songs wed play to work, love to labor, within the larger cyclical rhythms of a human community that is harmoniously wed to nature," see Montrose, "'Sport by sport o'erthrown'," p. 548.

29. For an alternative view of this play's relation to Elizabeth, see Mark Thornton Burnett, "Giving and Receiving: *Love's Labour's Lost* and the Politics of Exchange," *English Literary Renaissance* 23 (1993): 287–313. For accounts of Elizabeth's relations with Alençon that take their courtship at face value, see Anne Somerset, *Elizabeth I* (New York: St. Martin's, 1991), pp. 308–30; Carolly Erickson, *The First Elizabeth* (New York: Summit Books, 1983), pp. 323–30; and J. E. Neale, *Queen Elizabeth I* (Garden City, N.Y.: Doubleday Anchor, 1957), pp. 243–53. To the question of whether Elizabeth, a monarch, can be said to be using tactics, one may posit her relations, not just to the dominant ideology of male rule articulated, in the main, by her parliaments, but also to Catholic Europe's determination, following Pope Pius V's 1570 Bull *Regnans in Excelsis*, to depose her.

30. The story of Southampton's refusal to marry Burghley's granddaughter is told by Charlotte Carmichael Stopes, *The Life of Henry, Third Earl of Southampton, Shakespeare's Patron* (Cambridge: Cambridge University Press, 1922), pp. 34–40; A. L. Rowse, *Shakespeare's Southampton: Patron of Virginia* (New York: Harper and Row, 1965), pp. 53–7; and G. P. V. Akrigg, *Shakespeare and the Earl of Southampton* (Cambridge, Mass.: Harvard University Press, 1968), pp. 31–39. I focus in part on Southampton because there is much to recommend J. Dover Wilson's suggestion, *Love's Labour's Lost* (Cambridge: Cambridge University Press, 1923), that *LLL* was written during the plague years which produced the narrative poems Shakespeare dedicated to Southampton, "Venus and Adonis" and "The Rape of Lucrece." For alternative dates, see H. B. Charlton, "The Date of *Love's Labour's Lost*," *Modern Language Review* 13

(1918): 257–66, 387–400; and Alfred Harbage, *"Love's Labor's Lost* and the Early Shakespeare," *Philological Quarterly* 41 (1962): 18–36.

31. The Nérac embassy, suggested by Abel Lefranc, *Sous le Masque de "William Shakespeare"* (Paris: Payot, 1918), has been accepted by R. David, p. xxix, and Geoffrey Bullough, *Narrative and Dramatic Sources of Shakespeare,* (London: Routledge and Kegan Paul, 1957), 1: 429, among others. For *LLL*'s troubled relation to issues of topicality, see Albert H. Tricomi, "The Witty Idealization of the French Court in *Love's Labor's Lost*," *Shakespeare Studies* 12 (1979): 25–33; Hugh Richmond, "Shakespeare's Navarre," *Huntington Library Quarterly* 42 (1979): 193–216; and Mary Ellen Lamb, "The Nature of Topicality in 'Love's Labour's Lost,'" *Shakespeare Survey,* 38 (1985): 49–59.

32. In *Henry IV* (London: George Allen and Unwin, 1984), David Buisseret writes that in March 1572, Henry's mother Jeanne "sent for Henry to come to court, and went on towards Paris to make preparations for the marriage. . . . By 13 June, Henry had reached Chaunay. . . . There he learned that his mother was dead. . . . Then he continued on his way to Paris, very slowly, as if he were not looking forward to his marriage" (p. 7). For other histories of Henry of Navarre (later Henri IV of France), see Mark Greengrass, *France in the Age of Henri IV: The Struggle for Stability,* 2nd ed. (London and New York: Longman, 1984/1995); Irene Mahoney, *Royal Cousin: The Life of Henri IV of France* (Garden City, N.Y.: Doubleday, 1970); G. R. R. Treasure, *Seventeenth-Century France* (London: John Murray, 1966); Hesketh Pearson, *Henry of Navarre: The King Who Dared* (New York: Harper, 1963); and Andrew C. P. Haggard, *The Amours of Henri de Navarre and of Marguerite de Valois* (London: Stanley Paul, n.d.).

33. To my knowledge the only critic who recognizes that "where the play uses history, it uses it as something to escape from" is John Kerrigan, though he has the play escaping in the direction of escapism itself: *LLL* "offered its Elizabethan audience a reassuring light-hearted view of an alliance across the Channel which probably seemed in reality rather disturbing" (pp. 10–11).

34. The *liberation/resistance* distinction, like the *object/subject position* distinction used below, is David Halperin's, *Saint Foucault: Towards a Gay Hagiography* (New York and Oxford: Oxford University Press, 1995), pp. 56–7.

35. I rule out the possibility that Henry, knowing what was going to happen, intentionally walked into this slaughter because he felt caught by forces beyond his control. Note that the problem Henri faced is virtually identical to the problem we face as *LLL*'s audience. Like the events of 1572, *LLL* consists of at least two chains of signifiers, a strategic one, made up of the normative male activities we see taking place on stage (academy, sonnets, masque), that lead inexplicably to the play's problematic, ungeneric non-marriage ending, and a tactical one, constructed of these same activities, that, beginning *at a different place,* ends up leading to a non-nuptial ending that is, in its own way, comedic. It is only by analyzing both chains that the design/function of *LLL* becomes apparent, since it is only by seeing both chains *and their relationship to each other* that *LLL* is a comedy despite the fact that it does not "come out right" in conventional manner and form.

36. De Certeau, *The Practice of Everyday Life,* p. i.

37. Lawrence Stone, *The Crisis of the Aristocracy, 1558–1641* (London: Oxford University Press, 1965/1974), and *The Family, Sex and Marriage in England, 1500–1800*

(London: Weidenfeld and Nicolson, 1977). The latter was reviewed positively by Keith Thomas, *Times Literary Supplement* (21 Oct. 1977): 1226; negatively by E. P. Thompson, *New Society* (8 Sept., 1977): 499–501; and extremely negatively by Alan Macfarlane, *History and Theory* 18 (1979): 103–26, a review depending heavily on Macfarlane's earlier work, *The Origins of English Individualism: The Family, Property and Social Transition* (New York: Cambridge University Press, 1978). For social histories following Macfarlane's lead, see: Keith Wrightson, *English Society 1580–1680* (New Brunswick, N.J.: Rutgers University Press, 1982); Ralph A. Houlbrooke, *The English Family, 1450–1700* (London and New York: Longman, 1984); and J. A. Sharpe, *Early Modern England: A Social History, 1550–1760* (London: Edward Arnold, 1987).

38. For studies of early modern adolescence, see: Paul Griffiths, *Youth and Authority: Formative Experiences in England, 1560–1640* (Oxford: Clarendon Press, 1996); Ilana Krausman Ben-Amos, *Adolescence and Youth in Early Modern England* (New Haven, Conn.: Yale University Press, 1994); Marjorie Garber, *Coming of Age in Shakespeare* (London: Methuen, 1981); Keith Thomas, "Age and Authority in Early Modern England," *Proceedings of the British Academy* 62 (1976): 205–48; Steven R. Smith, "The London Apprentices as Seventeenth-Century Adolescents," *Past and Present* 61 (1973): 149–61; and Natalie Zemon Davis, "The Reasons of Misrule: Youth Groups and Charivaris in Sixteenth-Century France," *Past and Present* 50 (1971): 41–75. For general studies, see: Erik Erickson, *Childhood and Society* (New York: Norton, 1950); Philippe Ariès, *Centuries of Childhood: A Social History of Family Life*, trans. R. Baldick (New York: Vintage, 1962); Peter Blos, *On Adolescence: A Psychoanalytic Interpretation* (New York: Macmillan, 1962); Aaron H. Esman, ed., *The Psychology of Adolescence: Essential Readings* (New York: International Universities Press, 1975); Aaron H. Esman, *Adolescence and Culture* (New York: Columbia University Press, 1990); and Alice Schlegel and Herbert Barry III, *Adolescence: An Anthropological Inquiry* (New York: The Free Press, 1991).

39. In 1552—according to S. Rappaport's *Worlds Within Worlds: Structures of Life in Sixteenth-Century London* (Cambridge: Cambridge University Press, 1989), p. 392–56% of the male population of London was under 30.

40. Clearly not all youths took advantage of this strong, or emergent, "adolescent" opportunity. Many would not have seen anything inadequate about things as they were and would have taken well-worn paths into dominant adulthood; others no doubt used this longer span of time to maximize the number of transgressive activities they could indulge in.

41. Henri thought he could marry Margot without also "marrying" Catholic France; Elizabeth knew she could not marry Alençon without also marrying Catholicism and patriarchy; Margot did not want to marry Henri because it would mean *not* marrying the Catholic social order (through her lover, Henri, the duc de Guise) she was one with and desired to remain one with. In fact, told by her mother, Catherine de Medici, that she would be marrying Henri of Navarre, Margot (according to her memoirs) responded as follows: "I made answere, that I having no other will but hers, it were superfluous, but I besought her seriously to consider that I was a Catholike, and that it would be a great affliction to me, to be married to one that was not of my Religion. Afterwards. . . . I replyed to her againe, that I had neither choice nor will, but what was hers, and besought her againe to remember, that I was a true Catholick." *The Grand Cabinet-Counsels Unlocked . . . Most excellently written . . . by Margaret de Valois*, trans. Robert Codrington (London: by R. H., 1658), p. 29.

42. Of emergent, strong adolescence there is virtually nothing, for example, in Ben-Amos's study. We are told that early modern adolescents "had few values that truly distinguished them from adults, and had few, if any, institutions which were wholly theirs" (p. 205). But this, as de Certeau shows us, is to miss the point. Strong adolescents appropriated adult values and institutions (e.g., academy, sonnet, masque) in order to exploit them tactically.

43. One reason Macfarlane disagrees so profoundly with Stone is that, unlike Stone, he refuses to consider the period's literary evidence: "The didactic, artistic and moralistic material in sermons, pamphlets, plays and poems has been little used [in my book]. Although I am reasonably familiar with such material, it seemed to me that one of the possible reasons for the distortion of English social history has been too heavy a reliance on upper class literature and on writing which stated what *ought* to happen" (p. 205). For Macfarlane to conflate dominant didactic and moralistic tracts with plays staged in emergent/transgressive theatres, not to mention representing plays and pamphlets as *upper class* literature, suggests the degree to which he excises from early modern culture the heterogeneous activities effecting many of the socio-cultural changes Stone records.

44. Michel de Certeau, *The Writing of History* (New York: Columbia University Press, 1988 [1975]), pp. 84–85.

45. The language for the second point is taken from David Halperin's *Saint Foucault*, pp. 61–62; that for the third is from Judith Butler's *Excitable Speech* (New York and London: Routledge, 1977), p. 156. For the claim that early modern England was always already uniquely adequate, if not virtually perfect, see Macfarlane's chapter on "England in Perspective" in *The Origins of English Individualis*m, pp. 165ff.

46. There is no doubt that Stone somewhat miscasts his central argument. By arguing, as he does, that early open lineage families were generally cruel and heartless, he asserts what he can't prove and what he neither needs to assert nor prove. The stronger argument is that these open lineage families only needed (that they were designed) to produce a heir and reproduce the existing symbolic order, and that, as a consequence, they didn't have to do, and often didn't do, anything but that. In this way his argument that, over time, marriages had to do something else, and did do something else, would be correct even if the something else they were doing was neither affectionate nor companionate. In short, Stone weakens his case by coming at these issues primarily from the perspective of the emotional aspects of marriage, as important as these are, rather than from the perspective of marriage's socio-economic functions. This sometimes causes him to focus more on a now largely invisible object, emotions, than on the crucial changes taking place in the *relations of power* that caused, and were caused by, such emotions.

47. Part of the subversive power of *commedia dell'arte* is that it both ridicules those who allow themselves to be reduced, and at the same time humorously displaces shame from those who had been reduced, to stereotypical identity-roles like pedant, braggart, clown.

48. Clearly this new form of individuality was available at the beginning of the sixteenth century in, most famously, Henry VIII's relations to marriage and Rome, but it was available only to what Bataille calls imperative and base heterogeneities (kings and criminals); moreover, for all its value, it was, psychically and socially speaking, disorienting, feared, and relatively forbidden, if not lethal, for anyone who was not king.

49. Margot no doubt wished retroactively that, at her marriage to Henri of Navarre, she had said "No" forecefully enough to prevent her brother, King Henri III, from being able, when she refused to say "Yes," to push her head down in a seeming gesture of compliance and consent, overruling her will, desire, and silence.

50. Slavoj Zizek, *The Sublime Object of Ideology* (London: Verso Press, 1989), p. 138.

51. Although the debate concerning Shakespeare's audience has usefully focused on identifying early modern playgoers in terms of class and gender, the category, strong adolescence, proves more helpful in identifying the "privileges" — i.e., education, empowerment, etc. — which audience members sought *from* early modern theatres than does the privileged or unprivileged status they brought with them *to* the theatres. For opposed versions of the class/gender approach, see Alfred Harbage, *Shakespeare's Audience* (New York: Columbia University Press, 1941), and Ann Jennalie Cook, *The Privileged Playgoers of Shakespeare's London, 1576–1642* (Princeton, N.J.: Princeton University Press, 1981).

14

"Leaving Out the Insurrection"

Carnival Rebellion, English History Plays, and a Hermeneutics of Advocacy

Simon Hunt

THE BOOKE OF SIR THOMAS MORE, submitted to the Master of the Revels for license in 1593 but not performed until much later, survives only in a fragmentary text. Written by Anthony Munday and at least five others, the manuscript is now something of a jumble: different hands, corrections, lacunae of various sizes, damage caused by both the effects of time and unfortunate attempts at repair. Although Hand D, one of six apparent contributors to the manuscript, is sometimes alleged to have been Shakespeare, for my purpose the most interesting contribution is that of Edmund Tilney, the Master of the Revels to whom the play was submitted. Holding this position between 1579 and his death in 1610, Tilney's everyday responsibility was to censor the dramatic works of Shakespeare, Marlowe, Kyd, Jonson and their contemporaries. The patent issued to Tilney in 1581 makes clear the tremendous extent of his editorial powers:

all and euery plaier or plaiers with their playmakers, either belonginge to any noble man or otherwise, bearinge the name or names of vsinge the facultie of playmakers or plaiers of Comedies, Tragedies, Enterludes or what other showes soever, from tyme to tyme and at all tymes to appeare before him with all such plaies, Tragedies, Comedies, or showes as they shall haue in readines or meane to sett forth, and them to presente and recite before our said Servant or his sufficient deputie, whom wee ordeyne appointe and auctorise by these presentes of all suche showes, plaies, plaiers and playmakers, together with their playing places, to order and reforme, auctorise and put downe, as shal be thought meete or vnmeete vnto himselfe or his said deputie in that behalfe.[1]

In his reaction to *Sir Thomas More*, Tilney fully exercises his mandate "to order and reforme". The opening scene of the manuscript submitted to the censor or his said deputy depicts a group of unhappy London "comons" lamenting the pernicious influence of "straungers" in their city.[2] A few scenes later this grievance erupts in violence as the rebels set fire to the houses of foreigners. Throughout the manuscript, Tilney has announced the changes he will require before licensing the play, going so far as to suggest the omission of entire scenes. In the margins of Scene I, written across the names of the speakers, stands a comment that reflects the gist of his concerns. "Leave out ye insur(rection) wholy," he demands, "& ye cause ther off." Tilney then suggests that the collaborators do "nott otherwise att your own perilles" (i. 1–19).

Tilney thus poses Munday, Hand D, and the other contributors to *Sir Thomas More* with what Stephen Greenblatt might call a "representational problem." In fact, this issue is closely related to what Greenblatt posits in "Murdering Peasants": "the representational problem posed by a victory over popular rebellion." At its most extreme, the depiction of the violent suppression of popular rebellion can result in an "uncanny convergence . . . in which the ruling elite, deeply threatened, conjures up images of repression so harsh they can double as images of protest." "The danger" in the depiction of victory over popular rebellion "is the effacement or, alternatively, the redrawing of boundaries, so that we perceive . . . betrayal instead of victory." Greenblatt also puts the question in rather cruder terms: "How can such buffoons [here he refers to the rebels in Shakespeare's *2 Henry VI*] be put down without embarrassment to the victors?"[3]

What Greenblatt's question suggests, however, is that before these buffoons are "put down" they are first somehow transformed from rebels to buffoons. In other words, the representational problem given voice by Tilney but present before his intervention is different from the one Greenblatt documents in "Murdering Peasants." In effect, the onstage depiction of popular rebellion is potentially subversive of the established order in at least two ways. First there is the danger Greenblatt notes, that victory over rebellious peasants will resemble betrayal; second there is the risk, implied by Tilney's response, that the rebellion in question might present an ideological threat, even a viable alternative, to the dominant power. As Greenblatt shows, one effective answer to the problem of victory over popular rebellion is the "separation of rhetoric and violence" in which the dominant power that wins a victory over rebellious peasants is somehow distanced from the actual act of quelling the rebellion.[4] However, before this dynamic comes into play, a text that would find the approval of a figure like Tilney must first find some means of seeming to leave out the insurrection, the subversive potential of the rebellion it depicts. This first representational problem, that of the potential ideological threat inherent in the depiction of popular rebellion, must be resolved before the second, that of achieving victory without betrayal, even becomes an issue.

For Elizabethan writers of English history plays, these problems constituted a particularly treacherous territory. On the one hand, while representing history with anything resembling literal accuracy was perhaps not the genre's most stringent requirement, the excision of entire insurrections from depictions of well-known historical periods was surely a great deal for Tilney to ask. On the other hand, given what Greenblatt describes as the "unrest and class hostility that afflicted England sporadically throughout Elizabeth's reign," the danger of staged subversion leading to actual unrest in the theaters was very real.[5] Even if history demanded that rebels could not be left out "wholy," then writers of history plays still found themselves under intense pressure to omit the ideologically subversive portion of rebellion, what Tilney might call the "insurrection." Munday and his collaborators responded to this dilemma in a way that is paralleled by Shakespeare in *2 Henry VI* (1590) and by the anonymous author of *The Life and Death of Jack Straw* (1587–90). All of these playwrights associate the rebellion they depict with the Elizabethan stage clown and with the alternation between carnivalesque misrule and the everyday. As such, they participate in what Richard Helgerson has identified as "an associative cluster that could . . . be manipulated as a unit. Festivity discredited rebellion; rebellion discredited festivity; and both discredited the clown and the common people he represented."[6] Moreover, a discussion of this strategy provides a uniquely useful occasion for considering a representational problem of recent historicist work in literary studies: the debate over the relationship between such cultural forces as "subversion" and "containment". I close the present essay by arguing that a hermeneutics of advocacy is one way of side-stepping this claustrophobic binary and generating historicist readings more attentive to the subtle everyday negotiations of history.

One such negotiation, the carnivalization of popular rebellion, is perhaps most readily apparent in a series of rewritten scenes which have been appended to *Sir Thomas More*. While it is perhaps dangerous to speculate as to whether these scenes were added before or after the play was submitted, it seems clear that the changes were made in an attempt to make the play more acceptable to the censor, that is, to make it less clearly subversive of the established order as represented by Tilney. In this context, one of the most interesting changes to the rewritten rebellion scene is the addition of a character identified simply as "Clowne" (iv[a]. 65), who takes several lines originally written to be said by "all." This change serves to undermine the universality of the uprising's ideology as it is expressed in the first version. Instead of being expressed by the united voice of the common people, such sentiments as "fier the howses" (iv[a]. 25) are now spoken by a character who also utters such nonsense as "come come wele tickle their turnips wele bu(tter ther) boxes shall strangers Rule the Roste [yes] but wele baste [yt] the roste come come a flawnt a flaunte" (iv^a. 1–3). In *Jack Straw*, similarly, the Peasants' Revolt of 1381 counts among its number a character identified in stage directions as "Tom Miller the Clowne," who suggests that a dead man can be reanimated if someone would "blow wind in his tayle."[7]

In both these cases, the close association of rebellion with an everyday figure of the Elizabethan stage, the clown, tends to render the rebellion ridiculous. Furthermore, although our knowledge of the Elizabethan clown's stage activity is largely based on speculation and conjecture, Walter Cohen, among others, has noted the way in which both much of the clown's scripted language and especially his tendency to improvise "violated the mimetic quality of the drama both by its nonsensical turns and by its anachronistic approximation to the speech of his audience. In this respect the clown may be said to have called attention to the reality of the theater."[8] At once a carnivalesque figure opposed to the world of the everyday and a reflection of the quotidian concerns of an audience whose onstage representative he sometimes seems to be, the stage clown stands as a pivotal figure in a complex network of associations and identifications. In the plays I consider here, both by drawing attention to a reality external to the dramatic fiction of particular plays, and by making the rebels seem ridiculous by their association with him, the clown serves in part to undermine the potential of onstage rebellion as a viable alternative to the established order.

In Shakespeare's *2 Henry VI*, no character is explicitly identified as the clown. However, Shakespeare's depiction of Jack Cade, the leader of Cade's Rebellion of 1450, suggests that he is the character that probably would have been played by the company's stage clown. Throughout his first speech, Cade is frequently interrupted by one of his men, Dick Butcher, who comments wittily on Cade's claims of nobility:

Cade: Therefore am I of an honourable house.
Butcher: Ay, by my faith, the field is honourable; and there was he born under a
    hedge.[9]

Butcher's jest identifies Cade with both of the principal meanings of the word "clown" identified by David Wiles. Born under a hedge, he is clearly a "countryman." He is also the "principal comedian," since he is the butt of the onstage humor. In both these ways, figures like Cade, *Jack Straw*'s Tom Miller, and the unnamed clown of *Sir Thomas More* are closely associated with what Wiles has called "the paradigms of festival." In fact, Wiles argues, the clown of the Elizabethan stage descended from the traditional Lord of Misrule and remained "a surrogate Lord of Misrule."[10] This connection between such clowns and the Lord of Misrule is clear in Cade's interaction with Butcher: Cade is simultaneously the leader of these peasants and an object of ridicule for them; his status, in a moment of carnivalesque inversion, is both high and low.

Not only are the rebellions in these plays linked to carnival indirectly through the institution of clowning, the everyday embodiment of carnival on the early modern stage, but more direct connections are also common. Cade, for example, even before he appears on stage, is described as "like a wild Morisco" (III. i. 365), linking him with the Morris dance, an important part of traditional carnival celebrations. Such references suggest that these playwrights were aware of "the practice," identified by C. L. Barber, "of mocking individuals by identifying them with traditional holiday roles."[11] Thus, on the most superficial level, the allegation that Cade is a carnivalesque figure serves, like his clownishness, to render ridiculous the rebellion with which he is associated.

Echoes of festive and carnivalesque practices occur frequently throughout these plays. For example, that Cade has been "seduc'd" by the villainous York "To make commotion, as full well he can,/Under the title of John Mortimer" (III. i. 356–59) links him to the tradition of festival disguise noted by Peter Burke and Thomas Pettitt.[12] Another form of carnivalesque disguise is represented in the actions of Doll Williamson in *Sir Thomas More*; she announces herself "a Captaine" (i. 99–100) among the rebels and later enters wearing "a shirt of Maile, a head piece, sword and Buckler" (iv. 410–11) and thus reflects rituals of festive cross-dressing. Similarly, the title character's assertion in *Jack Straw* that "I came for spoile and spoile Ile have" (III. i. 758) echoes the strain of carnival identified by Pettitt which involved "the extortion of money from people travelling along the road."[13] This carnivalesque antagonism toward outsiders or "straungers" also finds expression in the Ill May Day rebellion depicted in *Sir Thomas More*. One of the rebels, George Bettes, announces the rebels' intentions to harrass aliens in terms that explicitly refer to festival behavior: "on May day next in the morning weele go foorth a Maying, but make it the wurst May day for the straungers that ever they sawe" (ii. 95–97). Even the anti-intellectualism of the Peasant's Revolt in *2 Henry VI*—for example, when the rebels sentence to death a hapless clerk who admits he can write his name, or the hysterical and oft-quoted cry "The first thing we do, let's kill all the lawyers" (IV. ii. 76–77)—finds parallels in carnival traditions.

In fact, all of these instances share what might be called the ideology of carnivalesque inversion, an ideology that has largely supplanted the apparent ideological bases of the rebellions which these plays claim to depict. Each of the three plays I have discussed so far uses as historical sources Hall's and Holinshed's *Chronicles*. However, all of the playwrights in question have muted much of the economically and politically charged, potentially still-controversial material in the historians' accounts. To take just one example, although Shakespeare's primary historical source for *2 Henry VI* was Holinshed's accounts of Cade's rebellion of 1450 and also of the Peasants' Revolt of 1381, Shakespeare elides the historian's descriptions of the peasants' grievances.[14] Instead, the leader of Shakespeare's rebellion is a puppet of the scheming Duke of York and espouses the ideology of carnivalesque inversion and misrule:

There shall be in England seven halfpenny loaves sold for a penny; the three-hooped pot shall have ten hoops; and I will make it felony to drink small beer. All the realm shall be in common, and in Cheapside shall my palfrey go to grass. And when I am king, — as king I will be, — . . . there shall be no money; all shall eat and drink on my score; and I will apparel them all in one livery, that they may agree like brothers, and worship me their lord. (IV. ii. 65–70)

Strikingly, although Cade claims he wants to establish a kind of communism in which "all the realm shall be in common," his larger concern seems to be establishing himself as a carnival king or Lord of Misrule. Thus, he returns repeatedly to images of himself as king — as king he will be.

I should observe that I am referring here primarily to the "official" Folio text of *2 Henry VI*. Taking note of the play's complicated textual history, William C. Carroll observes that the early, "bad" Quarto version of the play includes such potentially controversial material as the Duke of Suffolk tearing up a commoners' petition complaining of his acts of enclosure, events apparently invented by Shakespeare.[15] Such potentially subversive instances, however, had been largely excised by the time the play was reconstructed into the Folio text.

The author of *Jack Straw* allows more explicitly socio-political commentary into his play than survives in the Folio version of *2 Henry VI*. Such material is present, for instance, in the form of the rhetoric of Parson Ball, a priest associated with the *Jack Straw* Peasants' Revolt. The rebellion begins as an interpersonal confrontation between the play's title character and the tax collector he believes has molested his daughter. Soon, however, Ball counsels Straw and some of his neighbors to arms in a stirring speech which looks both forward and backward to an idyllic, communal social organization and, in doing so, questions the very structure of Elizabethan society:

England is growne to such a pass of late,
That rich men triumph to see the poore beg at their gate.
But I am able by good scripture before you to prove,
That God doth not this dealing allow nor love.
But when *Adam* delved and *Eve* span,
Who was then a Gentleman.
. . . .

But follow the counsell of John Ball,
I promise you I love yee all:
And make division equally,
Of each mans goods indifferently,
And rightly may you follow Armes,
To rid you from these civill harmes. (I. i. 78–109)

However, when Ball's comrades do follow arms, this utopian vision once again is in tension with a more carnivalesque notion of rebellion. Jack Straw's immediate response to this speech is to propose making Ball himself "Archbishop of Caunterburie,/And Chaunceller of England" (I. i. 117–18). The other military leader of the Peasants' Revolt, Wat Tyler, meanwhile, crows "Wele be Lords my Maisters every one" (I. i. 127), a declaration which is echoed several times in the course of the play.

In short, then, this rebellion is not based on Ball's principle of "division equally," but on the principles of misrule and inversion, which do not seek to change society so much as simply to turn it upside down, making peasants into "Lords" and "Kings." Thus, Jack Straw's uprising here, like Shakespeare's rendering of Cade's rebellion, and like the carnival festivities which both reflect, follows what Barber has called the "Saturnalian Pattern," in which festival behavior is a temporary "release" from everyday behavior. According to this pattern, Barber tells us, "The release of that one day was understood to be a temporary license, a 'misrule' which implied rule . . . a license [which] depends utterly upon what it mocks: liberty is unable to envision any alternative to the accepted order except the standing of it on it head." Thus "The misrule works, through the whole dramatic rhythm, to consolidate rule."[16] In this sense, for an Elizabethan audience, familiar with the forms and rhythms of popular festivals, these onstage rebellions would have seemed like nothing more than a brief holiday, inevitably to be subsumed into everyday life before long. All of this, perhaps, casts an ironic light on Jack Cade's battle cry in 2 Henry VI: "Then are we in order when we are most out of order" (IV. ii. 189–90).

This process of carnivalization is more difficult to trace in Sir Thomas More because of that text's fragmentary condition. Moreover, in spite of the instances I cite earlier, the rebels in the play do not always seem particularly carnivalesque. Throughout the pre-revision version of the play, the comedy provided by the rebels seems to invite the audience to laugh with the rebels rather than at them. Even explicit references to carnival like Bettes's "weele go foorth a Maying" are not inadvertent echoes of carnival behavior, but self-conscious manipulations of carnival institutions. The link between this Ill May Day rebellion and Barber's Saturnalian pattern is further undermined by the clarity and seriousness of the former's ideological aims. Munday and his co-authors quote directly and extensively from Holinshed's account, and the uprising against the pernicious influence of foreigners comes across as focused, planned, and controlled. In the following speech, for example, the rebel Lincoln reads from a written statement he has prepared, denouncing "strangers" in terms which would resonate powerfully for a London audience of the 1590s:

Aliens and straungers eate the bread from the fatherlesse children, and take living from all the Artificers, and the entercourse from all Merchan(ts wherby povertie is so much encreased, that every man bewayleth the miserie(of other, for crafts men be brought to beggerie, and Merchants to needines. (i.83–86)

In short, then, Edmund Tilney's reaction to the first draft of this play is not terribly surprising. However, given what we have seen in *2 Henry VI* and *Jack Straw*, it is also not surprising that the collaborative playwrights added the "clowne" to their revisions in an attempt, as we have seen, to carnivalize the play.

Interestingly, *Sir Thomas More* also shares with the other two plays a final phase in Barber's Saturanlian pattern: the scapegoating of the Lord of Misrule. As Barber, Burke, and others have documented, such "mockery kings . . . are frequently turned on by their followers, tried in some court, . . . and burned or buried in effigy to signify a new start."[17] In these plays, while the vast majority of the rebels are eventually pardoned for their misdeeds, the leaders of each rebellion — Cade in *2 Henry VI*, Jack Straw, Parson Ball, and Wat Tyler in *Jack Straw*, and Lincoln in *Sir Thomas More* — are killed. What is more, in each case, as in Greenblatt's reading of *2 Henry VI*, victory is accomplished not by royal or noble forces but, through the vehicle of a privileged commoner, by "a separation of rhetoric and violence." Thus, just as Alexander Iden kills Cade in Shakespeare's play, the Lord Mayor of London slays Jack Straw, and Thomas More (not yet "Sir") subdues the Ill May Day rebels; each is subsequently knighted for his actions. In this way, the association of popular rebellion with clowning and misrule serves both to undermine the potential subversiveness of placing rebellious peasants onstage and also to provide at least a partial solution to the "representational problem" with which Greenblatt is concerned in "Murdering Peasants."

Thus far, I have in effect been arguing for a pattern of what some might call "containment," although I have deliberately avoided using the c-word more than once. In order to explain my reluctance, I would like to consider very briefly another play, Thomas Heywood's *1 Edward IV*, probably first performed in 1599. Although Heywood's rebels seek to distance themselves from earlier rebellions — "We do not rise like Tyler, Cade, and Straw" — they are "desperate, idle, swaggering mates" whose ideology is that "we will be kings tonight."[18] Not surprisingly, these rebels are just as much carnivalesque buffoons as the others I have discussed. What is striking about the play, however, is that the rebels are not the only clowns. This category, relatively secure in the other plays I have discussed, here bleeds quite freely into other categories like citizen, nobleman, even king. Thus the citizen Josselin, whose speeches almost invariably dissolve into "and so forth," is just as ridiculous as any of the clownish rebels he fights against. The character who was almost certainly played onstage by the company's professional clown, Hobs the "Tanner of Tamworth," meanwhile, operates separate from the central power relationships of the play.

Still, it is Hobs's partner in these scenes, King Edward himself, who is *Edward IV*'s most surprising clown. Conspicuously absent from the battle to defend his crown, Edward seems content to let citizens put down peasants rather than fighting himself. Speaking in clownish prose while the nobles around him speak in aristocratic verse, he amuses himself as an unpredictable trickster, linking himself both with festival traditions of disguise and with the tradition of the carnivalesque stage clown as the "principal game-maker" of the stage, to use Wiles's phrase.[19] Twice, in episodes summarized by the title page to *1 Edward IV*, Edward disguises himself in order to manipulate his subjects: "his merrie pastime with the Tanner of Tamworth, as also his love to faire Mistress Shore, her great promotion, fall, and miserie, and lastly the lamentable death of both her and her husband" (3). In the first of these instances, as critics have variously argued, it is possible to read a monarch achieving a moment of essential contact with his subject, Hobs.[20]

In his second disguise, however, Edward dons a disguise in order to try to persuade Jane Shore, a merchant's wife, to become his concubine. Whether it is read traditionally as seduction or more accurately as harassment, even rape, the king's conduct initiates a chain of events which ruptures the Shore marriage, forces Jane into sexual transgression, renders both Jane and her husband poor and miserable, and eventually (in *2 Edward IV*) leads to their deaths. The play's apparent critique of Edward's carnivalesque behavior is reinforced by the fact that Jane Shore and her husband Matthew appear throughout *1 Edward IV* as paragons of Elizabethan middle class virtue, embodying the values of marriage, fidelity, hard work, humility, love, valor, chastity, philanthropy, and deference to hierarchy.

Elsewhere I argue that Heywood's *Edward IV* plays thematize a tension between two kinds of domesticity — the citizen domesticity of the Shores and a potentially lethal royal domesticity — and that this tension seems to support Edward's assertion, upon first sight of Jane Shore, that his is a "traitor heart."[21] I include an attenuated version of this argument here to suggest that it is entirely possible for popular rebellion, the carnivalesque, and the English history play to be combined in a way that does not add up to "subversion contained." Indeed, a discussion of the first three plays I treat here which read "carnival" as other than a kind of temporary license — or which made more of the clown's potential to invite identification on the part of the audience members whose everyday language he sometimes apes — would surely produce readings rather different from mine. In any case, as Peter Stallybrass and Allon White remind us, "the politics of carnival cannot be resolved outside of a close historical examination of particular conjectures: there is no a priori revolutionary vector to carnival and transgression."[23] There remains only the process of examining the workings of these opposing but perhaps complementary dynamics within individual texts and at particular moments of their reception.

What Stallybrass's and White's remark suggests is that, by extension, plays and other instances of cultural work cannot be divided simply into those which subvert and those which contain, to employ the binary as it has figured in some recent historicist work.[23] Such cultural interventions remain open to an infinite variety of (re)constructions at the interpretive hands both of those who are witnesses to the original event and of those who visit it retrospectively. Thus they tend to defy the vocabulary of subversion and containment, or at least the reductively simple binary structure in which this vocabulary has sometimes appeared.

In fact, it seems to me, as to some other recent critics, that this polemic is largely a false one. No one argues that there is no such thing as true subversiveness or, for that matter, that every introduction of potentially controversial material is necessarily subversive. Even Stephen Greenblatt, who is usually associated with the containment side of the debate, acknowledges that "the identification of the orthodox ideology that informs a particular text by no means obviates the possible presence of genuinely subversive elements." Indeed, Greenblatt's notion of "recording," a process in which "power," because it "thrives on vigilance," registers potentially subversive voices so that they may be "brought into the light for study, discipline, correction, transformation," seems to demonstrate that a merely binary construction of subversion / containment is inadequate.[24] Valerie Traub concurs, writing that "the process of containment is inherently unstable," while Jonathan Dollimore asserts that "nothing can be intrinsically or essentially subversive . . . [subversion] cannot be guaranteed a priori, independent of articulation, context and reception."[25] Thus the two terms of this polemic, while they are certainly opposing valences, are not the polar opposites they may at first seem to be. Rather, they are closely related dynamics which more often than not appear together as twin faces of the remarkable and/or everyday moments that comprise history. As Greenblatt would have it, "the apparent production of subversion . . . is the very condition of power."[26] Alan Liu, however, takes this paradoxical construction even further, writing that "containment is the very form of subversion."[27] In this context, I would suggest, it is worth remembering that the metaphor here is not one of destruction or of negation, but of containment. In other words, at the same time that a text and a dominant ideology enclose a subversive voice, they also preserve that voice, encoding it into text. Dollimore makes a similar assertion in *Radical Tragedy*: "the very condition of something's containment may constitute the terms of its challenge."[28] Such ideas, in short, open a space for a text which is at once "subversive" and "contained," which, indeed, is subversive precisely because it has been contained.

According to Liu, what is necessary to convert contained subversion into active subversion is "an advocate willing to be put at risk,"[29] someone perhaps like a twentieth-century actor, director, or reader. When this advocate endeavors to activate the subversion within a text, in effect to open the container, he or she finds that the subversion remains intact precisely because it has been contained. It should be noted, of course, that an instance of "subversion" is not transhistorically potent, because the "power" or "powers" which it would seek to subvert are functions of history. In other words, a twentieth-century advocate's focus on particular textual valences of early modern plays can obviously have no effect on such sixteenth-century institutions of power as Elizabeth I and Edmund Tilney, except as they are viewed by history. Nonetheless, such textual valences as *Edward IV*'s apparent suspicion of royal misbehavior and the popular rebellion of the other three plays I have considered in this essay remain available for deployment, advocacy, in a variety of more or less analogous historical situations. The irony is that the forces that serve apparently to undermine the ideological potential of the popular rebellions depicted are also the very forces that enable these rebellions to be depicted at all in the face of routine pressures like those represented by Edmund Tilney and to remain present for subsequent readers and audiences.

It is within what might be called a "hermeneutics of advocacy," then, that I wish to read these plays, choosing to discuss not only their mechanisms of "containment," but more importantly the fissures in and ironically preservative effect of such containment. To this extent, my practice might be seen as analogous to, if not as "presentist" (in the sense of a concern not so much for the past as for the uses the present makes of its past) as, that of Alan Sinfield in his recent *Faultlines*. Calling for a discourse of "dissidence" rather than subversion—a move which shifts agency from the text to its critic—Sinfield extends his readings of Shakespeare's plays to include imagined productions, productions which aim, as he says of one play, "to check the tendency of *Julius Caesar* to add Shakespearean authority to reactionary discourses."[30]

In closing, however, I want to remember that the will to become an advocate or a dissident does not lead inevitably to political success. As I have endeavored to demonstrate, everyday human agency is never so transparent, not least because the reception of any text is an ongoing process. It should be noted, moreover, that the sometime New Historicist concern with cultural moments as contained or subversive — but in any case defined by the position of their agents with regard to a monolithic power — represents a considerable misprision of the work of Michel Foucault, in so many ways the starting point of this branch of cultural studies. In his later work especially, but also throughout his career, Foucault insisted that "there is no relationship of power without the means of escape or possible flight."[31] Typically, he put the matter even more succinctly in an informal remark: "People know what they do; they frequently know why they do what they do, but what they don't know is what what they do does."[32] In other words, cultural workers may certainly intervene at specific moments in history. However, their very interventions can become the site for contestation or, in Liu's term, advocacy, thereafter. The ironic case of Edmund Tilney and *The Booke of Sir Thomas More* is relevant, if perhaps not exemplary, here. Performing his daily duties as Master of the Revels, Tilney sought to have excised the play's "insurrection." Notwithstanding his intentions, his contribution to the manuscript has remained ever since a component of the play's place in English literary history — as a curiosity, as a clue to the interactions between early modern theaters and their censors, as a locus for the discussion of such matters as rebellion and subversion and dissidence. While it is quite obviously possible, then, for human agents to advocate deliberately dissident or reactionary positions, it is also the case that no cultural work can simply be reduced to the personal or political motivations of the agent behind it or to a category like subversion or containment. In this sense, as Parker Douglas argues, "cultural practices are best seen as actions which are properly known through their consequences."[33]

Notes

1. Quoted in Frederick S. Boas, *Queen Elizabeth, The Revels Office, and Edmund Tilney*, 1937 Elizabeth Howland Lecture (London: Oxford University Press, 1938), p. 19. Boas provides a useful, concise, and generally accurate account of Tilney's life and career.

2. Anthony Munday et al., *The Booke of Sir Thomas More*, ed. W. W. Greg (London: Malone Society, 1911), Scene iii, Line 323 and Scene i, Line 97. All other citations of this play refer to this edition and will appear in the text.

3. Stephen Greenblatt, "Murdering Peasants: Status, Genre, and the Representation of Rebellion," *Representations* 1, 1 (1983): 23.

4. Greenblatt, "Murdering Peasants," p. 23. A useful sampling of the substantial historical literature that attends to early modern popular rebellion is *Rebellion, Popular Protest, and the Social Order in Early Modern England* ed. Paul Slack (Cambridge: Cambridge University Press, 1984). See also Roger B. Manning, *Village Revolts: Social Protest and Popular Disturbances in England, 1509–1640* (Oxford: Oxford University Press, 1988). Both suggest, as does Greenblatt, that the most important Tudor responses to rebellion were ideological at least as much military, stressing the cultural importance of order as well as imposing it through force.

5. Greenblatt, "Murdering Peasants," p. 14.

6. Richard Helgerson, *Forms of Nationhood: The Elizabethan Writing of England* (Chicago: University of Chicago Press, 1992), p. 222. In the chapter entitled "Staging Exclusion," Helgerson writes about these and other texts in terms similar to those I am using here, occasionally using the same evidence. His central focus, however, is on several crucial shifts in Shakespeare's practice as a writer of English history plays during the 1590s, shifts which contributed to the emergence of an authors', rather than a players', theater. My primary concern is less with Shakespeare or any other particular individual than with a representational strategy available to early modern dramatists and the ways in which that strategy allows for a consideration of current methods of historicist research. Slack — in the introduction to the anthology cited above — concurs that "the connection between rituals of revolt and rituals of 'misrule' has frequently been stressed in recent work." However, he insists "the point can be exaggerated" (p. 11). In other words, although early modern observers often noted connections between carnival and rebellion, Helgerson's "associative cluster" is not merely a "natural" conglomeration of phenomena, but a *deliberate* association made by individuals at particular historical junctures.

7. *The Life and Death of Jack Straw*, ed. Kenneth Muir and F. P. Wilson (Oxford: Malone Society, 1957), Act I, scene i, lines 39–40 and Act I, scene i, line 47. All other citations of this play refer to this edition and will appear in the text.

8. Walter Cohen, *Drama of a Nation: Public Theater in England and Spain* (Ithaca, N.Y.: Cornell University Press, 1985), p. 178.

9. William Shakespeare, *The Second Part of Henry the Sixth*, in *The Riverside Shakespeare*, ed. G. Blakemore Evans (Boston: Houghton Mifflin, 1974), Act IV, scene ii, lines 49–51. All other citations of this play refer to this edition and will appear in the text.

10. David Wiles, *Shakespeare's Clown* (Cambridge: Cambridge University Press, 1987), pp. 12, 110, 17–18, 21.

11. C. L. Barber, *Shakespeare's Festive Comedy: A Study of Dramatic Form in Relation to Social Custom* (Princeton, N.J.: Princeton University Press, 1959), p. 53.

12. Peter Burke, *Popular Culture in Early Modern Europe* (New York: Harper and Row, 1978), pp. 182–85. Thomas Pettitt, "'Here Comes I, Jack Straw': English Folk Drama and Social Revolt," *Folklore* 95, 1 (1984): 14. In addition to the specific debts cited in these notes, I owe much of my understanding of "carnival" and the "carnivalesque" to Burke and to the germinal work in this field: Mikhail Bakhtin, *Rabelais and His World*, trans. Hélene Iswolsky (Bloomington: Indiana University Press, 1984). Another useful source is Michael D. Bristol, *Carnival and Theater: Plebeian Culture and the Structure of Authority in Renaissance England* (New York: Methuen, 1985). A thorough account of the actual calendar customs behind English carnivalesque ritual is

provided by Ronald Hutton, *The Rise and Fall of Merry Englnd: The Ritual Year 1400–1700* (Oxford: Oxford University Press, 1994).

13. Pettitt, p. 14.

14. For example, Cade's line in Shakespeare's play "my mouth shall be the parliament of England," (IV. vii. 14–15) seems to derive from this passage in Holinshed's description of the 1381 rebellion: "within foure daies all the lawes of England should come foorth of his mouth." By contrast, few of Holinshed's more controversial comments find their way into Shakespeare's play. Of the 1381 rebellion, for example, Holinshed writes that "the commons of the realme [were] sore repining . . . for the pole grotes that were demanded of them," and that "they were sore oppressed . . . by their landlords." Similarly, in his chronicle of the 1450 rebellion, Holinshed meticulously lists the "Articles proponed by the commons against the duke of Suffolke" and "The complaint of the commons of Kent, and causes of their assemblie on the Blackheath." Neither instance is quoted in the Shakespearean text.

15. William C. Carroll, *Fat King, Lean Beggar: Representations of Poverty in the Age of Shakespeare* (Ithaca, N.Y.: Cornell University Press, 1996), pp. 137–8. Carroll goes on to demonstrate the extent to which the Folio version rewrites the crucial figure of Alexander Iden from a "potential encloser," as he had appeared in the Quarto, into "an emblematic version of the happy rural man" and thus makes him more "legitimate" (138–139). As Carroll's acute reading of the play's response to early modern poverty suggests, *2 Henry VI* actually underwent a process analogous to that I trace here in *Sir Thomas More*. Other useful considerations of this play include Michael Hattaway, "Rebellion, Class Consciousness, and Shakespeare's *2 Henry VI*," *Cahiers Elisabethains* 33 (1988): 13–22; Phyllis Rackin, *Stages of History* (Ithaca, N.Y.: Cornell University Press, 1990); Robert Weimann, *Shakespeare and the Popular Tradition in the Theater* (Baltimore: Johns Hopkins University Press, 1978); and Richard Wilson, "A Mingled Yarn: Shakespeare and the Cloth Workers," *Literature and History* 12 (1986): 164–80.

16. Barber, *Shakespeare's Festive Comedy*, 3–5, 10, 205, 214.

17. Ibid., p. 207. See also Burke, *Popular Culture*, 185.

18. Thomas Heywood, *1 Edward IV*, *The Dramatic Works of Thomas Heywood*, ed. J. Payne Collier, 4 vols. (London: Shakespeare Society, 1851) 1: 9, 18, 30. All other citations of this play refer to this edition by page number and will appear in the text.

19. Wiles, p. 3.

20. See, for example, Helgerson, *Forms of Nationhood*, 232, and Anne Barton, "The King Disguised: Shakespeare's *Henry V* and the Comical History," in *The Triple Bond: Plays, Mainly Shakespearean, in Performance*, ed. Joseph G. Price (University Park: Pennsylvania State University Press, 1975), p. 95.

21. Heywood, p. 60. I offer a fuller version of my reading of Heywood's *1 Edward IV*, plays in my unpublished paper "Woman Killed with Kingness: Jane Shore and the Threat of the Royal Domestic." I should note here, however, that *2 Edward IV* in many ways complicates the argument I am making about its predecessor, not least because of Jane Shore's apparent suggestion that she has suffered violence at the hands — more precisely the feet — of her husband. (I am grateful to Patricia Fumerton for reminding me of this instance and for her insistence that a reading of even the first play as an idealized vision of domesticity should account for Matthew Shore's anxiety about his wife's involvement in economic business.) Even so, the Shores seem to die a sanctified

death at the end of the second play, reunited and apparently martyred by their suffering at the hands of their king.

22. Peter Stallybrass and Allon White, *The Politics and Poetics of Transgression* (Ithaca, N.Y.: Cornell University Press, 1986), p. 16. Along the same lines, Slack—in the "Introduction" to the anthology cited above,—note 4, asserts the consistent "conservatism of popular aspirations" in early modern rebellion (6).

23. A useful summary of the debate I address here is provided by Jonathan Dollimore's "Introduction" to *Political Shakespeare: Essays in Cultural Materialism*, 2nd ed., ed. Jonathan Dollimore and Alan Sinfield (Manchester: Manchester University Press, 1994). Indeed, most of the essays in this volume, and particularly those by its two editors, participate in the discussion of these issues. Each editor contributes a new essay to the 1994 second edition. In his, Sinfield agrees with many who have asserted a difference between U.S. and British practice in historicist criticism: "North American new historicists have tended to find power containing resistance; British cultural materialists to stress the potential for dissidence" ("Heritage and the Market, Regulation and Desublimation," p. 260). My aim here is neither to contest nor to reinscribe such a distinction, but rather to explore the intersections between the kinds of readings that Sinfield and others characterize by emphasis and by geographical origin. Louis Montrose has made a related argument. In his "New Historicisms" he asserts that "The binary logic of subversion-containment produces a closed conceptual structure," in part because, as I argue, it is based in a reading of Foucault that "makes no theoretical space for change or contestation" (in *Redrawing the Boundaries: The Transformation of English and American Literary Studies*, ed. Stephen Greenblatt and Giles Gunn (New York: Modern Language Association, 1992), pp. 402–3.

24. Stephen Greenblatt, "Invisible Bullets: Renaissance Authority and its Subversion," *Glyph* 8 (1981): 42, 50–51. Hugh Grady, in an essay that is in part a defense of Greenblatt against the charge that his theory of containment is too ironclad, argues that even in "Invisible Bullets" Greenblatt's work allows for more "negotiation" than is often realized ("Containment, Subversion—and Postmodernism," *Textual Practice* 7, 1 [Spring 1993]). Implicitly making a similar point, Theodore B. Leinwand advocates "negotiation" as a useful critical tool for sidestepping the limitations of subversion-containment, although he makes relatively little of previous circulations of the term, most obviously in the title of a book of Greenblatt's (*Shakespearean Negotiations: The Circulation of Social Energy in Renaissance England* [Berkeley: University of California Press, 1988]). Leinwand: "a negotiation-based model of social relations that can account for change or for resistance to change has the significant advantage of recognizing that the lower orders are not limited to a choice between quietism and insurrection" ("Negotiation and New Historicism," *PMLA* 105, 3 [May 1990]: 480).

25. Valerie Traub, *Desire and Anxiety: Circulation of Sexuality in Shakespearean Drama* (London: Routledge, 1992), pp. 145–46. Dollimore, "Introduction," *Political Shakespeare*, p. 13.

26. Greenblatt, "Invisible Bullets," p. 57.

27. Alan Liu, "Wordsworth and Subversion, 1793–1804: Trying Cultural Criticism," *Yale Journal of Criticism* 2, 2 (1989): 87.

28. Jonathan Dollimore, "Introduction to the Second Edition," *Radical Tragedy: Religion, Ideology, and Power in the Drama of Shakespeare and his Contemporaries*, 2nd ed. (Durham, N.C.: Duke University Press, 1993), p. xxi. See also Carroll, who, usefully

rehearsing some readings of *2 Henry VI* with regard to the subversion/containment issue, writes, "I see the issue here as less a subversion/containment dichotomy being worked out in the writer's ideological practice than the unexamined coexistence of these forces" (*Fat King, Lean Beggar*, p. 156 n. 31).

29. Liu, "Wordsworth and Subversion," p. 87.

30. Alan Sinfield, *Faultlines: Cultural Materialism and the Politics of Dissident Reading* (Berkeley: University of California Press, 1992), p. 21. Hugh Grady, in a related move, calls for critics of the Renaissance to make "a straightforward self-situation in the postmodern era on the grounds that there is no other choice, except that of disguising the set of concepts which one inevitably uses to approach and 'read' an alien culture" (p. 42).

31. Michel Foucault, "Afterword: The Subject and Power," in *Michel Foucault: Beyond Structuralism and Hermeneutics*, ed. Hubert L. Dreyfus and Paul Rabinow, 2nd ed. (Chicago: University of Chicago Press, 1982), p. 225. For my reading of Foucault, I am partly indebted to my colleague Jon Connolly. Catherine Belsey made a related point in her talk at the 1994 MLA Convention, arguing (and here I paraphrase from memory) that the time has come to cease defining all cultural phenomena of early modern England primarily in terms of their relationship to monarchy ("Shakespeare: The Next Generation," Panel 658: "Rethinking Shakespearean Tragedy," Modern Language Association Convention, San Diego, Calif., 29 December 1994).

32. *Michel Foucault*, ed. Dreyfus and Rabinow, p. 187.

33. Parker Douglas, "'Everything's Different; Nothing's the Same': Notes Against the Logic of Ahistoricism" (unpublished paper), p. 25.

15

Graffiti, Grammatology, and the Age of Shakespeare

Juliet Fleming

"A big part of graffiti is to be able to appreciate the past."
— Dream, graffiti writer from Oakland[1]

I

AT THE END of the *Welspring of wittie Conceights* (1584) is a set of "Certaine worthie sentences, very meete to be written about a Bed-chamber, or to be set up in any convenient place in a house."[2] In the appendices to Thomas Tusser's *A hundreth good points of husbandry married unto a hundreth good poynts of huswifery* (1570) is a series of something called "Husbandly posies"—"Posies for the Hall," "Posies for the Parlour," "Posies for the Guest's Chamber," and "Posies for thine own bedchamber" (see Appendix to this essay).[3] These two sets of poems bear witness to the surprising fact that the Elizabethan house-holder was advised to write on his, or her, own walls. Evidence that such advice was followed is furnished by two Hertfordshire properties, on whose interior walls selections from Tusser's posies can still be read (Figures 1 and 2). I propose that drawing and writing on walls was widely practiced in Eliz-abethan and Jacobean England; that it was sanctioned there in ways that are foreign to ourselves and troubling to the categories within which we recognize graffiti; and that this is something that we have not cared to know about the age of Shakespeare.

Catching me writing my name on the wall of the gym, the headmistress of my junior school once uttered the memorable line "Do *I* come to *your* house and write on the walls?" The proposition was traumatic not only because we think of graffiti writing as being a largely adolescent activity, but also because while writing on the walls of schools, prisons, municipal toilets, and other public places has to be specifically forbidden, the prohibition against writing

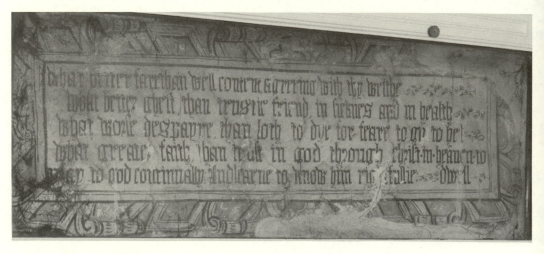

Figure 1. Wall-painting, Pirton Grange, Pirton, Herts. Text gathered from Tusser, pp. 291–93 (see Appendix).
  what better fare than well content, agreeing with thy welthe
  what better ghest, than trustie friend, in sicknes and in health
  what worse despayre, than loth to dye for feare to go to hel
  what greater faith than trust in god, through christ in heaven to dwell
  Pray to god continually: And learne to knowe him rightfullie
By permission of the Royal Commission on the Historical Monuments of England, © Crown Copyright.

on the interior walls of a house is, for us, a deeply internalized one.[4] The distinction between texts that are attached to, and texts that are written on, the interior of the house will suggest itself here, but it is one that the Elizabethans did not themselves make. A wall-painting recorded in a church at Llantwit Major, Glamorgan by E. Clive Rouse, part of a decorative scheme dated 1604, comprises a painted frame (Figure 3). The space it demarcates asks to be filled; but to wonder whether this is more properly done by pasting a document into place, or by writing or drawing directly onto the plaster, is to encounter what today appears to be a characteristic joke within Elizabethan decorative art. Refusing to understand the difference between what is "real" and what is not (so that the thing representing *is* the thing represented) the Llantwit frame proposes a representational economy that is finally unsusceptible to neo-classical questions of reason and taste. Here we encounter, and will want to resist, what Foucault calls "the very language of things."[5]

Early modern English contains no term to denote graffiti writing — a fact suggesting not so much that the vice was unknown, but that the activity was

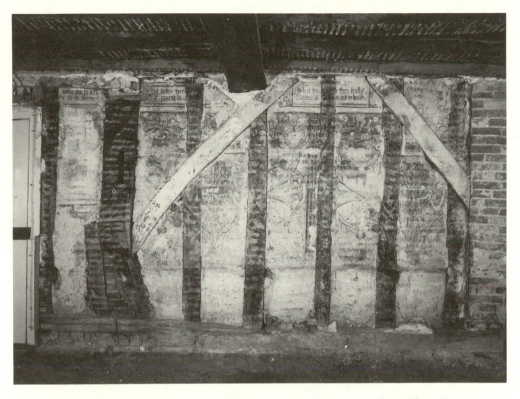

Figure 2. Wall-painting, Ansell's End Farm, Kimpton, Herts. Text adapted from Tusser, p. 291 (see Appendix).
   [What better thought, than think on] God, and daily him to serve
   [What better gift than to the poor, that] ready be to sterve.
   What better fayre [than well content, agreeing with thy welthe]
   What myrthe to . . .
   What better Gheste, then trustie friends, in sicknes and in health
By permission of the Royal Commission on the Historical Monuments of England, © Crown Copyright.

not distinguished from other writing practices, and not yet considered a vice.[6] Like pornography, with which it often shares a site, graffiti in its modern sense is an effect of categorization. In its political dimension it appears against the grid of what we understand to be the difference between public and private, professional and amateur, authorized and unauthorized.[7] But modern graffiti is also a form of painting or writing that, uniquely, announces itself as being written "on" something. It thus puts into play the analogous thematics of surface and depth, presence and absence, which together comprise the gram-

Figure 3. Drawing by E. Clive Rouse of a church wall-painting at Llantwit Major, Glamorgan, dated 1604. By permission of the Conway Library, Courtauld Institute of Art.

matological dilemma of writing in its material aspect. It is the insistent visibility of the material remainder that constitutes the scandal of modern graffiti;
a writing that, exceptionally, is understood to be *filling space*. That the Elizabethans did not see it this way, or rather that they saw most or all writing as
having both dimension and location, is one of the burdens of this essay.

Graffiti, almost by definition, is produced in media and on sites that make
its long survival unlikely. Scratched rather than chiseled, or written in the even
more ephemeral media of charcoal, chalk, marking stone, smoke, and blood,
early modern graffiti was presumably swiftly obliterated. Graffiti does survive,
notoriously, on the interior walls of the Domus Aurea in Rome, whose ancient
and delicate decorative paintings are partially obscured by the signatures and
comments of the fifteenth- and sixteenth-century artists and tourists who came
to see them.[8] The Domus Aurea has been taken as evidence that the impulse to
write graffiti is simply human, and simply transgressive. But in the last thirty
years a very wide range of drawings and inscriptions, both religious and secular, has been recovered and documented from the interior walls and pillars of
England's churches, and provides incontrovertible evidence that graffiti writing was once sanctioned in ways now foreign to ourselves.[9]

The difficulty of recognizing the graffiti of the past in its own terms is
illustrated by Susan Sontag's essay on the paintings of Pieter Saenredam
and Gerhard Houckgeest, seventeenth-century Dutch painters whose spare
church interiors display their own signatures as if scratched on the church piers
along with the other graffiti drawings recorded there. Against the visual evidence of Saenredam's "Interior of the Buurkerk, Utrecht" (1644), which
clearly shows adult graffiti writers at work, Sontag argues that graffiti would
have been "invariably read . . . as the trace of small children," and understands
its presence in the paintings as a "mild profanation" of the sacred space, and a
gesture of self-deprecation on the part of the artist, "as if he too, were an artless
vandal." Correctly noting that the graffiti seems to be "without aggression" in
the paintings, Sontag is led to theorize a past world in which "trespass is not a
threat," so that the graffito functions as a sort of Protestant gargoyle, "an
element of charm in the majestic visual environment."[10] It would be simpler,
and I think more correct, to theorize a world in which graffiti is not a trespass.

In fact, medieval and Renaissance church graffiti is so common in England that Doris Jones-Baker recently developed a taxonomy of its customary
locations and forms: giants and windmills on towers; boats low down on
pillars; priests' names and dates on the jambs of the priest's door; and portraits
of traditional parish "characters" such as the local giant cut in the places where
their costumes and props were stored.[11] Part of the church wall was sometimes
set aside to serve as the parish noticeboard: erasures were made by water,

scraping, or successive coats of limewash, the careful removal of which now reveals drawings and inscriptions of all kinds. Surviving graffiti constitutes an important record of religious and secular parish life: Jones-Baker notes that the *majority* of fourteenth-century musical notation survives in the form of church graffiti, where it was written as a mnemonic aid to church musicians and officials. Church walls are also the register for political events, signatures and portraits of local people, burial inscriptions, and secular drawings, mottoes and comments.[12] Post-Reformation graffiti documented by Violet Pritchard in churches around Cambridge include an Elizabethan gravedigger with his implements, flowers, the reminder "Mors comparatur umbre que semper sequitur corpus" ["Death is like a shadow, which always follows the body"], and the lines "fare well all clere Melawdy / fare well all ladyes and."[13] Izaak Walton records that after Donne's burial, "some unknown friend, some one, of the many lovers and admirers of his vertue and learning; writ this *Epitaph* with a cole on the wall, over his grave," in the church where he was buried:

Reader! I am to let thee know,
Donne's Body only, lyes below:
For, could the grave his Soul comprise?
Earth would be richer then the skies.[14]

After centuries of interior alteration much less graffiti writing survives in secular interiors. But in the course of her search for church graffiti, Pritchard documented several instances in the domestic buildings of Cambridgeshire. At Sawston Hall, the house where Mary Tudor was staying when she heard of Edward's death, Pritchard found a graffito of the head of a Spanish soldier and two inscriptions in a stone mantelpiece: "Owine male donique male scribe" ["Owen writes an evil script when writing evil things"]; and "Igne levatus hyems" [from Ovid's *Remedia Amoris*: "Winter is alleviated by fire"]. In the Old Vicarage at Little Wilbraham, three inscriptions survive on a fireplace. The first is a riddle:

I am in the fier and yet am cold
Let him that can this riddle unfold
Yf the fier be little and wether cold
'Tis easy this riddle to unfold.

Underneath a different hand proposes a solution: "I hope I do this riddle unfolde / In sayinge that this stone is coulde." The third inscription is the incomplete "Amore sau [. . .]co sauciando perio periendo spero, sperendo rem in iscor" ["By love I am wounded. By wounds I gain experience; by

Figure 4. Graffiti signatures of Robert Spalding (fellow 1592–1604) and Gabriel Duckett (fellow 1563–72) from the fireplace in the Old Treasury, St. John's College, Cambridge. Courtesy of the Master, Fellows, and Scholars of St. John's College, Cambridge.

experience hope; by hoping . . ."].[15] Over the fireplace in the Old Treasury at St. John's College, Cambridge, are several signature inscriptions by former fellows of the college, some of them dated. Among those identified by Malcolm Underwood are Roger Ascham (1542), John Taylor, Thomas Fowle, Thomas Randall (1575), Gabriel Duckett (1570), William Fulke (1565), Laurence Washington, Walter Barker (1572), William Coell (1572), James Smith (1577), Edward Alvey (1574), Thomas Playfere, and Robert Spalding (Figures 4 and 5). Excusing one disreputable practice by adducing another, Underwood speculates the names were written under the influence of wine served in the auditor's chamber at the times of account.[16] I am arguing, instead, that graffiti writing was as common, and as unremarkable, in domestic interiors as it was in the churches of early modern England.

Figure 5. Dated graffiti signature of Edward Alvey (fellow 1570–76) from the fireplace in the Old Treasury, St. John's College, Cambridge. Courtesy of the Master, Fellows, and Scholars of St. John's College, Cambridge.

II

Although I and others sometimes use it as a noun singular, the word graffiti is a plural noun; and, as if to illustrate how strangely inflected are the notions of agency that center on its production, there is no verb to describe the action whose mark or trace the graffito is. In eighteenth-century England the Italian term *sgraffiato*, derived from the Latin to cut or scratch in stone, became current in the context of pottery manufacture to refer to the process of cutting through a glaze to expose different-colored clay underneath (pottery so deco- rated is known as "incised ware"). The difficulty of locating the graffito — the idea that it is at one and the same time *imposed on* and discovered *beneath* the surface of a wall, and can therefore be thought of both as a wound and as an instance of recovery (or, rather differently, as being at once additive and an index of wear) — is a paradox that has continued to haunt the term; dictating, for example, our own distinction between graffiti which culpably obscures the past and graffiti as a potent record of that past.

By the middle of the nineteenth century, the word *graffiti* did begin to imply the operation of the unauthorized activity whose results decorate and articulate our own public spaces, but the term was still sheltered from opprobrium by its imbrication with an antiquarian historiography. Following the publication in 1856 of Raphael Garucci's *Graffiti of Pompeii*, the best-known graffiti were those which had been uncovered there, and they seemed to nineteenth-century commentators such as J. A. Symonds to have the "power to reconstruct the past and summon as in dreams the voices and forms of long since buried men."[17] Symonds does not see graffiti as the signature of an irresponsible newcomer, but as the trace of a person long-vanished. Graffiti writing has been accorded paradoxical value as a form of expression whose infantile or atavistic character allows it to function as a conduit for instinctive or unconscious forces. Within an aesthetic economy that understands art as being born from a personal resistance to culture, expressions of "authentic ferocity" are read as the hallmarks of genius; while the marginal and overlooked may be privileged as the depositories of authenticity.[18] Ancient graffiti (which historians distinguish from formal inscriptions on the uncertain grounds that the former are done "in a free hand") are still sometimes read as if they constituted a special form of the minor mode: one in which voices of the past, unmodified by dictates of genius, official form, or imperial ideology, registered themselves and were miraculously preserved.[19]

The reality effect that historical graffiti can produce depends on its being associated with voice rather than with writing. But graffiti does not rely on the conventional illusion of voice as the transparent medium that guarantees the speaker's self-presence. Instead of being opposed to the dead letter of writing, graffiti's voice is heard, for example by Symonds, as something itself spectral, "the voices . . . of long since buried men." A thing undead, graffiti's voice generates uncanny effects. Its simple utterance, "X her mark," prompts questions that are rarely addressed to writing outside the realms of lyric poetry. Who speaks? from where? (what do you want of me?). Graffiti in history arrests our attention by suggesting that a voice may be detached from the subject—may be in fact an object or foreign body within the subject. The hysteria with which the Anglo-American world today encounters its own graffiti has a primarily political dimension.[20] But, as the medium of the urban poor, graffiti is overdetermined. For wherever it appears, the graffito stages—and allows its viewers to indulge in—the proposition of a radically dispossessed self.

Graffiti writing may not have held quite the same lesson for the early modern English, whose intellectual economy was predicated on a socially constituted subject and notions of authorship that were collective, aphoristic, and inscriptive, rather than individualist, lyric, and voice-centered.[21] Operating on a natural world divinely marked for human notice, and dealing with truths it understands to be already extant, early modern writing is readily perceived by its practitioners as tending toward non-subjectivity — that is, toward a writing that requires no subjective position of enunciation. If I write a sentence from Tusser on my wall ("What better bed than conscience good, to pass the night with sleep?"), whose utterance is it? Neither mine nor Tusser's: it is a commonplace, it "speaks for itself." So Erasmus celebrated proverbs as "symbols" in which ancient wisdom was "contained." "They were so deeply respected in old times," he adds, "that they seemed to have fallen from heaven rather than to have come from men. 'And *know thyself* descended from the sky' says Juvenal."[22] The strange effects produced on us by Elizabethan wall-writing result in part from the fact that in it we encounter the denotative writing of the past through the prism of a reading practice predicated on modern notions of subjectivity.

III

The term "worthy sentence" ("meete to be written about a Bed-chamber") is a tautology, for the Renaissance *sentence* is already a wise saying that announces itself as such. It is written "in a pointed manner": one designed to indicate its special provenance among the various registers (classical, Biblical, proverbial) of the exhortational mode. The word "posy," on the other hand, is a syncopated form of poesie: its sixteenth-century meanings are not always distinct from those of its parent category, but include the short poem accompanying the picture of an emblematic device, a small collection (usually culled from a larger "garden") of the "flowers" of rhetoric, and a motto written on a ring or a piece of tableware.[23] Graziano derides Nerissa's ring in *The Merchant of Venice* as "a hoop of gold, a paltry ring, / That she did give me, whose posy was / For all the world like cutler's poetry / Upon a knife — 'Love me and leave me not'" (5, 1, 147–50). While formally a posy must be short ("as woman's love, or the posy of a ring" says Hamlet), its defining characteristic is to be written in such a way that its material embodiment forms an important part of its meaning. The posy, in short, is a saying or poem that is pointed by being written *on* something.

In *The Arte of English Poesie* (1589), George Puttenham defines a posy as "a short epigram . . . printed upon . . . banketting dishes of suger plate" and taken home at the end of the feast by each guest as a kind of party favor. "Nowadays," he continues, posies are more commonly painted "upon the backsides of our fruit trenchers of wood" or used "as devises in rings and armes and about such courtly purposes."[24] For Puttenham, the posy is the exemplary form of poetry at the court of Elizabeth I. Pinned to trees and curtains, set upon conduits, and wrapped around gifts; or plaited into bracelets, embroidered onto clothes, and copied into books, the posy plays a crucial role in the material exchange of favors that articulates life at court. As material forms, posies were classified according to a once fluid and now invisible taxonomy of location. Samuel Daniel, for example, comments, "This word *mot* signifieth as much as *Gnome*, a short sentence or Posie, whose places are divers. Some use to set them upon gates, as that which (according to the Poet) was set on Hell gate."[25] All writing is written on something: the posy is the written form that calls attention to that fact. Under "normal" circumstances (the circumstances in which text is legible as such) the paper and ink that subtend it — and constitute its writing — are invisible; and any material facts that such a writing may record about itself ("For paper I am") will be glossed as textual effects. It is only when we encounter writing where we do not expect to see it, wrought in materials or on surfaces that then become visible as "writing matter," that we confront the material properties of the trace.[26]

Since material properties can only be encountered as metaphors, this is a confrontation that itself takes place in language. But it is one assimilated with some difficulty to the triumph of form over matter (meaning over thing) on which the operation of language depends. The recurrence of flowers in Elizabethan wall paintings is less "naturalistic" than it seems today: the flower is a flower of rhetoric, it appears on the wall as a metaphor literalized or inverted. A collection of flowers on a wall, a posy, is a figure for a text. Appearing before us as if they were metaphors written backwards, painted flowers reveal themselves not as things, but as a *desire* for that fusion between figure and thing that Foucault takes to be characteristic of early modern thought (Figure 6). This is a desire that, except under special circumstances, we no longer share.

It is worth insisting that the posy — a piece of writing with physical extension — cannot exist as text in the abstract. To make a distinction that would have been incomprehensible to his readers, Tusser's "Husbandly Posies" are patterns for posies rather than the things themselves: it is the householder who, copying them onto her walls or cutting the book in order to paste them there, makes a posy from a text. It follows that within the history of English literature posies as such have not survived. Read within the context of the "Elizabethan Miscellany," the posy is at once condemned for and relieved of its material form and purpose. To the extent that these are remembered — "These sentences following were set upon conduits in London, against the day that King James came through the city, at his first comming to the Crowne" — the posy appears quaint.[27] But the Elizabethan quaint is a category that pre-

Figure 6. Wall-painting over a fireplace from Number 2, Lower Farm, Barley, Herts. By permission of the Royal Commission on the Historical Monuments of England, © Crown Copyright.

sumably comes into visibility at the same time as that of the essentialized, abstracted text. Pilgrimage to Shakespeare's birth-place — and for that matter the less ludicrous but no less dusty labor of editing his works — presupposes the existence of a Shakespearean text beyond the accidents of the written trace. It is as if, today, the literary effect depended on the denial or occlusion of certain forms of matter.

But the Elizabethans understood reading and writing differently, as procedures for the gathering, storage, and redeployment of well-framed wisdom.[28] Within such a regimen, writing is that which frames truth to catch the eye or memory: like the stylistic devices of brevity or ornament, writing can, *in and of itself*, add weight to a sentence.[29] In *The Art of Memory* (1621), John Willis lists the procedures of condensation and displacement that produce memorable representations. Such representations or "ideas" can be either "direct" (where the image of a goat stands for a goat) or "oblique . . . whereby the thing to be remembered is obliquely or indirectly signified." Willis distinguishes three types of oblique idea: the "relative" (that is, the metonymic), the "subdititial" (the metaphoric), and the "scriptile" (the written): "a Scriptile idea is, whereby the thing to be remembered, is supposed to be written on a plaine white table hanged up in the midst of the opposite wall." Within the imagined space of his memory system, Willis advises that ideas be stored in the places they would occupy in real life. Thus a "libell or Epigramme" is "supposed to be written in a paper, and pasted upon the opposite wall"; if the idea is "a Proclamation or Title page of a Booke," it should be "pasted unto the wall"; if it is "a new pamphlet . . . it is fastened to the wall with nailes."[30] Tessa Watt has described early modern alehouses as places where printed texts and visual imagery were disseminated. She notes contemporary accounts of inns with "rows of ballads" pasted on the walls, and cites William Cornwallis's description of an inn where "not a Poste, nor a painted cloth in the house, but cryes *Feare God*."[31] As Watt's work shows, inns and alehouses were not unique in this respect: the Elizabethans did not buy their books ready bound, and hard covers compete with walls as the proper place to store or display at least some kinds of written text. Putting itself on display for the purposes of memory and education, striving (even in its new print formats) to be decorative, Elizabethan writing everywhere embraces its own materiality.[32]

IV

It is the working assumption of local historians that the writing that survives on the walls, doors, and windows of the Elizabethan interior has been copied

from more properly "textual" sources; which is certainly the procedure suggested by Tusser and Fister.[33] Surviving inscriptions can occasionally be traced
to proverb collections, or to the influential emblem books of Alciati and
Whitney: in *Have with you to Saffron Walden* Nashe scoffs that Erasmus's
Adagia have been "all snatcht up for painter's posies."[34] To Erasmus himself,
the posy is a proverb materialized, the proverb is a posy *in potentia*; "*Sustine et
abstine*: Bear and Forbear. For a long time now [these two words] have been
current as a proverb among educated men, and well do they deserve to be
inscribed on walls and columns everywhere, and to be engraved on every
ring."[35] In Little Morton Hall, Cheshire, two lines survive engraved on a
window: "Men can no more knowe a woman's mind by kaire/Than by her
shadow judge what clothes she weare." It is tempting to read the lines as deriving from Donne's "Twicknam Gardens": "Nor can you more judge woman's
thoughts by teares/Then by her shadow, what she weares" (ll. 24–25). But in
this instance we cannot be certain that the graffito does not predate the poem;
nor that Donne, whose undatable poems are highly self-conscious about their
own locations, did not find or indeed write some of his best lines on walls.
Thomas Coryat regularly copied down verses he encountered written on or in
houses on his Continental travels, and Nicholas Bacon presented Jane Lumley
with a manuscript copy of the *sententiae* he had painted in his long gallery at
Gorhambury.[36] The contents of Elizabethan commonplace books are likely to
have been as regularly read off as written onto windows and walls.

According to the sermon given at her funeral, Anne Clifford decorated
the walls, hangings, and furniture of her bed-chamber with "sentences or
sayings of remark":

> She would frequently bring out of the rich Store-house of her memory, things new and
> old, Sentences, or Sayings of remark, which she had read or learned out of Authors and
> with these her Wals, her Bed, her Hangings, and Furniture must be adorned; causing
> her Servants to write them in Papers, and her Maids to pin them up, that she, or they, in
> time of their dressing, or as occasion served, might remember, and make their descants
> upon them. So that, though she had not many Books in her Chamber, yet it was dressed
> up with the flowers of a library.[37]

Like Montaigne, who wrote fifty-four sayings from Biblical and classical
sources onto the rafters of his library (many of which reappear in his *Essais*),
Clifford is here engaged in an intellectual practice — the culling and deployment of the "flowers" of wisdom — that is highly characteristic of English and
continental humanism.[38] And while parietal writing (that is, writing done
directly onto the wall) is vulnerable to social derogation in the early modern
period (as one of George Herbert's "Outlandish Proverbs" has it, "A white

wall is the paper of a foole"), the English humanists and those they influenced may have felt the stigma of charcoal on whitewash no more keenly than they felt the stigma of print.[39] The practice of early modern wall-writing may then have materially informed not only memory systems based on imagined interior "places," but also the mental topography of the intellectual system that manifested itself in the keeping of commonplace books.

In fact, I imagine the whitewashed domestic wall as being the primary scene of writing in early modern England. In 1585 Samuel Daniel noted that "men all naturally take delight in pictures, and even little children as soon as they can use their hands at libertie, goe with a Cole to the wall, indeavouring to drawe the forme of this thing or that."[40] Presumably it was not only children who availed themselves of the writing space provided by the whitewashed wall. The writing that survives from the Elizabethan period was produced by people who had the technological and financial resources for the laborious procedures of securing paper, pen, and ink.[41] The poor, the hurried, and those (it may have been practically everybody) unconcerned with the extensive circulation and long survival of their *bons mots* wrote with charcoal, chalk, stone, and pencil. That the bulk of early modern writing was written on walls, and was consequently both erasable and in our own scheme of things *out of place*, is a proposition with consequences for current assumptions about the constitution and statistics of literacy and schooling in the early modern period.[42] But, beyond this, it prompts us to imagine, in an age to which is ascribed the inauguration of "proper" writing, a widespread, and in contemporary terms multiply "undisciplined" writing practice: one within which writing and drawing are not fully distinguishable; defacement operates as a principle of textual production; the page is no longer an important boundary; and the written product cannot be taught, reproduced, or sold as a commodity. Elizabethan wall-writing is, in short, graffiti by another name.

V

In Puttenham's work, posies belong within a larger class, the "epigramme," a category of writing that, "short and sweete (as we are wont to say)," includes the posy, the epitaph ("an inscription such as a man may commodiously write or engrave upon a tomb in few verses"), and the anonymous public inscription.[43] Puttenham considers the best contemporary examples of epigrams to be those associated with Pasquino, one of Rome's "speaking statues," on whom, according to John Florio, "all Satires, Pasquins, rayling rimes or libels are fastened and fathered," a practice that continues to this day (Figure 7).[44]

Figure 7. "Il Balbuino," one of Rome's speaking statues. Photo, Juliet Fleming.

Spoken, according to the conceit, by the statue itself, the epigram (or "pas-quinade") allows expression of those "bitter taunts, and privy nips" that erupt within men in society. Directed sometimes against a neighbor and sometimes, in carefully contained circumstances, against the State, the epigram registers the oppositional, playful, and somatic impulses of the civil subject.[45] In the case of the pasquinade, the epigram attains the nonsubjective status of Erasmus's proverb ("'Fallen from the skies', says Juvenal") when it takes its place as a public utterance "fathered" on a mute object.

The location of Puttenham's epigram in Elizabethan England and Augustan Rome associates it with graffiti in the modern sense:

> . . . this *Epigramme* is but an inscription or writing made as it were upon a table, or in a window, or upon the wall or mantell of a chimney in some place of common resort, where it was allowed every man might come, or be fitting to chat and prate, as now in our tavernes and common tabling houses, where many merry heads meete, and scrible with ynke, with chalke, or with a cole such matters as they would every man should know, and descant upon.[46]

Puttenham does not especially deprecate such writing, which he associates with the dissemination of information from an anonymous source. Under different circumstances Jonson's Lovewit displays equal equanimity when he returns from the country to discover that graffiti writers have been busy in his London house:

> Here, I find
> The emptie walls, worse than I left 'hem, smok'd,
> A few crack'd pots, and glasses, and a fornace,
> The seeling filled with *poesies* of the candle:
> And MADAME, with a *Dildo*, writ o' the walls. (*The Alchemist* 5, 5, 38–42)[47]

"Poesies of the candle," usually glossed as stains caused by candle smoke, can also mean (what to the modern householder would be much the same thing) verses, slogans, or signatures written on the ceiling in candle smoke: additions to the word Madam, and the drawing of a dildo — or alternatively to the text of a ballad called "Madam with a dildo," or to a portrait of a woman with a dildo — that have already been written on Lovewit's walls.[48]

Tolerance of anti-social activities is one of Lovewit's characteristics; and his easy embrace of smoke-writing is not shared by the speaker in Herrick's "Hesperides," who includes in his list of necessities for a happy retirement home a modest but weather-proof roof "And seeling free / From that cheape *Candle Bawdry.*" In Beaumont and Fletcher's *Philaster* (2, 4, 147–50), the King vows to expose the courtesan Megra, "make ribal'd rimes, / And sear thy name with candles upon walls." Megra threatens to retaliate by publicizing the Princess's love affair: "Your dear daughter shall stand by me / On walls, and sung in ballads, anything." In the opening scene of *The Alchemist* Face threatens to hang Subtle "in picture," "write thee up bawd in *Paules*," and "have all thy tricks . . . told in red letters: And a face, cut for thee / Worse than GAMALIEL RATSEY'S" (1, 1, 90–102). Herford and Simpson gloss "red letters" as alluding to "rubricated titles and headings of old books"; but red ochre stone is one of the more common media in which Renaissance wall-writing survives, and the notorious center aisle and churchyard of St. Paul's Cathedral is a likely site for the exposure threatened by Face: a graffiti portrait of Subtle on the gallows, with slogans describing his crimes.[49]

The elaborated taxonomy (almost a rule of genre) that once determined the appropriate materials, locations, and subject matter of Elizabethan wall-writing has, like most of the writing itself, been lost. Candle smoke seems to be a derogated medium, proper vehicle for the set of sexual anxieties whose parietal articulation may have constituted the primary discourse of pornography in early modern England. But even candle writing is by no means uniformly reproved, and should be read in the context of the widespread practice of graffiti writing in other media. When Spenser's Colin Clout says of the English court that "all the walls and windows there are writ, / And full of love, and love, and love my deare" (ll. 776–77), or when the speaker in Fulke Greville's poem records how he used to find his name "by Myra finely wrought" in the chimney, we have tended to read the lines as if the locations they ascribe to poetry were metaphorical. Thus the occasion for Donne's poem "A Valediction on my name, in a window" ("My name engraved herein, / Doth contribute my firmness to this glass") is assumed to be imaginary, and its extrapolation into a meditation on signature appears duly "conceited." But as Rosemary Freeman notes, the sixteenth century was an age when "it was natural and intelligible for a man to scratch an emblematic poem on his friend's window pane, taking the brittleness of the glass as his 'picture' and his theme."[50] The practice of writing on windows is attested both in poems such as Herbert's "The Posy" ("Let wits contest, / And with their words and posies windows fill"); and in the survival from the period of inscribed window panes, and of "writing rings" (diamonds set in high bevels with one point outwards) designed to mark glass.[51]

If John Foxe is to be believed, Princess Elizabeth used such a ring to record her deliverance from her enemies. Leaving Woodstock, where she had been under house arrest, Elizabeth "wrote with her diamond, in a glass window, 'Much suspected by me / Nothing proved can be. Quoth ELIZABETH, Prisoner.' "[52] Less well supplied during her imprisonment in the Tower, Lady Jane Grey still managed "certain pretty verses written . . . with a pin: 'Do never think it strange,/Though now I have misfortune;/For if that fortune change,/The same to thee may happen./Jane Dudley."[53] Such poetry forms part of the considerable archive of verse that survives from the period scratched and carved into prison walls; and is evidence of a type of graffiti writing familiar today.[54] But Thomas Fuller records a line written by Raleigh on a window at court: "Fain would I climb yet fear I to fall," to which the Queen is alleged to have replied by writing underneath "If thy heart fails thee, climb not at all."[55] In *Ar't Asleep Husband* (1640) Richard Brathwaite remarks: "I have sometimes read written in a window with a diamond, by one, it seemed, who was not settled in his Choice . . . these lines *If I might chuse, I knowe not which were best,/She that is naked, or is neatly dresst.*" Brathwaite found an answering opinion on another pane: "*If I might chuse, I'de have her such ane one/As shee was first created, bone on bone:/And in that naked-nature posture have her/When th'Serpent with an Apple did deceive her.*"[56]

In *The English Gentleman and English Gentlewoman . . . with a Ladies Love lecture* (1641), Brathwaite records three further instances of window-writing conducted antiphonally between men; as well as the sentiments of four "brave resolved" women, who expressed "the nobleness of their thoughts in these proper imprezes, which with their Diamonds they left writ in the panes of their own chamber windowes":

The device of the first was this:
  It is not in the power of fate
  To weaken a contented state.
And the second scornes to fall short of her resolution
  Fortune may sundry Engines finde,
  But none to raze a noble minde.
The third in contempt of Fortune, inlargeth this subject:
  Should fortune me distresse,
  My minde would be no lesse.
The fourth, to shew her affection true Toutch, attests her constancy in this:
  Fate may remove
  Life, but not love.[57]

These small collections, if not invented by Brathwaite, constitute the imperfect register of an interactive, material, and popular poetic practice whose thematic resources include a debate concerning the comparative permanence of texts and their material supports.[58] Where Donne argued that his name, and the poem inscribed above it, "doth contribute my firmnesse to this glasse," the devices "left writ" by Brathwaite's constant women have a more obvious, but still complicated relation to the written trace. Each poem begins by taking the firmness and indelibility of window writing to illustrate its proposition that something (contentment, nobility, love) will survive a general ruin; and each immediately realizes that it is precisely the solidity of such writing that threatens it with destruction. Windows break, walls fall, writing will be erased.

There is extensive literary and non-literary evidence that the early modern English did not hesitate to write on walls as well as windows. One of the few surviving poems of Elizabeth I, "O fortune, thy wresting wavering state" was written on a wall at Woodstock, where it was seen and copied down by Paul Hentzner in 1597.[59] A character in John Grange's *Golden Aphroditis* (1577) relieves his feelings at having been denied access to his mistress by writing "*Veni, vidi* . . . upon the gallerie doore," while another entertains his fellow guests by writing "with a redde oker stone upon the skrene of the hall" a long and riddling poem that invites a written response.[60] In W. M.'s *The Man in the Moone* (1609) Fido advises the lover "If shee useth you hardly either in words or deeds, or countenanceth any of your enemies or evill willers, set it downe in your table-bookes, and write it upon the wal in your bed-chamber, that you may at al times better remember them: and consider if she tendered you she wold not wrong you."[61]

Together with political commentary, personal slander, and the performance of signature, erotic fixation is still recognizable as an appropriate theme for graffiti writing. Less easily assimilated to that category are the games, recipes, school lessons, memorials, house rules, prayers, extracts from the Bible, memoranda to the self, and advice to others that the early modern Europeans wrote on their walls.[62] John Hoskyns drew portraits of his servants, with Latin distichs, on the outside walls of Morehampton, his country seat.[63] John Dee noted that the Prague study of the astronomer Hájek was decorated with "things manifold written very fairly," "very many *Hieroglyphical* Notes *Philosophical*," "verses over the door," and a description of the alchemist's work on the south-side wall.[64] The seventeenth-century English account of Nicholas Flamel's successful projection records that, in the process of puzzling over the symbols discovered in an ancient book, the French alchemist "caused to bee painted within my *Lodging*, as naturally as I could, all the figures and portraicts of the *fouwth* and *fifth* leafe."[65] In the country parson's house described by George Herbert, "Even the walls are not idle, but something is written or painted there which may excite the reader to a thought of piety; especially the 101 psalm, which is expressed in a fair table, as being the rule of a family."[66]

In Chapman, Jonson, and Marston's *Eastward Ho* (1605) Touchstone traces his fortune as master goldsmith to the sober practices described in and exemplified by the writing on his shop walls:

Did I gain my wealth by ordinaries? no! By exchanging of gold? no! By keeping of gallants' company? no! I hired me a little shop, bought low, took small gain, kept no debt book, garnished my shop, for want of plate, with good wholesome thrifty sentences — as, "Touchstone, keep thy shop, and thy shop will keep thee"; "Light gains make heavy purses"; "'Tis good to be merry and wise." (1, 1, 52–60)

A successful merchant whose social values are both criticized and ratified, Touchstone is a familiar figure on the early Jacobean stage. By the beginning of the seventeenth century, proverbs are perhaps coming into conflict with new notions of subjectivity, originality, and authenticity in writing; and the emphatic redundancy of Touchstone's "wholesome thrifty sentences" — "'Tis good to be merry and wise" — seems designed to reflect criticism both on the practice of reducing philosophy to a set of personalized truisms, and on a generation and a class for whom moralizing is, at least on stage, fast becoming a signature effect. Read as the engrossing of common to particular interests, the humanist intellectual practice of textual "gathering" now appears emblematic of a mercantile success predicated on an otherwise unlocatable lack of generosity. For Touchstone holds that capital is founded in the first instance on the industry and thrift of his own class — "Did I gain my wealth by ordinaries? no!" — and is thus able to imagine the capitalist mode of production as one that has called itself into being — "Touchstone, keep thy shop, and thy shop will keep thee." The sense (palpable to us, as it may not have been to his contemporaries) that there remains something unaddressed in Touchstone's account of the genesis of his fortune registers itself here as a contradiction between his economic and intellectual practices. Instead of "plate" Touchstone hoards "sentences"; he wisely puts his money to work at the same time that he apparently takes texts out of circulation to display them on his walls. Within a fully capitalist regime such as our own, Touchstone is revealed as a fetishist of the text — someone who inappropriately values writing for its magical efficacy in his own life. His misappropriation of the essentialized, abstracted text is underwritten by what now appears to be the old-fashioned and inappropriate practice of materializing text as wall-writing.

VI

The simple visibility of graffiti as such vanishes when it is considered within a culture which practiced a wide variety of wall-writing.[67] The Elizabethan interior as it has survived under the auspices of the National Trust presents us with a potent instance of domestic peace. Chastely whitewashed, or wrapped in the decorous and domestic pleats of the famous "linen-fold" panelling, it seems to preserve for us the graceful silence of the pre-commodity home. In fact, brightly painted walls and ceilings formed the decorative focus of most rooms in Tudor and Stuart England; surviving rooms display an exuberance of color and design that, together with the inclusion of *trompe l'oeil* and figurative effects, and a tendency to continue patterns over studs, panels and beams, proves uncongenial to modern taste.[68] Tapestry and wainscotting apart, Tudor and Stuart methods of interior decoration included ballad sheets and tables pasted directly onto the wall, or attached to cloth hangings; "wall papers" produced specifically for the purpose by printers who recycled spoiled pages by printing decorative patterns (sometimes incorporating mottoes) on their backs; and painted cloths.[69] These last so regularly contained writing that they became known for their sententiousness: Shakespeare's Tarquin reminds himself, "Who fears a sentence or a old man's saw / Shall by a painted cloth be kept in awe" (*The Rape of Lucrece*, 244–45); while an exchange between Jacques and Orlando (*As You Like It* 3, 2, 266–70) equates painted cloths and posy rings as the sites for the moral truism: "J: You are full of pretty answers. Have you not been acquainted with goldsmith's wives, and conn'd them out of rings? O: Not so; but I answer you right painted cloth, from whence you have studied your questions."[70]

From the middle of the sixteenth century until the beginning of the seventeenth, wall painting was perhaps the most common form of interior decoration. Painted walls (and, for that matter cloths) are not best understood as "poor man's tapestry": each constitutes a medium and a practice with its own technical opportunities and sophisticated generic conventions, and each found a place in wealthy as well as more modest interiors. Documenting more than three hundred surviving wall-paintings in the 1930s, Reader classified them as "arabesque" work in black and white, "naturalistic" floral ornament painted in rich colors, panels divided by strapwork and filled with cartouche, representations of tapestries and other hangings, and figure subjects taken from contemporary pastimes and from Biblical and classical sources.[71]

Any of these decorative schemes could contain writing: as a whole they comprise a field of art that deserves more serious critical attention than it has hitherto received. Produced in a period that spans the English Reformation, Elizabethan wall-painting necessarily addresses itself to the vexed (and state-legislated) imbrication of word and image: its ideal analysis would proceed under the aegis of a calligraphic term (perhaps *calligramme*, or the more contemporary *graf*, if *graffiti* will not do) that encompassed word and image, and did not presume to know the difference between writing and painting.[72] Archaeological evidence shows that the writing on the interior walls of the Elizabethan house included Biblical verse and commentary, prayers, heraldic mottoes, injunctions to fear God and obey the Prince, exhortations to charity and righteous living, and reminders of mortality. Typical of the last, with its tropes of flowers and clay, and its theme of the insubstantiality of earthly life, is the inscription recorded by Reader from a farmhouse in Chiddingly, E. Sussex:

In lyfe theare ys no suer staye
For fleashe as flower doth vade awaye
This carcas made of slyme and claye
Must taste of deathe theare is no waye.
While we have tyme then lett us praye
To god for grace bothe night and daye.[73]

Stoke Poges Manor House, built by the Earl of Huntingdon in 1553, has a series of painted sayings in one room, of which Reader found the following still legible: "Feare the Lord, Obey the Prince," "Love thi neighbour," "Beware of Pride," "Speak the truth," and "Bear no malice"; on the wall of a four-room cottage in Chalfont St. Peter was the black-letter inscription: "When any thing thou takest in hand to do or Enterpryse/fyrst marke well the fynall end there of that maye Aryse. Fear God."[74] Surviving political statements are common and unanimously conservative, ranging from the ubiquitous "Obey the Prince" to the inscription of Elizabeth's motto, "Semper Eadem" at an inn in County Dublin. While such exhortations may suggest the extensiveness of Tudor state supervision, or the possibility that public and private spheres were not yet distinct from each other, slogans such as "God save the Quene" (like the coronation mugs that are the very type of British domesticity) may serve instead to remind us that an active embrace of ideology is a reassuring thing. The Elizabethan domestic interior may have been comfortable to its occupants not because it offered refuge from state interference, but because it provided a personal field within which the subject who had learned to desire his own ideological subordination was permitted — indeed instructed — to write.

Such, after all, is the burden of the two nearly identical passages from Deuteronomy (6: 4–9; 11: 18–21) that underpin the practice of wall-writing in post-Reformation England (Figure 8).[75] Tyndale rendered the first as follows:

Hear Israel, the Lorde thy God is Lorde only and thou shalt love the Lorde thy God with all thyne hearte . . . And these wordes which I commaunde the this day, shalbe in thine herte and thou shalt whett them on thy childer, and shalt talke of them when thou art home in thyne housse and as thou walkest by the waye, and when thou lyest doune and when thou rysest upp: and thou shalt bynde them for a sygne uppon thyne hande. And they shalbe papers of rembraunce betwene thyne eyes, and shalt write them uppon the postes of thy house and uppon thy gates.

Figure 8. Wall-painting over a fireplace at Feering House, Feering, Essex. Text from Deuteronomy 6: 4–9. Photo, Peter Rogers, reproduced courtesy of Margaret Carrick.

Against this passage, which is crucial to the Reformation project of a vernacular Bible, Tyndale inserts the barbed marginal note, "It is heresy with us for a laye man to loke of gods worde or to reade it." He goes on to explain his choice of the term "whett" (from the Hebrew root ShNN, to sharpen or repeat), as meaning "exercyse": exercise your children in God's commandments, and put them into use or practice ("ure") with them. The gloss to the Geneva Bible comments on Tyndale's term "some read, ye shall whet them upon thy children: to whit, that they may print them more depely into memorie." The Christian has God's truth imprinted in her mind and heart through education as well as through Grace: the impossible pedagogic trajectory whereby repetition is transformed into memory can be explained, here as nowhere else, as the action of Grace itself.

The Reformed Christian is thus advised, following Deuteronomy, to rehearse God's truth in conversation, bind it on hand and brow, and copy it onto walls. Luther pleased himself with imagining "the whole Bible to be painted on houses, on the outside and the inside, so that all can see it"; while Calvin, sensitive to the fact that the distracted householder may need to be continually reminded of his duty, advised, "Let us have Gods lawe written, let us have the sayings of it painted on our walles as in tables, and let us have things to put us in minde of it early and late."[76] Calvin holds memory aids to be so necessary that God *repeats* the injunction to write them (Deuteronomy 6: 4–9; 11: 18–21)—thus enacting what Calvin understands to be the burden of both passages: "This repetition therefore is not superfluous, where God telleth us again, th[at] it is good for us to have his lawe written everywhere."[77] (In a different register, the repetition of something already known may produce an experience akin to the transformation of unconscious into conscious material; the subject remembers, but only *at the moment of repetition*, both what it knows and that it knew it all along).[78]

Some Reformers showed themselves more chary of the prosthetic nature, and the material dimension, of such mnemonic devices. The Bishop's Bible (1578) glosses Deuteronomy 6: 9 by explaining that the injunction to write "upon the postes of thy house, and upon thy gates" means nothing "but continual meditation of the lawe"; while Joseph Hall, arguing that it is not the outward show but "the heart and reins are those that God looks after," used the same passage to illustrate the difference between Christians and Pharisees:

God charged them to binde the Law to their hand, and before their eyes, *Deut. 6* wherein, as *Jerome* and *Theophylact* well interpret it, he meant the meditation and practice of his Law: they, like unto the foolish Patient, which when a Physitian bids him take that prescript, if they could but get a list of parchment upon their left arme next their heart, and another scroll to be upon their forehead . . . thought they might say with *Saul, Blessed be thou of the Lord, I have done the commandment of the Lord.*[79]

But surviving wall-writings such as the Chiddingly inscription suggest that the pious Elizabethan did indeed go to bed at night and wake in the morning in the written shadow of the Lawe: "Therefore at night call unto minde/how thou the daye hast spent: /Praise God, if naught amisse thou finde: /if ought, betimes repent."[80]

Such admonitions, concerned as they are with testing, counting, and timeliness, are overdetermined in their early English context, posing both in their content and in themselves the crucial question of whether there *is* ever time or place for repentance. *Pace* Calvin, the repetition of God's law within a predestined world is precisely superfluous; the wall-written prayer (and by extension any prayer) is reduced to the statement of an intention to pray. What, after all, following Deuteronomy, should one write on posts, gates, and frontlets for the eyes? — nothing more nor less than the injunction to do so. But what has one done in doing this? The answer, even for Calvin, is nothing at all, for the only "true decking," the one that makes us acceptable to God, is already to "beare his Lawe *in minde*." Calvin attempts to displace the carnal potential of the writing practices he endorses by displacing it first onto women (who he finds would do better to beautify their bodies, clothes, and houses with "remembrance of Gods lawe" than with "bracelets and other fine toyes"); and then onto the Jews, who in their use of mezzuzot and tefillin took an "excellent lesson" and "turnd it into a charme and sorcerie . . . lyke to the *Agnus Dei* in popery, and such other geugawes as the papists hang about their necks."[81] For Calvin, to believe in the efficacy of words in their material dimension is to commit precisely the idolatry that the passage warns against. So, even as he writes on his walls, the Reformed Christian must "marke that God will not bee served by the wrytynge of some sentence of his lawe upon a post or a doore, or at the entry of a house," and undertake instead the impossible achievement of ensuring that law is "so engraven in our heartes, as it may never be wiped out again."[82] Impossibly, and therefore fruitfully, Reformed Christianity structures itself across the problem of the signifier, the problem that is the material dimension of language.

VII

The set of anxieties that graffiti has the power to cause within the differently constituted modern home finds powerful expression in a passage from Daniel (5: 5–30):

In the same hour came forth fingers of a man's hand, and wrote over against the candles upon the plaister of the wall of the king's palace, and the king saw the part of the hand that wrote . . . and this is the thing that was written MENE, MENE, TEKEL UPHARSIN . . . This is the interpretation of the thing, MENE: God hath numbered thy kingdom and finished it. TEKEL: Thou art weighed in the balance and found wanting. PERES: Thy kingdom is divided and given to the Medes and the Persians. . . . In that night was Belshazzar King of the Chaldeans slain.

The sinister charge of this passage derives from the way in which it positions the coming of death as a truth at once too certain and too terrible to be known.[83] Belshazzar's magicians can read but cannot understand the writing on the wall: its interpretation is reserved for Daniel, famous in the Authorized version for his skill at the "shewing of hard sentences and dissolving of doubts" (Daniel 5: 12). *Mene* is from the Hebrew root to count or number, *Tekel* from the root to weigh; *Peres* from the root to divide: each word can also signal a unit of money: a mena, a shekel, a fraction of a shekel. The inscription can thus be translated either as "Counted: pounds, shillings, and pence," or as "Counted: numbered, weighed, and divided."[84] It is Daniel's correct interpretation of the inscription that instantiates its fatal meaning: in the same moment that the prophet speaks, Belshazzar is weighed and found wanting, his kingdom divided, his death sealed.

Patricia Parker argues that the figure of the partition or wall is used in the Bible to evoke the deferred but relentlessly approaching end of days; and writing on the wall still figures for us, as it did for Belshazzar, the sinister and strangely collapsible hiatus between a sentence and its execution.[85] It is not death itself but the coming of death that has the power to transfix the terrified king: Belshazzar's unexplained end ("in that night was Belshazzar . . . slain") is determined by his own thanataphobia, and figures "the strange paradox of the suicide who voluntarily seeks death in order to free himself of [an] intolerable thanataphobia."[86] Cousin to the oracle, which drives its victims to the doom it seems to warn against, the writing in Belshazzar's palace operates within twentieth-century narratives of subjectivity as an instance of repression's capacity to fixate the subject at a particular site, where he or she awaits in terror the return of the repressed.

The appearance of the mysterious writing on the wall has subsequently become a master parable in narratives of the uncanny — "that class of the terrifying which leads back to something long known to us, once very familiar," as Freud put it in his famous essay.[87] Among the phenomena that produce intense feelings of being in the presence of the uncanny he included coincidences or repetition effects which "force upon us the idea of something fateful and inescapable" (as when the reappearance in daily life of a certain number suggests itself as an indication of an allotted span of life); a hand cut off at the wrist (especially one able to move on its own); death, live burial, and the return of the dead. The story of Belshazzar's feast, with its disembodied writing hand, its enigmatic inscription, and its numerical puns that seem both to predict and to bring about the king's death, underwrites all subsequent instances of writing on the wall, and adds its legendary freight to more localized effects of the uncanny. But a point Freud deems worthy of "special mention" is that an uncanny effect is "often and easily" produced when "a symbol takes over the full functions and significance of the thing it symbolises." Today, this means that we find ourselves in the presence of the uncanny wherever writing puts itself in the place of the text.

In Donne's "Valediction of my name, in the window," a poem whose burden may be summarized as "I've written my name in your window, and now you can't get rid of me," the graffiti signature implies both permanency (self-sameness) and death:

As no one point, nor dash,
Which are but accessaries to this name,
   The showers and tempests can outwash,
   So shall all times finde mee the same;
You this intirenesse better may fulfill,
   Who have the patterne with you still.

The name dies and survives in the writing: dies because it cannot be where writing is; survives in the iteration effect of the material trace. Today the uncanny effect of wall-writing depends in part on the dizzying collapse of language into its material forms with which graffiti seems to present us: words flee, writing remains — and remains to speak in the voice of the undead. But it is a marked fact that in the age of Elizabeth, in spite of Reformation concern over idolatry, written language does not seem to be aspiring to full transparency, and is still tending to accord sentience to its own material supports. In Pittleworth Manor, Hants., Reader recorded a wall decorated with a pattern of pomegranates and foliage, painted as if on a brocade tapestry.[88] The "tapestry" appears to hang in folds, evoking, as if it were a curtain that could be withdrawn, an impossible space behind itself. Attached to the "surface" of the imaginary cloth, and so appearing to float on the wall (as Donne's signature floats, unlocatably, on glass) is the saying: "Thus lyving all waye dred we death and diing life we doughte." The saying is conventional, but pointed here by a staged collision between text and writing: without a wall you cannot have space; without writing you cannot have text. If the counterfactual wish to pass through the surface of a wall, or alternatively to enter an imaginary deep space within it, is a figure for a modern apprehension that demands and awards itself transparency of language, the Pittleworth wall-painting is able at once to account for and deny that demand.

By the second half of the sixteenth century, plaster was made according to a process that produced intense heat, and columns of steam, from cold limestone. It furthermore required the admixture of animal hair: and so offered a rich metaphorical field for those who wrote about, on, and in it.[89] Blood, charcoal, marking stones of all colors, smoke, lead, and diamonds on glass have further properties of their own; and each could draw on the overdetermined terms "shade" or "shadow," terms which can mean to portray, draw, or paint; to reflect, imitate or follow; to prefigure or foretell; to show forth or cover over.[90] The shadow is a trace or spectral form (one from which the substance has departed), and the type of what is fleeting or delusive (a figure for life itself). Glossing the phrase "Nebula in pariete: A shadow on the wall," Erasmus comments, "Ausonius in one of his letters . . . speaks of shadows on a wall as things of no substance, like dreams: 'Have you never seen,' he says, 'a shadow painted on a wall?' The title of the poem appended to that letter interprets this as something frivolous and empty; for a shadow is a thing too insubstantial to be represented in colour."[91] Using its own locations and material status to signal and elaborate its recurrent themes of signature, death, and the end of days, and their common tropes of flowers, bodies, wounds, shadows, farewells, and graves, Tudor graffiti everywhere embraces and acknowledges the complex anxieties contained even in the graffito's most simple and paradigmatic instance, "I was here."

Appendix

From *The Welspring of wittie Conceights* trans. William Fister (London: Richard Jones, 1584).

Certaine worthie sentences, very meete to be written about a Bed-chamber or to be set up in any convenient place in a house:
1. The good Son, grafteth goodnes, whereof salvation is the fruit
   But the evil planteth vices, the fruit whereof is damnation
2. Therefore, at night call unto minde
   how thou the daye hast spent:
   Praise God, if naught amisse thou finde:
   if ought, betimes repent.

From Tusser, *Five hundred points of good husbandry etc.* (1573).

¶ POSIES FOR THE HALL
1. Friend, here I dwell, and here I have a little worldly pelf,
   Which on my friend I keep to spend, as well as on my self. . . .
¶ POSIES FOR THE PARLOUR
1. As hatred is the serpent's noisome rod;
   So friendship is the loving gift of God.
2. The drunken friend is friendship very evil;
   The frantic friend is friendship for the devil.

3. The quiet friend, all one in word and deed
   Great comfort is, like ready gold at need. . . .
¶ POSIES FOR THE GUEST'S CHAMBER
1. The sloven and the careless man, the roynish nothing nice,
   To lodge in chamber, comely deckt, are seldom suffered twice. . . .
¶ POSIES FOR THINE OWN BEDCHAMBER
2. What better fare than well content, agreeing with thy wealth,
   What better guest, than trusty friend, in sickness and in health?
3. What better bed than conscience good, to pass the night with sleep,
   What better work, than daily care, from sin thyself to keep?
4. What better thought, than think on God, and daily him to serve,
   What better gift than to the poor, that ready be to sterve?
6. What worse despair, than loth to die, for fear to go to hell?
   What greater faith than trust in God, through Christ in heaven to dwell?

Notes

I am grateful to Phillippa Berry, Richard Corum, Jonathan Crewe, and Carla Freccero, who each invited me to speak on this topic; Jayne Archer, Crystal Bartolovich, Georgia Brown, Mark Burnett, Muriel Carrick, Katherine Craik, Ian Donaldson, Margreta de Grazia, David Kastan, John Kerrigan, Tom Luxon, Jeremy Maule, Peter Stallybrass, and Malcolm Underwood for furnishing me with examples of wall-writing; Seth Schwartz, who provided Hebrew and Latin translations; and Phillipa Berry, Claire McEachern, Dympna Callaghan, Stefan Collini, and Lowell Gallagher for their perceptive comments on earlier versions of this essay.

1. "Brothers need to start knowin' where it started from. There's a lot of writers out there who are just comin' out the blue and not knowin' a damn thing about the history of graffiti, you know? I think a big part of graffiti is to be able to appreciate the past. I'm talkin' about brothers like Phase 2, Skeme — the man Skeme from New York, mad skills, you know? Its cool to know that a lot of the writers out here, that are old school, have heard of these brothers and have much respect for them. You know, a lot of youngstas comin' up have never heard of them." Dream in *Urb magaseen* 27 (1993): 49.

2. *Welspring of Wittie Conceights*, trans. William Fister (London: Richard Jones, 1584), N3ᵛ.

3. Thomas Tusser, *Five Hundred Points of Good Husbandry, together with a Book of Huswifery* (London: Lackington, Allen, and Co., 1812 [1573, 3rd ed., enlarged]), pp. 287–92.

4. So deeply internalized is the modern prohibition against domestic graffiti that ancient historians read the survival of graffiti as "evidence" that the building or room in question had a public function. See also Alfred Loos: "With children it is a natural phenomenon, their first artistic expression is to scrawl on the walls erotic symbols. But what is natural to the Papuan and the child is a symptom of degeneration in modern man." Loos, "Ornament and Crime," in *Alfred Loos: Pioneer of Modern Architecture*, ed. L. Münz and G. Künstler, trans. Harold Meek (London: Thames and Hudson, 1996), p. 226.

5. Michel Foucault, *The Order of Things: An Archaeology of the Human Sciences* (London: Vintage Books, 1973 [1966]), p. 59.

6. For a good account of graffiti writing as a contemporary practice see Susan Stewart, *Crimes of Writing: Problems in the Containment of Representation* (Oxford: Oxford University Press, 1991), pp. 206–33. Reading graffiti as a signature effect, one that exists not "in the singular work, but in a process of rampant reproduction" and so figures "a crime in the mode of production," Stewart argues that the tradition of graffiti writing should be dated only from the late 1950s and the early 1960s. For a longer and excellent cultural history of graffiti see Adam Gopnik and Kirk Varnedoe *High and Low: Modern Art/Popular Culture* (New York: Museum of Modern Art, 1991), pp. 66–99.

7. Sylvia Ann Grider demonstrates the way in which conceptions of graffiti vary between cultures by arguing that Mexican-Americans do not regard graffiti as a defacement of public property. Sylvia Ann Grider, "*Con safos*: Mexican Americans, Names, and Graffiti," *Journal of American Folklore* 88 (1975): 132–42.

8. Nicole Dacos, *La Découverte de la Domus Aurea et la formation des grotesques a la Renaissance* (London: Warburg Institute, 1969), pp. 139–60.

9. Church graffiti from the same period have been found in Norway and in France: see M. Blindheim, *Graffiti in Norwegian Stave Churches c. 1350–1550* (Oslo: Universitetsforlaget AS, 1985); and Asger Jorn et al., *Signes gravés sur les églises de l'Eure et du Calvados* (Copenhagen: Édition Borger, 1964). A member of the Situationist International movement (1957–61), Jorn understood the graffiti he documented as an expression of the spirit of popular liberation against authority; see Anne-Charlotte Weinmarck, *Nordisk Anarkiism* (Arhus: Kalejdoskop Forlag, 1980), p. 85; and Gopnik and Varnedoe, *High and Low*, p. 91.

10. Susan Sontag, "The Pleasure of the Image," *Art in America* 75 (November 1987): 126, 130. For further discussion of Saenredam's church paintings, one which usefully stresses the lack of a clear boundary between painting and writing in Dutch art, see Svetlana Alpers, *The Art of Describing: Dutch Art in the Seventeenth Century* (Chicago: University of Chicago Press, 1981), pp. 169–221.

11. Doris Jones-Baker, "The Graffiti of Folk Motifs in Cotswold Churches," *Folklore* 92, 2 (1981): 169–85.

12. Doris Jones-Baker, "Medieval and Tudor Music and Musicians in Hertfordshire: The Graffiti Evidence," in *Hertfordshire in History: Papers Presented to Lionel Munby* (Hertfordshire Local History Council, 1991), pp. 22–45; and idem, "English Medieval Graffiti and the Local Historian," *The Local Historian* 23, 1 (February 1993): 3–19.

13. Violet Pritchard, *English Medieval Graffiti* (Cambridge: Cambridge University Press, 1967), p. 54.

14. Izaak Walton, *The Lives of Dr. John Donne, Sir Henry Wootton, Mr Richard Hooker, Mr George Herbert* (London: Thomas Roycroft, 1675), p. 77.

15. Ibid., pp. 171–80; translation mine.

16. Malcolm G. Underwood, "The Old Treasury and Its Graffiti," *The Eagle* 68, 288 (1980): 23–26.

17. John Arthur Symonds, *Greek Poets* (London: A and C Black, 1873), p. 242. Raphael Garrucci, *Graffiti de Pompéi*, 2nd ed. (Paris: Benjamin Duprat, 1856). For a brief account of the historical documentation of Pompeian graffiti, see Gopnik and Vardenoe, who are themselves led to conclude, "On these walls, as nowhere else, a

wealth of oaths and imprecations, drawings and historical references, prayers and obscenities, put the flesh (sometimes all too weak and human) of daily life back onto the noble skeleton of an idealized ancient culture" (Gopnik and Vardenoe, *High and Low*, p. 70).

18. Gopnik and Vardenoe, *High and Low*, pp. 72–74.

19. As its title suggests, this is the governing assumption of Helen H. Tanzer's *The Common People of Pompeii: A Study of the Graffiti*: "Messages, tags of verse, pleasant thoughts of friend and sweetheart, bits of self-glorification and the like all allow the people to reveal themselves to us" (Baltimore: Johns Hopkins University Press, 1939), p. 83.

20. See S. Stewart, *Crimes*, p. 209.

21. See Mary T. Crane, *Framing Authority: Sayings, Self, and Society in Sixteenth-Century England* (Princeton, N.J.: Princeton University Press, 1993), p. 6.

22. D. Erasmus, *Collected Works of Erasmus*, 86 vols. (Toronto: University of Toronto Press, 1982–92), 31: 13.

23. Robert Hayman represents himself as having gathered flowers and "intreated slips" from the spacious garden of "Owen's booke . . . to make himself a poesie" in *Certaine Epigrams out of the first foure bookes of the excellent Epigrammatist, Master John Owen*, trans. R. Hyman (London: Roger Michell, 1628). For a useful discussion of the posy as a metaphor for a collection of rightly-chosen rhetorical "flowers" see Crane, *Framing Authority*, pp. 177–79.

24. George Puttenham, *The Arte of English Poesie*, ed. E. Arber (Kent, Ohio: Kent State University Press, 1970 [1589]), p. 72. For trencher verse see *Proceedings of the Society of Antiquaries* (1885): 207–16; (1888): 201–23; and A. H. Church, "Old English Fruit Trenchers," in A. H. Church et al., *Some Minor Arts as Practised in England* (London: Seeley and Co., 1894), pp. 47–54. In Donne's poem "To Sir Henry Goodyere" the poet chides himself for offering moral truisms, when "Tables, or fruit-trenchers teach as much" (l. 44).

25. *The Worthy Tract of Paulus Jovius, contayning a discourse of . . . Imprese*, trans. Samuel Daniel (London: Simon Waterson, 1585), A5r.

26. The term "writing matter" is taken from Jonathan Goldberg, *Writing Matter: From the Hands of the English Renaissance* (Stanford, Calif.: Stanford University Press, 1990). Following Derrida's suggestion in *Grammatology*, Jonathan Goldberg undertakes a local "cultural graphology" — a study of the material practices, institutions, and ideologies of English Renaissance handwriting. As he points out, the book centers "on the formations of a new "high" literacy, and on the manuals directed at this ideological project," and "can only glance at the sites that these books preclude, sites that vitally contradict their regulatory aims." *Writing Matter*, p. 9. This essay remains indebted to the theoretical formulations of Goldberg's work as it examines some "alternative" sites of Elizabethan handwriting.

27. *Percy Society Reprints* (London: Percy Society, 1851) 3: section 2, p. 71.

28. See Crane, *Framing Authority*, pp. 12–38.

29. See Tessa Watt, *Cheap Print and Popular Piety* (Cambridge: Cambridge University Press, 1991), pp. 217–53.

30. John Willis, *The art of memory so far forth as it dependeth upon places and ideas* (London: W. Jones, 1621), p. 47; see also Watt, *Cheap Print*, p. 221.

31. Watt, *Cheap Print*, p. 219.

Graffiti, Grammatology, and the Age of Shakespeare   347

32. Rosemary Freeman argues that the sixteenth century enjoyed "a very much closer relation between literature and decoration than has ever existed since" and uses her study of emblems to illustrate both "the literary nature of contemporary decoration" and "the decorative nature of contemporary literature." Rosemary Freeman, *English Emblem Books* (New York: Octagon Press, 1966), p. 98.

33. See, for example, Watt, p. 192, and Muriel Carrick, "Wall Paintings in Feering and Kelvedon," *Historic Buildings in Essex* (Publications of the Essex Historic Buildings Group, 2, September 1985), pp. 328–39. Izaak Walton records the disastrous progression from book to wall of a witticism ("Legatus est vir bonus peregrere missus ad mentiendum Reipublicaie causa" — An ambassador is an honest man sent to lie abroad for the good of his country) that Henry Wootton wrote in a companion's commonplace book: "As it was, it slept quietly among other sentences in this *Albo*, almost *eight years*, till by accident it fell into the hands of Jasper Scioppius, a Romanist, a man of restless spirit and a malicious pen; who with books against King *James* prints this as a principle of that religion professed by the King, and his Ambassador Sir Henry Wootton, then at Venice, and in Venice it was presently after written in several glass windows, and spitefully declared to be Sir Henry Wootton's." Isaak Walton, *Reliquae Wottonianiae* (London: T. Maxey, 1651), sig. C1ᵛ–C2.

34. Thomas Nashe, *Have With You to Saffron Walden* (London: John Danter, 1596).

35. Erasmus, *Collected Works* 34, 10.

36. Thomas Coryat, *Coryat's Crudities* (Glasgow: James Maclehose and Sons, 1905 [1611]), pp. 2, 91, 213. Elizabeth McCutcheon, *Sir Nicholas Bacon's Great House Sententiae* (English Literary Renaissance Supplements 3, 1977). Bacon also had sentences on his porch, in his hall, in the small banqueting house in his orchard, and on the door to the oak wood, (McCutcheon, p. 18).

37. Edward Rainbowe, *A Sermon Preached at the Interrment of Anne, Countess of Pembroke* (London: R. Royston and H. Broom, 1677) p. 48. Cited in Barbara Lewalski, *Writing Women in Jacobean England* (Cambridge, Mass.: Harvard University Press, 1992), pp. 139–40.

38. For Montaigne's sentences, "tracées au pinceau sur quarante-six solives et deux poutres transversales," and the two commemorative inscriptions written on the wall of his study, see P. Bonnefon, "La Bibliothèque de Montaigne," *Revue d'Histoire Littéraire de France* (July 15, 1895): 313–71.

39. George Herbert, *Outlandish Proverbs: Selected by Mr G. H.* (London: T. Paine, 1640), #839.

40. *Worthy Tract*, A1ᵛ.

41. See Goldberg, *Writing Matter*, pp. 59–107.

42. For example, Harold Love's passing assumption that "the teaching of writing in petty schools must always have been hindered by the absence of desks" and David Cressy's definition of literacy as "the ability to set down words on paper" will be affected by the proposition of a widespread practice of wall-writing. See Harold Love, *Scribal Publication in Seventeenth-Century England* (Oxford: Clarendon Press, 1993), p. 87; and David Cressy, *Literacy and the Social Order: Reading and Writing in Tudor and Stuart England* (Cambridge: Cambridge University Press, 1980), p. 59. Using the capacity to append a signature to a document as his literacy test, Cressy concluded that more than two-thirds of men and more than four-fifths of women were illiterate in

seventeenth-century England: "Their marks ranged from the simple scrawl of someone who had *never held a pen* to the elaborate sketch or diagram of another whose dexterity was some compensation for his illiteracy" (emphasis mine). Cressy's illiteracy rate consequently includes not only those who can read but not write, but also those who can write with charcoal or marking stone but not with ink.

43. Puttenham, *The Arte of English Poesie*, pp. 68–72. The term 'epigram' is derived from the Greek term for inscriptions on the stones, pottery, and papyri of Archaic Greece. Examples include the two lines on 'Nestor's goblet'; the imperfect sentence that survives on a Dipylon jug; and the brief address in which a tombstone or votive tablet typically "spoke" to the passerby. For a brilliant account of the poetics of the "speaking object" see Jesper Svenbro, *Phrasikleia: An Anthropology of Reading in Ancient Greece*, trans. Janet Lloyd (Ithaca, N.Y.: Cornell University Press, 1993).

44. Puttenham, p. 69. John Florio, *Queen Anna's New World of Words* (London: M. Bradwood, 1611), p. 30. For another English account of Pasquil and his fellow statue Marforio see Fynes Moryson, *Itinerary*, 2 vols. (New York: Macmillan, 1907 [1617]), 1: 288. "At one end of this market place, in a corner of a street opposite to a publicke Pallace, is the statua of Pasquin, upon a wall or a private house, which hath neither armes nor feet, they being cut off by passengers in the night. For all libels, even against the Pope himself, use to be made in forme of a dialogue, and fastened upon the statua of Pasquino, and another of Marforio . . . they two bearing the persons one of the question maker, the other of the answerer."

45. See Thomas Elyot's introduction to his *Pasquil the Playne* (London: Thomas Berthelet, 1540 [first ed. 1533]), A2ʳ: "Pasquillus, that speaketh moste, is an image of stone, sittinge in the citie of Rome openly: on whom ones in the yere, it is leful to every man, to set in verse or prose any taunte that he wil, agayne whom he list, howe great an asate so ever he be." For a brief comment on the use of graffiti for unofficial political commentary in early modern Italy see Peter Burke, "The Uses of Literacy in Early Modern Italy," *The Social History of Language*, ed. P. Burke and Roy Porter (Cambridge: Cambridge University Press, 1987), pp. 36–37.

46. Puttenham, *The Arte of English Poesie*, p. 68.

47. I follow Herford and Simpson in reproducing the typography of the Folio (London: W. Stansby, 1616), where small capitals usually denote a proper name, italics a proper name or a term or art.

48. Since the word dildo[e] both means refrain, and can operate (like hey nonny nonny) as a nonce word that makes up a refrain, and since a candle could be used as a dildo, this does not begin to exhaust the meanings of "MADAM, with a dildo, writ o' the walls." The dildo is the maternal phallus—the nothing that draws everything toward itself—so such meanings are in any case inexhaustible. But see Stephen Orgel, "On Dildos and Fadings," *American Notes and Queries* 5 (1992): 106–10.

49. *Ben Jonson*, ed. C. H. Herford, Percy Simpson, and Evelyn Simpson, 10 vols. (Oxford: Clarendon Press, 1950) 10: 58. Harold Love argues that early seventeenth-century news of the type traded in the nave of St. Paul's was an "oral commodity," which passed "with no reliance on writing . . . the nave of the church was no venue for reading." Love, *Scribal Publication*, p. 195. While the reading and writing of graffiti are rarely registered in the historical record, their likely presence complicates the nature of such "oral "exchanges.

50. Freeman, *English Emblem Books*, p. 7.

51. The poem's first stanza records Herbert's "personal motto," "*Less than the*

least/Of all thy mercies, is my posy still." *George Herbert and Henry Vaughan*, ed. Louis L. Martz (Oxford: Oxford University Press, 1986), p. 474. In "Dulnesse" the poet castigates himself by remembering his earlier work: "Where are my lines then? my approaches? views?/Where are my window songs?" On diamond writing rings see H. C. Smith, *Jewellery* (London: Methuen, 1908), p. 260.

52. John Foxe, *Actes and Monumentes* (London: J. Day, 1563), p. 1714.

53. Foxe, *Actes and Monumentes*, p. 922.

54. E. A. H. Fenn, "The Writing on the Wall," *History Today* 19, 1 (June 1961): 419–23.

55. Fuller, *The Worthies of England* (London: J. G. W. L. and W. G., 1662), Mmr; cited in L. Bradner, *The Poems of Queen Elizabeth I* (Providence, R.I.: Brown University Press, 1964), p. 7.

56. Richard Brathwaite, *Ar't Asleep Husband* (London: R. Best, 1640), p. 10.

57. Richard Brathwaite, *The English Gentleman and English Gentlewoman* (London: John Dawson, 1641), pp. 256, 448, 451.

58. Ibid., p. 430. See also Brathwaite's description of the "wanton damasella who portrayed the affection of her heart in as light an imprese; writing these lines with her Diamond in a window: '*The choicest Cates soon'st cloy the appetite,/One is too stale a dish to feed delight*'" (143); and the wronged wife, "when like a *fruitfull vine*, shee had brought forth many faire and promising branches to a debaucht husband, by whose profuser courses, her hopes which she has stored in her numerous progeny, perished, and her selfe through griefe irrecoverably wasted; she wrote these pensive lines with a Diamond in her Chamber Window, to give a living shadow to her lasting sorrow: *Up to the Window sprung the spreading Vine,/The dangling Apricocke, and Egglantine;/Since when, that vine, and branches too were found,/Shred from their root, laid sprawling on the ground*" (351–52).

59. Paul Hentzner, *Itinerarium* (Nuremburg, 1612), p. 144; cited in Bradner, *Poems*, p. 71.

60. John Grange, *The Golden Aphroditis* (London:. H. Bynneman, 1577) Llvʳ–M.

61. W. M., *The Man in the Moone* (London: J. Windet for N. Butter, 1609). *Percy Society Reprints* (London: Percy Society, 1851), 24: 46.

62. Watt documents the extensive range of painted and printed texts produced for the walls of Christian households in the late sixteenth and early seventeenth centuries. Watt, *Cheap Print*, pp. 217–53. To "set" something in a table may be to do no more than arrange the lines for easy and memorable reading.

63. Louise Osborn, *The Life, Letters, and Writings of John Hoskyns* (New Haven, Conn.: Yale University Press, 1937), pp. 20–56 and 212–3; Mark T. Burnett, "The Trusty Servant": A Sixteenth-Century English Emblem," *Emblematica* 6, 2 (Winter 1992): 244.

64. John Dee, *A True and Faithfull Relation of What Passed for Many Yeers between Dr John Dee . . . and Some Spirits* (London: D. Maxwell for T. Garthwait, 1659); see R. J. W. Evans, *Rudolf II and His World: A Study in Intellectual History, 1576–1612* (Oxford: Clarendon Press, 1975), p. 204.

65. Nicholas Flamel, *Nicholas Flamel his Exposition* (London: T. Walkley, 1624 [1612]), p. 16.

66. George Herbert, *A Priest to the Temple. Or, the Country Parson* (London: Benjamin Roke, 1675), p. 49.

67. The following account is dependent on the work of Reader, who recorded

surviving English domestic wall paintings in the 1930s. Francis Reader, "Wall-paintings of the 16th and early 17th centuries recently discovered in Bosworth House, Wendover, Bucks.," *Archaeological Journal* 87 (1930): 71–97; idem, "Tudor Mural Paintings in the lesser houses of Bucks.," *Archaeological Journal* 89 (1932): 116–73; idem, "Tudor Domestic Wall-Paintings I," *Archaeological Nournal* 92 (1935): 243–86; idem, "Tudor Domestic Wall-Paintings II," *Archaeological Journal* 93 (1936): 220–62. Watt usefully elaborates Reader's work (Watt, *Cheap Print*, pp. 179–53).

68. Following Reader, Watt puts the height of the vogue for English wall-painting at 1530–1580, and suggests that its decline may be attributable to "the growing ownership of paintings and prints as we now know them [which] changed ideas about what 'art' should be, and made the use of every odd surface for painting seem old-fashioned and inferior" (Watt, *Cheap Print*, p. 199).

69. In 1568 Herman Schinkel, a Delft printer, answered charges that he had printed prohibited ballads by claiming "that they were printed in his absence by his servant, and on his return he refused to deliver them and threw them in a corner intending to print roses and stripes on the other side, to paper attics with" (*Notes and Queries* NS 11 [July 1856]); see also Reader, "Tudor Mural Paintings," p. 163. H. Jenkinson, "English Wall-Paper of the Sixteenth and Seventeenth Centuries," *The Antiquaries Journal* 15 (1925): 237–53 argues that, although very few have survived, decorated printed papers were "both plentiful and popular in their day," and were used not only to decorate walls but also to cover books and line boxes.

70. Reader, "Tudor Domestic Wall-Paintings I," p. 246. Watt, *Cheap Print*, p. 219.

71. Reader, "Tudor Mural Wall-paintings," pp. 119–20.

72. The term *calligramme* was used by Apollinaire to describe his experimental poem-pictures. Guillaume Apollinaire, *Calligrammes* (Paris: Gallimard, 1918). An imagistic arrangement of text (*non rebus sed verbis*, as it were), the calligramme has its own ancient, modern, and post-modern history. Like the rebus, of which it is the inverse, the calligramme stages the confrontation between word and image which graffiti more quietly ignores. According to Gopnik and Varnedoe, it was Garrucci (1856) who extended the meaning of graffiti to include drawings as well as inscriptions. Gopnik and Varnedoe, *High and Low*, p. 70. For discussion of the Protestant tradition of "visual stories" see Watt, *Cheap Print*, pp. 185–85, 224, where she notes the term "table" describes a broadside or painting "caught somewhere between decorative 'imagerye' and the schematic arrangement of printed words."

73. Reader, "Tudor Mural Paintings," p. 121. For a fuller description of this inscription and the decorative scheme that contained it see Philip Mainwaring Johnston, "Mural Paintings in Houses: with Special Reference to Recent Discoveries at Stratford-Upon-Avon and Oxford," *Journal of the British Archaeological Society* NS 2 (1932): 75–100.

74. Reader, "Tudor Mural Paintings," p. 120.

75. The text of the first passage survives on a wall in Feering House, Essex; see Carrick "Wall Painting," p. 6, and Watt, *Cheap Print*, p. 217.

76. See Ernest B. Gilman, *Iconoclasm and Poetry in the English Reformation: Down went Dagon* (Chicago: University of Chicago Press, 1986), p. 35; and Watt, *Cheap Print*, p. 185.

77. John Calvin, *Sermons on Deuteronomy*, trans. Arthur Golding (London: Henry Middleton, 1583), p. 473.

78. Regina M. Schwartz, *Remembering and Repeating: On Milton's Theology and Poetics* (Chicago: University of Chicago Press, 1993), p. 5 cites this passage in the context of a discussion of repetition and memory. On the importance of the classical *sententia* as a form that is not only memorable in itself, but has the power to bring the reader to consciousness of what she knows, and so appears to "speak the language of oracles," see McCutcheon, *Sir Nicholas Bacon's Sententiae*, p. 45.

79. Joseph Hall, *Works*, 2 vols. (London: E. Brewster, 1634), 1: 379.

80. Fister, *Welspring*, N3ᵛ.

81. Calvin, *Deuteronomy*, p. 276. Samuel Purchas, by contrast, describes Jewish observance as the type of prophylaxis acceptable to Calvin: "*The sentence* Hear Israel etc. *and another sentence is to be written on the postes of the House.* He which hath his *Phylacteries* on his head and arms, and his knots on his garment, and his Schedule on his doore, is so fenced he cannot easily sinne." Samuel Purchas, *Purchas his Pilgrimage* (London: W. Stanby, 1613), p. 154.

82. Calvin, *Deuteronomy*, p. 473.

83. For an account of early modern exegesis of Daniel 5, see Eileen Reeves, "Daniel 5 and the *Assayer*: Galileo reads the handwriting on the wall," *Journal of Medieval and Renaissance Studies* 21 (1991), p. 12.

84. *Peake's Biblical Commentary*, ed. M. Black and H. H. Rowley (London: Thomas Nelson and Sons, 1962), p. 596.

85. Patricia Parker, *Literary Fat Ladies: Rhetoric, Gender, Property* (New York: Methuen, 1987), p. 14.

86. Otto Rank, *The Double: A Psychoanalytic Study*, trans. Harry Tucker Jr. (Chapel Hill: University of North Carolina Press, 1971), pp. 77–78. Rank quotes Dorian Gray, "I have no terror of Death. It is only *the coming* of death that terrifies me." See also Schwartz, *Remembering*, p. 102.

87. Sigmund Freud, "The Uncanny," *Standard Edition of the Complete Psychological Works of Sigmund Freud*, 24 vols., trans. James Strachey (London: Hogarth Press, 1953–73), 17: 217–56.

88. Reader, "Tudor Domestic Wall-Painting I," p. 277. Watt, *Cheap Print*, pp. 205–9.

89. The practice of mixing animal hair in plaster is a fact remembered in *A Midsummer Night's Dream* both by Thisbe, who begins her lewd and inadvertent analogy between the wall and the body of her lover with "My cherry lips have often kiss'd thy stones,/Thy stones with lime and hair knit up in thee" (5, 1, 193–94), and by Theseus, who defends Snout's performance of the wall by asking "Would you desire lime and hair to speak better?" (5, 1, 163).

90. Graphite (called plumbago, English antimony, or black lead) was discovered in Borrowdale in the middle of the sixteenth century; before this, lead styluses were commonly used to rule lines and margins and to draw on paper. See Henry Petroski, *The Pencil: A History of Design and Circumstance* (New York: Alfred Knopf, 1990).

91. Erasmus, *Collected Works*, 33: 210.

Contributors

ANN JENSEN ADAMS is associate professor of the History of Art and Architecture at the University of California, Santa Barbara. She curated the exhibition and authored the catalog of *Seventeenth-Century Dutch and Flemish Paintings from New York Private Collections* (1988). She also edited the anthology, *Rembrandt's "Bathsheba Reading King David's Letter"* (1998), and, along with many articles, is author of the forthcoming *Public Faces, Private Identities: Portraiture and the Production of Community in Seventeenth-Century Holland*.

JUDITH C. BROWN was a professor in the History Department at Stanford University and is now Dean of the School of Humanities at Rice University. She has published two books — *In the Shadow of Florence: Provincial Society in Renaissance Pescia* (1982) and *Immodest Acts: The Life of a Lesbian Nun in Renaissance Italy* (1985) — as well as articles in *Renaissance Quarterly* and in *Rewriting the Renaissance: The Discourses of Sexual Difference in Early Modern Europe*, ed. M. Ferguson et al. (1986).

RICHARD CORUM teaches English at the University of California, Santa Barbara. He has published on Milton and Shakespeare in the anthologies, *Milton and the Idea of Woman*, ed. Julia M. Walker (1988) and *The Pleasures of History: Reading Sexualities in Premodern Europe*, ed. Louise Fradenburg and Carla Freccero (1996). He is also author of the forthcoming *Understanding Hamlet*.

FRANCES E. DOLAN is associate professor of English and an affiliate of the History Department and the Women's Studies Program at Miami University in Ohio. She is author of *Dangerous Familiars: Representations of Domestic Crime in England, 1550–1700* (1994) and editor of *The Taming of the Shrew: Texts and Contexts* (1996). Her current project is a study of gender and constructions of Catholicism in seventeenth-century England.

JULIET FLEMING is an assistant lecturer in the Faculty of English, Cambridge University. The essay in this volume is taken from her current project, "The Arts of English Poesie," an investigation into the material writing practices of early modern England (*Reaktion*, forthcoming).

PATRICIA FUMERTON is associate professor of English at the University of California, Santa Barbara. As well as articles published in *Representations*, *ELH*, and *English Literary Renaissance*, among other journals, she is author of *Cultural Aesthetics: Renaissance Literature and the Practice of Social Ornament* (1991) and is currently at work on a book titled "Spacious Voices/Vagrant Subjects in Early Modern England."

RICHARD HELGERSON is professor of English at the University of California, Santa Barbara. In addition to numerous essays and reviews, he is author of *The Elizabethan Prodigals* (1976), *Self-Crowned Laureates: Spenser, Jonson, Milton and the Literary System* (1983), and *Forms of Nationhood: The Elizabethan Writing of England* (1992).

SIMON HUNT is in the final stages of completing his Ph.D. in English from the University of California, Santa Barbara. He was an assistant research-writer for the *Norton Shakespeare Workshop*, ed. Mark Rose (1997), and is working on the "staging" of succession, 1598–1608. He teaches English at the Santa Catalina School in Monterey, California.

STEPHANIE H JED is associate professor of Italian and Comparative Literature at the University of California, San Diego. She is author of numerous articles in journals and essay collections as well as of *Chaste Thinking: The Rape of Lucretia and the Birth of Humanism* (1989). She is currently at work on a book project entitled "Reorganizing Knowledge: Feminists, Librarians and the Italian Nation."

SHANNON MILLER is assistant professor of English at Temple University. She is author of *Invested with Meaning: The Raleigh Circle in the New World* (University of Pennsylvania Press, 1998) as well as articles on Shakespeare, Jacobean city comedy, and Aemilia Lanyer's poetry. She is currently at work on a project that explores motifs of violence in the writings of Renaissance women.

LENA COWEN ORLIN is Research Professor of English at the University of Maryland, Baltimore County and Executive Director of the Shakespeare Association of America. She is author of *Private Matters and Public Culture in Post-Reformation England* (1994) and *Elizabethan Households: An Anthology* (1995). Her current work explores the material culture of the early modern household.

KAREN L. RABER is assistant professor of English at the University of Mississippi. Her published work on women writers and Renaissance closet drama has appeared in *Studies in English Literature* and *English Literary Renaissance*. The article in this volume is part of another book-in-progress, titled "Country Contentments': A Cultural History of Renaissance Country Recreations," which will cover treatises and writings on "huswifery" as well as country pastimes like hawking, angling, horse and hound racing, and hunting.

DEBORA SHUGER is professor of English at the University of California, Los Angeles. She is the author of *Sacred Rhetoric: The Christian Grand Style in the English Renaissance* (1988), *Habits of Thought in the English Renaissance: Religion, Politics, and the Dominant Culture* (1990), and *The Renaissance Bible: Scholarship, Subjectivity, and Sacrifice* (1994), as well as editor (with Claire McEachern) of *Religion and Culture in Renaissance England* (1997).

DON E. WAYNE is associate professor of Literature at the University of California, San Diego. He is author of *Penshurst: The Semiotics of Place and the Poetics of History* (1984) and has published numerous essays on topics in early modern literature and culture as well as on contemporary theory and cultural criticism. His recent publications include an article in *The Consumption of Culture, 1600–1800*, ed. Ann Bermingham and John Brewer (1995), and a study of hegemony in estate poems and in the iconography of Hardwick Hall, in *Soundings of Things Done: Essays in Early Modern Literature in Honor of S. K. Heninger Jr.*, ed. Peter E. Medine and Joseph Wittreich (1997).

Index

Acknowledgments

The idea for this volume arose out of a series of Renaissance Studies conferences held annually at the University of California, Santa Barbara between 1991 and 1996. Among the many UCSB faculty and graduate students (some now holding positions at other institutions) who aided in these projects, we owe special thanks to: Shannon Miller, Cynthia Skenazi, Richard Corum, Robert Williams, Roze Hentschell, Bret Rothstein, Jon Connolly, Claire Busse, Jessica Winston, Jennifer Hellwarth, Todd West, Julia Garrett, David Ziegler, and Dwight Brooks. Our warm thanks to these untiring fellow-laborers in Renaissance fields. Thanks as well to those UCSB institutions that generously supported our efforts: the Renaissance Studies Program, English Department, Interdisciplinary Humanities Center, Graduate Division, Women's Center, and Department of French and Italian.

In formulating this volume, we partly drew on these conference proceedings but also reached well beyond them. The everyday task of evaluating and organizing papers was greatly aided by the always reasoned advice of our colleague, Richard Helgerson. To him we owe a special thanks. We are also grateful to Leah S. Marcus for her clear-sighted reading of the manuscript, which helped guide our revisions.

Much of Patricia Fumerton's article "Homely Accents" previously appeared in *ELR* as "Subdiscourse: Jonson Speaking Low," (*English Literary Renaissance* 25 [1995], 76–96) and a version of Juliet Fleming's paper has appeared in *Criticism* 39,1 (Winter 1997): 1–30. In addition, Judith Brown's essay was previously published in a different, Italian version, in *Quaderni Storici* 29,1 (April 1994): 117–42. Thanks to these journals for allowing us to republish and, in the case of *Quaderni Storici*, also to translate these papers.